BANDITS,
CAPTIVES,
HEROINES, AND SAINTS

Cultural Studies of the Americas

George Yúdice, Jean Franco, and Juan Flores, Series Editors

continued on page 333

BANDITS, CAPTIVES, HEROINES, AND SAINTS

Cultural Icons of Mexico's Northwest Borderlands

Robert McKee Irwin

Cultural Studies of the Americas Series
Volume 20

University of Minnesota Press
Minneapolis
London

Portions of chapter 2 were previously published as "Toward a Border Gnosis of the Borderlands: Joaquín Murrieta and Nineteenth-Century U.S.–Mexico Border Culture," *Nepantla: Views from South* 2, no. 3 (2001): 509–37; reprinted with permission of Duke University Press. Portions of chapter 3 were published as "Ramona and Postnationalist American Studies: On 'Our America' and the Mexican Borderlands," *American Quarterly* 55, no. 4 (2003): 539–67; copyright American Studies Association; reprinted with permission of The Johns Hopkins University Press; and as "The Legend of Lola Casanova: On the Borders of Border Studies," *Aztlán: A Journal of Chicano Studies* 30, no. 2 (Fall 2005); reprinted with permission of the Regents of the University of California and the UCLA Chicano Studies Research Center.

Published by the University of Minnesota Press
111 Third Avenue South, Suite 290
Minneapolis, MN 55401-2520
http://www.upress.umn.edu

Library of Congress Cataloging-in-Publication Data

Irwin, Robert McKee, 1962–
    Bandits, captives, heroines, and saints : cultural icons of Mexico's northwest borderlands / Robert McKee Irwin.
        p. cm. — (Cultural studies of the Americas ; 20)
    Includes bibliographical references and index.
    ISBN: 978-0-8166-4856-6, ISBN-10: 0-8166-4856-5 (hc : alk. paper)
    ISBN: 978-0-8166-4857-3, ISBN-10: 0-8166-4857-3 (pb : alk. paper)
    1. Mexico, North—Historiography. 2. Mexican-American Border Region—Historiography. 3. Popular culture—Mexico, North.
4. Popular culture—Mexican American Border Region. 5. Symbolism—Mexico, North. 6. Mexico, North—In literature. I. Title.
F1314.I79 2007
972'.1—dc22   2007008225

Printed in the United States of America on acid-free paper

The University of Minnesota is an equal-opportunity educator and employer.

12 11 10 09 08 07   10 9 8 7 6 5 4 3 2 1

To Rafael

CONTENTS

Acknowledgments

THIS PROJECT WAS POSSIBLE only with the support, assistance, and inspiration of a number of institutions and colleagues, each of whom deserves special mention.

My archival research was funded by Tulane University's Senate Committee on Research; by the Roger Thayer Stone Center for Latin American Studies, also of Tulane University; and by a Tinker Foundation grant from the University of Arizona's Center for Latin American Studies. I also was fortunate to receive a fellowship from the American Council of Learned Societies, the Social Science Research Council, and the National Endowment for the Humanities, which enabled me to take a sabbatical and dedicate a year to the elaboration of my manuscript. Finally, travel funding from the Office of the Dean of Humanities, Arts, and Cultural Studies at the University of California at Davis, along with Davis's Chicana/Latina Research Center, permitted me to make several research trips to tie up loose ends with my manuscript.

I am most grateful for the support shown by my former colleagues and students in the Department of Spanish and Portuguese at Tulane University during my initial years of research. Discussions with Marilyn Miller, Idelber Avelar, and Christina Sisk were of particular help to me, as was the support of Thomas Reese of the Stone Center for Latin

American Studies and my department's chairs—Christopher Dunn, Nicasio Urbina, and Maureen Shea. At UC Davis, my interactions with my graduate students Moisés Park, Valentina Velázquez, Barbara Gunn, Carlos López, and Gerardo Giambarazzio have been particularly fruitful.

The project took shape gradually, and as I began presenting pieces at conferences and publishing excerpts in scholarly journals, I received helpful feedback from scholars throughout North America, including Danny Anderson, Maarten van Delden, Javier Durán, Desirée Martín, Sergio de la Mora, Estelle Tarica, Kirsten Silva Gruesz, Silvia Spitta, Núria Vilanova, Claire Fox, Sophia McClennan, Fortino Corral, Claudia Sadowski-Smith, Deborah Cohn, Elizabeth Moreno, Maricruz Castro, Mónica Szurmuk, Carl Good, and Cristina Rivera Garza.

I must mention my indebtedness to the staffs of the library collections where I carried out my research: Tulane University's Latin American Library, the Fondo Reservado of the Hemeroteca Nacional de México, the Bancroft Library at the University of California at Berkeley, the archives of the Arizona Historical Society in Tucson, the Special Collections of the University of Arizona Library, the Instituto Nacional de Antropología e Historia archives in Hermosillo, the Library of the Universidad de Sonora, the New York Public Library, the California State Library, and the Pablo Martínez archives of the Instituto Nacional de Antropología e Historia in La Paz, Baja California. Most particularly helpful to me have been Hortensia Calvo, Paul Bary, and Guillermo Náñez of Tulane University and Walter Brem of UC Berkeley. I am also grateful to Miguel Tinker Salas for sharing his own research files with me.

Finally, just as invaluable as all the professional backing I have received has been the personal support of Rafael Díaz, especially during my sabbatical year when a single home office became the site of elaboration of both his dissertation and my book. Also, it goes without saying that this book would never have come into being without the legendary *chiles poblanos* of Dubravka Sužnjevíc.

INTRODUCTION

LET ME BEGIN BY SKETCHING a few scenes from Mexico's northwestern borderlands in the latter half of the nineteenth century:

A middle-aged woman wandered through downtown Hermosillo hawking trinkets in the street. She was dressed as a Seri Indian and her facial tattoos indicated that she was not merely donning a costume. Yet her physical features were clearly those of a white woman. Locals might have guessed her identity, recalling the story of a lovely *criolla* carnival queen who had been taken captive by Seri warriors, then seduced by the savage allure of their chief. The marriage of a privileged *criolla* to an enemy leader—for the Seri, seen as the most savage of the indigenous groups of Mexico's northwestern borderlands, remained autonomous and at war with "civilized" Mexico—was still shocking to the Sonorans who recognized Lola Casanova as she passed through the rapidly modernizing city of Hermosillo.

Perhaps around the same time, a livestock rancher in northern Sonora lived out his last years in anonymity. He managed to do so despite the fact that he had been a hero to Mexicans of the borderlands a few decades earlier. Having migrated north as a young man to seek his fortune in gold rush California, he was violently disillusioned by the brutal racism of Anglophone settlers. After witnessing the rape of his wife and murder of his brother, and suffering countless personal humiliations, he turned into a vengeful social bandit, terrorizing all Alta California. Some believed he had been hunted down by government agents, and that his severed head, preserved in alcohol in a large jar, proved his death; others knew that that head was not actually his, and that Joaquín Murrieta had made his heroic escape back to Sonora where he would live a long and productive life.

This was also the time that a lady from Guaymas was belatedly lauded for her heroism of a few decades earlier. Count Gaston de Raousset Boulbon, the gallant French filibuster, had led an invasion of the Mexican Northwest from Alta California, with the intention of liberating the region from Mexican oppression and opening up the prospect of French colonization. Raousset was rebuffed not only by the Mexican military but also by local residents, including an Indian teenager who would grow up to be the most fearsome Yaqui rebel ever to challenge Mexican authority, and a very proper upper-class lady who could not condone bad manners even in a desperate filibuster. But the heroine of the day was not the notorious Cajeme nor the elegant Guadalupe Cubillas, but a modest housewife, Loreto Encinas de Avilés, who ran through the streets of Guaymas, wailing baby in her arms, sounding the warning that the French filibusters were about to attack.

Also in this long ago era, a young *mestiza* girl began exercising astounding curative powers and preaching a rhetoric criticizing the oppression of indigenous peasants at the hands of the government and the Catholic Church. She became a living saint to many, inspiring numerous rebellions and eventually prompting President Porfirio Díaz to banish her to Arizona, where she would continue to incite revolt. She was a veritable Mexican Joan of Arc, and her adventures presaged the Mexican revolution, but Teresa Urrea, La Santa de Cabora, would die a humble death in the United States where she would no longer be revered as a healer but mocked as an example of backward Mexican superstitiousness.

These anecdotes, all products of history, legend, gossip, and literary imagination, hint at some of the cultural meanings conveyed by these icons of the contact zone that is the U.S.–Mexico border. Many of these figures play a role in national history. Others are better known in the United States than in Mexico. Yet none are as significant to any national imaginary as they are to that of the borderlands. Their stories—as they develop over time, diverging and shifting, intersecting, echoing, and contradicting each other—signify heavily on borderlands culture. They are cultural icons whose multiple and ever-changing histories define the culture of Mexico's northwestern borderlands in the late nineteenth century as distinct from that of either Mexico or the United States, or even of the U.S. southwestern borderlands. The contact zone of the Mexican Northwest developed a culture very much its own following the U.S.–Mexico war of the 1840s, a multilayered culture whose relations to the cultures of the Mexican national mainstream, the imperialist United States, and its emerging Mexican American minority of the Southwest are indicative of the complex web of social and cultural hierarchies that ruled everyday life in North America in the era of manifest destiny.

Frontier Territory

In 1848, a monumental change occurred in the area of Mexico that is today the country's northwestern borderlands. The present Mexican state of Sonora and surrounding territories including the Baja California peninsula and western Chihuahua, which had once been situated in the middle of Mexico's vast northwestern frontier territories—more or less in the middle of nowhere, far away from central Mexico and farther away from any foreign country—now found themselves sharing a border with the United States, a country that had just aggressively seized half of Mexico's lands and seemed poised to grab for more.

The Spanish word "frontera" can be translated to English as "border," "borderlands," or "frontier." The case of the area that became in 1848 Mexico's northwestern borderlands makes clear the inadequacy of the Spanish term. While "border" is a term designating very clearly the delimitations between two entities—regardless whether such a delimitation can ever really be defined with precision—"borderlands" and "frontier" are much broader terms, both referring to extensive swaths of territory, and neither implying clear-cut limits of any kind. In nationalistic terms, a "frontier" is an area located far from the center of the nation, a peripheric zone that abuts not a neighboring nation but unconquered wilderness. Mexico's northwestern frontier territories in the early 1800s were vast terrains, sparsely populated by a mix of *criollo* settlers and indigenous peoples, distant from the nation's center in terms of transportation, communication, and culture. Largely unprotected by the national military, Mexican settlers struggled with the unconquered indigenous groups for whom these territories had been an undisputed homeland for generations. Although in Spanish colonial times many native peoples had been more or less subdued in frontier missions and gradually assimilated into Mexican *criollo* culture, others remained in violent rebellion against white colonizers, making some parts of the region virtually uninhabitable by *criollos*. Thus, alongside the tales of glory of northwestern Mexico's early *criollo* pioneers exist parallel sagas of the heroic defense of native lands by tenacious indigenous nations, such as those of the Seris and the Yaquis.

The Borderlands

When in 1848 these frontier territories abruptly became Mexico's northwestern borderlands—a territory no longer fading out into an ever more barbarous oblivion but directly adjoining a powerful and rapidly modernizing neighbor—all the issues outlined above remained and would be further complicated by the region's new role as defense outpost against potential incursions by the increasingly imperialistic United States. The rhetoric of manifest destiny evoked threat after threat of invasion, annexation, or colonization of northwestern Mexico, if not by the United States itself, then by U.S.–based adventurers. The attraction to California of adventurers from all over the world, seeking their fortunes in the gold rush of 1849, further complicated the cultural mix of the borderlands, and soon northwestern Mexico became the target of California–based French invaders as well. In addition, as parts of the Mexican Northwest began to develop economically, immigration to Alta California spread south, leading to new cultural conflicts as Mexicans struggled to live alongside new arrivals—most notably, immigrants from China—who brought with them cultural practices utterly incomprehensible to

Mexican *fronterizos*. If that were not enough, the Mexican borderlands' proximity to the United States (and distance from central Mexico), notwithstanding whatever antagonisms were in play at any moment, brought about an economic interdependency that would closely link Mexican *fronterizos* to their northern neighbors. Such associations were often painful, as Mexico's image in the United States was hardly that of an equal partner. Mexico's *fronterizos* needed to confront and correct Yankee prejudices in order to better foster the economic relationships on which their project of modernization depended. This push and pull with their new neighbor, along with the increased clashes brought about by growing internationalization, further complicated the already conflictive state of social and cultural relations in the region.

A Cultural Contact Zone

According to Mary Louise Pratt, a "contact zone" is a social space "where cultures meet, clash, and grapple with each other, often in contexts of highly asymmetrical relations of power, such as colonialism, slavery, or their aftermaths" ("Arts" 34). Pratt, seeking new critical paradigms to address contemporary trends of globalization, proposes "an optic that decenters community (and its corollary, identity) to focus on how social bonds operate across lines of difference, hierarchy, and unshared or conflicting assumptions" ("Criticism" 88). Rather than setting about to draw conclusions regarding national culture, Pratt suggests that "a contact zone perspective decenters community to look at how signification works across and through lines of difference and hierarchy[;] . . . borders are placed . . . at the center of concern while homogeneous centers move to the margins" (ibid.).

I would add that a critical approach that focuses on zones of cultural contact may be productive not only to address contemporary "postnational" concerns. In fact, in many if not all historical moments and local contexts, official or mainstream national culture is only one cultural force at work, always in dialogue with cultural production that voices perspectives of multiple cultural communities, whether they be communities of shared ethnic, gender, foreign national, class, religious, or other identities marginalized in a national context.

The border paradigm commonly used to address the contact zone between Mexico and the United States is useful, but limited in that it tends to imply a binary vision, composed only of a monolithic (white, Anglophone) United States, a monolithic (*mestizo*, Hispanophone) Mexico, and combinations thereof (often limited to the Mexican American hybrid). A contact zone perspective does not suggest a limitation to a binary view.[1] The culture of the U.S.–Mexico borderlands, after all, is the product of more than just a simple summation or fusion of two national cultures. The two national monoliths are present, but so are local perspectives based on, for example, class and ethnic identities as well as other national affiliations (including, as we will see, Chilean, French, and Chinese).

The recent surge of interest in the multicultural U.S. Southwest has made "border studies" into a major node of inquiry in the context of both American studies and Latin American studies. Studies of the borderlands emphasize "local relations of conflict and cooperation among ethnic and linguistic communities and the relative autonomy and heterogeneity of their cultural practices with respect to national centers" (Gruesz 91–10). This is certainly the case of the U.S. Southwest, undoubtedly one of the key contact zones Kirsten Silva Gruesz had in mind when she articulated the concept cited above.

However, a similar interest in the Mexican Northwest as a contact zone or as an integral part of a larger cross-border contact zone has not materialized. Like the U.S. Southwest, the Mexican Northwest has a long history of conflicts between white colonizers and often resistant indigenous groups. As in the U.S. Southwest, clashes between Mexican and U.S. cultures have been a part of everyday life for over one hundred fifty years. And parallel to the U.S. Southwest's history of receiving immigrants from all over the world, the Mexican Northwest's history also reflects the interest of certain foreign populations (such as the Chinese or the French) in migrating to or even taking over the region. Finally, the Mexican Northwest, particularly in the late nineteenth century, shares with the U.S. Southwest a distance from its nation's center that not only locates it on the periphery of national culture but at times puts it at odds with the national. The Mexican Northwest, the "other borderlands," would appear to be as exemplary a cultural contact zone as the U.S. Southwest, and it is time that it received significant attention within a framework of inquiry that goes beyond the regional or the national.

To understand the complexities of cultural contact in the borderlands, it is necessary to gain access to multiple perspectives and to see how dialogues and rhetorical confrontations between different groups have played out in history. Therefore, rather than look at individual texts, I have chosen to look at multiple texts that treat similar subject matter. Nick Couldry proposed a "cultural studies" methodology of textual analysis based on a "textual environment," a context of intertextual dialogue formed by "(a) flows of texts, (b) flows of meaning (across and within texts), and (c) movements of potential readers within (a) and (b)" (80). The idea is to study not "texts as objects" but "textual processes" of (multiple) signification (86). I have chosen to work with several cultural icons of the late-nineteenth-century borderlands: figures who appear and reappear at multiple historical moments, and from multiple cultural contexts. The intercultural dialogue that results around these icons through literature, journalism, historiography, film, legend, and so on facilitates insight into the dynamics of cultural relations among the multiple groups sharing the space of the contact zone of the U.S.–Mexico borderlands.

Cultural Icons of the Borderlands

The term "cultural icon" is one common in everyday usage, but poorly treated in academic discourse. Part of the reason for this is that it is a concept that has come into common use only recently, and usually only to refer to figures associated with mass communication and consumerism. However, it is a particularly useful category for interrogating the context of a cultural contact zone because it is a robust category that allows for multiplicities of meaning in ways that similar discursive genres such as myth and legend do not.

The term "legend," for example, tends to refer to a story belonging to a particular place and a particular people. Legends tend to exist outside history or in opposition to official history. They exist in popular culture, representing oral traditions and folklore. While legends' protagonists may have a life beyond the context of the legends about them, their roles in history, literature, or film tend to be seen as separate from their participation in legend. Often the legend is seen as a source text on which other stories are based, although it is the legend and not the stage play or the historic facts that carries the weight of cultural meaning for those to whom the legend belongs.

Myth is something more culturally weighty than legend because, as Roland Barthes asserts, "it transforms history into nature" (129). While a legend does bear cultural meaning, it does so in a less narrow way. Legendary characters may be rough, shape shifting, and contradictory. La Santa de Cabora of borderlands lore was at once an innocent girl and a hard-nosed revolutionary; she is not a mythological character because she is not a "poor, incomplete [image], where the meaning is already relieved of its fat, and ready for a signification" (Barthes 127). She is too messy for that: her meaning is variable, debatable. While some have tried to make a myth of her (as the Mexican Joan of Arc), her baroque image resists. Barthes writes:

> Myth . . . purifies [things], it makes them innocent, it gives them a natural and eternal justification, it gives them a clarity which is not that of an explanation but that of a statement of fact . . . In passing from history to nature, myth acts economically: it abolishes the complexity of human acts, it gives them the simplicity of essences, it does away with all dialectics . . . , it organizes a world which is without contradictions because it is without depth. (143)

A cultural icon is not a myth because its iconic status is dependent upon dialectics and multiple layers of meanings. A "cultural icon" is, according to a pair of dictionary definitions, either "a very famous person or thing considered as representing a set of beliefs or a way of life" *(Cambridge International Dictionary)* or "a person or thing regarded as a representative symbol, especially of a culture or movement" *(Oxford English Dictionary)*. Nicola Miller, who studies Latin American intellectuals as cultural icons, understands the latter as "artifacts of veneration," "objects of consumerism," and "vehicles of facilitation, . . . symbolic of values, desires and options" (62).

Miller concludes her study of such icons as José Martí, José Carlos

Mariátegui, and Gabriela Mistral by stating that "icons are touchstones of . . . 'intrinsic meaning': they are telling about the cultural concerns of any particular moment in history" (75). Cultural icons are more than legends because they exceed the confines of the narrative story; they are capable of producing meaning on their own, outside of their stories. As protagonists of multiple stories, their meanings differ among different audiences; they are not myths, evocative of fixed essences. For this reason, I question Nicola Miller's final statement about cultural icons; to reiterate, she claims that icons "are telling about the cultural concerns of any particular moment in history, but . . . *do not allow for tension, conflict or debate* about those concerns" (75, emphasis mine).

Miller's objective is to understand how major Latin American intellectuals came to be not only icons of their national cultures but also agents of unification to Latin American culture as a whole, and it is not my point to argue about whether figures like Diego Rivera and Gabriel García Márquez really signify strongly and univocally to the point of silencing tension, conflict, and debate within a national or continental context. However, I will argue that a cultural icon of the borderlands can only be constructed around the inevitable tensions, conflicts, and debates that determine the cultural complexity of a contact zone.

Yet another reference defines a cultural icon as

> a famous individual who has transcended "mere" celebrity to come to represent a given *Zeitgeist* to a sizable part of the world. As such, a cultural icon is not simply a *famous face* but a complex, multi-layered personage who reflects the conflicts and contradictions of his or her time. (*The Free Dictonary.com*, emphasis in original)

Given that the focus of this study is precisely on the cultural conflicts of the borderlands and the contradictions in interpretation of their histories in different places or among different groups, the cultural icon would seem to be a most useful critical tool. An icon may incorporate legend or even myth but is not limited to a single story or cultural meaning. An icon more likely attains its status as such for its elasticity, its attractiveness to multiple peoples, and its ability to signify differently in multiple contexts.

This study, then, employs the cultural icon concept to look at how multiple groups including Mexicans and gringos, Chicanos and Chileans, Seris and Cherokees, intellectuals and balladeers, novelists and filmmakers, politicians and neighborhood gossips, opposition journalists and state historians have all appropriated well-known figures of borderlands legend and retold their stories, creating meanings for their own audiences. The cultural icons of the borderlands in fact thrive on the tensions and conflicts their stories arouse in the multiple agents of their telling. My objective, then, is to analyze the shifting and conflicting significations communicated by the often-told stories surrounding these borderlands icons at the many different moments and in the many different cultural contexts in which they are produced and reproduced, interpreted and reinterpreted.

While the focus is on icons that emerged in the late nineteenth century, and significant attention is paid to the representations of those icons during that timeframe, all of them have lived on into the twentieth and twenty-first centuries, and their meanings have continued to evolve over time. Their cultural meanings have also varied significantly according to the context in which the retellings of their stories have been produced and the ideological goals and prejudices of those who have produced those retellings. While the stories behind the icons may have common origins and share some key elements, the meanings conveyed are different when produced for a postrevolutionary Mexican nation audience, for one of the manifest destiny–era U.S. Southwest, for surviving twentieth-century indigenous cultures of the borderlands, for late-twentieth-century Chicanos, and so on. This comparative study aims to understand the contact zone centered on the Mexican Northwest through an interpretive reading of the multicultural dialogues about a handful of the region's cultural icons.

A Transnational Approach

While traditional historiography or literary criticism might work well to capture many of the important elements of the cultural diversity of the borderlands, such approaches often fail to grasp their transnational significance. Regional histories and literary histories of the Mexican Northwest tend to lock themselves into national contexts in terms of both bibliography and the conclusions they draw. Despite obvious similarities, no one has ever compared the Lola Casanova legend to *Ramona*, Helen Hunt Jackson's romantic novel of the U.S. Southwest. No one has ever explored the polemic between Mexican centrist nationalism, U.S. racism against Mexicans, and regional pride that led to the publication of the northwestern borderlands' first literary book, Aurelio Pérez Peña's *Heroína*.

But the links and antagonisms between the Mexican borderlands and the United States (and, likewise, the Mexican nation) are undeniable. The culture of the Mexican Northwest was often a more visible, tangible slice of Mexico to *gringos* of the Southwest than was a centrally produced and promulgated Mexican national culture; the borderlands often served as a synechdoche of the national for *gringos* looking for nearby investment opportunities and trading partners. On the other hand, *fronterizos* had to face *yanqui* misconceptions and prejudices about Mexico more directly than other Mexicans because of their proximity to and frequent dealings with their neighbors across the border. The culture of the borderlands reflects the ideas, feelings, and lifestyles of the people living in the borderlands, but it also reflects their reactions to other external representations of their culture that they must face. This study aims to capture this transnational aspect of cultural production by tracing out the cultural trajectories of these icons, all of which tend to travel and to produce multiple meanings about the borderlands from multiple locations.

While the discrete locations of cultural production mentioned above may be impossible to fully distinguish from each other (e.g., regional contexts often carry national implications; the minority discourse of U.S. Chicanos may also contain elements of U.S. nationalist or Mexican nationalist thinking), and it would be dangerous to make assumptions of purity regarding the identity categories implicitly associated with the writers and the intended readers of or the groups represented in the works discussed, for purposes of comparison most texts nonetheless can be linked most prominently to one context or another. I do not believe that in any case these categorizations are so rough or imprecise as to dilute the validity of the accompanying analysis.

Textual Analysis in a Preliterary Culture

This focus on diverse perspectives and meanings further draws the study beyond the confines of "la ciudad letrada"—that is, the region's elite urban *criollo* oligarchy of poets, historiographers, or essayists (Rama)—to intellectual outsiders, including less-educated classes and indigenous groups. The study's scope of inquiry includes literature, historiography, journalism, cultural criticism, legend, *corrido*, film, biography, even gossip—whatever sources are available—in order to construct as diverse a range of representation as possible.

Literary production in the northwestern borderlands in the late nineteenth century hardly existed. Regional historiography had scarcely come into being in those years. And although still a severely limited enterprise until essentially the last decade of the nineteenth century, journalism, on the other hand, was being produced in the region since the 1840s. Its analysis, along with that of the limited literary and historiographic sources of the period, does facilitate inquiry substantially. Letters, *corridos*, biographies, legends, and oral histories together with literature, historiography, and journalism constitute a mass of material substantial enough to draw interesting conclusions and to furthermore represent a diversity of views. For example, all these icons eventually became protagonists of important literary works, but each had existed quite prominently beforehand in popular legend.

In many cases, these icons' trajectory was from legend to literature to history, in that order. And although popular legend is the most ephemeral, least straightforward of these three forms to trace or fix, in this study it is the genre that most often informs all others. If the novels of Francisco Rojas González on Lola Casanova or of Brianda Domecq on Teresa Urrea are the best-known versions of these icons' stories, it is their immense popularity in local legend that made those novels possible.

And while traditional genre categories may in fact apply to the texts under examination here, a close examination reveals a multidirectional interdependency among genres. Borderlands historiography often bases itself on literature, on fiction—after all, Yellow Bird's Joaquín Murrieta novel was published long before Murrieta was admitted into historiography of any kind. The authority of eyewitness testimony asserts itself in literary fiction, the most prominent example being Heriberto Frías's novel *Tomóchic*. Legend and rumor inform chronicles that disguise themselves as history, as with tales of Lola Casanova that continue to circulate around western Sonora. Newspaper accounts and history texts often prove to be less reliable than novels—Brianda Domecq's literary portrait of La Santa de Cabora is certainly more believable than representations of Teresa Urrea in journals such as the *New York Times*. Literary critics trump official historiography on decades-old local legends, as Edith Lowell's M.A. thesis brings Seri versions of the Lola Casanova legend into dialogue with borderlands history. Despite the fact that two texts about the same cultural icon may not agree on much, all these narrative genres seem to inform each other and draw from each other in unpredictable ways, revealing the operation of what Néstor García Canclini calls interclass *mestizaje* (71). Elite urban *fronterizos* participate just as actively as peasant or indigenous classes in popular forms of cultural production such as oral history and legend, and these popular forms in turn invariably inform later reconstructions of these legends in literature and historiography. Journalism, a form of mass cultural production that caters both to wealthy elites and to the literate and semi-literate working classes, also serves as a cultural bridge, interpreting popular cultural expression from an elite perspective and planting seeds to promulgate legend. Guadalupe Cubillas's role in the filibuster Raousset Boulbon's surrender was not well known and might have been forgotten entirely had it not been reported in newspapers.

Bandits, Captives, Heroines, and Saints

The chapters that follow carry out this analysis of a diversity of texts about a handful of major cultural icons of the Mexican borderlands in order to draw from them cultural significations regarding (1) Mexican borderlands culture of the late nineteenth century, which is in fact the main object of inquiry here; (2) Mexican borderlands culture as it continued to evolve through the twentieth century; (3) Mexican national culture and how it has interpreted and influenced the culture of the northwestern borderlands at different historical moments; (4) U.S. culture and how it has understood, interacted with, and often drawn strong responses from the culture of Mexico's northwestern borderlands; (5) the regional culture of the U.S. Southwest and how it has interacted with that of the region directly to its south, that of northwestern Mexico; (6) the increasingly substantial Mexican American culture of the United States and its own relationships to that of the Mexican Northwest; and (7) indigenous cultures of the Mexican borderlands, particularly as they remain apart from and often oppose the *criollo, mestizo,* and/or national mainstream at different times.

The first chapter, "The Other Borderlands," focuses on academic discourse and its neglect of Mexico's borderlands as such. It critiques American studies for paying lip service to postnationalism while remaining exclusively focused on the cultural production of the United States and for resisting multilingual or multinational dialogue, particularly in Spanish or with Mexican or Latin American scholarship. It likewise critiques Mexican studies for its addiction to nationalist premises that understand the northwest only as a region of the nation and not as a contact zone and neglect the regional diversity of indigenous Mexico. Latin American studies similarly has enthusiastically incorporated U.S. Latino/a cultures into its realm of inquiry without sufficiently expanding regional or minoritarian focus within the outdated area-studies paradigm on which the field was founded. The chapter finally advocates a transamerican approach to U.S.–Mexico border studies, an approach that highlights the importance of Mexico's northwestern borderlands— "the other borderlands"—in understanding the highly conflictive context of North America from a postnationalist perspective.

Each of the chapters that follows introduces the case of a particular icon or set of icons and traces out the evolution and multiple deterritorializations and reterritorializations of its representations over the past century and a half across the Americas (and sometimes beyond), and across multiple genres of cultural production.

Chapter 2, "The Many Heads and Tales of Joaquín Murrieta," reviews the multiple biographies of the social bandit from his childhood in Sonora to his vengeful rampage around Alta California and his decapitation (and beyond). It follows his jarred head around the museums of California even as Murrieta himself reportedly goes on living peacefully back home in Sonora, and traces his representations through a series of shocking plagiarisms and unexpected recontextualizations that keep his name alive as an important cultural hero on both sides of the border—not to mention in Chile—to this day.

Chapter 3, "Lola Casanova: Tropes of *Mestizaje* and Frontiers of Race," looks at how regional written culture avoided the disturbing legend of Lola Casanova's rejection of white society and her marriage to a "savage" Indian—that is, until national culture briefly embraced it (only to rebuff it as too radically anti-Malinchista). Only then did regional culture reluctantly incorporate Lola Casanova—whose legend had lived on quite vigorously in popular oral histories of both Seri Indians and *criollo* and *mestizo* Sonorans—into its pantheon of cultural icons.

Chapter 4 takes a slightly different approach. Titled "The Heroines of Guaymas," it looks at the many competing versions of the history of the filibuster invasions of Gaston de Raousset Boulbon into Sonora in the early 1850s, drawing attention to how the addition to this borderlands drama of a number of local supporting players—Raousset's Mexican girlfriend; Doña Loreto Encinas de Avilés, the legendary heroine of Guaymas; Guadalupe Cubillas, whose rigid decorum elicited Raousset's surrender; José María Leyva, Mexican patriot turned Yaqui insurgent hero—transforms a simple conflict between Mexico and France into a complex representation of the borderlands in relation to both Mexico and the United States. In particular, the independent journalist Aurelio Pérez Peña's play *Heroína*, along with his journalism, reflects significantly on race relations in the borderlands and on the daunting and unavoidable shadow cast by the United States over the culture of the Mexican borderlands.

The final chapter, "Of Sedition and Spiritism: La Santa de Cabora," looks at the reception of the larger-than-life figure of Teresa Urrea in Mexico City, Sonora, Chihuahua, Arizona, New York, California, and elsewhere by worshippers, spiritists, government officials, protorevolutionaries, mothers of gravely ill children, and latter-day admirers. It traces her extraordinary life from the hut where she grew up as a bastard girl to the ranch of her wealthy father, to the town of Tomóchic where her worship as a living saint sparked one of the most bloody and horrific stories of the Porfiriato. It follows La Santa de Cabora into exile across the border to Arizona and Texas, and later into California, where she embarked on a cross-country tour as a healer and performer.

The book closes with an epilogue that summarizes how the various icons in question have signified in the different cultural contexts in which they have come into play: those of the United States, the Chicano Southwest, indigenous Mexico, the Mexican nation, and the Mexican Northwest.

In order to piece together the shifting and conflictive meanings of these icons in the borderlands contact zone from which they emerged, it has been necessary to carry out a study that crosses borders of nation, language, time, discipline, and genre. This kind of methodology is what I believe border studies requires. Although my largely archival research has limited the scope of my project and forced me to favor certain kinds of sources over others (namely, those most likely to find their way into print, whether directly or indirectly, versus those more inaccessible to scholars of U.S. or Mexican literature or history—oral histories and legends, especially those of indigenous cultures), I believe its methodology has produced a sufficient diversity of representation to draw valuable conclusions regarding the complexities of the culture of the Mexican northwestern borderlands as seen from a transamerican perspective.

CHAPTER ONE

THE OTHER
BORDERLANDS

UPON **THE** **SIGNING** of the Treaty of Guadalupe Hidalgo in 1848, a new border was established between the United States and Mexico in western North America. Like the western United States, northwestern Mexico was "frontier" territory, populated only sparsely, except by indigenous groups, many of whom remained autonomous and unincorporated into the Mexican nation. Prior to 1848, Mexico's northwestern frontier also included the lands ceded to the United States as a result of the U.S.–Mexico war of 1846–48. Now suddenly Sonora and Baja California found themselves on the border, politically severed from their former Mexican frontier neighbors, territories that would become the U.S. states of California and Arizona. This does not, however, imply that Mexico's Northwest was to abruptly become culturally distinct from the new U.S. Southwest. Writes the Chicano cultural critic José David Saldívar: "First carved out in the midst of U.S. imperialism by the Treaty of Guadalupe Hidalgo (1848) and the Gadsden Purchase (1853), the U.S.–Mexico borderlands have earned a reputation as a 'third country,' because our southern border is not simply Anglocentric on one side and Mexican on the other" (8).

Saldívar's 1997 study of borderlands culture, *Border Matters*, features readings of works by Mexican American artists and writers such as

Américo Paredes, Gloria Anzaldúa, and El Vez in a study that aims at
the following: "By analyzing a broad range of cultural texts and practices (*corridos*, novels, poems, paintings, *conjunto*, punk and hip-hop songs,
travel writing, and ethnography) and foregrounding the situated experiences facing Chicanos/as, *Border Matters* puts forth a model for a new
kind of U.S. cultural studies, one that challenges the homogeneity of
U.S. nationalism and popular culture" (ix). Saldívar's book, then, is not
about the entirety of U.S.–Mexico borderlands experience as the prior
quote implies, but about the borderlands of Chicanos/as, a borderlands
positioned against "the homogeneity of U.S. nationalism"; in other
words, it is about the U.S. Southwest.

Border Matters is an important book because it took the lead in a
movement on the part of scholars of Mexican American culture in the
United States to "remap American cultural studies" to reflect the heterogeneity of U.S. culture, particularly with regard to its Chicano components. This incursion of identity politics into the field of American
studies, frequently through scholarship categorizing itself as "border
studies," has transformed the field.[1] The "new" American studies now
advertises itself as "multicultural," "postnationalist," and even "transamerican."[2] Yet, most of these projects of borderlands cultural studies
limit themselves at the border, as if the U.S. Southwest were detached
culturally from the Mexican Northwest. This of course was not the case
in 1848, nor is it so today.

Referring to the establishment of the new national border in the
mid-nineteenth century, the historian Oscar Martínez writes:

> Mexican Americans . . . and Mexicans felt deeply the impact of
> the boundary in the formation of lifestyles, attitudes, and cultural
> orientations. Although the border separated Mexican Americans
> politically from Mexico, physical proximity kept them tied to their
> roots culturally and socially . . . Their compatriots . . . on Mexican
> soil found themselves insulated from American political domination
> but not from economic and cultural influences; that reality, coupled
> with sheer geographic remoteness from the core of the nation,
> assured that the *norteños* or *fronterizos* . . . would develop societal
> patterns distinct from the rest of Mexico. Thus the presence of the
> border played a fundamental role in converting border Chicanos and

Mexicans into entities that stood apart from the mainstream societies
of each nation. (*Troublesome Border* 5)

Nonetheless, the great interest in understanding the borderlands of the
U.S. Southwest has obscured the Mexican borderlands from scholarly
inquiry in the U.S. academy. This chapter looks at how border studies
has taken shape in Mexico and the United States from multiple perspectives and in multiple contexts, paying particular attention to the
treatment of Mexico's northwestern borderlands of the late nineteenth
century.

Its focus, then, is decidedly not national. While the national perspectives of Mexico and of the United States will be considered, particularly as they are applied to the discursive evolution of the various icons
in question here, the point is not to use the cultural history of the Mexican borderlands in order to better understand U.S. national paradigms.
I believe it is a greater priority to break ground on studying the Mexican borderlands from a transamerican perspective without centering
the study on the United States. Nor is my purpose to revise Mexican
national paradigms from the perspective of the national periphery. I
assume here that U.S. and Mexican national cultures are already sufficiently well understood. The point of border studies is to shift the focus
to key contact zones such as the Mexican Northwest to better understand cultural relations among multiple groups (not just nations).

Mexico's Borderlands in American Studies

American studies, including the related fields of Chicano studies and
southwestern studies, has been a major locus of scholarly investigation
regarding the U.S.–Mexican borderlands. The best of such investigations have contributed strongly to what Ramón Saldívar articulates to
be "an opposition reconstruction of American literary history"—and of
U.S. cultural history in general ("Narrative Ideology" 20). However,
the decentering process in American studies is not new to the last few
decades. Many have located an important moment in American studies
with regard to the borderlands in the 1890s with Frederick Jackson
Turner's historic address to the American Historical Association,"The
Significance of the Frontier in American History."[3] Turner famously

argued that westward movement of the American frontier throughout the nineteenth century was key to the formation of the U.S. national character. The frontier, which he defined as "the meeting point between savagery and civilization" (3), as it moved ever westward, away from old Europe and into the virgin wilderness of the West, "advanced and carried with it individualism, democracy, and nationalism, and powerfully affected the East and the Old World" (35). He gave the speech at a time when the western United States was largely "settled" and its "savage" indigenous groups mostly subdued. He launched his frontier hypothesis that it was the process of westward settlement and frontier culture that had formed the core of U.S. culture at a time when the country would need to refocus and assume new goals: "For nearly three centuries the dominant fact in American life has been expansion. With the settlement of the Pacific coast and the occupation of the free lands, this movement has come to a check" ("The Problem of the West" 219).

Turner's persuasive reading of U.S. history turned attention from both the eastern United States, seen until then as the nation's political, cultural, and spiritual center, and from Europe, which had been taken for granted to be the point of origin for American culture.[4] Turner posited an American exceptionalism, identifying expansionism as the guiding principle of national cultural formation. However, Turner "believed that the particularism of the colonial past gave way to a homogeneous people. In affirming that unprogressive European cultural traditions could not enter this West, Turner . . . did not imagine Native Americans, African Americans, or Mexican Americans as part of the deep fraternity of the American people."[5] The Americanist Brook Thomas links Turner's thinking with that of Josiah Strong, author of the 1885 treatise *Our Country*, a text promoting a messianic message of manifest destiny, in which the racially superior white Protestant Anglo-Saxons were on a divine mission to "civilize" not only the existing territory of the United States but also Mexico, Central and South America, the Pacific islands and Africa, "and beyond" (Thomas 285). While Turner did not project the blatant racism of Strong, his radically expanded vision of U.S. culture clearly did not recognize its inherently imperialist underpinnings.

A couple of decades later, Herbert Eugene Bolton launched another vector of historical inquiry with his publication of *The Spanish Borderlands* (1921). Bolton challenged then conventional notions of U.S. history's having origins only in the East and in English colonialism. Bolton promoted the incorporation of the Spanish colonial heritage of the U.S. South and West into the field of U.S. history. Bolton did not sell his turn to the borderlands as a potentially new dominant paradigm of inquiry for U.S. historians but as an important interrogation that had until then been excluded from national historiography. His Spanish borderlands confined itself initially to the U.S. side of the border; however, eventually the "Bolton school" would go on to expand its work into Latin American history, most particularly the history of Mexico, extending U.S. history into a much more broadly defined history of the Americas. Bolton wrote for a U.S. audience, his goal being to open the minds of U.S. history students beyond the limits of traditional U.S. history studied in isolation from its geographical context in the Americas. Bolton most clearly articulated his vision in 1932 in his own address to the American Historical Association, "The Epic of Greater America," in which he recalled Turner's frontier thesis when he asked, "Who has tried to state the significance of the frontier in terms of the Americas?" (quoted in Weber, 36), only to go on to challenge its limitations.

Bolton's work, focused as it was on colonial times, did little to draw attention beyond U.S. culture, except by pointing toward its distant Spanish colonial past. Many in the United States were already familiar with the Spanish past through novels such as Helen Hunt Jackson's exceedingly popular *Ramona*, an emblematic text in the late-nineteenth-century construction of the U.S. Southwest's "Spanish fantasy heritage." This nostalgic reinvention of pre-nineteenth-century Alta California was animated by "gracious Spanish grandees, beautiful *señoritas*, and gentle Catholic friars [who] oversaw an abundant pastoral empire worked by contented mission Indians" (David Gutiérrez 70). This idyllic construction of New Spain contrasts distinctly with U.S. notions of Mexican culture in the nineteenth and early twentieth centuries, which portrayed Mexico as backward, uncultured, corrupt, and immoral. Mexico in the 1920s and 1930s remained a discrete and inferior other, unrelated to U.S. culture except in its Spanish colonial past, which it shared with part of the United States. Contemporary Mexico, along with its literature, historiography, and popular culture, was of little interest to the Bolton school.[6]

Unfortunately, Bolton's was not a first step that would invoke others to exceed his intentions and further recontextualize U.S. cultural history and the notion of America in hemispheric terms. American studies in general has been largely guided, historically, by what some have called the "myth and symbol school," which promoted a series of traditional icons, metaphors, heroes, rituals, and narratives that together formed the basis of collective consciousness and national subjectivity.[7] It was not until the last decades of the twentieth century that another major intellectual movement would again push the U.S. Southwest to the forefront of American studies, this time as the field was driven to pay the Mexican American culture of the southwestern borderlands significant attention. The rise of Chicano studies drew the intellectual focus of American studies away from mainstream cultural myths to the margins of U.S. culture with explorations of such themes as migration, hybridity, cultural conflict and resistance, and intercultural influence. This time, Mexico's role was not that of an idealized colonial era past; the context of the borderlands profoundly linked U.S. and Mexican histories and contemporary cultures in ways that had been ignored as much by Boltonians as by Turnerians and adherents to traditional American studies methods.

José David Saldívar proclaimed in 1997 that "the invocation of the U.S.–Mexico border as a paradigm of crossing, resistance, and circulation in Chicano/a studies has contributed to the 'worlding' of American studies and further helped to instill a new transnational literacy in the U.S. academy" (xiii). The term "worlding" is misleading, however; Chicano studies certainly brought multiple perspectives into American studies discourse and rightfully recognized Mexican culture's presence in U.S. culture both in the borderlands as well as in the national mainstream. Still, Chicano studies' center of inquiry by definition was the Mexican American population of the United States, and as a result its studies of the borderlands have always tended to focus on the U.S. side of the border. In some ways, this limitation is perfectly reasonable: the Mexican American culture of the U.S. Southwest deserves to be recognized as an important and long-standing force in U.S. culture. Still this

U.S. bias has produced some unintended side effects that have caused a problematic imbalance in scholarly production on the borderlands in general, as we will see.

Another recent trend in American studies is the "postnationalist" impulse. The goal of this movement is to make American studies "less insular and parochial, and more internationalist and comparative," and "to revise the cultural nationalism and celebratory American exceptionalism" of previous generations (Curiel et al. 2). It aims to be "critical of U.S. hegemony and the constructedness of both national myths and national borders" (Curiel et al. 3). Among its gripes with American studies is the field's tendency to produce a homogeneous vision of U.S. national culture and history. Regarding the role of Mexican Americans: "Chicanos . . . remain perpetual latecomers, cast in the role of 'recent' immigrants and foreign nationals, as if the War with Mexico did not predate the Civil War" (Curiel et al. 4).

Here, the field of American studies is clearly responding to Saldívar and other U.S. Chicana/o border theorists of recent years whose work has challenged the disciplinary and linguistic bounds of American studies. However, the degree to which this new postnationalist American studies truly goes beyond the borders of the United States is open to question. The work of Chicano studies scholars has certainly drawn attention to the inadequacy of nationalist paradigms to discuss the southwestern borderlands. Chicano studies and postnationalist American studies scholars then are reading U.S. national culture from the multiple perspectives of the United States' multiethnic population and its many communities of immigrants (and their descendents) from all over the world—which is not the same thing as truly expanding American studies beyond national geopolitical boundaries. The borderlands of postnationalist American studies still tends to limit itself quite strictly at the U.S. border, as if it were being patrolled by the immigration police.

In her 2004 presidential address to the American Studies Association, Shelley Fisher Fishkin asserted, "if the circle of critics and colleagues with whom we regularly share our work all live in the United States, if we assume the subject of our study is by definition what transpires within U.S. borders, and if all are comfortable reading or speaking no language but English, many of us see nothing amiss. We may snicker at the residents of Gopher Prairie for their conviction that 'Main Street is the apex of civilization.' But shouldn't we recognize the hint of a similar arrogance and ignorance at work when we assume that the United States represents the apex of American Studies scholarship, and that whatever American academics 'do not know' can't possibly be worth knowing?" (36). This is not to say that the project of postnationalist American studies is not transformative—it has indeed expanded the field of inquiry of American studies and posed productive challenges to commonly accepted notions of American history and culture. Still, it must not overstate its case.

For an example, let us turn briefly to the recent anthology *Postnationalist American Studies* (2000), edited by John Carlos Rowe. The chapter that focuses most on the U.S.–Mexico borderlands is the excellent analysis by Shelley Streeby of the Joaquín Murrieta legend in goldrush-era California (see chapter 2). Murrieta was born in Sonora and migrated to Alta California in the early 1850s. His legend has taken many forms, and Murrieta has played many roles, from criminal desperado to social bandit to soldier of *la raza*. His story has been told and retold many times both in the U.S. Southwest and in Sonora (and elsewhere). Yet Streeby's "postnationalist" reading of the Murrieta story cites no Sonoran sources. In fact, its only two Spanish-language sources were both published in the United States, and despite its focus on *corridos*, it leaves out M. A. Serna Maytorena's *En Sonora así se cuenta* (1988), the definitive study on Sonoran *corridos*, which includes three different versions of the Murrieta ballad. A suggested teaching syllabus provided by Streeby includes no Spanish-language or Mexican sources at all. True, her focus is not Sonora but 1848 California. Nonetheless, a glance at the circumstances that brought Murrieta from Sonora to California and the differing significations of his myth back in his homeland would have added an interesting postnationalist perspective to the story, and the only way to engage effectively in a postnationalist context is to open dialogue with the scholarship produced abroad, if only just across the border.

The "new" American studies, like postnationalist American studies, pays lip service in its most recent incarnation to its pretensions of "address[ing] the problems of understanding the many different societies of the western hemisphere and its strategic border zones" (Rowe, *New American Studies* xv), and to its claims that "we should know that today the study of U.S. cultures is necessarily bilingual" (xvii). It insists that its "new interest in border studies should include investigations of how the many different Americas have historically influenced and interpreted each other" (53). It proposes "establishing intellectual and cultural contact zones where a certain dialectics or dialogics of cultural exchange is understood to be a crucial aspect of how the field of American Studies is constituted and how the related territories of the Americas and the United States ought to be understood" (57). Once again its intentions challenge racist and imperialist biases of the field, but in practice so far it has been disappointing.

John Carlos Rowe, whose proposals, quoted above, point to a new comparativist movement in American studies, and who also edited the above-mentioned definitive anthology on postnationalist American studies, does little to back up his lofty ideas. In his own essay on Joaquín Murrieta (and it is telling that in it he uses the common Anglophone spelling, "Murieta"), a text focused on the 1854 John Rollin Ridge novel and U.S. "Indian removal" policy, he makes no citation of any Latin American or Spanish-language text. There is no evidence of the Murrieta legend's circulation in a multilingual contact zone. The article, taken from Rowe's book *Literary Culture and U.S. Imperialism* (2000),[8] in fact does just what the author himself warns the new American studies against: "comparative cultural study can often reinforce, rather than transform, national and cultural hierarchies and even contribute to the sort of cultural imperialism it is intended to criticize and overcome" (*New American Studies* xvi). By ignoring scholarship written in Spanish and produced in Latin America, Rowe's and Streeby's scholarship perform just such an act of intellectual imperialism. Mexican and Spanish-language scholarship is routinely rendered invisible by American studies scholarship, even that which exhibits the best intentions of inclusiveness. Postnationalist American studies may indeed promote the U.S.–Mexico borderlands as a major center of intellectual inquiry, but it is a center skewed ever northward that still firmly maintains an apparently impenetrable intellectual wall at its Mexican edge.

For a Mexicanist observer of the posturing of the new Americanists, there are many ironies. If a Mexican scholar on the borderlands omits from her or his bibliography an important U.S. source, the reason is likely that the U.S. text was unavailable in underfunded Mexican libraries and that it was too expensive to obtain individually. However, Mexican border studies scholars would be seen as remiss if they did not look beyond national scholarship. In American studies, however, foreign scholarship routinely goes unnoticed, despite its availability in U.S. university libraries or through interlibrary loan.

This is not to say that all scholars working in American studies or Chicano studies retain old-school parochialist methodologies. Oscar Martínez, a former director of the Center for Inter-American and Border Studies at the University of Texas at El Paso, is a professor of borderlands history who is active in both American and Latin American studies. His work transcends disciplinary boundaries and draws from multilingual and multinational sources. Upon reading the first page of *Troublesome Border* (1988), his study of the history of political and social conflicts between the United States and Mexico in the borderlands, that "Americans are largely unaware that Mexicans also view their northern border with concern, and at times even alarm" (1), it is clear that not only is Martínez not a traditional or even "new" Americanist but that he understands perfectly the shortcomings of American studies. Americans are unaware of Mexico's point of view on the borderlands because Americans, like the Americanists who teach them American history and cultural studies, remain complacently uninformed about the world in which their country exists, even when it comes to its immediate neighbors. Unfortunately, Martínez's approach to border studies is rare among Americanists.[9]

This, however, is not to say that Mexico never enters the discussion, particularly when it comes to Chicano studies. In fact, texts like Gloria Anzaldúa's *Borderlands/La Frontera* (1987) have been a major tool in introducing the Mexican cultural heritage of Chicanos into American studies discourse. Anzaldúa does employ a Spanish-language bibliography, citing such prominent Mexican intellectuals as Octavio Paz and José Vasconcelos and examining Mexican cultural icons such as the Virgin of Guadalupe, the Aztec goddess Coatlicue, and the tragic heroine of indigenous legend La Llorona. Anzaldúa also writes in *pocho*, freely mixing Spanish into her English narration. Anzaldúa's borderlands are richly

Mexican. However, they also exhibit a serious shortcoming, made apparent in a list of borderlands types that she elaborates: "Chicano, *indio*,
American Indian, *mojado*, *mexicano*, immigrant Latino, Anglo in power,
working class Anglo, Black, Asian" (109). While her list clearly includes
Mexicans, including of course Mexicans on the U.S. side of the border,
it totally overlooks borderlands Mexicans on the Mexican side of the
border. Anzaldúa's concern is the U.S. Southwest, not the Mexican north,
and therefore she does not bother to list *norteños* among her cast of borderlands characters. Nor does she concern herself with their unique culture anywhere in her book.

   Likewise, her treatment of indigenous Mexico follows mainstream
Mexican nationalist discourse that treats the national past as that of the
Aztecs (e.g., Coatlicue, Tonantzin-Tonantsi for Anzaldúa); her borderlands is Aztlán, mythical homeland of the Aztecs, and her Chicanos are
"the *aztecas del norte*" (23). But the Aztecs—whose empire was based in
Tenochtitlán, today Mexico City—were not known to have had a great
cultural presence in what are the present-day borderlands (although they
may have passed through there at some point). Utterly erased from
Anzaldúa's vision of Mexico are the indigenous peoples of the northern
borderlands, some of whom—the Yaquis, the Mayos, the Seris—continue
to have a major cultural impact on the region (see especially chapters
3, 4, and 5). When Mexico does enter American studies discourse, it
tends to be in a simplified form in which it is reduced to its national
stereotypes, and the cultural diversity that defines Mexico's northern
borderlands is largely ignored.

   Therefore it is not surprising to read American studies scholarship
that states confidently (citing no sources) that "Mexican literature flourished in the northern Mexican borderlands prior to and after 1848"
(Calderón and Saldívar 2). Such a statement would surely be shocking
to the experts on Mexican borderlands literature, who do not find any
kind of "flourishing" literary industry developing in Mexico's Northwest, for example, until well into the twentieth century. Indeed, its first
published book of literature, Aurelio Pérez Peña's *Heroína* (1897), has
been largely forgotten and remains unread even by most experts on
Sonoran literary history because there were no literary institutions to
preserve or even critique it at the time it was published (see chapter 4).

It was uncovered as an archaeological artifact might be, buried deep in the archives of the Bancroft Library of the University of California at Berkeley, only a few years ago.

The Mexican borderlands literary critic María Socorro Tabuenca mounts a rigorous attack on border studies in the United States, claiming that its obsessive and exclusive focus on the U.S. side of the border has "resulted in the invisibilization of the literature that originates in the northern borderlands of Mexico" (86).[10] In a more recent collaboration, Mexico-based Tabuenca and the U.S.–based Mexicanist Debra Castillo argue:

> It is important either to take both sides—the United States and
> Mexico—into consideration or to be specific about which side one
> is going to talk about or study and to recognize the material and
> metaphorical differences involved in such transnational analyses.
> Otherwise, the "intellectual colonialism" from which the Mexican
> border has suffered to this day will be perpetuated. (4)

They go on to point out that while Chicano literature may occupy a marginal, minority position in U.S. culture, "when it is put into the perspective of a transborder literary project, the disparity vis-à-vis Mexican border literature is clear" (6).

Castillo and Tabuenca recognize that part of the reason why Mexican border literature occupies a subordinate place in relation to U.S.— including Chicano—border literature is the fact that northern Mexico's publishing industry is smaller and more poorly funded. Fewer books are published, and those that do get printed see a smaller distribution. The same applies to borderlands criticism and historiography. There is a greater abundance of U.S.–based border studies criticism, and there is a greater access to academic journals and university presses that publish in English. However, this is not an excuse for the new American studies to fail to seek out Mexican scholarship. As Kirsten Silva Gruesz puts it regarding her own "transamerican" approach to American studies: "the challenge . . . is not to integrate Latinos to an existing national tradition, but to reshape that tradition in a way that recognizes the continuous life of Latinos within and around it" (211). Whether or not Mexicans would recognize themselves as "Latinos," her point is clear:

American studies scholarship must do more than just study the Latin American immigrant element of U.S. culture; it must broaden its scope of inquiry into those Latino cultures of the United States and also into the Latin American cultures to which they remain connected. And, of course, scholarship that goes beyond the traditional bounds of American studies must dialogue with scholars of the fields into which it expands.[11] Unfortunately, despite some gestures in this direction, American studies has not yet been able to break out of its nationalist habits, and the majority of its border studies projects have tended to confine themselves to the U.S. Southwest.

Mexico's Borderlands in Mexican Studies

Mexicanists, as I have mentioned, who study Mexico's borderlands are typically more likely than Americanists who study the U.S. Southwest to consult scholarship from the other side of the border. For example, volume 4 of *Visión histórica de la frontera norte de México* (2nd edition, 1994), edited by David Piñera Ramírez, routinely cites U.S. sources such as J. Fred Rippy and Oscar Martínez. In fact, as Latin Americanists are aware, it is the very same colonial hierarchies of knowledge that discourage Americanists from seeking out intellectual dialogue with Latin American and Latin Americanist scholars that necessitate cross-border citations for Mexican investigators of the northern borderlands. The citation of U.S. scholarship validates Mexican research in a way that the citation of Mexican scholarship does not for U.S. scholars, particularly those working in American studies.

Nonetheless, border studies among specialists in Mexico has also tended to limit itself in ways that have deflated its importance when viewed from a transamerican perspective. The first problem regarding the study of the Mexican borderlands by Mexicans and Mexicanists has always been what Luis Leal calls "the powerful centrifugal force operating in every aspect of Mexico's life and culture" ("Mexico's Centrifugal Culture" 111). Mexican national culture has tended to construct itself in a centralist fashion, with the cultures of its geographic periphery consistently given less importance than those of Mexico City and the surrounding states of central Mexico.

Tabuenca elaborates on the same theme by asserting that until the last decades of the twentieth century, "Mexico's northern borderlands continued to be seen as 'land of savages' [*tierra de bárbaros*] in national discourse" (106). Mexico's efforts since its independence to establish a profoundly rooted national culture have consistently marginalized its borderlands states. Mexico's periphery's tensions with the center were acute from the beginning, as border states found nineteenth-century national governing structures to favor central states. Border states, separated from the capital by huge distances, mountains, jungles, and difficult terrain, felt isolated from the heart of the nation and developed regional cultures that were in many cases quite distinct from national models. For example, Mexico's Northwest had few cultural links to the Aztecs, to the Virgin of Guadalupe, and other national symbols. And as *fronterizos* rejected mainstream national culture, Mexico City's cultural *caudillos* ignored borderlands culture. Aside from its reputation as a barbaric frontier territory, the north is too close to the United States, and as a result its culture is often seen as contaminated by U.S. influence. And just as Mexican nationalist culture has marginalized its peripheries, Mexican studies has also tended to focus its attention on the national and on the central.

This is not to say that the Mexican academy (along with Mexicanist scholarship in the United States and elsewhere) has not directed any attention to Mexico's northwestern borderlands. However, its efforts in this area have, like those of Americanists with regard to the U.S. borderlands, been surprisingly parochial, particularly when it comes to nineteenth-century projects. The most common treatment is that of the Mexican borderlands as a regional culture (often articulated in state-based terms: e.g., Sonoran history, the literature of Baja California Sur), a small piece of the larger national culture.

For example, Piñera's aforementioned *Visión histórica* presents the northern borderlands' history from 1850 to 1910 in three chapters (each one representing a different temporal period), with each chapter broken down by state, so that each of the six border states (Chihuahua, Coahuila, Nuevo León, Tamaulipas, Sonora, and Baja California) receives equal and individualized attention.[12] Its focus is on putting together state histories like pieces of a puzzle that together form that of the nation.

Likewise, volume 3 of *Historia general de Sonora* (2nd edition, 1997), co-ordinated by Juan Antonio Ruibal Corella, structures its content, the history of the northwestern borderlands state of Sonora, largely through national paradigms, following a national periodization (e.g., independence, the war with the United States, the era of *la Reforma*, the French occupation, etc.).

César Sepúlveda, in his *La frontera norte de México: Historia, conflictos 1762–1983* (1983), refers repeatedly in his prologues to his subject of inquiry as "our" borderlands, making clear the Mexican context from which he speaks. Again, while he treats national conflicts with the United States—including the 1846–48 war, the filibuster invasions of the 1850s, the various political conflicts over the border, and so forth, his attention remains focused on the Mexican side. Although of course his bibliography includes many U.S. sources, including books by Herbert Eugene Bolton and David Weber, among many others, his study is not comparative. It is once again a piece of Mexican history, Mexican national history.

A look at Sergio Ortega Noriega's *Un ensayo de historia regional: El noroeste de México 1530–1880* (1993) further demonstrates the dominance in Mexican borderlands historiography of a regional focus that refuses to venture beyond a national context. Here the author addresses his Mexican readers (presumably an audience from central Mexico, where the book was published) "who wish to know the history of the Northwest, a region that occupies a less than modest place in the 'histories of Mexico'" (7). Ortega Noriega's object is to give the borderlands the attention it has previously lacked in the context of national historiography. Interestingly, when confronted with the changes in the borderlands' geography during the course of the vast time period of his study, he chooses to limit himself in utterly national terms. For him, the Northwest is "the cluster of states of Sinaloa, Sonora, Baja California and Baja California Sur, to which I necessarily must add the southern part of the U.S. state of Arizona as well as part of California for the period in which they were territories of New Spain and the Mexican Republic" (11). It is as if suddenly in 1848 and again in 1853 the cultural unity that linked Alta California to Baja California and what has become Arizona to Sonora terminated with the signing of a pair of treaties.

Still, as Ortega Noriega's work makes clear, the study of colonial North America complicates historiography as presented in strictly national terms. A closer look at the field of Mexican colonial historiography sheds additional light on the problem. In accordance with the "centrifugal force" exerted by Mexican national culture, as mentioned by Leal above, Mexican colonial historiography has tended to maintain its focus principally on central Mexico (and secondarily on Yucatán), paying quite limited attention to the northern borderlands. On the other hand, we have seen that as early as the 1920s, Herbert Eugene Bolton called for the incorporation of the history of Spanish colonial North America into a broadly defined American history. Bolton and his followers naturally followed up with a historiography that focused on present-day U.S. territories such as Alta California but also expanded southward, most especially into northwestern Mexico, thereby "invad-[ing] the domain of historians of Mexico" (Weber 66). The Mexican historian José Cuello proposed in a 1982 essay "a counterattack" (Weber 68): the reincorporation of the colonial history of what is today northern Mexico into Mexican colonial historiography, but with the caveat that this project be limited at the current national border. "The Borderlands field, he suggested, was a disreputable partner from whom historians of Mexico should seek a divorce. Borderlands history, he argued, is not 'an integral part of the Latin American historical field because the conceptual structure which organizes Borderlands history and selects its methodologies and themes belongs to the field of United States history'" (Weber 68, quoting Cuello). Since it is the U.S. academy (the Bolton school and its descendents) that has provided the conceptual framework for the field, Cuello holds that the intellectual disparities that have shaped national historiographies are so severe as to make cross-border inquiry—even when considering periods prior to the establishment of contemporary national borders—dangerously problematic.

Likewise, Mexicanists working in the United States have been relatively obsessed with the national paradigm in their dealings with the region. A major U.S.–based study, Stuart Voss's *On the Periphery of Nineteenth-Century Mexico* (1982), positions its major focus (the histories of the northwestern states of Sonora and Sinaloa) once again in a national context, mapping out the process by which the northwestern

Mexican periphery "became part of the larger national experience" (xv). Voss concerns himself with the period leading up to the Mexican revolution, examining "how a region on the periphery of Mexico in time became not only an ongoing part of the nation, but eventually its center" (xv). While Voss's interpretation of borderlands history is perhaps more radical than that of some other historians, it once again limits itself to the national paradigm.

A variant to this nationalist vision is the perspective of frontier studies. Just as Frederick Jackson Turner argued that the frontier was a central force in shaping national culture in the United States, a few scholars have investigated the nature and the significance of Mexico's northern frontier. However, David Weber notes that Mexico's frontier has never achieved the prominence in national discourse that the U.S. frontier did with Turner:

> The Anglo-American frontier may or may not have promoted
> democracy, as Turner argued, but, because Americans widely believe
> that it did, the idea itself is of considerable importance. In Mexico,
> however, there has been no counterpart to American idealization
> of frontier life. No myth about the salubrious impact of the frontier
> exists on which a Mexican Turner might construct a credible
> intellectual edifice. (51)

Such a comparative approach is not quite transamerican, as it maintains its focus on the relation of the frontier to tropes of national culture, whether in the United States or Mexico, and is blatantly U.S.–centric in its imposition of a major U.S.–specific discourse onto the study of Mexico.

Nonetheless, it has produced some interesting conclusions, namely, that a cultural transformation did occur toward the end of the nineteenth century in which "[t]he movement of [U.S.] capital into northern Mexico also reshaped northern Mexico from a frontier (a state-facing-nonstate process) into a borderlands, an area (or processal geography, better said) linked to another state (the U.S.) by capital and the cross-boundary movement of people" (Heyman 53). This "frontier to border transition" (Mora-Torres 4) coincides not just with the arrival of U.S. capital to the Mexican north but with "[t]he end of old-style 19th-century *caudillismo*, the defeat of the Indians, the decline in contraband and banditry" and the integration of northern Mexico "into a centralized political system."[13] This transition interestingly links the Mexican borderlands both to the United States, with which it became increasingly connected in economic terms, and to central Mexico, to which it became better integrated politically. More importantly, by the late nineteenth century, the borderlands came to enjoy improved transportation—most importantly rail lines—which made the region more accessible in both directions. All of the above developments established more solid cultural links in both directions as well. Nonetheless, the vast majority of Mexican studies scholarship on the borderlands has tended to emphasize the national over the transamerican context in its treatment of the period.

Mexico's Borderlands in Latin American Studies

Similar comparative approaches are not uncommon in Latin American studies. In particular, the frontier concept of U.S. history has been adapted for comparative use in Latin American contexts on numerous occasions, with results of varying degrees of interest. Weber summarizes some of the principal conclusions of this trajectory of Latin American studies scholarship, noting first that in Latin America, the physical environments of frontier territories (e.g., the Argentine pampa, the Amazon jungle) tended to differ significantly from those in the United States (40). While this is true for much of Latin America, the climate and topography of northwestern Mexico are in fact quite similar to those of the U.S. Southwest. Second, the particular kinds of relationships between national cultures and unincorporated indigenous groups of frontier zones often differed in Latin America when compared to those seen in the United States, with U.S. policies of annihilation contrasting sharply with Latin America's promotion of assimilation (41)—although, once again, in the Mexican Northwest, while some *mestizaje* and the absorption of certain indigenous groups into the mainstream did occur, regarding other less docile groups (e.g., the Seris, the Yaquis), Mexican frontier policy was often nearly parallel to U.S. policy in the Southwest. Third, Latin Americanists have contrasted Turner's "environmentalism"—that is, the notion that the land, climate, and conditions of the frontier had a decisive impact on pioneer settlers and, ultimately, on U.S. culture—with the Latin American case, in which the impact of frontiersmen and the culture they brought with them to the frontier was a transformative factor in the shaping of frontier culture (and not vice versa) (42). Once again, in the particular case of the Mexican borderlands, the difference is not so obvious. While it is clear that Mexico's frontier did not produce the same kind of cultural metaphors that the U.S. frontier did, the Mexican historian Silvio Zavala's conclusion that "the insecurity of life in the Mexican north and the instability of a docile Indian labor force 'stamped the character of the northern people with a certain temper and energy'" (quoted in Weber 44) suggests some clear parallels as well.

This is not to say that Latin Americanists are comfortable with any "frontier hypothesis," or even with the notion of frontier as a major node of inquiry. Recall that "frontier" is usually understood as a contact zone where the edges of civilization (settlement) and barbarism (unconquered wilderness) overlap. Regarding pre-twentieth-century Latin America, as David Weber and Jane Rausch point out:

> Geographic areas may have a low man-land ratio, but they are rarely "unsettled," and areas that urbanites see as "wilderness" have nearly always contained their own distinctive indigenous civilizations. Moreover, native societies usually have regarded themselves as at the center rather than on the frontier. As used by the invading culture, the word *frontier* has had a decidedly ideological quality. (xiii)

For this and other reasons mentioned above, the frontier paradigm has not had a central presence in Latin Americanist scholarship on the borderlands.

What is seen clearly in these more comparative studies that are approached from a broadly Latin American perspective is a tendency to gloss over or utterly overlook the specificity of the case of northern Mexico. After all, unlike the cases of Patagonia, the Amazon jungle, or the Peruvian Andes, Mexico's northern frontier directly abuts the United States. It follows then that its relationship with the United States would be different from that of other parts of Latin America with the North American behemoth, and that U.S. culture, particularly

U.S. southwestern borderlands culture, would play a greater role in its constitution and evolution. Therefore, comparative Latin American frontier studies have not been helpful in illuminating the specific case of Mexico's Northwest.

Still, to the extent that many such studies do at least mention northern Mexico, if only as an exception to predominant patterns common to other parts of Latin America, they are more helpful than what seems to be the latest trend in Latin Americanist border studies. Latin American studies, despite its historical formation as a cold war–era area studies discipline defined in strictly national and geographic terms, has striven in recent years to adapt itself to a changing world in which immigration to the United States from Latin America has produced significant cultural changes to mainstream U.S. culture. In other words, Latin American studies has branched out into Latino studies, overlapping in many cases with the same style expansion as that seen in American studies.

This interdisciplinary overlap has been productive in many ways. It has begun to pressure disciplinary boundaries of both American studies and Latin American studies and to point to the importance of bilingualism.[14] However, as Latin American studies follows Latin American immigrant communities in their northward trajectory, the field must be careful not to duplicate problematic hierarchies of knowledge that imbue the field of American studies. It is problematic but at least understandable that the border studies produced and read by Americanists and scholars of Chicano studies may limit itself too rigidly to questions of interest north of the border without considering or consulting the borderlands of northern Mexico. However, when the same mistake is repeated by Latin Americanists, it is alarming.

In 1984, Richard Griswold del Castillo wrote a review article for the *Latin American Research Review* titled "New Perspectives on the Mexican and American Borderlands," in which he reviewed five recent books, three published in the United States, and two in Mexico. Despite the title's suggestion that the works would address both "the Mexican and American borderland," all five books dealt exclusively with "the American southwest" or the cultures "north of the Río Bravo." While Griswold judges the texts in question to be "synthetic" as they "integrate both American and Mexican perspectives" (200), their focus is exclusively upon the populations and cultures of the U.S. Southwest.

In 2002, Benjamin Johnson, in the same journal, published the review essay "Engendering Nation and Race in the Borderlands," again reviewing a cluster of recently published books treating the U.S.–Mexico borderlands, which Johnson defines as "the region on either side of the border that now divides the United States and Mexico" (259). Once again, all six texts addressed the Mexican American populations of the United States to the exclusion of those of the Mexican side of the border. Four of the texts focused on gender issues in specific U.S. Southwestern states including New Mexico, Arizona, and California; the other two texts were novels written by the *Tejana* Jovita González, both set in southern Texas. This time all six books were published in the United States.

It is unlikely that either of these critics set out to exclude texts on northern Mexico from his survey of border studies scholarship; it is more probable that each reviewed the most recently published and well-received texts that were available within the particular thematic limits implied by their chosen topic. However, it is noteworthy that neither critic found it strange that the particular collection of books he ultimately did review focused exclusively on one side of the border. Whether these omissions reflect publication patterns, the journal in question's relationships with Mexican publishers, or the possibility that the Mexican borderlands are simply not very interesting to many Latin Americanists cannot be ascertained—although the absence of any mention of the influential border studies scholarship of the prolific *tijuanense* José Manuel Valenzuela Arce, for example, is remarkable. The prominence of scholarship on the U.S. Southwest at the expense of scholarship on the Mexican borderlands within the context of Latin American studies is lamentable.

An interesting example of a Latin Americanist branching out beyond the disciplinary and geopolitical confines of his field is the recent work of the U.S.–based Argentine cultural studies scholar Walter Mignolo. His *Local Histories/Global Designs: Coloniality, Subaltern Knowledges, and Border Thinking* (2000) proposes a revision of knowledge production that decenters the mainstream academy of western Europe and the United

States, refocusing attention on thinkers from the borderlands. Proto-typical is the Chicana intellectual and poet Gloria Anzaldúa, who for Mignolo complements mainstream academic knowledge with that pro-duced by people like her, intellectuals from subaltern cultures (5–6). Mignolo introduces the term "border gnosis" to refer to the "hidden" philosophies and epistemologies of traditional cultures that intellectu-als from such communities bring into mainstream academic discourse (9–11). He writes:

> Border gnosis as knowledge from a subaltern perspective is knowledge
> conceived from the exterior borders of the modern/colonial world
> system, and border gnoseology as a discourse about colonial knowledge
> is conceived at the conflictive intersection of the knowledge produced
> from the perspective of modern colonialisms (rhetoric, philosophy,
> science) and knowledge produced from the perspective of colonial
> modernities in Asia, Africa, and the Americas/Caribbean. (11)

Mignolo's study obviously goes well beyond the context of the U.S.–Mexico borderlands or even his own field of Latin American studies.

However, to the extent that the book is a Latin Americanist's theo-rization of the hybrid thinking of the borderlands between countries like the United States and Mexico, and that the Chicana Anzaldúa is his much-lauded intellectual role model from that region, it is interest-ing to observe once again that the U.S.–Mexico borderlands is reduced to the U.S. Southwest, and that the Chicana who published on the U.S. side, taught at U.S. universities, and wrote more in English than in Spanish is featured, while no Mexican borderlands figure from the Mex-ican side who writes principally in Spanish or specializes in the culture and history of the Mexican borderlands appears. Anzaldúa, we will recall, has been criticized for her reductive representation of Mexico. Writes the Mexican borderlands critic Socorro Tabuenca, referring to Anzaldúa's seminal *Borderlands/La Frontera*:

> In Anzaldúa's text, despite the crossing of borders and different
> worlds . . . , the geographical border and the relations between Mex-
> ico and the United States are essentialized. U.S. whites are presented
> as "them" and minorities as "us" . . . ; between these two worlds, a
> third country arises, "a border culture" . . . But this third country . . .
> is also a metaphoric culture narrated from the first world. (89)

Mignolo's idealization of the widely admired Anzaldúa serves to reinforce the hierarchies of knowledge that his book aims to assail. Chicano
studies, largely accepted into the U.S. university system in the fields of
both American studies and Latin American studies, may remain a minority discourse in the United States, but it plainly outranks Mexican border studies.

Some of the issues that have come up in the global context of Latin
American studies resound emphatically for U.S.–Mexico border studies. Mignolo writes of the "asymmetry of language" to reflect not only
the subordinate position of languages like Spanish in relation to English but the relative hierarchies of languages in general within the context of academic discourse (231). Indigenous languages, of course, which
in many cases have relatively few speakers, carry very little prestige and
are not capable of reaching a significant audience, particularly when
compared with Spanish, the dominant language throughout much of
Latin America. Yet despite the large number of Spanish speakers in the
Americas, its academic status (both globally and oftentimes even within
Latin America itself) is inferior to that of English.

These issues of academic power have plagued the field of Latin American studies since its rise in the United States during the cold war. The
Chile-based cultural critic Nelly Richard discusses a major product of
U.S.–based area studies: "Latin Americanism," a concept analogous to
the "orientalism" studied by Edward Said. Richard objects to the "academic distribution of disciplinary knowledges that administer and cer-
tify the value and meaning of Latin American cultural practices" (3). She
is one of several Latin America–based intellectuals who "have sharpened
their critical knives on what they regard as a major Latin Americanist
sellout of Latin America into the global market taking place primarily,
if not exclusively, through the U.S. academy" (Moreiras 240). If Latin
American studies has contended with issues of the greater power and
prestige of U.S. publications, work carried out in English, and U.S.–
based conferences, when the subject becomes the borderlands, such issues
become more pronounced. Those who dominate are not only U.S.–
based scholars who publish in English but scholars whose work focuses
on U.S. culture, albeit a peripheral aspect of U.S. culture: the Mexican
American Southwest.

A Transamerican Approach

We have seen that American studies, Mexican studies, and Latin American studies have all proven inadequate in their treatment of the U.S.–Mexico borderlands. American studies focuses almost exclusively on the U.S. side of the border and is unaccustomed to and poorly equipped for dialogue with scholars located outside the U.S. academy who do not work in English. Mexican studies tends to view the borderlands as a region whose culture is a marginal element of a Mexican national whole in which the role of the United States is that of foreign nation and not a country whose own borderlands share hybrid cultural traits with the neighboring Mexican borderlands. Latin American studies has turned to the borderlands by expanding its scope into the Mexican American Southwest, opening dialogue directly with Chicano studies scholarship, and in the process has neglected the Mexican borderlands.

I am advocating, then, for a transamerican approach to U.S.–Mexico border studies. A transamerican methodology studies the histories and cultures of a contact zone such as the U.S.–Mexico border from the multiplicity of perspectives that are relevant to the analysis of any shared cultural space in the context of the Americas. Given that the borderlands—both sides of the border—are inherently multicultural, they demand just such an approach to the study of their history and culture. Generally speaking, both Mexican and U.S. perspectives must be amply considered to gain a valid understanding of life in the borderlands; however, it is a gross simplification to reduce either Mexico or the United States to a monolithic cultural vector. Issues of class, gender, race, religion, region, and so forth will often split apart the national into competing components. Furthermore, the nineteenth-century borderlands were populated as well by groups of people who fit into neither national category, or into both. Immigrants (from Mexico or the United States into the other country) and children of mixed marriages of U.S. and Mexican parents, for example, might often identify as cultural hybrids. Unassimilated indigenous groups (e.g., Yaquis, Apaches) and immigrants from other countries (e.g., France, China) might fit into neither category. One of the borderlands' most fascinating traits is their multiculturalism.

Such an approach has occasionally been applied to the contact zone of the U.S.–Mexico borderlands. Miguel Tinker Salas's *In the Shadow of Eagles: Sonora and the Transformation of the Border during the Porfiriato* (1997) centers its interrogation on the Mexican state of Sonora, but it soon becomes apparent that Sonora is inseparable economically, socially, and culturally from neighboring Arizona: "The establishment of a border did not restrain foreign capital, nor did it restrict cultural interaction. As Mexicans and Americans came into contact, a far-reaching exchange of customs took place on both sides of the international line, producing a complex web of social and cultural interrelations" (2–3). The Sonoran historian Juan Antonio Ruibal Corella comments: "It will not escape the contemporary observer that although it is true that the present day Sonoran is strongly influenced by North American culture . . . it is no less true that the Sonoran influence in Arizona is so considerable that . . . one might speak of transculturation occurring between both countries" (132). Tinker Salas's study is transamerican because, although it does take Sonora as a starting point, it does not limit itself in scope to one or the other side of the border. Moreover, its bibliography deals amply with primary sources and scholarship on and about both the Mexican and the U.S. borderlands.[15]

My objective in this study is to examine the cultural trajectories of several icons of the Mexican northwestern borderlands, viewed through a transamerican lens, taking into account multiple perspectives from both sides of the geopolitical border, drawing upon information in both Spanish and English (and occasionally French). Until now, no discipline's conventions of border studies actively promote such an approach, one that is comparative without being biased toward the U.S. borderlands or toward national cultures, one that recognizes the cultural differences found on each side of the border while at the same time remaining aware of the cross-cultural links within the regional context of the borderlands that prevent the absolute separation of the two sides into discrete cultural entities.

But before beginning to examine the cultural icons that will bring the late-nineteenth-century Mexican Northwest to life, I must elaborate, so that there may be no doubt, on why the other borderlands, the Mexican Northwest, are of interest beyond their own local context.

The Other Borderlands

Those who are not very familiar with northwestern Mexico might imagine that the region has received limited attention within the sphere of border studies for several reasons. It is not the multicultural space that the U.S. Southwest is because the migration between Mexico and the United States moves only from north to south. The Mexican Northwest is a monolingual Spanish space populated only by Mexicans, and Mexicans who are not even interested, despite the proximity, in crossing over into the United States. As such, it is not a region whose multiculturalism defies Mexico's national imaginary in the way that the Chicano Southwest does in the U.S. context. Nor is the Mexican Northwest the space of cultural hybridity that the U.S. Southwest is. It has no special cross-border cultural significance for the United States that would make it the equivalent of Aztlán for Mexicans, that is, a space of postcolonial transgression or resistance. And while, for Chicanos, a deconstructive view of the border may be spiritually liberating, for Mexican *norteños*, the border is always the border: it is a legal limit that can only be crossed at great personal and economic risk and/or expense. All of these ideas are misconceptions.

I will argue that like the U.S. Southwest, the Mexican north is first and foremost a cultural contact zone whose heterogeneous inhabitants, *los fronterizos*, are culturally distinct in many ways from their compatriots from the central part of the country. A closer look at the other borderlands turns out to be as deconstructive an exercise as an interrogation of the Chicano Southwest. The Mexican borderlands are culturally linked to and distinct from both mainstream Mexico and the United States. It is a zone of multicultural jumble, and of cultural hybridity, in whose shaping migration has played a significant role. It is also a primary zone of resistance to U.S. imperialism. All of these characteristics that have drawn attention to the U.S. Southwest are also present and frequently prominent in the culture of the Mexican Northwest. And the late nineteenth century, when the current border was first forged and the Mexican borderlands essentially came into being, is when all of these issues first became critical to the understanding of the region.

One critic writes:

One would think that the borderlands, that part of North America
where the United States and Mexico meet, would be a particularly
rich site for work in cultural studies. The American Southwest and
its counterpart in northern Mexico have a complex mix of Native
American, Latino, and Anglo peoples, a mix that has given birth to
a rich culture or complex of cultures. (Dasenbrock xvi)

Even Gloria Anzaldúa, who, as we have seen, not only ignores the Mexican borderlands but often reduces Mexican culture to nationalist clichés,
recognizes that "borderlands are not particular to the Southwest" and
that "the borderlands are physically present wherever two or more cultures edge each other" (19). The border studies scholar Claire Fox explains that "imperialist expansion creates dominant and marginal groups,
geographic centers and peripheries, but also . . . under circumstances
of prolonged interaction, mutual influences among peoples are inevitable."[16] We will see that in the case of the Mexican Northwest, it did
not require a very prolonged interaction to set in motion the inevitable
mutual influences; in some ways, they began to emerge almost immediately following the establishment of the border.

The Mexican cultural critic Roger Bartra writes, "When we approach
a border, the first thing we worry about is how to cross it" ("Introduction" 11); I might add that the second thing we worry about is to how
to keep others from crossing it. The establishment of the border set off
in Mexico a series of cultural syntheses and cultural clashes, of influences and resistances, of crossings and blockings, all of which would
quickly solidify the cultures of the region as distinctly hybrid.

The case of the Mexican Northwest, like that of the U.S. Southwest, is particularly interesting because the border was established in
the middle of frontier territory. The borderlands became a cultural contact zone between two countries, but the U.S. Southwest and the Mexican Northwest were also national frontiers. The borderlands historian
Juan Mora Torres writes: "The early years of border development did
not follow any kind of blueprint because neither the Mexican government nor the United States had the capacity to police and administer
the societies at the edges of their territories" (6). Yet from the start, the
U.S.–Mexico borderlands were "unique and volatile because this is one

of the few regions in the world, if not the only one, where two large nations that are so different come into permanent contact" (273).

But it is not only two well-defined units of nation that come into contact. In the nineteenth century, if any one region of Mexico represented the Mexican nation, it was what Barry Carr calls "the Mexico City-Puebla-Veracruz axis" along with perhaps Oaxaca (1). The Northwest was and is decidedly not representative of national culture. In racial terms, Silvio Zavala points out that the resistance to *mestizaje* in the north distances the region from Mexico's national image as a mixed race country:

> If a balanced mixture of ethnic stocks may be considered the symbol of what is Mexican, it is possible that the people of the old northern frontier meet this standard. On the other hand, there are scholars who hold that the great number of northerners are ethnically creole . . . If Mexican nativism is based on the blending of the ancient civilization of the sedentary Indians and that of the Spaniards, then the central provinces rather than the northern must have originated the distinctive Mexican character. (Zavala 44–45)

The image of the north is multiethnic, but not *mestizo*.

The local idiosyncrasy of the northwestern borderlands goes beyond the merely racial to embrace the cultural. "*Norteños*," writes Oscar Martínez, "are said to be different in their manner of thinking, speaking, acting, and dressing" (*Troublesome Border* 107); there were, in the late nineteenth century, even movements to establish political autonomy, as small separatist movements advocated an independent "Republic of Sierra Madre" (108). A regional identity has historically permeated the north, distinctly marking difference from the national model, even as many *norteños* came to be ardently patriotic in the face of the physical proximity to the Yankee imperialist threat (Tinker Salas 3). Resistance to U.S. military might, however, has not usually translated into cultural isolation or economic protectionism. In fact, in the late nineteenth century, Mexico's Northwest more than any other region of the country welcomed U.S. economic development to the point where its economy gradually became "an appendage to the US economy."[17]

The unique position of states such as Sonora on the U.S. border made the United States a more important element of regional culture, whether in the form of the menacing other or as the prized wealthy neighbor. A late-nineteenth-century Sonoran governor, Manuel Gándara, once described his state as "the gateway to the republic and the bulwark of Mexican nationalism" (quoted in Tinker Salas 99, his translation). Still, again and again, scholars of the Mexican borderlands insist that like Chicanos of the U.S. Southwest, Mexican *fronterizos* would never be as Mexican as those of the region surrounding Mexico City. In the nineteenth century, "Northern Mexico became a permanent zone in which the economies and cultures of two nations that were in many ways worlds apart engaged each other, creating a unique region different from the interiors of both Mexico and the United States" (Mora-Torres 9). The border was, as we know, formed following the U.S.–Mexican war of the 1840s. Many of the issues brought about by the signing of first the Treaty of Guadalupe Hidalgo of 1848 and then the Treaty of la Mesilla (known in the United States as the Gadsden Purchase) that followed in 1853, particularly those regarding everyday life, were not national but regional—and significantly transamerican—in nature. The consequences to the new Mexican Northwest, the new borderlands, were much more material than they ever would be to politicians, businessmen, and military leaders in Mexico City. Regional difference was felt not only by the *norteños* themselves but by national leaders who made it a priority in the decades following the French Intervention to "unify Mexico" by bringing the north into the mainstream of national politics and culture, in an effort that the historian Juan Mora-Torres calls "the taming of the north" (8–9). But it would not be until the era of the Mexican revolution that the north became prominent in national culture and northerners became visible as national leaders (Carr 1).

Ironically, the late-nineteenth-century efforts to integrate the northern borderlands into national culture in Mexico were synchronous with a liberal trade policy that encouraged U.S. economic investment and development in Mexico. Naturally, economic connections became strongest in the border region. In this way, Mexico's attempts to solidify and consolidate national culture over the full expanse of its territory coincided with a dilution of national integrity in those same borderlands as they became ever more connected to U.S. culture. The Northwest was no longer a frontier, a distant outpost, but was quickly becoming a well-populated, rapidly modernizing center of economic development; these modern borderlands no longer seemed so distant from either the center of Mexico or the U.S. Southwest. Once railroad links in both directions were complete in the 1880s (Gracida Romo 34–38), northwestern Mexicans had the option of traveling both ways and of becoming both more and less connected to Mexico.

To the extent that travel to the United States, access to U.S. products, and contact with U.S. visitors and businesspeople became easier and more common, it seemed to *norteños* that "the official border that separated the United States from Mexico was . . . a fictional device" (Fernández 87). Of course, "the new boundary had different meanings to different people, classes, and communities" (Mora-Torres 23). For merchants and investors, for laborers anxious for any kind of work, for secessionists, for patriots, for smugglers, for fugitives on the run, for migrants from Central Mexico, and so forth, the border might offer widely varied opportunities or hurdles and might signify vastly different concepts.

Border Indians

This diversity of meaning becomes most apparent when looking at those least affiliated with the national cultures of either country. In the mid- to late nineteenth century, numerous indigenous groups continued to live in relative autonomy in the Northwest, participating minimally in mainstream Mexican culture, and certainly not assuming a national or even a regional Mexican identity. The historian Oscar Martínez describes the situation as follows:

> If the initial encounter with whites marked one major turning point in the history of the borderlands Indians, the creation of the U.S.– Mexico border marked another. The region's indigenous groups had to grapple with external controls imposed by the white man, including the restriction of physical movement beyond approved international limits. Those tribes that lived at or near the border would find it especially difficult to adjust to the new way of life. (*Troublesome Border* 54)

The Apaches, for example, would become notorious border crossers, taking advantage of the fact that the Mexican military was prohibited

from pursuing them across the border by raiding Mexican northern settlements at will. The Treaty of Guadalupe Hidalgo initially provided
that the United States would keep borderlands indigenous groups from
making such raids, and the United States made what Mexico considered only a half-hearted effort to follow through.[18] However, it "seemed
incomprehensible to the indigenous peoples for Americans to demand
that they stop attacking Mexicans, a common enemy" (Martínez, *Troublesome Border* 58).

Martínez describes other cases of indigenous border crossers including Kickapoos who crossed from the United States into Mexico to avoid
persecution, and Yaquis who crossed from Mexico into the United States
for the same reason (*Troublesome Border* 74). If many *norteños* maintained a distinct regional identity, this does not mean that they did not
also identify as Mexicans; groups such as the Yaquis and the Seris, on
the other hand, identified neither as Mexicans nor as *norteños*. They did
live in the same borderlands as the Mexicans and the *gringos*, but the
national identity categories through which they understood the region
were more complex. The Yaquis, left alone until the late nineteenth century, in fact declared their autonomy in the 1870s, resisting both Mexican control and incursions by U.S. developers into their lands. The
indigenous component makes it impossible to define the borderlands in
any combination of terms that limit themselves to a U.S.–Mexico binary.

The indigenous groups making major cultural impacts in late-
nineteenth-century northwestern Mexico include not only the belliger-
ent mostly U.S.–based Apaches, the stubbornly resistant Seris, and the
sometimes cooperative, sometimes rebellious Yaquis and Mayos but also
several other groups who still had a regional presence, although they
were largely assimilated into local culture. This latter category includes
the Pimas, the Ópatas, and the Pápagos. Cynthia Radding has shown
how, particularly in rural and working-class sectors of Sonora, *mestizaje*
was common and racial categories tended not to be fixed by blood, instead often being determined by more economic factors. Nonetheless,
due precisely to the difficulties that the elite classes had in controlling
the more resistant autonomous groups mentioned above, white Sonorans in particular constructed regional identity employing images of
white civilization in opposition to indigenous barbarism.

The Mexican borderlands historian Alejandro Figueroa Valenzuela summarizes the diversity among indigenous peoples of the state of Sonora in the latter half of the nineteenth century—it is worth quoting his excellent summary in detail—as follows:

> In general, the Indians were conceived as "savage" beings . . .
> However . . . , the people who called themselves civilized . . . found
> that some were more "primitive," "barbarous" and "savage" than
> others . . . [T]hose who defended their territory, their political
> autonomy and their ethnic identity were positioned on the lowest
> part of the social development scale and on occasion their humanity
> was questioned . . . Upon the Seris and Apaches, civilization had to
> be imposed at any cost, exterminating them or stripping them of all
> their natural resources of subsistence so that they would ultimately
> disappear from the map . . . [T]he Ópatas, Pimas and Pápagos . . .
> were no longer "so wild" . . . The process of the loss of their identity
> and their integration into the regional mixed race population was
> seen as being due to an innate characteristic, like a virtue proper to
> their race that permitted them to abandon their traits of barbarism . . .
> The Yaquis and Mayos turned out to be more disconcerting for
> Sonorans . . . Both groups . . . performed as the most capable workers
> in the State and they stood out for their strength, resistance and
> intelligence; however . . . their rebellions in defense of their territorial
> rights, customs and political integrity were catalogued as a symptom
> of their "bloodthirsty impulses." ("Los indios" 153)

These peoples' complex place in Mexican borderlands history must not be overlooked, nor reduced to a monolithic notion of "savages," nor conflated with a reductive national image of indigenous (usually Aztec) Mexico.

The indigenous groups of greatest interest here, then, are not the peaceful assimilators but those who insisted upon separating themselves culturally from mainstream Mexico, namely, the Apaches who contin-ued to thwart settlement projects in northern Mexico with cross-border raids from the United States through the nineteenth century; the Yaquis who sometimes participated in Mexican society without ever relinquish-ing cultural autonomy and, when threatened by Mexican incursions into their traditional lands, defended themselves valiantly; the Mayos, culturally similar to the Yaquis, though more willing to cooperate with

Mexican governmental authorities, but who rebelled occasionally when provoked; and the Seris, known as the most "barbarous" of all groups, who despite their small numbers, lived isolated from creole society in the Sonoran desert, resisting military and paramilitary harassment and maintaining their autonomy through most of the nineteenth century.

The treatment of the "Indian question" is difficult in the context of the Mexican Northwest. While the Seris clearly have their versions of the Lola Casanova story, and the Yaquis and Mayos participated actively in Teresa Urrea's rise as a cultural icon of the Mexican Northwest, their perspectives cannot be captured easily. The translations of their views of history and legend to English or Spanish for academic audiences are inevitably problematic, particularly when some researchers assume that transparent dialogue, dialogue uninhibited and unaltered by hierarchies of political power and long histories of distrust, can be carried out with "native informants" from the ivory towers of the academy. After all, as James Clifford has noted, "Ethnographic writing is allegorical at the level both of its content (what it says about cultures and their histories) and of its form (what is implied about its mode of textualization)" (98). He adds further, "Much of our knowledge about other cultures must . . . be seen as contingent, the problematic outcome of intersubjective dialogue, translation, and projection" (109). While some academics have called for "a return to local epistemology" (Varese 149) or some form of "border gnosis" (Mignolo 9–11), much of the available research on these relatively marginal indigenous groups (compared, for example, to the nationally more visible Mayas or Zapotecs) does not make clear how researchers worked to overcome such difficulties when extracting data from their informants. For example, Seri versions of the Lola Casanova legend reported by the literary scholar Edith Lowell do not address who translated them into English or Spanish, nor does Lowell question their validity even though she obtained them only indirectly, through missionaries. While it would be a mistake to exclude indigenous perspectives from a study on the borderlands as contact zone, it is unfortunate that available sources on indigenous cultures of the borderlands are more fraught with issues of reliability than other sources studied here.

Los Forasteros

The other important social group that adds complexity to any analysis of the late-nineteenth-century northwestern Mexican borderlands is the region's immigrants. And aside from the many *gringos* who wandered south, whether to make money, or to flee problems, or simply to enter into Mexican culture in true *fronterizo* style—as was the case, for example, of Juan Robinson, who married a Mexican woman and was a leading citizen in Guaymas for decades—the largest immigrant group in the region was the Chinese. Migration is often assumed in the case of Mexico to refer to the emigration of Mexicans to the United States. For this reason immigrant populations in Mexico are frequently overlooked.

In the case of the Mexican borderlands, Chinese immigration began to take root in the 1870s and increased significantly in the 1880s when the Chinese Exclusion Act became law in the United States. The Chinese started up numerous small businesses, frequently establishing themselves in communities that were growing rapidly due to foreign investment in mines and factories, and most often these businesses served the working-class Mexicans who went to live and work in these areas. Borderlands elites in cities such as Guaymas and Hermosillo resented the economic inroads the Chinese were making and engaged in active campaigns to curb their immigration. When Porfirio Díaz signed a trade agreement with China in 1893, *fronterizos* of the Mexican Northwest were outraged (Hu-Dehart, "La comunidad china" 195).

Attitudes in Mexico's northwestern borderlands regarding immigration were often as censorious and blatantly racist as they were in the United States. In fact, it appears at times that Mexico's *fronterizos* felt compelled to imitate *gringo* prejudices in order to demonstrate their own cultural similarity to their neighbors. It is, of course, ironic that the same xenophobic prejudices that were ruining many once wealthy Californios and driving many Mexican immigrants—including the *sonorense* Joaquín Murrieta—to crime were commonplace among their cousins back in the Mexican Northwest, only now directed against the region's own group of exotically foreign immigrants, the Chinese. The multicultural Mexican Northwest exhibits a subtle diversity that reveals an interesting and rarely analyzed aspect of Mexican culture: its tendency (and during the Porfiriato this quality was quite prominent) to assume a hegemonic or even imperialist role when it can. Compared to the United States, Mexico is subaltern, but when dealing with Chinese immigrants (or with Central Americans on Mexico's forgotten "other borderlands"), Mexicans comfortably shift into their role of higher status or greater power.[19] This is not to say that there was resistance to all forms of diversity in the Mexican northwestern borderlands of the late nineteenth century. Alfonso Iberri, describing the city of Guaymas in the last decades of the nineteenth century, the same time when journalists like Aurelio Pérez Peña were initiating a propaganda campaign against the Chinese (see chapter 4), recalls a cosmopolitan population with a great variety of immigrants from all over the world, mentioning examples from no less than twenty different countries of Europe, the Americas, Africa, and Asia.[20]

The border that northwestern Mexico shares with the southwestern United States is something of a paradox. While it links the two cultures—or rather two sets of cultures—that have formed on either side to the point of making it inconceivable not to look at the region in terms of its cross-border alliances or even cultural units, it also reinforces difference, particularly as the late-nineteenth-century borderlands came to be a testing ground for questions of national autonomy. With the constant threats and rumors of filibuster invasions, Apache incursions, and political annexation, and with the Mexican borderlands never connected closely enough with the Mexico City–centered Mexican nation, it was not until well into the twentieth century that the fear that the United States might in one way or another seize or absorb the Mexican Northwest, particularly Sonora and Baja California, would subside (Martínez, *Troublesome Border* 52). For this very reason, many have concluded that up-close exposure to U.S. culture may have actually buttressed both traditional regional identity and a national identity that the region had previously resisted assuming (Tinker Salas 259). The borderlands is the part of Mexico that has worked most closely with the Yankees, has come closest to Yankee annexation, and has—as early as the gold rush of 1849—been Mexico's main point of departure for emigration to the north, but it is also the area of the country that has had to work hardest to resist the power of the United States, despite the uneven terms of the struggle.

A wave of northward emigration in the gold rush era had "nefarious consequences" for Sonora and left Baja California "practically depopulated" (Ruibal Corella 115). Through the 1870s, rapid development in both Alta California and Arizona continued to attract emigration from Mexico's Northwest, making settlement of the area a major problem. Sonora's then governor, Ignacio Pesqueira, estimated that the state had lost 14 percent of its population to northward migration in those years (Voss 183). From the moment in which the border was established, the economic attractions of the north were a major temptation and over time the Northwest would become a platform for the national tradition of emigration to the United States that continues to today.

Conclusion

In synthesis, the complex layers of Mexican borderlands hierarchies with respect to such factors as race, class, migration, and degree of assimilation (particularly regarding indigenous groups) reveal Mexico's northwestern borderlands to be a hybrid culture as multifaceted as that of any other borderlands territory. It is the degree of difference between Mexico and its U.S. neighbor, the Northwest's regional distinctiveness from Mexican national culture, its variety of culturally autonomous and semiautonomous indigenous groups, the complex relations between the Northwest and both the Mexican center and its conflictive neighbor to the north, the growing presence of immigrants, the regular flow of emigrants, and the long history of the region as a frontier outpost that make the Other Borderlands unique. More than the U.S. Southwest, in fact more than any other place in the world including perhaps even the Caribbean, the Mexican borderlands presents a case study of the direct and constant head-to-head clash of a rich and powerful country with a much poorer and weaker one. The fact that these two lands share an immense border, whose borderlands region exhibits a wealth of cultural diversity, make these Other Borderlands a fascinating study of transamerican culture for Mexicanists, Latin Americanists, and Americanists alike.

The U.S. Southwest is famous for producing such symbols of U.S. culture as cowboys, pioneers, and 49ers; it also has produced major cultural icons for both Anglo and Mexican Americans including Zorro, Ramona, and Geronimo. The Mexican Northwest, too, has produced its own fascinating cultural icons including the social bandit Joaquín Murrieta; the transgressor of racial prohibitions Lola Casanova; the forgotten heroines Loreta de Avilés and Guadalupe Cubillas; and the protorevolutionary mystic Teresa Urrea, La Santa de Cabora. With the exception of Murrieta, none of these figures is as well known (outside the Mexican borderlands) as the U.S. Southwestern icons listed above; and, even in the case of Murrieta, few people —whether in the United States or in any part of Mexico aside from the northwestern borderlands—are familiar with the Mexican borderlands cultural contexts from which they arose. The following chapters are meant to reposition these borderlands icons in a transamerican context that goes beyond traditional disciplinary boundaries to reveal the cultural ramifications of the various intercultural interactions that occurred in the contact zone that was the Mexican Northwest in the late nineteenth century.

CHAPTER TWO

THE MANY HEADS
AND TALES OF
JOAQUÍN MURRIETA

I N THE EARLY 1850S in gold rush Alta California, a band of Mexicans under the leadership of Joaquín Murrieta became notorious for its bloody assaults on and murders of miners and other inhabitants of the region. Many California communities lived in a state of terror as daily news stories reported one attack after another, often in multiple regions of the state. Soon a reward was offered for Joaquín's head. That summer, Captain Harry Love and a troop of California Rangers set off after the Mexicans, eventually killing Murrieta and his notorious henchman, Manuel García, who went by the nickname Three Fingered Jack. They beheaded the former and cut the hand off the latter, preserving them in jars of alcohol to display around the state to prove that the Mexican bandits had at last been defeated.

Those are the basic components of the legend of Joaquín Murrieta. However, from the early newspaper reports and the first literary representations of Murrieta to the hundreds of reformulations of the legend in novels, plays, *corridos*, poems, histories, movies, and the like over the past century and a half in California and the United States, France, Spain, Chile, and Mexico by *gringo*, Native American, Chicano, Sonoran, Latin American, and even Russian writers, it seems that no one can agree on the many details of the case. Consensus occurs even less on the cultural meanings evoked by the many retellings of the Murrieta legend.

Is it Murrieta or Murieta or Muriata?[1] Was there one Joaquín, were
there five, or even more? Was Murrieta from Sonora or Chile? Was he
dark haired or blond? Was he killed by Harry Love or by someone else?
Or did he escape and die two days later from wounds unrelated to the
shootout with Love, or did he flee back to Sonora and not die until many
years later, of old age? Was his wife named Rosa, Carmela, or Carmen?
Did he act out of revenge, desperation, or a sadistic urge to kill? Did
he exist or is he a mere literary invention? Was his head destroyed in
the 1906 San Francisco earthquake or can it still be seen today?

Writes the borderlands cultural critic José Manuel Valenzuela Arce,
"Myth is not validated in historical truth, but in its social functionality"
(15). Murrieta as a mythical figure is a source of Mexican pride in the face
of anti-Mexican prejudice in the United States, yet, more than a myth,
he is a cultural icon whose shape-shifting persona performs a diversity of
functions in the many contexts in which it has flourished. As María Rosa
Palazón Mayoral puts it, Murrieta can be found "wherever an imagination creates him or protects him, or assimilates him and feels represented
by him . . . Joaquín is a hub of projections" (49). Joaquín Murrieta's legend endures as long as the cultural conflicts it puts into play—conflicts
based on differences in race and national origin in the U.S.–Mexico
borderlands, or in the Americas in general—remain unresolved.

Most representations of Murrieta appear to be works of fiction,
though each claims basis in historic fact. And while some texts do present themselves as history, venerable historians such as Hubert Howe
Bancroft brazenly cite the foundational Murrieta novel by Yellow Bird
(aka John Rollin Ridge) as primary source material (Joseph Henry Jackson, "Introduction" xxxviii), and José Vasconcelos, in his Mexican history text, went so far as to base his Murieta on a 1936 Hollywood film,
The Robin Hood of El Dorado (Leal, "Introducción" 63). Many versions
of the story, moreover, that appeared as the original work of a given
author were in fact largely plagiarized from earlier versions. One such
plagiarism, the 1904 version commonly attributed to Ireneo Paz, was in
fact likely only published from his print shop, with neither an author nor
translator listed (Wood 77–78); the translator Frances Belle's erroneous
attribution of Paz as author, however, was reaffirmed and authorized by
Paz's eminent grandson Octavio Paz, who, in contradiction to all literary

history previously published on Ireneo Paz's oeuvre, cited the Murrieta text as the work "of my grandfather" in 1997 ("Silueta" 7), and by Luis Leal, who published the newest edition of the text listing Paz as author.[2] In short, the Murrieta story is so malleable since there is no original, no master version; its evolution has always been through hybrid fictional/nonfictional genres of questionable origin.

Murrieta, writes María Mondragón, "is an unreliable historical character who slips between ethnic identities," "a shapeshifter" (179). This description of the Murieta character in the 1854 Ridge novel serves to convey how Murrieta, the legend, shifts in and out of Wild West pulp fiction in the United States, Sonoran historiography, Chilean theater, and Chicano nationalist poetry, assuming different cultural significance in each.

Murrieta, then, is in many ways a typical borderlands icon, representing no one group, signifying in multiple directions to multiple audiences. But while some of his shifting identities have been well fleshed out in recent years—notably the California outlaw, the Chicano icon, the Chilean anti-imperialist rebel, and even the Mexican national hero—his cultural significance in his home Mexican borderlands state of Sonora has remained largely ignored by Murrieta scholars outside Sonora. Murrieta did achieve his fame in California, but he was born in Sonora and may have also died in Sonora. His migration to gold rush California and struggles on the U.S. side of the border are emblematic of Mexican borderlands life in the early years following the U.S.–Mexico war, and his notorious reputation in California signified heavily in Sonora. It signaled both the tensions of race and nation in the late-nineteenth-century borderlands, and also the implications in northern Mexico of the (usually negative) images being promoted in the U.S. southwestern borderlands of Mexican culture, and reflected the ambivalence Sonorans felt regarding their northern neighbors.

The Construction of an Icon 1850–54

In January 1848, the Treaty of Guadalupe Hidalgo not even signed yet, gold was discovered in Alta California, and within months the madness that was the California Gold Rush was in full swing. The proximity of

Sonora's largest population centers to the border, the lack of active plans of economic development in the state, and the new insecurity felt by Sonorans upon suddenly finding themselves living not only in an area known for its hostile indigenous groups but also in a territory abutting that of an unfriendly neighbor, high on a wave of expansionism, put Mexico's new borderlands in a precarious state from the start. Many Sonorans could not resist the attraction of the gold rush, and migrants from Mexico's Northwest were among the first of the so-called 49ers to arrive in Alta California, with approximately ten thousand Sonorans crossing into the state between 1848 and 1850 (Susan Johnson 61). Among them, encouraged by a brother who migrated before him, was a young Sonoran named Joaquín Murrieta.

At first, he was just another Mexican immigrant. In a few years he would be the most wanted man in the territory and his ultimate execution would be cheered by thousands. Yet what is of interest here is not the biography of a man but the construction of a legend. In the first years of the decade of the 1850s, Joaquín Murrieta did not exist in the public imagination.[3] While some evidence suggests that a loose gang of bandits, one of whom was the young Murrieta, began stealing horses and gold, and in many cases murdering its victims, as early as 1850, no names of its members became public knowledge, nor were they exclusively Mexican.[4]

In fact, it was not until 15 December 1852 that the name Joaquín Murrieta reached the public eye in a story from San Francisco's *Alta California*.[5] The story concerns the November murder of General Joshua Bean. Ana Benítez, an apparent mistress of Murrieta, upon interrogation admitted that her lover was a member of the gang responsible for the killing, but she contended that another man, Cipriano Sandoval, was the murderer. However, another of the gang members arrested, Reyes Feliz, claimed that Murrieta was the real killer. In any case, Murrieta escaped, but this high-profile crime brought attention to a violent band of Mexicans, and public interest would only become more concentrated in the coming year (Thornton 15).

January 1853 was when publicity regarding what seemed to be a rampage of crimes committed by a band of bloodthirsty Mexicans really took off. The *San Joaquín Republican* began a series of frequent reports on a band of robbers and murderers made up of "the most notorious Mexican desperadoes of the country" (26 January 1853, reprinted in Latta 36). They were accused of all kinds of crimes including stealing bags of gold dust, terrorizing and sometimes murdering their victims, making off with horses, indiscriminately attacking *gringos*, pillaging miners' and traders' camps, and generally menacing the population of the region from Los Angeles up past San Francisco to Sacramento. The band's leader was identified only as "Joaquín."[6]

The reaction of readers was swift and violent. By late January, hundreds of men joined a posse to hunt down the Mexicans. Two Mexican suspects were promptly lynched. However, the campaign went well beyond the usual brand of mob justice meted out on individuals. The *San Joaquín Republican* further reported:

> At the same time they resolved to burn the habitations of the Mexicans indiscriminately . . . The entire Mexican population has been driven from San Andreas and the forks of the Calaveras . . . If an American meets a Mexican he takes his horse, his arms, and bids him leave . . . We understand that a Mass Meeting was held at Double Springs, on Wednesday morning, and resolutions passed . . . making it the duty of every American citizen at all events to exterminate the Mexican race from the county. The foreigners should first receive notice to leave, and if they refused they were to be shot down and their property confiscated. (29 January 1853, reprinted in Latta 38)

The conflict had escalated most rapidly and was not about to moderate. In February, the "desperate" and "notorious outlaw, Joaquín" was in the headlines daily with all kinds of violent crimes attributed to him and his followers. The *Los Angeles Star* observed at one point that Joaquín seemed to be "in four counties and ten townships in the same day."[7] The historian Frank Latta notes that the quantity of crimes being reported in diverse locations "required at least four Joaquíns" (43), and he accounts for five Mexicans named Joaquín known to be in the area at the time: Joaquín Murrieta, Joaquín Carrillo Murrieta, Joaquín Juan Murrieta, Joaquín Valenzuela, and Joaquín Botellier (43)—the latter two also sometimes referred to as Joaquín Ocomorenia (or Nacomoreno) and Joaquín Botellas, respectively.[8]

However, the newspapers continued to use only the first name,

Joaquín, in their news stories. In mid-February, the *San Francisco Whig* came up with a short biographical sketch of Joaquín, which asserted that he had been born in Jalisco and was thirty-five years old. It further claimed:

> He is chief of a notorious band of robbers now infesting the vicinity of Mexico, and though living in California, has a regular chain of communication with his associates in his native country. He has been known to enter the capital cities disguised as a friar . . . He is about six feet in height, and of immense muscular strength; is well versed in the use of arms, and in disposition cruel and sanguinary. He has a dark, sallow complexion, and during the Mexican war was known to wear a coat of armor.[9]

From this story came a whole range of features that would evolve and shape the Murrieta myth. First, it was made clear that he was an immigrant (and not a Californio, that is, a Mexican native of Alta California), that his network of bandits was vast and international in scope, that he was a shape-shifter and master of disguise, that he was almost superhuman (tall, strong, used armor), and that his hatred for the United States dated back to his exploits in the U.S.–Mexico war. While Latta claims that this description is a "composite of all five Joaquíns" (43)—competing descriptions identified him as light haired and light skinned or swarthy (Latta 11)—more importantly it began to flesh out the villainous public figure.

By the end of the month, the governor of Alta California had put up a reward of one thousand dollars "for the capture of Joaquín" (*San Joaquín Republican* 23 February 1853, reprinted in Latta 48). The description issued the previous week of a Mexican superman would probably not have been very helpful in identifying the governor's target. Meanwhile, the waters got muddier as the same report revealed: "Strong evidence has been obtained that some bearing the name of Americans, are connected with Joaquín's band."

Then, in early March, a last name was at last provided. However, it was not Murrieta, but Carrillo.[10] The Joaquín Murrieta suspected in the late 1852 murder mentioned above had apparently been forgotten. Meanwhile, reports continued coming in from all over the state through the following months. At times it seemed that any crimes in which any Mexicans were implicated were attributed automatically to the ubiquitous Joaquín—still usually not given a last name.

However, the *San Francisco Herald* printed a detailed story on Joaquín on 18 April that added several memorable particulars to Joaquín's public image. First of all, it reported a conversation that Joaquín had with a rancher in which it was revealed that the young Mexican had actually met many visitors from the United States while growing up in Mexico and was a great admirer of them and their culture. He was not from criminal stock but from "a good family" and had received "an excellent education" (quoted in Thornton 82). He had come to the United States with a dream for a better life, "thinking to end my days in California as a citizen of the United States" (quoted in Thornton 81). The report went on: "But he had been oppressed, robbed and persecuted by the Americans in the placers—had lost $40,000—been driven from a piece of land—had been insulted and grossly maltreated without justice—had been flogged—and he was determined to be avenged for his wrongs four fold. He had robbed many—killed many, and more should suffer in the same way" (quoted in Castillo and Camarillo 47–48). This justification for Murrieta's life of crime would have a major impact on the formation of his legend.

Two other key events were also reported in the same story. First, it noted that early one Sunday morning in Stockton, a well-dressed young Mexican rode into town and noticed a poster advertising that Joaquín was wanted, dead or alive. Defiantly, he dismounted and wrote under the text of the poster: "I will give $10,000 myself," signing his name "Joaquín" before riding off (quoted in Castillo and Camarillo 47; see Figure 1).

The story went on to recount an anecdote in which several Mexicans knocked on the door of a house in the Salinas Plains, asking for refreshments. At least one of the heavily armed men was wearing a false beard and moustache. The host chatted with his visitors, apparently in English, asking, since they said they had just come from the placers, for news of the famous Joaquín. The disguised man replied, "I am that Joaquín, and no man takes me alive, or comes within one hundred yards of me with these good weapons" (quoted in Castillo and Camarillo 47;

see Figure 2). At this point Joaquín began to frankly tell his story to his rancher host, as mentioned above. These latter two events—that involving the reward poster, and that of the unmasking in which Murrieta cried, "I am Joaquín"—would become key features of the legend.

Around this time, the first visual representation of Joaquín appeared in the form of an engraving. The *Sacramento Steamer Union* published the portrait on 22 April 1853 (1; see Figure 3). Here, Joaquín entered the public imagination as a very dark-skinned figure, with long black hair,

Figure 1. "Joaquín Murieta: Dead or Alive." Cartoon from San Francisco Chronicle, *1853.*

Figure 2. *"I Am Joaquín!" Illustration from "The Life of Joaquín Murieta"* (California Police Gazette, *1859*). *Reprinted with permission of the California State Library.*

Figure 3. *"Portrait of Joaquín."* Sacramento Steamer Union, *1853. Reprinted with permission of the California State Library.*

his dress including elements of indigenous garb (a shawl-like garment with a geometric design lay across his shoulders) and perhaps that of a pirate (a scarf wrapped around his head), and partially concealing a gun.

Then in early May the *San Francisco Herald* revealed another key detail: "The real name of the bandit is Joaquín Muliati." This story also confirmed that Joaquín "speaks English fluently" (quoted in the *San Joaquín Republican* 7 May 1853, reprinted in Latta 61). However, Joaquín Muliati soon morphed into the five Joaquines as reports a few weeks later revealed that the government had formed a posse of California Rangers, under the leadership of Captain Harry Love, to capture "one or either of the five Joaquins, viz: Joaquin Muliati, Joaquin Ocomorenia, Joaquin Valenzuela, Joaquin Botellier and Joaquin Corrillo" (*San Joaquín Republican* 30 May 1853, reprinted in Latta 64).

It was still really just Joaquín, any Joaquín, who needed to be caught. The gold rush historian Susan Lee Johnson comments:

> It is hard to know whether the proliferation of Joaquins represented Anglo attempts to explain the geographic spread of reported depre-dations or instead reflected information gathered from months of chasing the supposed perpetrators. Most likely, both phenomena were at work and were mutually reinforcing. New intelligence about the bandits, who were reported to number in the hundreds, came in from each self-appointed posse, but somehow only men with the name Joaquin stuck in Anglo memories. (38)

The *Alta California* of San Francisco, several months later, would re-call, "Every murder and robbery in the country has been attributed to 'Joaquin.' Sometimes it is Joaquin Carrillo . . . ; then it is Joaquin something else, but always 'Joaquin!'" (23 August 1853, quoted in J. H. Jack-son, "Introduction" xxvi).

In any case, the hunt was on, and reports of the Rangers' progress came in regularly. Then, on 30 July, word reached the newspapers that Harry Love and his men had finally caught "the bandit Joaquin" (now only one and not five) and had his head along with that of his accomplice, Three Fingered Jack (Latta 67–69). These initial reports of Joaquín's death did not bother to identify which of the many proliferating Joaquines was the one so artfully decapitated.

Three Fingered Jack was another well-known Mexican bandit of the day and was thought to be Joaquín's second in command. As in the case of Joaquín, there is a great deal of confusion as to who this man was. Latta claims he was Manuel Duarte (15); Thornton identifies him as Bernardino García (14); Leal names him as Manuel García ("Introducción" 14); and Rojas contends his name was Juan Manuel García and that Joaquín Valenzuela and not García was Murrieta's first lieutenant (*El "Far West"* 58). Humberto Garza identifies Manuel Duarte, nicknamed "Tres Dedos," as a figure distinct from "Juan Tres Dedos" or "Three Fingered Jack," whose real name was Juan Manuel García (5).

The *San Joaquín Republican* assumed "that Joaquin Valancuela (not Carrillo) has been killed" because it was this Joaquín, well known as a horse thief, who was a frequent "companion" of Three Fingered Jack (2 August 1853, reprinted in Latta 70). However, Harry Love would confirm a few days later that he and his men had in fact killed "the notorious robber Joaquín Muriatta" (*San Joaquín Republican* 6 August 1853, reprinted in Latta 71). It is this designation that began to firmly root the name Muriatta (or Murieta or Murrieta) into the popular imagination as *the* Joaquín. But this is not to say that there was no public debate on the topic.

As early as 12 August, Joaquín's head went on display, pickled in an oversized jar of whiskey.[11] Some witnesses agreed that it was the famous Joaquín's, while others did not. The *San Francisco Chronicle* believed that the traveling exhibit was organized by "unscrupulous tricksters" and that Joaquín was now "enjoying the cool breeze of Sonora, Mexico, without his head, since that is here."[12]

There remained some confusion not only as to whom the head belonged but also with regard to which of the numerous Joaquines was the one everyone wanted dead. The *San Francisco Herald* printed the following letter to the editor on 19 August 1853:

> Señor Editor Herald: As my capture, or supposed capture, seems to be the topic of the day, I will, through your kindness, inform the readers of your valuable paper, that I still retain my head, although it is proclaimed through the presses of your fine city, that I was recently captured, and became very suddenly decapitated.

The letter was signed Joaquín Carrillo (reprinted in Latta 643).

Despite the apparent confusion, the name Joaquín Muriatta became established to the public as the name of the famous Mexican bandit. The reputation of this Joaquín was further advanced when, on 23 August, the *Alta Calfornia* of San Francisco dug up the story, forgotten for most of the year, about Joaquín Murrieta's suspected involvement in the Bean murder, originally reported the previous December (Castillo and Camarillo 43).

With the passing of time, Joaquín Murrieta's reputation would continue to mushroom, while the other Joaquines would fade from public memory. No one except the most avid enthusiasts of California history reads these old newspaper stories anymore; still, their influence cannot be underestimated, particularly because they provided the basis for the first literary representation of Murrieta that firmly established him as a major cultural icon of the borderlands.

The Invisible Joaquín in the Mexican Press

The scandal caused by the banditry in Alta California in the early 1850s did not take long to reach Mexico. Mexico City's *El Siglo XIX* was the first to take up the story, editorializing on the content of an article from the *San Francisco Times and Transcript* of 31 January 1853. The editorial, dated 15 February 1853, expressed great alarm at what was going on at the time in Calaveras County. While the article made a brief reference to "Mexican thieves," its principal concern was the hyperbolic reaction of the Anglophone residents of the county. The following quote repeats much of what has already been cited in the above section, but seen (as readers of *El Siglo XIX* would have seen it) in isolation from the context of the highly publicized crimes that created the panic, the actions of the citizens of Calaveras County seem even more outrageous:

> In Calaveras County, on account of the presence of some Mexican thieves, the people have risen up against the Mexican population, burning all houses of Mexican inhabitants, disarming their neighbors, and expelling all Mexicans from the county. There was a meeting in Double Springs in which it was agreed to exterminate the Mexican race. Mexicans who refuse to leave the county will be shot and their properties confiscated. Stirred by the most just indignation, we

extracted this news, which we believe to be true, and in which we see a new effrontery to Mexico for which our government must seek satisfaction . . . The conduct of the Americans is unjustifiable; it is an affront to their own laws and to the rights of people. Whatever our internal situation may be, the government must not let this horrible insult pass unnoticed.[13]

The context, for Mexicans, was not one of uncontrolled crime in Alta California. Mexico City newspapers of the mid-nineteenth century were reporting other stories about postwar relations between the United States and Mexico that continued to cause alarm among Mexicans for entirely different reasons. For example, on 7 February 1853, *El Universal* printed the translation of a story from the *Weekly Picayune* of New Orleans entitled "Another Project of Annexation," referring to an active expansionist movement in the southern United States. It noted that the *Alta California* of San Francisco had published a series of articles on "the fertility and vast resources" of Baja California, summoning the spirit of "manifest destiny" (2). *El Universal*'s response—that the *Picayune* was a "propagator of piratical doctrines" (3)—was not meant to be figurative rhetoric, considering that the launching of filibuster expeditions from New Orleans and San Francisco to seize control of different parts of Mexico, Central America, or the Caribbean was commonplace at the time, and the latest assault—by French count Gaston de Raousset Boulbon—had just been put down in Sonora (see chapter 4). Given the apparent enthusiasm of the *gringos* to obtain even more territory than the vast expanse they had snatched from Mexico in the 1840s—and the border, in fact, was still in dispute and would remain so until the realization of the Gadsden Purchase in 1854— it was no surprise to newspaper readers in Mexico City that the citizens of Calaveras County were on a murderous rampage to "exterminate" any and all Mexican residents of the region.

An editorial printed a couple of days later expressed further outrage at the actions of the *gringos* of Calaveras County, which it described as "barbarous and contrary not only to the rights of individuals, but to any idea of religion and humanity, even in the Middle Ages"; their brutality is "comparable only to that of the most backwards tribes of Africa."[14] The complaint is articulated in clearly national terms, as an issue of "national honor."[15]

By the end of March, *El Universal* was providing a little more local context, noting that the radical actions of the *gringos* of California were a reaction to a campaign of pillage, robbery, and "shocking murders" committed by a "party of Mexican thieves" under the leadership of "a robber named Joaquín" (29 March 1853, 2). The more complete context in no way assuaged the reaction of the Mexican editors, who promptly followed up with an editorial just as irate as that of *El Siglo XIX* in which they articulated a similar call to action on the part of the Mexican government toward a country "whose only interest with respect to us consists of annihilating us" (*El Universal* 31 March 1853, 1).

The Mexican journals focused minimally on the alleged crimes of the Mexican bandits, concentrating instead on the outrageous response of Wild West Californians. Joaquín's name was mentioned only in passing, and when his last name was reported, upon his beheading, the "famous captain of the bandits" was identified as Joaquín Carrillo (*El Siglo XIX* 19 August 1853). The name Murrieta did not enter Mexican public discourse during his lifetime.

Even in Sonora, where Joaquín Murrieta was born, his exploits in California did not become well known in the 1850s. One reason is that the newspaper industry in Sonora was in its infancy. The only journal in circulation was the government-sponsored *El Sonorense* of Ures, much of whose weekly space was devoted to official documents such as legislation, military communiqués, proclamations, and so on. The small amount of space remaining—usually a page or less per week—was divided among local reporting, reprints of articles from other journals (most often from Mexico City) on stories of national or international scope, advertisements or announcements, and occasionally literature (usually poetry). It would not be until the last decade of the century, with the rise of journals such as *El Imparcial* of Guaymas (see chapter 4), that an independent newspaper industry whose coverage included significant local content would begin to thrive in the northwestern Mexican border states (Moncada O.).

El Sonorense, of course, did concern itself with border issues, including social problems arising in Alta California and other former Mexican territories. The 2 March 1849 issue, for example, reported a brutal mass murder committed by five Anglo-American deserters of the U.S.–Mexico war whose victims included a Mexican woman who was in the process of giving birth in a California mission. The crimes went "not only unpunished but not even pursued due to a lack of [police] authority" (4). Another story reports a border crime, this time on the Sonora side, again committed by "a squadron of bandits" from the United States, that ended in the brutal robbery and hanging of an eighty-year-old priest (15 June 1849, 2).

Other articles expressed alarm at the mass migration of *sonorenses* to Alta California to mine gold, or generally to seek their fortune, leaving the state ever more vulnerable to raids or assaults by Apaches and Seris.[16] The Calaveras County scandal—reaching *El Sonorense*, whose offices were isolated from the world at large in the desert town of Ures, then the state capital, only after a delay of several months, via Mexico City's *El Siglo XIX*—was just one more horror story of the savage treatment of Mexicans in the borderlands to the journal's readers in Sonora. The story (quoted at length above) concluded with the following succinct editorial commentary: "We do not need to comment on the preceding incident. All Mexicans, particularly Sonorans, will see from it the luck that awaits them in California" (25 March 1853, 4). As in Mexico City, the greatest impact of the story came from the shocking racist behavior of the Anglo- Americans: "Strange conditions are found in the United States, in that populace that wishes to be a model for everyone else; there together with the most refined civilization appears the most degraded barbarity."[17] The name Joaquín (Carrillo, Murrieta, or otherwise) never reached the nascent print media of late-nineteenth-century Sonora.

The Travels and Transformations of Yellow Bird's Joaquín Murieta

In 1854, only a year after the adventures of Joaquín Murrieta ended in Alta California's newspapers with his decapitation at the hands of California Rangers, a novel was published. *The Life and Adventures of Joaquín Murieta, the Celebrated California Bandit* promised to recapture the excitement of the previous year, as well as to flesh out the character of the fearsome Mexican villain whose bloody exploits had terrorized the California countryside.

First, a very brief summary of the book's plot should be given, as this novel would become the best-known source of information on the bandit. Joaquín Murieta was a young Mexican who migrated to the United States with the best intentions, to make his fortune legally. Once in California, he witnessed the rape of his wife and the lynching of his brother for a crime he did not commit. The same sadistic and racist white Anglo-American miners who carried out these acts then proceeded to flog Joaquín: he was driven to banditry by the barbarous treatment to which he was subjected in gold rush–era California. He then set about to exact revenge on the Anglo-American race. The story is messier than one of a focused national hatred—Joaquín had many white Anglo friends and even collaborators, including one named Mountain Jim. Meanwhile, a leading member of his band, Three Fingered Jack, was pathologically cruel and often killed for no reason—in contrast to the sympathetic Joaquín. Their victims, in addition to the detested Yankees, often included Chinese miners, other foreigners, or even Mexicans. The adventure ends with Joaquín's death and beheading at the hands of Harry Love, a tragic but necessary finish. Still, the novelist's premise is explicitly stated in one of his concluding paragraphs:

> The story is told. Briefly and without ornament, the life and character of Joaquín Murieta have been sketched. His career was short, for he died in his twenty-second year; but, in the few years which were allowed him, he displayed qualities of mind and heart which marked him as an extraordinary man, and leaving his name impressed upon the early history of this State. He also leaves behind him an important lesson that there is nothing so dangerous in its consequences as *injustice to individuals*—whether it arise from prejudice of color or from any other source; that a wrong done to one man is a wrong to society and to the world. (Ridge 158, emphasis in original)

The historian Susan Johnson observes, "Once Ridge published his tale of atrocity and its retribution in 1854, Anglo recollections of unprovoked Mexican attacks on mining camps would never again seem so credible" (46).

The book's author listed his name as Yellow Bird, although many knew him as John Rollin Ridge. Part Cherokee, he often wrote under his Cherokee name. The "Publishers' Preface" brashly announced this fact, asserting that "the author is a 'Cherokee Indian,' born in the woods—reared in the midst of the wildest scenery—and familiar with all that is thrilling, fearful, and tragical in a forest-life" (2). Ridge's publishers clearly meant not only to send a social message but to excite readers' lust for adventure.[18]

Yet his novel on Murieta was more than a "thrilling, fearful and tragical" adventure story. From the very first paragraph, the narrative adamantly inserts itself into "the early history of California" (7). The text cites journals such as the *Marysville Herald* (21) for their accounts of the crimes attributed to Joaquín and his associates, and Ridge's California readers undoubtedly recognized many details taken directly from widely read (uncited) news stories from such journals as the *San Francisco Whig*[19] and the *Daily Herald,* also of San Francisco.[20] Its protagonists, Joaquín Murrieta, his bloodthirsty sidekick Three Fingered Jack, the captain of the Rangers Harry Love, well-known victims such as General Bean, and many others previously identified in news stories further demonstrated the historical accuracy of Ridge's adventure novel. Ridge had clearly done a good deal of research on his hero's life, and it is not surprising that the novel, in addition to achieving a certain respect from its readers in 1854 California, would later become an important reference for historians and biographers.[21]

Ridge's novel was also an inspiration for multiple re-elaborations of the story, some of which have been called overt plagiarisms. In the 1850s, several retellings of the Murrieta tale emerged that did not appear to copy Ridge, including one serialized adventure story in the short-lived *Pacific Police Gazette* under the title "Joaquin the Mountain Robber, or The Bandits of the Sierra Nevada" and another a few months later in the 1854 incarnation of the *California Police Gazette* under the similar title "Joaquin, the Mountain Robber! or Guerilla [sic] of California,"[22] both of which came out a few months before Ridge's book was published (Thornton 85–86).

Charles E. B. Howe's 1858 play *Joaquín Murieta de Castillo* did apparently make free use of the Ridge novel, although it added other elements, including an evil priest whose villainous nature contrasts with that of the aristocratic Joaquin, a Cuban-born Spanish nobleman. Howe's Joaquin was only marginally involved with a group of bandits led by a ruffian named García (Three Fingered Jack) and his death at the hands of the California Rangers came only after Joaquin's wife had been raped and killed, prompting him to swear, "Revenge, with its unholy light, takes possession of my soul!" (49). Howe's Joaquin did not have time to commit the crimes he is known for, and his image remains the one projected earlier in the play when he saved potential victims from his ruthless bandit colleagues. One female character asked rapturously, "How can we thank you, our noble preserver; and how can I repay you for your timely protection of my family? I know you are good as you are wildly beautiful" (33). There is no surviving evidence that indicates that the play reached a significant public or exercised much influence in its day (Thornton 94).

However, the anonymous version of the Murieta story published by the 1859 reincarnation of the *California Police Gazette* in serialized form, and soon after in book form, plagiarized directly and extensively from Ridge's original and did reach a wide audience.[23] This latter version and its illustrations, engravings by Charles Nahl,[24] became well known and forever established the visual image of Murrieta as a dark-haired *mestizo*, despite numerous conflicting reports that he had actually been light skinned and fair-haired (see Figure 4). Although Ridge published a new edition of his Murieta book in 1871, its impact in the nineteenth century was mostly indirect.[25] For it was the 1859 *California Police Gazette* version, which included several minor details that distinguished it from Ridge's version (notably the name assigned to Murieta's wife: Carmela, as opposed to Rosita in Ridge), that was later translated (also uncited— in other words, plagiarized) into other languages (Leal 20–26).

. The first translation was in 1862, into French by Robert Hyenne, who listed himself as author. In 1867, the Chilean Carlos Morla Vicuña translated the pirated Hyenne French version into Spanish (listing himself—C. M.—as translator and Hyenne as author) and converting Murieta, until then always portrayed as a Mexican, for the first time into a Chilean. In 1871, Carlos Nombela incorporated numerous episodes of the Morla translation into his own epic novel *La fiebre de riquezas: Siete años en California*. An independent translation of the *Police Gazette* story, again presenting itself as an original piece of work, appeared in serial form in the Spanish-language journal *La Gaceta* in Santa Barbara,

Figure 4. Joaquín Murieta. *Painting by Charles Christian Nahl (1859). Courtesy of Robert B. Honeyman Jr. Collection, The Bancroft Library, University of California, Berkeley.*

California, in 1881.[26] The *California Police Gazette* plagiarism, then, was important in bringing the Murrieta legend from the realm of local folklore into that of world literature. Since it and not the Ridge novel was the version most read in the nineteenth-century United States, and the one on which French, Spanish, Chilean, and U.S. Hispanic translations were based, it is worth noting how it differs from the Ridge text from which it drew so freely.

Shelley Streeby notes a few key differences between the two texts. Although she classifies both in the genre of sensationalist crime fiction, she judges that "[t]he *California Police Gazette* story is gorier and even more sensational than Ridge's, lingering over dripping blood, severed heads, and other body parts" ("Joaquín Murrieta" 171–72), and that it "identifies [Murieta] with the essentially depraved and bloodthirsty" Three Fingered Jack, who in Ridge serves more to provide contrast to Murieta's more noble impulses ("Joaquín Murrieta" 179). While Ridge wished to introduce his Murrieta tale into California history, the *Police Gazette* emphasized Joaquín's role in that history as a Mexican and a criminal: "In other words, while Ridge implies that the citizens of California need to think about how race prejudice turned Murrieta into a criminal, the *California Police Gazette* makes Murrieta into an example of an innate, alien criminality" ("Joaquín Murrieta" 173). In both cases justice wins out in the end as the notorious bandit Joaquín is finally killed, but Ridge puts American racism at the root of the violence: had his Murieta been treated fairly upon his arrival to California, such a "truly wonderful man" (Ridge 7) with "a mild and peaceable disposition" (8), a "frank and cordial bearing" (9), and "perfect good humor" (12) would never have turned criminal; the *Police Gazette*, on the other hand, aims "to make a hero out of a representative of the state—namely, Harry Love . . . —and . . . to racialize Mexicans by identifying them both as essentially foreign and as similar to so-called 'savage' Indians" (Streeby, "Joaquín Murrieta" 171). In the *California Police Gazette*, Ridge's tragic hero turns into an evil villain who issues the battle cry: "my arm is nerved for the work of destruction, and the life-blood of the Americans shall flow as freely as the mountain stream" (anon., *Joaquin Murieta, the Brigand Chief* 6).

What emerges in the vast array of literature that developed out of both the Ridge and the *Police Gazette* texts is a Joaquín Murrieta who is both heroic and demonic, both sensationalized and romanticized. Critics have complained that Mexican bandit figures in the United States "have been depicted either as fictionalized and romanticized folk-myth personalities or as murderous, blood-thirsty, thieving outlaws" (Castillo and Camarillo 1). Murrieta is clearly both.

For example, Henry Llewellyn Williams made his 1865 Joaquin Murietta a "monster" (H. L. Williams 2) comparable to, but more awful than, "a whole roster of famous European criminals and highwaymen" (Thornton 96). A 1944 history of California insisted that Joaquín was "a cutthroat Mexican bandit."[27] Frances Belle, translator back to English of the Mexican translation of the *California Police Gazette* plagiarism of Ridge, in her translator's preface, proposes to tell the story of the "lawlessness" of "the terrible Joaquin Murrieta" along with that of "the brave men who risked their lives to rid the country of" such "outlaws" (ix). But just as often, Murrieta was made into a romantic hero. Joseph Badger, in his *Joaquín, the Saddle King* (1881), portrayed his Joaquín as a blond Spaniard who fought on the U.S. side in the war with Mexico, thereby becoming "a hero to all North Americans" (Leal, "Introducción" 41). Charles Gray, in his 1912 *A Plaything of the Gods*, constructed his Murieta as kin to Spanish royalty on his mother's side and a descendant of great *tlaxcalteca*[28] kings on his father's (6) in a tale set in "old California," where Murieta was raised by a priest in a picturesque mission. The familiar story of revenge later became one of social banditry, as Murieta and his followers went pursuing justice for the poor and helpless by robbing the rich. This image was reinforced a few decades later in a book that would make a major mark on the Murrieta legend, Walter Noble Burns's *The Robin Hood of El Dorado* (1932), which was soon after made into a Hollywood film of the same name (1936). In these versions, again Three Fingered Jack is the "murderous Bad Mexican," contrasted with Murrieta, "a courtly bandit who serenades beautiful women" (Thornton 122). Hollywood's Murrieta has been compared to other cinematic Spanish-speaking romantic heroes of the borderlands such as Zorro and the Cisco Kid.[29] Even among Californios in the late nineteenth century, views of Murrieta are often at odds with each other. The prominent Californio Mariano Guadalupe Vallejo, in his *testimonio* to the California historian Hubert Howe Bancroft in the 1870s, claimed that many young Mexicans and Californios who had experienced injustice at the hands of the *gringos*, "thirsty for vengeance, took off to join the band of Joaquin Murieta and under the command of this fearsome bandit they were able to avenge some of the wrongs inflicted upon them by the North American race" (quoted in Sánchez, *Telling Identities* 290). In contrast, Antonio Franco Coronel (in a similar *testimonio*) "goes to great pains to dismiss . . . the generally held belief that Californios as a group were supportive of the bandits" (Sánchez, *Telling Identities* 291), whom he saw as "a murderous lot" (292).

The many reworkings of the Murrieta legend by novelists, filmmakers, historians, biographers, poets, and playwrights in the United States, particularly in California, are too numerous to mention. Murrieta's role in California history is as indelible as the individual elements of his legend are largely unverifiable. The cacophony of competing representations only adds to the confusion.

Despite this diversity of representation, there are clear patterns in terms of the cultural meanings assigned to him. For example, the Murrieta legend is often deployed and reshaped to promote racial harmony. The 1962 opera *Joaquín Murieta*, written by the Canadian-born Italian American Cesare Silvio Claudio, "endeavors to reconcile the three ethnic and cultural groups of Alta California: that is, the Native Americans, the Hispano-Californios, and the Yankees" (Albert Huerta, "Joaquín Murieta" 529). This particular allegory of racial integration calls for the invention of an indigenous wife and a white Anglo-American lover of Joaquín. Such schematic racial allegories hardly resemble the whole of multicultural reality of a California whose ethnic diversity also extended to significant populations of Chinese and French immigrants, for example, and whose Spanish-speaking population included Californios, Mexican immigrants, Yaqui immigrants from Sonora, Chileans, Peruvians, and others. In other words, the context of gold rush California is too complex to address with facile oppositions of Mexican versus Anglo or white versus nonwhite.

In a similar vein, although Joaquín is often constructed as a romantic hero, critics have observed that the cultural difference Murrieta portrays often serves to promote racist assumptions. Lydia Hazera points, for example, to an otherwise sympathetic portrayal of Murrieta (renamed Juan Moreno) in Charles Snow's 1929 pulp novel *The Fighting Sheriff.* When the novel's Harry Love character is faced with the opportunity to kill Moreno/Murrieta, he cries, "'I can't do it! It's too hellish, I am a white man.' The obvious inference is that 'white men' do not resort to sadistic measures, in contrast to dark-skinned men like Mexicans" (Hazera 205).

These U.S. representations of Murrieta, while sometimes critical of U.S. racism, do not easily avoid it themselves. The very fact that it is the bandit Murrieta and not the novelist María Amparo Ruiz de Burton or the well-respected Californio Mariano Vallejo who is perhaps the best remembered Mexican American of nineteenth-century California history is itself troubling. But it was not only in the United States that Joaquín Murrieta emerged as a folk hero of the gold rush.

What Ireneo Paz Did or Did Not Write

In 1999, Arte Público Press published a new edition of *Vida y aventuras del más célebre bandido sonorense, Joaquín Murrieta: Sus grandes proezas en California*, attributing authorship to Ireneo Paz. This book was first published in 1904 in Mexico City. Later editions also appeared in Los Angeles. Raymund Wood made clear in 1974 that "it is extremely unlikely that Ireneo Paz wrote the work" ("Ireneo Paz" 77). Apparently Paz, in publishing this Spanish edition of the *California Police Gazette* story in 1904, acquired the Spanish-language copyright. Interestingly, Luis Leal writes, "we discovered that the version published by don Ireneo Paz is nearly identical to that of the *Gaceta* of 1881" ("Introducción" 26). Thus, Paz was neither author nor translator of this work but merely publisher of a translation that had been done by an anonymous employee of a Santa Barbara newspaper several decades earlier.

Still, this version is significant in bringing Murrieta to Mexican readers for the first time. It also made an important move in reclaiming Murrieta as Mexican, when previous Spanish versions in circulation in Europe and the Americas had insisted that he was Chilean. This was also the first version to insist on a correct Mexican spelling of Murrieta's last name, heretofore always Murieta.

While this translation made no significant changes to its *California Police Gazette* plot, since it is the first Murrieta story to have any impact in Mexico, it is worth reviewing a few elements of the story, particularly with regard to how the protagonist was positioned vis-à-vis both Mexico and the United States.

Murrieta, again, was a messy character. He had the best intentions early in his life and was driven to crime by racist *gringos*. Generally speaking, he stuck to his goal of meting out revenge against those who had wronged him, but on many occasions, often under the evil influence of the bloodthirsty Three Fingered Jack, Murrieta's gang would kill indiscriminately. Victims included not only *gringos* but also Chinese and other immigrants and sometimes even Mexicans. And without Ridge's editorial remarks that essentially blamed Joaquín's terrible acts on the circumstances that shattered his dreams of a better life in the United States, Murrieta emerged as much less a romantic hero than in Ridge, or than in later English-language texts such as those of Gray or Burns.

However, his nationality is key. Leal surmises, "Ireneo Paz published the life of Joaquín in 1904 undoubtedly motivated by the desire to bring him back to Mexico" ("Introducción 26). Nonetheless, the story follows the *Police Gazette*'s (and Ridge's) critical attitude toward Mexico. Ridge, for example, did not mince words in explaining why his Murieta migrated to California: "he became tired of the uncertain state of affairs in his own country, the usurpations and revolutions which were of such common occurrence"; furthermore Joaquín was "[d]isgusted with the conduct of his degenerate countrymen" (8). The Paz version, following the *California Police Gazette*, is more detailed and personal in its treatment of Mexico's defects, implicitly laying blame on the government of Mexico's most enduring, though not necessarily popular, leader in the era prior to Murrieta's emigration, Antonio López de Santa Anna.

Joaquín was from Sonora, but (in the *Police Gazette* and in Paz, but not in Ridge) went to Mexico City in 1845 at the age of sixteen to work as a stable boy on the estate of President López de Santa Anna. Santa Anna himself never appeared as a character, but it was among his employees that young Joaquín was humiliated upon being sabotaged in an equestrian competition (Ireneo Paz 98–99). To U.S. readers of the *Police*

Gazette or its mutations, the incident may have recalled the reputed corruption and petty rivalries that had kept the Mexican federal government in a state of constant disarray during the first decades of independence. To Mexican readers of the Spanish translation, particularly those from the borderlands, it more likely signaled the arrogance and prejudice that Mexicans of the capital so frequently exhibited toward those from the provinces. While for *gringo* readers Joaquín's conflict with his peers in Santa Anna's stables may have intimated a blow to the young man's identity as a Mexican, which later motivated his self-exile, for Mexican readers—and above all for Sonorans or others from peripheral territories—the conflict with the *chilangos* more likely solidified his regional identity as a *norteño*.

Joaquín's feelings toward the *gringos* were ambivalent in Paz. He was discomforted by "the invasions that the Yankees had more than once carried out into Mexico's rich dominions" (101). However:

> Joaquín had come into contact with several North Americans, and although he was not in agreement with all their ideas, nevertheless disgusted with the weakness of those of his people, he had sometimes felt that he had not been born in the land of independence and liberty. He would often compare the laziness, the slovenliness, the apathy and the submissive character of his compatriots with the energy, activity and culture of the Americans, especially with respect to their eternal love for freedom. (101)

The national context of his thinking then turned regional when he added, "had his picturesque and peaceful little home located in one of the most beautiful valleys of Sonora not offered so many attractive features, Joaquín would have abandoned his nationality forever" (101).

Joaquín's gripes clearly were with Mexico, the nation, and with the haughty citizens of Mexico City who were running it, not with his beloved Sonora. It is also significant that after the murder of Joaquín's first wife, Carmen, he did not seek a *gringa* or even a *california* wife, but instead returned to Sonora to marry his former neighbor, Clarita (112–13), further demonstrating his attachment to his homeland, understood in regional and not in national terms.

The Mexican novel, which saw at least six editions between 1904

and 1923 (Wood, "Ireneo Paz" 79n3), made a significant contribution
to the legend of Murrieta by asserting his Mexican nationality and his
Sonoran identity. Moreover, although based closely on one of the most
anti-Mexican English-language versions of the legend, it gave a Mexican voice to the published retelling of the tale for the first time.[30]

Back in the USA: The Rediscovery of Yellow Bird's Joaquín Murieta, a Great "American" Novel

The success of the pirated reworking of Yellow Bird's original Murieta
novel in the *California Police Gazette* was quite disheartening to the
author. Ridge publicly accused the journal of plagiarism when it first
published its anonymous Murieta text in 1859 (Walker 257). Ridge's
novel, meanwhile, had gone out of print. A new 1871 edition was billed
as a third edition, undoubtedly to point out the vast similarity of the
Police Gazette edition to Ridge's original. In Ridge's preface to this third
edition, he declared irately, "A spurious edition has been foisted upon
unsuspecting publishers and by them circulated, to the infringement of
the author's copyright and the damage of his literary credit—the spurious work, with its crude interpolations, fictitious additions, and imperfectly designed distortions of the author's phraseology, being by
many persons confounded with the original performance" (quoted in
Walker 257).

However, it is not this revised and polished version that is best known
to readers today since the edition currently in circulation is based on
the 1854 original. In fact, it was the 1955 edition, published by the University of Oklahoma Press, that would attain a widespread twentieth-
century readership, overshadowing the renown of that of the *Police
Gazette* and eventually earning a remarkable level of respect among literary and social historians. Not only was Yellow Bird's Murieta novel
the first novel published in English by a Native American author but
it was also one of the first historical novels about the racial conflicts in
the postwar Southwest. Much has been written about the text in recent
years, and it is not necessary for the purposes at hand to analyze all
recent criticism. However, several of the recent readings of the novel
are worth mentioning.

Contemporary critics agree that "Ridge exploits every hyperbolic resource of language to render his protagonist Byronically attractive" (Kroeber 5); that "[b]y retaliating against white aggressors," Ridge's "trickster-bandit attempts to order the world of the frontier oppressed" (Lape 79); and that "the novel exposes the precarious positioning of 'savagery' and 'civilization' within the dominant historical discourse" (Mondragón 173). Yet all three of the critics cited above approach the text less through the perspective of its protagonist than through that of its Native American author. Their readings of "the complexity of Ridge's identity, of Indian identity in general, and of American identity" (Mondragón 173–74) often leave aside what the novel—so often read, it must be remembered, as historiography and not as fiction—communicates about its Mexican protagonist or to a Mexican reader. Murieta, master of disguise, is a derivation of "the traditional mythological Trickster" of Native American cultures (Lape 57), and there are many other good reasons for which the study of this novel should be revived by scholars of Native American cultural studies, but this is only part of the story.

Another school of criticism approaches the novel as not so much a text of Native American literature as one of American literature, a story about American culture. Writes John Lowe, "Joaquin speaks not only for the poor but also for the racially and ethnically oppressed, all denied 'space' at the feast of America" (120). Ridge's Murieta undoubtedly gained the sympathy of U.S. English-speaking readers not as an ethnic other but as a man who represented the contradictory ideological vectors of national identity that demanded the acculturation of new immigrants to the United States, and at the same time promoted a rugged individualism as the key to the American spirit. John Carlos Rowe writes, "For Ridge, Joaquín's sublimity embodies the identity that U.S. culture ought to cultivate in a democratic society: self-reliance based on an ability to harness natural power and to defy social conventionality. In Ridge's portrait, Joaquín is decisively *American*" (*Literary Culture* 117, emphasis in original).

Important as this revival of Ridge has been for the revisions and expansions of the field of American studies as proposed by the so-called new Americanists (see chapter 1), the weakness in this new body of criticism on the Yellow Bird Murieta novel mimics a weakness in the American studies approaches to the borderlands in general: a lack of knowledge and/or interest in the history and culture of the Mexican borderlands, where the real Joaquín Murrieta apparently was born and where he is remembered today, for example, by members of the International Association of Descendants of Joaquín Murrieta.[31] American studies' tendency to resist bilingual scholarship and inter-American dialogue with the Mexican academy continues to restrain the field within a "house of mirrors," as Djelal Kadir puts it (21).

The lack of attention to a Mexican borderlands perspective goes beyond the obvious lack of knowledge of Spanish on the part of many scholars who pretend to be experts on Murrieta. Lowe, for example, assumes that the Murieta spelling used by Ridge is correct, maligning a California tourist guidebook for spelling Joaquín's last name with a double "r" (117). And if Yellow Bird, himself not much of a Spanish speaker, was nonetheless able to transform the Muliati and Muriati of the California newspapers into a much more Spanish-sounding Murieta, it is shocking that Karl Kroeber cannot even manage to copy this name correctly, referring repeatedly to the novel's hero as Joaquin Murietta, even when citing Ridge's book title.

Spelling errors aside, declarations about the Mexican American experience among American studies critics too often ring false. Timothy Powell enthusiastically seeks to revive interest in Ridge's novel for its "multicultural complexity": Ridge's "*Joaquin Murieta* does not fit easily into the binary critical framework of center/margin, colonized/colonizer, oppressor/oppressed, that for the last two decades has been used as a critical tool for recovering the voice of the 'Other' in American history and literature" ("Historical Multiculturalism" 186). His study of Ridge's writings teases out "conflicting feelings of a deep-seated racial rage at white society and an equally powerful desire to be included into 'America'" (196)—so far, so good. He then attempts to show that Ridge's narrative draws from multicultural sources including the Anglo-American-style historical romance novel, Cherokee myth, and Mexican popular culture (199–202). In the latter case, he makes the claim that "[a] literary archaeology of Ridge's novel reveals . . . that the narrative development of *Joaquin Murieta* can be traced back to Mexican American *corridos*" (200). True, the *corrido* was in the process of becoming an established genre of Mexican cultural expression in the borderlands right around the time when Ridge wrote his novel, and multiple *corridos* that recount the Murrieta legend do exist and may have even begun to take form before Ridge wrote his book.[32] However, there is no indication that Ridge had any contact with the Mexican migrants who are likely to have improvised or repeated ballads on Murrieta, nor that he would have been capable of following musical pieces sung in Spanish. Ridge's research was carried out primarily through reading English-language newspaper reports, and there is no evidence that he ever sought out the perspective of Mexican Americans, particularly among the mostly illiterate balladeers who were the most likely to have made Joaquín into a Mexican borderlands folk hero through their music. In short, the narrative development of the novel cannot in any way be "traced back to the Mexican American *corridos*"; in fact far more convincing is Bruce Thornton's argument that a well-known Murrieta *corrido*—the earliest recorded version, from the 1930s—"clearly derives from the *Police Gazette* story" of 1859.[33] Powell, whose bibliography includes no Mexican or Spanish-language sources, is unqualified to bring Mexican cultural forms into his discussion and would have been better off focusing on Native American or U.S.-American perspectives like the other Americanist critics mentioned above, incomplete though such an approach may have been.

This is not to say that no representations of Murrieta in the United States have been sufficiently complex to accurately reflect the multicultural borderlands that produced his legend. The most complete study of Murrieta was the life project of the amateur historian Frank Latta, who spent decades rooting through archives, hunting down rumors and family histories in Sonora, and reading everything he could find on Murrieta and his associates. The result, a 650-page volume of Murrieta lore and rough interpretations of often contradictory data, is Latta's masterpiece, *Joaquín Murrieta and His Horse Gangs* (1980). Latta's mass of information, much of it unreliable, all of it fascinating, in the end is a mess of contradictions—"exasperating" in the words of one historian (Susan Johnson 346n6).

For example, he delves meticulously and relentlessly into the fate of Joaquín's severed head. First he conjectures that the head displayed in 1853 could not have been that of Joaquín Murrieta, who he believes died in a shooting a few days after his alleged beheading—for Latta, the head belongs not even to one of the other Joaquines (some have speculated that it was the head of Joaquín Valenzuela, for example) but to an Indian named Chappo. Latta had previously produced sources confirming that Joaquín Murrieta was a "huero" [sic],[34] which for him proves that the bottled head, described as that "of a typical California Indian: very dark complexion, inky-black hair and eyes" (608), could not have belonged to the famous bandit.

Latta traces the bottled head to a series of owners until it ends up in a museum of anatomy and science curiosities in San Francisco. While the commonly accepted story is that the head perished there in the 1906 earthquake, Latta claims that he himself went to see the head on display after the earthquake. He writes, "I do not remember exactly where Dr. Jordan's Pacific Museum of Anatomy and Science was located in 1906, but it was in the 700 block on a street a short distance north of Market Street. And that building was neither shaken down nor burned" (613). Just as he, seventy-four years later, appears poised to provide his eyewitness report proving that Joaquín's head survived the earthquake, he goes on to recount that he and his friend, upon entering the "Pathological Room," became so sick that they "bolted for the door" and "couldn't eat for two days" afterward (613). Not only could he not place the museum at the address where all sources listed it as being located but he did not actually see anything to contradict the reports of its destruction (and that of the all-important head).

This colorful tale is typical of Latta. He follows all kinds of leads, many of them vague memories of aged informants, who often were reporting what they remembered being told by their own long-deceased elderly relatives. The quantity of data he collected is impressive, but the text itself is utterly confusing. And perhaps for this very reason, Latta's is the classic and most authoritative study of Murrieta. Murrieta and the borderlands from which his legend sprung were anything but neat and easily comprehensible.

Joaquín in Chile

Meanwhile, Joaquín's trajectory in Chile has not concerned itself so much with issues of Native American identity, American exceptionalism, or postmodernist multiculturalism as it has with U.S. imperialism in the Americas. In order to make its point relevant to Chile, this literature has had to kidnap Murrieta and make him Chilean. The struggle for representation in which Murrieta has been deployed goes beyond the local context of the U.S.–Mexico borderlands to signify in the context of the Americas.

Mexicans of nearby Sonora and their compatriots from further south were not the only ones to make gold rush–era California their destination. Immigrants arrived from all over the world, and ports such as San Francisco made the region far more accessible to Latin Americans from Pacific coastal countries than to Europeans or even to Easterners. Peruvians and Chileans in particular quickly established a significant presence in California. However, U.S. racism that had initially been directed primarily toward Mexicans soon came to lump all Spanish speakers into the same demonized category of "greasers," who were stereotyped as dark-skinned *mestizos* and seen as racially inferior to white Europeans.

Stories of racial prejudice and violence soon reached the South American homelands of these immigrants. Chilean culture apparently was just as much in need of a redeeming hero in the face of Yankee effrontery, and it seems that just as soon as the Chilean Carlos Morla got his hands on Robert Hyenne's translation of the *California Police Gazette* version of the Murieta story, one of what would become many Spanish-language editions of the novel began to circulate in Chile, with Murieta identified as Chilean less than a decade after his putative death.

In the 1930s, there was a resurgence of interest in Chile as Antonio Acevedo Hernández wrote a dramatic work entitled simply *Joaquín Murieta*. Acevedo's story is based largely upon the well-known (in Chile) version of Hyenne (Pereira Poza 81), but the context of its cultural signification is notably distinct, moving beyond the local to the hemispheric. Acevedo summoned not the ghost of Santa Anna but that of the South American independence hero Simón Bolívar, as his text exhorts Latin Americans to "unite, move towards the ideals of Bolívar, and form a single and great power that will counteract the actions of all who dominate unreasonably" (quoted in Pereira Poza 83).

Thirty years later, a new generation of Latin Americans became acquainted with Murieta as a Chilean icon of anti-imperialist resistance when the Chilean poet Pablo Neruda dramatized his life once again in the cantata *Fulgor y muerte de Joaquín Murieta*. Moreover, if there was any doubt at that time as to Joaquín's nationality, Neruda quashed it, declaring vociferously, "Joaquín Murieta was Chilean. I have seen the proof" (quoted in Leal, "Introducción" 37). Neruda is more overtly combative in his rhetoric against "those who razed, enveloped in hatred, and trampled flags of errant peoples" and "those irascible crude warriors who have everything and want everything and mistreat and kill everything" (Neruda 137). Murieta would seem to represent a third-world everyman faced with the brute force of the greed and power of the wealthiest; racism is also a key theme as Neruda associates the California Rangers with the Ku Klux Klan (Alberto Huerta 49). While for some critics Neruda presents little more than "anti American clichés and Marxist bromides" (Thornton 139), he was in 1966 undeniably the most famous and influential writer to date to represent the legend of Murieta. One critic waxes, "The poetic word of Pablo Neruda will be the one that consecrates this figure that, through a fascinating and protean trajectory with many faces, will find its definitive place in the space of eternity" (Millares 212).

The exposure that Neruda gave the Murieta legend throughout Latin America and throughout the world[35] raised a red flag in the U.S.–Mexico borderlands where Murrieta, with double "r," had always been Sonoran. The Mexicanist historian James Officer felt obliged to put the matter of whether Murrieta was Chilean or Mexican to rest once and for all and went to Chile to investigate. There he discovered that the principal authoritative source for Chileans on Murrieta's Chilean nationality was the historian Roberto Hernández Cornejo, whose 1930 two-volume work *Los chilenos en San Francisco, California* identified Murieta as a Chilean bandit. However, writes Officer, "The many Chilean writers who base their designation of the Murrieta as a Chilean bandit on the work of Hernández Cornejo surely have read only the first volume because in the second Hernández himself begins to doubt" (131). He

then discovered that the root of Murrieta's Chilean identity was actually the Morla Vicuña translation of the Hyenne novel and that prior
to its publication, there seems to be no evidence whatsoever of the existence of a Chilean Murrieta (or Murieta) in California (131–32). Manuel
Rojas, too, made a point of refuting the Chileans, deriding them for being
unable to agree on Murieta's birthplace in Chile: Santiago or Quillota
or Valparaíso (*El "Far West"* 86).

The main contemporary Chilean authority on Murrieta, Carlos
López Urrutia, in fact had known for years that any real Murrieta that
may have existed was not Chilean. His 2001 publication of a new Spanish translation of the Yellow Bird novel includes as an appendix his article "El Murrieta chileno (la historia de un fraude literario)" in which
he reports that he brought the fruits of his own research on Murrieta's
nationality to Pablo Neruda himself: "'Was Neruda ignorant of this evidence?' the reader may ask. My answer is categorical: he was not ignorant of it, but he argued against it with a stubbornness and obstinacy that
defied logic" (141). Neruda insisted again and again: "I have irrefutable
proof that he was Chilean!" (141), but he was unable to produce it.[36]

López Urrutia, then, in doing a new translation of Ridge, with
Murrieta made Mexican again, is at odds with over a century of Chilean
literature and scholarship that made what was a much more parochial
figure of the U.S.–Mexico borderlands a revolutionary icon of hemispheric consequence in the context of the cold war. A Chilean Murrieta,
in absence of any monumental conflict between Chile and the United
States prior to the Pinochet coup, was more easily positioned as a hemispheric than a national icon, one who could "embrace the Latin American cause" with a "messianic" spirit (Pereira Poza 85). It is no surprise,
then, that López Urrutia's new re-Mexicanized translation was published in Mexico and not in Chile.

López Urrutia has not been the only Chilean to revive the gold rush
hero in recent years. Isabel Allende, in her *Hija de la fortuna*, reestab-
lishes Murieta as a romantic—and of course Chilean—hero. Allende
broadens the scope of the legend by incorporating also into her tale the
California journalist who "invents the character of Murieta as a 'Robin
Hood of California'" (Thornton 127), in other words, a rendering of
John Rollin Ridge himself, exploring the motivations behind the many

writers who have glorified (and demonized) the legendary bandit "to satisfy the common man's tastes" (Allende quoted in Thornton 127). Allende's Murieta (known as Joaquín Andieta), then, captures the "revolutionary fervor and passionate desire to champion the oppressed" (Thornton 127), and also the eagerness of others to tell his story, thereby evoking much more than the Mexican borderlands context in which Joaquín's conflicts inevitably play out. The broader, hemispheric context induced in the works of Allende's Chilean predecessors, and that of the writer who manipulates and embellishes facts and rumors to please an audience, gives an ephemeral shape to an ever-changing legend.

Murrieta Back in Mexico

Surprisingly, aside from Paz's *Vida y aventuras*, very little creative or scholarly work on Murrieta has been produced in Mexico. Beginning with the early popularity of Yellow Bird, it seemed that Murrieta "appealed predominantly to Anglo readers searching for a history of the new state" of California (Thornton 94). Some critics have gone so far as to imply that Murrieta is effectively a hero of an essentially U.S. legend who some "writers south of the Río Grande [have sought] to adopt as their own" (Alberto Huerta 48). In Latin America, Chile is the country that has most written about Murrieta. Nonetheless, in the last few decades, Murrieta has been the subject of several books published in Mexico.

The first is the historian Celso Aguirre Bernal's *Joaquín Murrieta: Raíz y razón del movimiento chicano*. Aguirre Bernal's Murrieta is cast as a Chicano hero, comparable to eminent national figures including the independence-era heroes Miguel Hidalgo and José María Morelos, and the revolutionaries Pancho Villa and Emiliano Zapata. This Murrieta has a unique characteristic of being "Mayo by nature, indigenous by his origin" (81), a notion Aguirre Bernal does not develop sufficiently to draw interesting conclusions. He situates his story within the history of the Mexican northwestern frontier and Aztlán, designating him a "precursor of the current Chicano movement" (79).

His reading is interesting because it locates Chicano resistance within a Mexican and not a U.S. context. His bibliography is fully Mexican: not one text is in English or was published in the United States. Oddly, he only dialogues with Chicanos or Chicano studies scholars—for example, Juan Bruce-Novoa, David Maciel—who publish in Mexico. His narrow national focus, parallel to that of many Americanist scholars in the United States, limits his work quite problematically, considering the wealth of material published on Murrieta in the United States, even from a Chicano studies perspective, which he ignores. He appears to be unaware of any of the novels on the topic, including the one commonly attributed to Ireneo Paz. Furthermore, he could easily have bolstered his (rather Manichaean) arguments of *gringo* racism and Mexican American heroism by browsing a few of the novels, histories, or biographies mentioned earlier in this chapter. Once again, it seems anti-intuitive to portray a borderlands icon in strictly national terms, or to pretend authority on a borderlands topic using a monolingual mononational bibliography.

A year later, Manuel Rojas authored another much more thoroughly researched study. Rojas published his work in the borderlands and applied a much broader research plan, citing numerous sources in both English and Spanish, and from Mexico, the United States, Chile, and France. However, like Aguirre Bernal, Rojas insists on a Mexican national context for Murrieta, painting him as a patriot. He sets out by signaling that his study responds to a call by the government "to go out and rescue those values that are proper to Mexicans" (*El "Far West"* 9); he finds these values in Murrieta, whose story, set in "the territories snatched from Mexico" by the United States (10), forms part of "the history of old Mexico, of amputated Mexico" (10).[37]

Rojas performed a very thorough investigation. Unlike many historians, particularly in the United States, who rely on John Rollin Ridge as their primary source on Murrieta, Rojas visited Sonora, and like the U.S. amateur historian Frank Latta before him, sought out evidence of the "real" Joaquín Murrieta in the area in which the bandit is thought to have grown up. His sources—principally the parish archives of the district of Altar, Sonora;[38] interviews of people claiming to be Murrieta's descendants; data previously assembled by Frank Latta (by similar means); even an exhumation of graves where he thinks Murrieta may have been buried in Sonora[39]—trace Joaquín Murrieta back to his birth in 1819.[40]

Moreover, Rojas audaciously posits a new theory regarding Murrieta's recalcitrance and banditry by placing Murrieta at the center of an organized plot whose goal was the "reannexation of California to Mexico" (*El "Far West"* 123). Rojas links Joaquín with a number of other outlaws—some of whom Frank Latta professes were often confused with him—implying that they all were likely in cahoots in a scheme that went well beyond the personal vengeance, banditry, and horse stealing with which they have generally been associated (124). Rojas moreover claims that Latta knew more than he let on in his 650-page tome on Murrieta, but that he "evaded" putting together certain evidence in order "to hide" their ramifications for fear that they would contradict "the 'official' history of the United States," which recognized no such organized military action on the part of Mexico.[41] Rojas accepts estimates that Murrieta's horse-thieving network counted a good two thousand men among its ranks. He writes, "It is tremendously significant that a 'thief,' 'murderer,' and 'desperado' would wish to join two thousand well armed men, all with horses . . . the reader will wonder, why? . . . to rob banks? . . . to assault Wells Fargo wagons?" (*El "Far West"* 125); he further asserts that the California Rangers were not a police but a paramilitary unit (129–31).

Rojas does not get much beyond the speculative stage in this line of inquiry and presents no evidence that is not circumstantial in nature, but he is adamant in his arguments. One critic complains that "Rojas's work ultimately suffers from the same limitations as Latta's . . . : the oral traditions cannot be shown to be independent of the literary creations that such traditions suspiciously resemble" (Thornton 133). Many of his claims, for example that the numerous allegations of brutal crimes attributed to Murrieta including several bloody murders of Chinese immigrants were all part of an organized persecution of Mexicans by the Anglo government, are not outlandish—even if U.S. sources have never thought to pursue them.[42] However, the veracity of his theory is less interesting perhaps than its very articulation. Although he moves beyond the linguistic and other bibliographic limitations of Aguirre Bernal by including a vast hodgepodge of sources from both sides of the border, he mimics his compatriot's desire to make of Murrieta a Mexican patriot and an important figure in nineteenth-century national history.

One other important theory that Rojas advances—here reiterating ideas previously put forth by Frank Latta (631–34)—is that Murrieta was not killed by Love and the California Rangers in July 1853. Rojas presents a range of evidence, including a letter he attributes to Joaquín dated after his supposed death (*El "Far West"* 142) and a reference making claims confirming his death in Sonora in 1879 (143). A popular theory was that Murrieta escaped punishment and returned victorious to Sonora where he lived a quiet life,[43] dying only decades after his adventure in California. This triumphant Joaquín gets the last laugh. He was never caught; his head was never displayed in a jar; the *gringos* never even figured out the truth. Whether or not there is any veracity in the theories presented by Rojas, his location of Joaquín in a glorious national history protagonized by Mexico's bravest patriots contrasts significantly with the majority of U.S. representations of Murrieta as a romantic hero or monstrous villain of the Old West. Murrieta was now a hero—much less softened by amorous adventures so often attributed to him in novels—not of the Old West, but of greater Mexico.

This new interest in Murrieta among Mexican historiographers perhaps inspired a new novel on Murrieta, Carlos Isla's *Joaquín Murrieta* (2002). Isla's version repeats many of the details of the Ireneo Paz *Vida y aventuras*, adding few elements of significance. However, given the new effort on the part of Mexican historians to recuperate Joaquín's story as part of national history and culture, one small difference between Isla and Paz is noteworthy. While Paz repeats the *California Police Gazette*'s final phrase: "This story can be considered, then, an integral part of the true early history of California," (242) Isla concludes: "This story can be considered, then, part of the history of Mexico" (152). If Murrieta still has not inspired enthusiasm in Mexico equal to what he has evoked in California or even Chile, Mexican culture's recent reappropriation of his legend signals a new resolution to reclaim his story for his birth country.

Chicano Joaquín

Quite similar to these Mexican readings of Murrieta are those that position Joaquín as an icon of Mexican American culture. These latter readings assume an understanding of U.S. culture that includes the cultural production of minority groups along with that of dominant ones, all interacting in a fragmented and unstable field of national signification. The Chicano Murrieta reasserts himself within U.S. culture no longer as a mere romantic hero of old California but as a symbol of defiant Mexican American participation in old Californian culture despite Anglo-America's attempts to exclude it. Mexican Americans, thus, take ownership of the Murrieta icon in order to deploy him to their ends.

In previous uses of Murrieta in the United States, even sympathetic ones such as that of Ridge, Mexican Americans remained passive objects. For example, returning to John Carlos Rowe's astute reading of Ridge, the Joaquín of *The Life and Adventures* "is decisively American" and the author "invests Joaquín's rebellious spirit with the zeal of revolution that Ridge identifies with the democratic aspirations of romantic individualism" (117). Joaquín is an American tragic hero because he is not permitted to fulfill the American dream he sets out to attain. The psychological profile of the Mexican protagonist of Ridge's novel—Joaquín as a recent immigrant who was ready to assimilate entirely to U.S. national ideal—was not constructed as the product of a dialogue with Mexican Americans of 1850s California.

Similarly, Mexican representations of Joaquín have tended to box him into the category of national hero. What in some *gringo* stories may be a tale of personal revenge, and what in the *California Police Gazette* and other Murrieta reworkings turns into a rabid violence that goes beyond reason, for Mexicans becomes an allegory of Mexican national defense against Yankee imperialism. Rojas's theory that Murrieta was part of a broad-based scheme to return Alta California to Mexico turns banditry into guerrilla warfare. Such binary thinking, however, may seem reductive to Mexican Americans, whose relationships to both Mexico and the United States frequently go beyond mere alliance to the former and animosity toward the latter.

The first translation of the Murrieta drama to reach Mexican Americans, *La Gaceta* of Santa Barbara's adaptation of the *California Police Gazette* narrative, later published in book form by Ireneo Paz, did not make significant changes to the text. However, as noted above, its significance to Mexican or Mexican American readers, particularly with respect to its implications regarding Joaquín's relationship to Mexico and to Sonora, was likely quite different from what Anglo-American readers would have understood. As one of the earliest Spanish-language novels published in the Southwest, it no doubt made an impact in establishing Murrieta as a key figure in Mexican American history for Mexicans on both sides of the border.

Perhaps the Los Angeles editions of the Ireneo Paz novel sparked a certain degree of interest in the Murrieta legend among Mexican Americans, for it is around the time of their publication that Murrieta began to appear in original (that is, not translated) Spanish-language literature in the U.S. Southwest for the first time. Adolfo Carrillo's short story "Joaquín Murrieta" was first published around 1922 in Los Angeles (López Rojo 9). Carrillo, a Mexican journalist exiled for political reasons who arrived in California via Havana and New York, was by no means a typical Mexican American immigrant, nor is his perspective typical of that of Mexican American sources on Murrieta. The Mexican critic Miguel López Rojo summarizes:

> Although the story teller is tough on the North American filibusters and adventurers, he does not criticize the annexation of Mexican territory by the United States government. Instead, he launches a fierce criticism against the leaders of the vanquished society: the Californio missionaries and patriarchs who were so idealized by other Hispanic and Anglo writers. (12–13)

López Rojo's conclusions, drawn from his reading of the entire collection of stories Carrillo published under the title *Cuentos californianos*, among which "Joaquín Murrieta" was one, note—despite Carrillo's proudly Mexican identity—a great deal of sympathy toward "the march of Anglo-american progress and bourgeois values" that changed the face of California after the U.S.–Mexico war, replacing a feudal social system heavily influenced by the old-fashioned regimen of the Catholic Church (22).

Carrillo's position, then, is not located within a binary scheme of Mexico versus the United States. His writing illustrates that while many Mexicans retain strong ties and identity links to their home country, many others prefer to assume a more "American" identity that leaves behind Mexican nationalist rhetoric. On the one hand, Carrillo's "Joaquín Murrieta" presents the binary view that opposes Mexico to the United

States in the character of Jack Tres Dedos, who killed *gringos* indiscriminately, criticized assimilated Californios, and tried to persuade
Joaquín to go back to Mexico. Jack was the savage, bloodthirsty one,
but he was also the one through whose voice a Mexican nationalist position is articulated. However, Joaquín was more moderate. While he was
dispossessed of his gold claim by some *gringo* miners, he directed his
vengeance toward not the United States but the band of ruffians who
raped and killed his sister. The band was led by an Irishman who arrived
in California after escaping from an Australian prison. Joaquín, once
his revenge was complete, continued marauding along with Jack and a
motley gang of Mexicans but never articulated his hatred in national or
racial terms. Finally, it was Joaquín who (against Jack's advice) fell in
love with the daughter of a Californio collaborator with the *gringos*,
who, "interested in the reward, sent detailed reports to the Governor
on Murrieta's plans" (96), leading to an ambush in which Joaquín died.

The text's political positioning is ambivalent. While it does articulate something of a Mexican nationalist stance, the character (Jack Tres
Dedos) through which it communicates these ideals is introduced as a
criminal (cattle rustler and horse thief) from the start, unlike Joaquín,
who had begun as an honest rancher, fisherman, and miner. Joaquín, the
good man turned bad due to the cruelty of an Irish criminal, had no
specific gripes with the United States, nor with *gringo*-friendly Californios. In the end, however, had Joaquín followed Jack's advice to drop
his "poche" [Americanized] girlfriend and go back to Mexico, the tragic
ending would have been avoided. Carrillo expresses, ultimately, a divided,
hybrid ideological posture that splits "between the values of the liberal
bourgeoisie and those of a racially and culturally Mexican identity"
(López Rojo 15).

Another exiled journalist, this one from Sonora, Brígido Caro (Moncada O. 32–33), penned a drama, again titled *Joaquín Murrieta*, which
"not only achieved success on the professional stage, but was also adopted
by the community for political and cultural fund raising activities"
(Kanellos 32). While these political uses of the play are suggestive, unfortunately no copy survives on which to perform a conclusive analysis.

However, the Murrieta legend's political possibilities were vividly
realized in 1967, when the Chicano activist Corky González wrote what

would become the emblematic poem of the Chicano movement, "I Am Joaquín." In the poem, Joaquín Murrieta is the Chicano everyman, a symbol of struggle to overcome racism in the United States. "I Am Joaquín" is, of course, the phrase of defiance that Murrieta purportedly uttered to a group of Anglo Californians at the peak of the Joaquín hysteria in 1853. Yellow Bird's Joaquín pronounced the famous phrase on multiple occasions (e.g., 51, 87).

González opens his poem with that mantra; he then sets up an opposition between a Mexican past embodied as "victory of the spirit, despite physical hunger" and a modern Anglo future represented by "that monstrous technical, industrial giant called Progress and Anglo success" (266). The poem makes Joaquín the first of many symbols of Chicano identity that include Cuauhtémoc, an anonymous "Maya prince" (267), Nezahualcóyotl, Cortés, Emiliano Zapata, the mountain Indian ("Yaqui, Tarahumara, Chamula, Zapotec, . . ." 271), and so on: in short, a whole parade of historic icons and symbols of Mexican and Mexican American identity. The poem touches upon key historic moments such as the Spanish conquest of the Aztec empire, the U.S.–Mexico war of the 1840s, and the Mexican revolution and enacts scenes from the struggles of everyday life of Mexican immigrants in the United States, placing Joaquín Murrieta at the center of it all. The poem ends in the rallying cry, "I shall endure! I will endure!" (279).

González, unlike Adolfo Carrillo, positions Mexican American culture as "a live continuation of Mexican culture" (Leal, "Introducción" 55). His identity politics reduces the Chicano experience to a clash between opposing forces, incapable of reconciliation. However, the poem's influence was profound, becoming "probably the most famous piece of Chicano literature; it has sold over two hundred thousand copies in various editions and has been frequently anthologized" (Thornton 137). A year later when Antonio Bernal painted Murrieta together with César Chávez in a mural at the United Farm Workers' Teatro Campesino Cultural Center in Del Ray, California, he was already following a new tradition of Murrieta's symbolic deployment.[44]

González's repositioning of Murrieta as a Chicano icon has naturally provoked the interest of Chicano studies scholars. Early (1970s) studies in the burgeoning field expressed a concern that "[a] substantial portion of Chicano history in the latter half of the nineteenth century is dominated by the presence of a sequence of Mexican 'bandits'" (Castillo and Camarillo 1). Disturbed by the degree of importance given to men who were essentially portrayed as criminals, scholars made an effort to recast border outlaws such as Murrieta as "social bandits," following the theory of Eric Hobsbawm.[45] The politics of Chicano studies, as it began to take institutional form in the 1970s, was clear, as Murrieta and other legendary bandits were described as exponents of "individual peasant insurrection" (Castillo and Camarillo 1). While an important early 1973 study by Pedro Castillo and Albert Camarillo warns, "There was, of course, the Mexican elite who was adamantly opposed to Chicano banditry" (2), Chicano studies concerned itself not with these elites but with the "peasant society" from which these social bandits emerged.

Frequently, the class warfare that such contentions imply is at odds with the complexity of the border culture of the Murrieta legend as portrayed in Carrillo or even Yellow Bird. One eminent Chicano studies critic declares that "while the majority of Anglo-Saxon literature refers to Mexican rebels as 'bandits,' Chicano historians and other experts in southwestern history understand many of these so called 'bandits' as revolutionary warriors or heroes of the resistance against the Anglo-Saxon invasion and classify them as precursors of the contemporary Chicano movement" (Herrera-Sobek 139). This posturing overstates the case and leads more crotchety critics to accuse Chicano studies scholars of "ethnic cheerleading" at the expense of sound scholarship (Thornton 142). And although their purpose may be mainly "to irritate a few American historians" (Humberto Garza x), their rhetoric—for example, Humberto Garza's discussion of "the genocide of Mexicanos and Mexicans by United States citizens" (33)—is oftentimes excessively one-sided. Meanwhile, their particular view of Mexican American culture as an extension of Mexican culture and an opposing force vis-à-vis Anglo-American culture aligns it strongly with Mexican nationalist critics such as Aguirre Bernal or Rojas, the latter of whom turns out to be a primary source for some Chicano studies scholars.[46]

In fact, in 1996, under the auspices of the International Association of Descendants of Joaquín Murrieta, La Cuna de Aztlán, a Mexicali-based publisher, put out a third edition of Manuel Rojas's landmark study, with text in both Spanish and English translation. Rojas's book was re-positioned—as the new subtitle, "Truthful Focuses for the Chicano Movement," makes clear—from a Mexican national to a Chicano point of articulation. Unlike the Chicano identity politics reflected in early studies such as that of Castillo and Camarillo, the work of a few pioneering Mexican Americans, all living in the U.S. Southwest, later works reflect a transnational community of Chicano nationalists whose political goals coincide with and are supported by a cadre of left-leaning intellectuals and activists from the Mexican side of the border. The Chicano activists' appropriation of Rojas's previously Mexican nationalist message is not an isolated incident; the Herrera Sobek text quoted above was in fact published in Tijuana, another new intellectual center of transborder, postnationalist research and activism.

Alfredo Figueroa, the president of the International Association of Descendants of Joaquín Murrieta, a Chicano, adds a new introduction, in which he takes up where Rojas leaves off. His Murrieta was at the head of an organized movement to "regain California" (1), whose initial goal was to round up and steal enough horses "to supply Joaquín's liberating army" (6). He claims that many of "Joaquín Murrieta's guerrilla veterans" retired in 1853 to northern Sonora where they "were just waiting for an opportunity to get revenge against the *gringos*" (2), an opportunity that they seized when Henry Crabb led his filibuster invasion into Sonora in 1857. Figueroa asserts that it was these retired *bandidos* from Murrieta's band who annihilated the invaders, decapitated their leader, and were soon lauded as the glorious heroes of Caborca. Since Rojas has the famous Joaquín living in Tecate at this time, it is not he but his men who have the last word in what for Figueroa is essentially an extension of the U.S.–Mexico war. The Mexicans do not regain Alta California, but nor do the Yankees seize control of Sonora. And it is *gringo* and not Mexican heads that roll.

If the Chicano agenda was spreading into Mexico, not all Mexican Americans on the U.S. side were necessarily arguing from the same position. Albert Huerta, a Jesuit priest and aficionado of California lore, uses a study of Murieta (note that he eschews the Mexican spelling), "Murieta y los 'californios': Odisea de una cultura" (1983), to rally against what he calls the "culturicidio" of old California (624), which he maintains began in 1833 with the Mexican state's appropriation of the Catholic Church's properties "including the 'missions' of Baja and Alta California" (619–20) and was furthered by the occupation of California by the capitalist and largely protestant United States in 1848 (622). Huerta is not a mainline Chicano activist; his concern is a fading regional culture of Hispanic California, an emphatically Catholic California. Huerta finds the legend of Murieta to be a key phenomenon in California's struggle against *culturicidio*, which in the end has thankfully not occurred:

> The setbacks due to the *culturicidio* studied here have not discouraged [the Hispano-Californian] from pursuing his goal of reestablishing the spiritual experience of the 'missions'. Without faith, the fate of the Hispano-Californian would be a tragedy for the history of the United States. With faith, the Hispano-Californian has withstood the blows of time. ("Murieta y los 'californios'" 649)

For Huerta, "Joaquín is a symbolic name that confirms the religious and regional values of the Hispanic-Californio" (Alberto Huerta 50).[47]

This is the same Father Albert Huerta who led the controversial Mexican American essayist Richard Rodríguez on a quest to see the still-preserved head of Joaquín Murrieta in the mid-1980s. Rodríguez is much more circumspect—and often frankly bemused—toward the Murrieta legend and its different appropriations by Americans, Chileans, Mexicans, and others, particularly when he is read in comparison with recent Chicano studies scholars such as Herrera-Sobek or Carlos Vélez-Ibáñez. Rodríguez seems particularly piqued by a rarely studied erotic element to the legendary hero, whom Rodríguez refers to as "a cutthroat Adonis," elaborating: "A friend who grew up in a small Valley town in the 1950s remembers that the city librarian kept two books from children, unless they had notes of permission from their parents. One was *Lady Chatterly's Lover*; the other was *The Life of Joaquín Murrieta with Illustrations*" (139).

While Rodríguez did his homework and discovered that the Murrieta head had been destroyed in the 1906 San Francisco earthquake, he nonetheless went along with Huerta when he "found the head" lying about in a defunct Old West museum in Santa Rosa (145). Rodríguez ironically reports that Huerta anxiously told him, "The head is expanding. I think it's going to explode" (148). Huerta's ultimate goal is to acquire the head (unfortunately, its owner does not wish to sell) so that he may persuade the state to fulfill its "obligation" to bury it, and, after a "solemn funeral mass," finally "bring [Murrieta] to rest" (136).

Rodríguez never attempts to put myth in opposition to historic fact, preferring to reconstruct Murrieta as a messy, contradictory, and unstable icon, not unlike the one who ultimately emerges from the most thoroughly researched studies such as that of Latta or Rojas. His brief anecdote nonetheless evokes the cultural complexity of the borderlands through its shifting and conflicting representations and rhetorical uses of the Murrieta story.

Joaquín in the Other Borderlands

Given that he is usually portrayed as having been born in Sonora, and sometimes rumored to have returned to Sonora to live after escaping death at the hands of the California Rangers, the infrequency of representations of Murrieta within the context of the Mexican northwestern borderlands is utterly remarkable. Scholars routinely tease out the cultural significations of his legend with regard to its contributions to notions of regional (California, the Old West), ethnic (Chicano, Mexican American, Native American), or national (Mexico, Chile) history and identity. However, they have ill considered the borderlands context from which the legend emerged, tending either to limit themselves to its cultural meanings on the U.S. side of the border only, or to consider its significations on the Mexican side of the border but only in a national context that subsumes Mexico's periphery into an unproblematized united whole.

True, nineteenth-century Sonora did not produce a major literary text comparable to Ridge's *Life and Adventures*, or even the *Police Gazette* plagiarism, and Murrieta did not become a major protagonist in Mexican borderlands newspapers in the 1850s as he did in California. However, this is not to say that he was not an important figure in Mexican borderlands culture in the years following his initial notoriety.

And while it is difficult over a century and a half later to trace clear evidence of how *fronterizos* interpreted the Joaquín Murrieta story when it filtered back to his homeland in the early 1850s, or of how the legend first developed in Sonora and Baja California, there is little doubt that a regional legend began to take form there in the latter half of the nineteenth century. The Murrieta of the northwestern Mexican borderlands is inseparable and distinct from the Mexican nationalist construction of Murrieta, just as it is inseparable and distinct from the Mexican American Murrieta of the U.S. Southwest.

Shelley Streeby makes a vital contribution to recent American studies debates on Murrieta by bringing discussion of the novels of Yellow Bird and the *California Police Gazette* in dialogue with the "important history of Chicana/o responses to the legend" ("Joaquín Murrieta" 181), among them the Murrieta *corrido* that has helped to make Murrieta "a pervasive symbol of resistance for people of Mexican origin in the United States" (180). Alfredo Figueroa draws attention to the subversiveness of the Murrieta *corrido:* "My uncles warned me not to sing this *corrido* in public because it was against the law to sing it in the United States" (3). Yet the first important published analysis of the Murrieta *corrido* appears not in a Chicano studies text but in a history of the *corrido* in Sonora, M. A. Serna Maytorena's *En Sonora así se cuenta* (1988), a text not cited by Streeby nor by other U.S.–based scholars who have studied the various forms of the Murrieta *corrido*, including Luis Leal. In Mexico, the *Corrido de Joaquín Murrieta* has usually been identified as a Sonoran (and not a Californian or Chicano) *corrido.*

My point here is not to invent a nationalist battle over which country is the rightful owner of the Murrieta *corrido* but to point out that the *corrido*, an oral tradition, is not easily rooted in any one place. Any borderlands *corrido* prominent on one side of the border is likely to be well known on the other as well. Even more than newspapers or novels or historiographies or biographies or even films, all of which have tended not to cross the U.S.–Mexico border and reach broad publics on both sides, the *corrido* is a cultural expression shared equally among Mexican Americans and Mexican *fronterizos*, although its cultural significance may differ in different contexts.

It is not a fixed form of cultural expression; *corridos* may evolve with every performance, and often they mutate into competing versions. It is thus impossible to tell what versions were sung one hundred fifty years ago or where. However, there are clues within existing versions that reflect on what the Murrieta legend meant not only to Mexican Americans living in the United States but also to Mexican *fronterizos* in the nineteenth century. Moreover, unlike novels, formal plays, movies, and historiographic essays, *corridos* are likely to be an expression of poor, often illiterate musicians, thus reflecting a different vision of regional (or racial or national) identity from that represented in the works of *letrados*, whose mark on culture tends to be much more tangible.

The Murrieta *corrido* clearly has its roots in the nineteenth century (Leal, "El Corrido" 13) and may have been sung in one form or another as early as the 1850s. The fact that Murrieta has been kept alive in the public imagination through the *corrido* for so long is a testament to the enduring relevance of his legend. In Serna Maytorena's study, the majority of the *corridos* he collects treat heroes or adventures of the Mexican revolution. Only a few make references to earlier periods, and no reference precedes the Murrieta legend. While the basic theme (Joaquín's heroic but tragic tale of vengeance) may draw directly from the newspaper stories of Murrieta in the 1850s, there are several aspects that were clearly added later. A few of the more interesting aspects of the *corrido* follow: seven versions, labeled A through G, were collected by Leal ("El Corrido" 18–22), and another three, noted here as H, I, and J, by Serna Maytorena (18–22).

In most versions, from the very beginning the narrator declares, "I am not American" (A-D, H, I), in some cases affirming, "I am Mexican" (F, G). Many versions add two further clarifications: "I am not Chilean" (A, G, J), mostly likely a response to the publication of the Morla translation of the *Police Gazette* Murrieta novel in San Antonio in 1929 or the wide publicity given the 1966 Neruda cantata; and "I came from Hermosillo" (A, B, F-J).

The vengeance theme is made clear in almost all versions—many of which recount the murders of Joaquín's brother (A-D, H-J) and his wife, Carmelita (A-C, H-J), and many also portray Joaquín as a social bandit who defends the Indians (A, B, F-J), steals from the rich (A, B, G, J), and tips his hat to "the humble" (A, B, G, J). A few versions make his vengeance something more than personal by portraying Joaquín as the leader of "troops" and applying other military terms (A, B, G, J), thus implying that Joaquín was involved in a patriotic military campaign against the United States. Most of these elements are familiar from well-known literary or historiographic versions of the Murrieta legend, and in the final analysis, there is nothing in any of the ten different *corridos* collected by Leal and Serna Maytorena that differentiates them significantly from the many versions of the legend in circulation.

However, read from the context of the northern borderlands, everything changes. Significantly, most versions place Joaquín's origins in Hermosillo, clearly not Chile, and, more important, clearly not central Mexico; Joaquín is a *fronterizo*. But Joaquín is not part of the nascent culture-constructing enterprise of the Mexican Northwest that would largely ignore him until the late twentieth century.

The earliest histories of the region from the era of the Porfiriato (e.g., Dávila) make no mention of him whatsoever. Eduardo Villa also leaves the *bandido* hero out of works such as his *Compendio de historia del estado de Sonora* (1937)—this despite the fact that Villa himself had been interpreter for Frank Latta to a surviving descendant of Joaquín's in 1936 and therefore was quite well informed regarding who Murrieta was (Latta 631). Sonora's earliest history textbook author, Laureano Calvo Berber, also omits Murrieta from his *Nociones de historia de Sonora* (1958).

Likewise, the great Murrieta novels have all been published in the United States, in Europe, in Chile, or in Mexico City, but never in Sonora. There is no equivalent of *Dolores o la reina de los kunkaks* (chapter 3) or *Heroína* (chapter 4)—landmark works of regional literature in northwestern Mexico—among the many novels, stories, and published plays on Murrieta, nothing to indicate the acceptance of Murrieta into the culture of literate Sonora prior to 1952, when Francisco Almada included a brief entry on Murrieta in his *Diccionario de historia, geografía y biografía sonorenses*. In Almada, Murrieta is hardly the great hero of the Mexican northwestern borderlands. The entry only mentions that "he was victim of abuses of the American authorities and, in vengeance, he dedicated himself to the career of banditry, committing crimes wherever he went" (494), a bland summary of the story that leaves out the more sensational features that had kept it alive in the public imagination for a century. In fact, there is nothing from Almada's *Diccionario* that gives the idea that Murrieta was admired by anyone, let alone that he had become a legendary hero.

Manuel Santiago Corbalá Acuña provides a few more clues in his 1977 history of Sonora. Corbalá has Murrieta emigrating to California with his wife, María Félix.[48] In this, the first published version of the Murrieta legend in Sonora that begins to enter into details of the story, María is raped by a *gringo* sheriff, whom Murrieta murders in revenge, "and not satisfied with that, he continued avenging that offense on all sheriffs who crossed his path" (259). Moreover, "as he was giving, he protected and aided the humble, especially if they were Mexican, thereby creating the legend of the generous, vengeful, daring and audacious bandit, valiant to the point of utter fearlessness" (259). Corbalá notes that his legend is a product of both authentic "astonishing facts and feats" and also "fantasy and tall tales" (259) but attributes its creation and persistence to a chain of oral history among Californians. In other words, Murrieta finally attains hero status among Sonora's *letrados* in 1977, but he is not embraced, and his heroism is shown to be of interest only to emigrant communities on the other side of the border.

The *corridos*, then, are quite important in that they not only exalt Murrieta as a Sonoran hero but do it in the face of his rejection on the part of Sonoran elite culture. After all, Murrieta was quite an ambivalent character. His legend contained heroic elements, but he was basically a criminal, a bandit who murdered with ease and who hated *gringos*. Was that the reputation that elite Sonora wished to portray of itself to its white neighbors, many of whom looked down on Mexicans in general and were known in the heat of the moment to propose outrageous acts such as the "extermination" of all Mexicans in Calaveras County? Whether or not Ireneo Paz (who lived in Mexico City) or the Mexican Americans of *La Gaceta* of Santa Barbara in Alta California wished to dramatize U.S.–Mexico relations as a bloody struggle, or perhaps even a race war, Sonoran elites—who needed to foster economic relations with their neighbors and also at some moments needed to do whatever was necessary to fend off the ever-encroaching spirit of manifest destiny—clearly preferred to celebrate its great *caudillos* such as Ignacio Pesqueira, its great politicians such as Ramón Corral, or even its great colonizers such as Padre Eusebio Kino rather than immortalize an emigrant bandit famous for terrorizing white Anglo California. Murrieta's severed head was a symbol of Anglo victory over Mexican banditry and recalled that of the *gringo* filibuster Henry Crabb. Murrieta was a symbol of border conflict, more likely to inspire war than the peace and collaboration in which many Sonorans wished to live alongside their Anglo American neighbors of Arizona and Alta California.

Murrieta did not represent Sonoran *letrados*. Murrieta did represent Sonoran farmworkers, Sonorans of little social standing, Sonorans who were likely to emigrate, as Joaquín once did, to the United States. Murrieta was of little interest to the wealthy Sonorans who were the ones with the means to establish shared notions of regional identity and culture through journalism, historiography, and literature. But to less formally educated Sonorans who learned their culture not through novels and history books but through songs and oral histories, Joaquín was a symbol of regional pride who has maintained importance there among "the humble" Sonorans he was said to have so respected for a century and a half.

By the 1980s, things were changing. Volume 3 of the *Historia general de Sonora* (1985) includes an excerpt from James Officer's aforementioned article establishing that Murrieta was Sonoran and not Chilean (in Ruibal Corella 117). The Sonoran historian Palemón Zavala Castro's 1985 history of nineteenth-century Yaqui resistance under Cajeme (see chapter 4) mentions Murrieta as a "bandido generoso" (112), hero to Mexican immigrants in California and emblem of Mexican defiance of Yankee racism. Zavala's brief summary of the legend concludes with a defiant satisfaction: "Many years later—still—the Americans wouldn't let any Mexican with the last name Murrieta enter the territories of California or Arizona" (113). Volume 4 of *Visión histórica de la frontera norte de México* (Piñera Ramírez, ed., 1987) includes a brief sketch of the Murrieta legend by José Jesús Cueva Pelayo in which Murrieta signifies a hero to modern-day Chicanos, a bandit to Anglo-Americans of his day, and a patriot "to his racial brothers" [sus hermanos de raza].

Aside from *corridos* and recent historiography, there is further evidence that Murrieta's memory has been kept alive in Sonora. The Murrieta historians Frank Latta and Manuel Rojas both decided to go to Sonora, not just to speak to historians or to scour archives but to

interview descendants of Joaquín Murrieta. The most interesting conclusion, hazy though it may be, that the authors drew from their interviews is that Murrieta was not shot and beheaded by the California
Rangers in 1853. Specifically, Latta interviewed—in 1936, with the help
of the Sonoran historian Eduardo Villa—a Señora McAlpin whose husband had claimed to be Joaquín's nephew and a witness to the bandit's
death. Whether or not the nephew, Tomás Procopio Bustamante—who,
according to his widow, became so obsessed with his uncle that he took
to using his name, sometimes tried to pass for the famous Joaquín, and
ultimately chose to become an outlaw to avenge his uncle (Latta 621–
22)—is a trustworthy source is questionable.[49] However, his widow
claimed he told her that Joaquín had not been involved in the battle in
which he was said to have died but instead was traveling to Monterey
at the time. On his way, he was shot in a skirmish with officers who did
not know who he was, and died a few days later. His wife buried his body
in secret at home (near San Francisco) so that no one would know he had
died (631–34).

Rojas uncovers conflicting family legends from multiple branches of
the Murrieta clan. Many swear that he must have died in California because he never returned to Sonora (*El "Far West"* 142). Others insist
that he died somewhere in the northern part of Sonora state (142, 191).
Others produce evidence that Murrieta may have lived in Tecate, Baja
California. Rojas hypothesizes that Murrieta returned to Mexico after
the famous showdown with the California Rangers, at which Rojas agrees
(with Latta) that Murrieta was not present, and which resulted in the
decapitation of his close associate, Joaquín Valenzuela. Discouraged from
continuing his mission to win back Alta California for Mexico, Joaquín
gave up his quixotic enterprise; Rojas concludes: "Murrieta lived his final
years traveling between Tecate and Cucurpe" (*El "Far West"* 198). These
sources place Joaquín's death in not 1853 but as late as the 1880s (198).

While the many strains of oral history on Murrieta in Sonora diverge
more often than they agree, what is clear is that they frequently reflect
a desire to see Joaquín escape the California Rangers, or even return
safely to Mexico, making his revenge even sweeter. The *corrido* likewise
avoids the final victory of the Rangers by portraying a living Joaquín.
Most often narrated in the first person (the Corky González poem most

likely took its inspiration from the *corrido*), the *corrido* allows Joaquín to tell his own story. Its defiant final lines, "I am that Mexican named Joaquín Murrieta" (Yo soy ese mexicano de nombre Joaquín Murrieta) (A, B, F-H), show Joaquín to be still alive. His death and decapitation never appear in these narrative ballads. The oral traditions of Sonora, then, more than any other genre of Murrieta lore, insist upon his survival.

Conclusion

If on the U.S. side of the border, representations of Murrieta play out in a battle of exoticizing and often racist constructions of a seductive but dangerous Mexican other versus hagiographic responses idealizing the same character as an ethnic or national hero, the Mexican borderlands have seen Murrieta in neither ethnic nor national terms. While the hagiographic position is echoed and even amplified in *corridos* and oral histories of the Mexican borderlands—and it must be emphasized that such forms of cultural production are nomadic and often establish themselves on both sides of the border—an opposing position can also be seen more prevalently in the Mexican Northwest than on the U.S. side. The position of *fronterizos letrados*, who have consistently played down or utterly ignored native son Joaquín Murrieta's historical importance, disputes his popular hero status, calling attention to a regional identity shaped by the pressures of the border. Sonoran elites were determined to project an image of civilization and not barbarous villainy, of compatibility with and not radical opposition to Anglo-America, of regional fortitude and not desperation in the face of threats of imperialistic incursions from the north. Elite culture rejected Joaquín Murrieta even as popular culture celebrated him—as more of a local than national hero.

A reading of Murrieta that fully incorporates his cultural significance on both sides of the border provides an insight into the full implications of the aftermath of the war of the 1840s and the rapid settlement of California throughout the region (and, by looking beyond the borderlands, for example to Chile, it signifies powerfully throughout the hemisphere). An approach of analysis of the legend that is both transamerican in scope and conscious of the cultural complexities of the borderlands is essential to obtaining such an insight.

CHAPTER THREE

LOLA CASANOVA: TROPES OF *MESTIZAJE* AND FRONTIERS OF RACE

O N 23 FEBRUARY 1850, a young *criolla* beauty named Dolores Casanova was making the short trip along with some relatives from her hometown of Guaymas to Hermosillo by carriage. Although the travelers were armed and prepared for a possible attack, they were unable to defend themselves from an assault by Seri Indians. Tensions had been high recently between the Seris and the Mexicans, and such attacks were not out of the ordinary. On this occasion, a bloody battle resulted, in which many of the traveling party were killed. Several of the survivors were kidnapped by the Indians, among them lovely Lola Casanova. One of the leaders in the assault, the young Seri Coyote Iguana, was attracted to Dolores. While she did not return his affection immediately, he eventually won her over during her captivity. Not only did Lola consent to give up her comfortable life in Guaymas and stay with the primitive Seris but she also accepted Coyote Iguana's proposal for marriage. She later bore several of his children.

This legend, subject over the years to many variations, usually ends without Lola's return to Guaymas. Lola is something of an anti-Malinche, and her story is an alternative paradigm of *mestizaje* that goes against well-known national tropes. Its recasting of race relations in the borderlands is in fact so shocking that despite the originality and romantic appeal of the story, it has never gotten a foothold into the realm of national culture in Mexico. Not even in the borderlands has it been sanctioned as a major legend of regional identity.

On the other hand, although it may still provoke a certain degree of astonishment or repugnance in some, it continues to fascinate multiple audiences. Lola Casanova, over a century and a half later, remains a popular icon of Mexican borderlands culture, her legend playing out the region's deep-rooted racial tensions. More important, her story contests liberal idealizations of nineteenth-century Mexican culture that would close a blind eye to these acute tensions that continued to provoke violence in the borderlands throughout the century.

National Myths of Mestizaje: Los Hijos de la Chingada

Mestizaje, although not a popular identity trope in Sonora nor a central rallying point for Mexican national identity until after the revolution of 1910, was gradually gaining acceptance in elite national culture in the second half of the nineteenth century. By the turn of the century, certainly, mixed-race Mexicans were increasingly visible in Mexican national culture. However, *mestizaje* in late-nineteenth-century Mexican literature followed a very limited range of defining tropes to which the legend of Lola Casanova in no way conformed.

The first and most basic trope of *mestizaje* in Mexican cultural production is that of the rape of Mexico by Spain. This encounter is typically represented allegorically through the figures of Hernán Cortés and La Malinche (aka Malintzin or Doña Marina). She was the indigenous maiden originally given to Cortés as a gift, who later would become his translator and lover. While on the one hand this representation of interracial relations implies the violence of armed conquest, with La Malinche being part of the spoils of war, on the other hand, she has traditionally been seen as a traitor to Mexico for collaborating with the enemy invaders. These interpretations are problematic, of course, because Mexico did not exist as such prior to the conquest, nor did Malintzin see herself as representing indigenous Mesoamericans as a whole. Indeed it is hard to charge her with responsibility to any group since her own people had betrayed her by giving her away as they would a jewel. Meanwhile, the

Aztecs, toward whose fall she did conspire, were in fact despised by many indigenous peoples of Mesoamerica for their own imperialist aggressions. Nonetheless, the representation of *mestizaje*, whether through La Malinche or other figures, traditionally followed the same paradigm. The male partner was white and the female indigenous. The female and her offspring were then incorporated into white colonial (and later national) culture. Although the new generation was not white, it was no longer exotically indigenous.[1] La Malinche appears repeatedly in nineteenth-century novels. Interestingly, the conquest of the Aztecs comes up as a theme first in Cuban, not Mexican, literature. The New World's first historical novel, *Jicoténcal*, was published in 1826 in Philadelphia and was written probably by a Cuban, possibly Félix Varela.[2] It featured two indigenous protagonists who become involved in one way or another with Cortés: the traitor Doña Marina (his lover) and the Tlaxcaltec heroine Teutila (the defiant object of his desire). Simultaneous with the various romantic and erotic interactions between the Spaniards and the Tlaxcaltecs and other indigenous Mesoamericans, there occurs a series of debates among the Tlaxcaltecs that result in their ultimate collaboration with the Spaniards, which in turn leads to the defeat of the Aztecs. In this novel's scenario of interracial relations, heterosexual bonding between whites and *indios* (and their product: *mestizaje*) is imagined as taking shape in any of several ways: by treachery and possibly rape (Cortés's treatment of Teutila), by treason and conspiracy with the enemy (La Malinche's collaboration with Cortés), or possibly even by love (the Spaniard supporting player Diego de Ordaz's noble affection for Teutila). In any case, should such a bond be realized, it is a given that the woman must give up her indigenous culture and identity, as Doña Marina does—and Teutila does not—and assimilate into Spanish culture. *Mestizaje* is about assimilation and civilization, about the gradual acculturation of indigenous Mesoamerica into Spanish or (now in the nineteenth century) *criollo* culture.

Multiple variations of the story of La Malinche appear in a number of other historical novels of the conquest of the Aztec empire, all with significant Mexican distribution in the nineteenth century, including the Cuban Gertrudis Gómez de Avellaneda's *Guatimozín* (1845),[3] the Yucatecan Eligio Ancona's *Los mártires de Anáhuac* (1870, and Ireneo Paz's *Amor y suplicio* (1873) and *Doña Marina* (1883).[4] The political goals of the authors may vary; nonetheless, the notion of a white male having his way with an indigenous female was commonplace in Mexican letters by the late nineteenth century, so much so that Mexican *mestizaje* came to be understood almost exclusively in these terms. When Ireneo Paz's grandson Octavio Paz articulated Mexican national identity as *mestiza* and designated Mexicans as "los hijos de la Malinche" in 1950 (59–80), these notions were already well engrained in the Mexican literary imaginary.

However, an alternative vision of *mestizaje* appeared in Mexican literature in the same era, one that was not constructed as an interracial bond between white *criollo* male and indigenous female. Ignacio Altamirano was Mexico's leading promoter of national literature in the late nineteenth century, and his greatest national novel is *El Zarco*.[5] *El Zarco*, like the novels by Ancona and Paz, deals with interracial romance but with a totally new formulation: this time the indigenous protagonist is male. Although he is portrayed as "ugly like the Indian he is" (67), Nicolás is the novel's romantic hero. Moreover, despite being ugly to some, including the *(criolla)* protagonist Manuela, he is a hard-working and successful blacksmith and good husband material (according to Manuela's mother). Manuela, however, is dazzled by the good looks and flashy clothes of the blue-eyed bandit known as El Zarco, so she runs off with him, only to discover that he is spineless, selfish, and callous. Nicolás is not white but lives in Yautepec, a place where "the entire population speaks Spanish, as it is composed of mixed races. Pure Indians have disappeared completely there" (4).

Like Altamirano, Nicolás is an Indian but is not an Indian. He looks like one and is identified as one, but he lives like any *criollo*. He is reasonably well educated, earns his living through *criollo* institutions, dresses *criollo*, and speaks only Spanish. It only makes sense that he would court a *criolla* like Manuela. Altamirano promotes a new trope of interracial romance that is finally realized when Nicolás marries Manuela's adopted sister Pilar. The lesson of the novel is that a good *criolla* like Manuela is better off not with flashy blond *bandidos* ("who are demons vomited forth from hell" [10], in the opinion of Manuela's mother), but with a good man like Nicolás, regardless of his race. After all, he is not a primitive savage but an "hombre de bien," an honest, upstanding citizen. And once again, as with La Malinche, it is the indigenous protagonist that gives up his culture and assimilates into *criollo* culture.

Here, of course, is the key to the shock value of the legend of Lola Casanova. The trope of *mestizaje* is not parallel with that of the familiar Malinche story in which the indigenous maiden is violated by the Spanish invader. Here the dangerous invader is the indigenous captor, and the violated maiden is white. This terror of a white virgin possibly being raped by indigenous savages, of course, provides the dramatic tension of a totally different trope of interracial relations : the captivity narrative. Before analyzing Lola Casanova's cultural meanings, it is worth looking at the racial ideologies promoted in nineteenth-century romantic narratives of captivity.

Terror on the Frontier:
White Damsels and Savage Raptors

American captivity narratives have in common the general scheme of fair white maidens being abducted by barbaric indigenous American captors.[6] The sexual violence implied in such narratives fed racial tensions among whites by portraying indigenous Americans as dangerously violent, animalistically irrational, and with a propensity to rape helpless females. In erudite literature and popular legend alike, such a threat became a national allegory that implied a need to subjugate indigenous insurgents in order to prevent the brutal violation of white civilization by unruly savages (Faery 10). Despite their predictable basic structure, each captivity narrative took its own shape and presented unique cultural nuances. Let us look at a few examples that circulated in the nineteenth-century borderlands.

On 27 July 1860, *La Estrella de Occidente*, Sonora's official state newspaper, printed the translation of a report originally published in the *Republican* of Saint Louis. Dated 9 April 1860, Tubac, Arizona, it recounts the "horrific details of the captivity, savage barbarity and sufferings of Mrs. Larina A. Page" (4). She was alone with a young female Mexican servant at her home in Arizona while her husband was out supervising Mexican laborers on his land when a band of Apaches attacked, ransacking the house and kidnapping the two women, tying them up and forcing them to walk behind them as they rode off on horseback.

They went on in this fashion for a full day, the women exhausted from being forced on at a rapid pace and terrorized with frequent threats that they would be killed. When Mrs. Page could no longer keep up, she narrates, "my savage captors resolved to kill me to put an end to their impatience. They stripped off my clothes including my shoes, leaving me in nothing but a shirt" (4). They then threw her down onto a rock, stoned her, "and soon left me there assuming I would die" (4). Although they had torn open her shirt, putting her "practically in a state of nakedness" (4), they had shown her only contempt and had never approached her sexually.[7] She then began walking, despite being injured and nearly frozen in the snowy mountains, until sixteen days later she finally reached home.

This captivity narrative is interesting for several reasons. First, it is told in the voice of the surviving victim herself, but more important it is told by an Anglo-American woman and is reprinted for a Sonoran audience. It is troubling that the fate of Mrs. Page's Mexican servant is forgotten. Clearly, in the context of the United States, it is the captivity of a (white) Anglo-American woman that is horrifying, not that of a (nonwhite) Mexican American. Apparently for the presumably white Sonoran reader, the fate of the presumably nonwhite Mexican servant was also of little consequence. That the white woman, Mrs. Page, survives is a comfort. In addition, for the Mexican reader, it is a tale from the other side of the border and therefore removed from the day-to-day life of Sonorans in Ures, Guaymas, or Hermosillo.[8] It also has a happy ending. The Indians are savage and cruel, but they are not murderers or even rapists—at least according to Page.

It is also significant that the captors were Apaches, a people residing primarily on the U.S. side of the border. The 1850s was a particularly tense time along the U.S.–Mexico border due to the frequent raids of U.S.–based Apaches into Sonora. The "guerrilla warfare" waged by the Apaches made northern Sonora "practically uninhabitable" and set in motion a series of serious conflicts between Mexico and the United States (Tinker Salas 62). The situation was such that "on the Mexican side, both in Chihuahua and Sonora, the Apaches had absolute control and no one dared take them on" (Antochiw 406). The Sonorans were bound by the Treaty of Gualdalupe Hidalgo from waging war with the Apaches across the border into U.S. territory until the 1880s (Tinker Salas 64); instead, they began offering rewards for delivering adult Apaches, dead or alive.[9] It was legal to "keep" children under fourteen "to educate in social principles."[10] Government-sponsored headhunting, of course, exacerbated tensions. Meanwhile, "most Sonorans, including top leaders . . . contended that Americans openly colluded with Apaches in their attacks on Mexico" (Tinker Salas 64). The rhetoric of manifest destiny in the United States was felt strongly in Mexico's Northwest, especially during the 1850s, when filibuster raids were commonplace and the hope for Sonora and Baja California to become the next two new U.S. territories was widespread in the U.S. Southwest. The mining speculator Sylvester Mowry wrote in 1864, "[The] Apache Indian [is] preparing Sonora for the rule of a higher civilization than the Mexican" (quoted in Tinker Salas 64). The thinking was that the Apache raids would drive the Mexicans out of Sonora "leaving to us (when the time is ripe for our possession) the territory without its population" (Mowry, quoted in Park 54).

This captivity narrative, then, would have reminded Sonoran readers of a danger lurking beneath its surface. A retelling of the kidnapping of Larina Page emphasized that Apaches were not necessarily exclusively in cahoots with the *gringos* at the expense of Mexicans. However, it also reminded Sonorans of the everyday danger posed by the marauding Apaches for Sonorans, whom they considered their absolute worst enemies. The historian Joseph F. Park writes:

> In 1859 . . . the [Apache] chief, Francisco, asked if the Apaches would still be permitted to steal from Sonora if the United States took the state from Mexico. The [U.S.] agent said that he thought not, and the old chief replied that "as long as he lived and had a warrior to follow him, he would fight Sonora, and he did not care if the Americans did try to stop him, he would fight till he was killed." (52)

It was a reminder of imminent danger, but a danger once removed.

A second borderlands captivity narrative presents a totally different set of lessons for a different audience. On John Russell Bartlett's exploratory journey to the region under the auspices of the United States and Mexican Boundary Commission in the early 1850s, he came across "a party of New Mexicans" in possession of "a young female and a number of horses and mules [all of which] had been obtained from [Piñal Apache] Indians" and all of which they planned to sell (303). Bartlett fussed at the New Mexicans, who "belonged to a people with whom the system of peonage prevails, and among whom, as a general thing, females are not estimated as with us, especially in a moral point of view" (306–7). Bartlett then proclaimed, "I therefore deemed it my duty—and a pleasant one it certainly was, to extend over her the protection of the laws of the United States, and to see that, until delivered in safety to her parents, she should be 'treated with the utmost hospitality' that our position would allow" (307). While the girl, whose name was Inez González, informed her rescuers that "[n]o improper freedom was taken with her person" (308) when with the Apaches, it is not made clear what "moral" conflicts had occurred with her purchasers, nor what Bartlett, so pleased to find himself in the role of hero to the damsel in distress, meant to imply with the word "hospitality," delivered as it was *entre comillas*.

In any case, the story of her captivity with the Apaches is as follows. While on an excursion to a fair at a neighboring town in northern Sonora, where she lived, the party with which she traveled was attacked by a band of Apaches who killed everyone except Inez, her two female servants, and a young boy. The other captives were sold separately, so she was left alone with her captors, who did not violate her but did rob her of her clothing "save a skirt and under linen" (308).

Once purchased by the New Mexicans, she was soon rescued by Bartlett, who made sure she was properly clothed. In addition, "she received many presents from the gentlemen of the Commission, all of whom manifested a deep interest in her welfare, and seemed desirous to make her comfortable and happy. But with all the attentions extended to her, her situation was far from enviable in a camp of over a hundred men, without a single female" (309). Once again, Bartlett maintains the sexual tensions central to a captivity narrative, while always simultaneously emphasizing the captive's safety with her benevolent *gringo* rescuers (many of whom had been soldiers during the U.S. invasion of Mexico only a few years earlier).

As they traveled down into Sonora, Bartlett continued to dote on his rescued captive. He dined with her daily, and in the Burro Mountains he adoringly named a spring after her: Ojo de Inez. Soon, they arrived at Santa Cruz, which would be the scene of Inez's dramatic reunion with family and friends, who had thought they would never see her again:

> The joy of the father and friends in again beholding the face of her whom they supposed was forever lost from them, was unbounded. Each in turn (rough and half naked as many of them were), embraced her after the Spanish custom: and it was long ere one could utter a word. Tears of joy burst from them all; and the sun-burnt and brawny men, in whom the finer feelings of our nature are wrongly supposed not to exist, wept like children, as they looked with astonishment on the rescued girl. (399)

Bartlett establishes himself not only as friend to the Indian-like ("rough and half naked") Mexicans but as their rescuer, a larger-than-life benevolent patriarch to the Mexican people. Given the constant conflict regarding the exact location of the border, the cross-border Indian raids, livestock rustling and smuggling, and cross-border escapes of runaway slaves, not to mention filibuster invasions, such an image would hardly have been bought by most Mexicans (and in particular *fronterizos*). But Bartlett wrote in English for a U.S. readership that would not take much convincing to be persuaded that Mexico would be better off having the United States managing its affairs and protecting its virgins.

The legend of Lola Casanova is different from either of these types of borderlands captivity narratives. First, the United States is absent from the foreground. Neither the victim nor any other protagonist in her drama is from that country. Still, it is clearly a drama of the contact zone. In the background lies the major social problem of the northwestern borderlands in the late nineteenth century: Mexico's inability to populate the region due to conflicts with indigenous groups and its consequent vulnerability to U.S. aggression, or stated another way, its inability to properly fortify its border against ever-threatening Yankee imperialism until it subjugated all insurgent indigenous groups. The legend of Lola Casanova served as a harsh reminder that the Seris, who remained a major problem along the northwest coast of the state until late in the nineteenth century, had to be conquered once and for all.

Second , there is no happy ending this time—at least not for *los fronterizos criollos*. While Lola herself might have fallen in love and come to enjoy life among the Seris,[11] such an idea was unthinkable for Sonorans for whom the Seris were primitives, savages, and well-established enemies to *criollo* Mexicans.[12] There is no heroic tale of escape or rescue. It is a story of defeat of *criollos* of Guaymas at the hands of *indios bárbaros*.

Third, and importantly, whether by consent or by force, Lola had sexual relations with Coyote Iguana and eventually became mother to at least one child by him. Neither Larina Page nor Inez González admitted to being sexually violated. Should it have become known that the presumably virgin Lola had been raped or impregnated by a Seri, she would have been shamed if not ostracized by her peers and would likely have been unable to ever marry. In short, this captivity narrative is beyond tragic: it is utterly shocking.

While Coyote Iguana may have spoken Spanish, he is no Nicolás. The historian Cynthia Radding has shown that for decades indigenous Sonorans had been assimilating into the mainstream. In nineteenth-century Mexico in general, and Sonora in particular, racial terminology often reflected not blood ties or ethnic heritage but "connotations of economic and social standing" (244). Acculturated dark-skinned Sonorans who had risen above the state of poverty were not viewed as *indios* and might even, under the right circumstances, marry white *criollos*. However, Coyote Iguana is clearly not one of these assimilated social climbers. He does not dress like a *criollo*, does not live among *criollos*, does not practice a *criollo* trade, and in fact considers himself an enemy of Mexico, acting as a leader in violent attacks on Mexicans, like the assault on the party of travelers in which Lola had been traveling the day of her abduction. The legend of Lola Casanova represents *mestizaje*, then, as the rape of *criollo* Mexico by insurgent *indios bárbaros*, or worse yet, the Malinche-like treason of *criollo* Mexico by a woman who rejects her own people to collude with the dark-skinned enemy. Lola Casanova's is a captivity narrative gone awry. Its happy ending of love and marriage twists social expectations beyond the recognizable and presents a jarringly scandalous vision of *mestizaje* that threatens *fronterizo* racial identity.

Race and Representation

Nineteenth-century *fronterizos*, much more so than Mexicans from other parts of the country, whose day-to-day dealings with the United States were more remote, were conscious of how they were portrayed on the other side of the border. They were aware that the image of Mexicans in the United States was one of dark-skinned, uneducated, uncultured mongrel peasants. The racial aspect was of particular significance as the rhetoric of manifest destiny often drew from scientific theories of race, which viewed darker races as inferior and saw miscegenation as degenerative, thereby justifying imperialist attitudes on behalf of whites. Regardless of the actual racial makeup of Mexico's population, *fronterizos* were sensitive to stereotypes that assumed Mexicans were *mestizos* who indiscriminately mixed with inferior races.

The historian Miguel Tinker Salas observes that northern elites strove to create an image of themselves as "somehow ethnically different from other Mexicans" (26). He explains: "Indian wars invariably hardened racial attitudes and broadly affected the society, including lower socioeconomic groups. Many individuals of mixed heritage made it a point to deny their indigenous roots," while elites made show of their European pedigree (26). Writes the historian Ramón Eduardo Ruiz of late-nineteenth-century Sonora: "Disgracefully . . . these notable fathers of progress also felt proud of being from good Spanish families, arranged marriages among their own, and looked down on their neighbors who did not have 'purity of blood' as inferiors" ("Los perímetros" 11–12).

This was not, of course, the view of Mexico and Mexicans held by most in the United States, a multiracial country that obsessed about maintaining its own racial purity and segregation and looked down upon its Latin American neighbors for their propensity for miscegenation. This was clearly the view that so frustrated *fronterizo* cultural elites— such as the journalist Aurelio Pérez Peña—who would make it their mission to defend northern Mexico's image as civilized and prudently controlled by white elites (see chapter 4).

Meanwhile, Pérez Peña's close friend and associate Francisco Dávila's 1894 book *Sonora histórico y descriptivo* directly confronts the prejudices of "some contemporary writers [who] . . . have exaggerated in the pages

of their newspapers the moral and material backwardness of Sonora"
(1). In the introduction to his book, which serves as a marketing tool
designed to attract foreign capital to the state, Dávila declares it his
goal "to record in these pages the state of advancement that Sonora has
achieved, proving . . . that in any part of our State, capital and life are
as safe as they are in the great population centers of the United States
and Europe" (3). Dávila's Sonora was as good as the wealthiest and most
powerful nations of the world because its Indian problem was largely
under control (Pérez Peña, "Carta" iii–iv), although it was still the case
in the 1890s that "the foreigner sees . . . lurking behind each one of our
rocks and shrubs the mouth of a rifle that, with a steady hand, the ferocious Apache aims at the breast of a defenseless settler" and "in the
mind of the man of the Old World every Sonoran looks like a mountain man with a harquebus on his shoulder and the traditional holster
and scimitar on his hips" (Dávila, *Sonora* 3). Dávila argued that Sonora
was no longer the Wild West, that it was now safe to settle there, and
that its riches were ripe for exploiting.

However, even in his descriptions of what Sonora had become, he was
careful to construct an image of a white Sonora, defined by its opposition to enemy Indians. Following a long chapter, "Districts and Their
Elements of Wealth" (254–306), is a chapter titled "The Tribes of the
State" (307–25) in which Dávila makes clear that these tribes are distinct and segregated from the implicitly white mainstream of Sonora
described in the previous chapter. Following the model of the United
States, regardless of the reality of interracial relations, Sonoran *letrados*
promoted their state's image as one of racial purity and white dominance.

A Digression: Borderlands Romance

Before returning to our analysis of the cultural significance of the Lola
Casanova legend in the Mexican borderlands, let us turn briefly to a
somewhat similar borderlands romance, also from the late nineteenth
century, but set in the United States, that of Ramona. Ramona was the
protagonist of the New Englander Helen Hunt Jackson's highly ac-
claimed and popular 1884 novel. A look at the cultural signification of
Ramona in both the United States and Mexico will provide some insight

into both how Mexico was understood at the time and why Mexico and
Sonora have resisted incorporating Lola Casanova into their respective
pantheons of national and *fronterizo* cultural icons.

Jackson's novel is an interracial romance with a twist. A brief plot
summary is in order. Ramona is a beautiful young girl raised in her aunt's
house in the U.S. Southwest shortly after the U.S.–Mexico war of the
1840s. Her aunt, *la señora* Moreno, is a proud Mexican *criolla*, a war
widow devoted to her sickly son, Felipe. Ramona falls in love with an
employee on the Moreno ranch, a Luiseño Indian named Alessandro,
much to her aunt's chagrin. And here is the twist: it turns out that her
aunt's deceased sister, that is, the woman whom Ramona has thought was
her mother, was in fact her stepmother. Ramona's father was a Scottish
sailor who had been in love with *la señora* Moreno's sister (also named
Ramona) but had lost her to another man while off at sea. The Scots-
man had had a daughter with an indigenous woman and had thought
that this daughter, Ramona (the novel's protagonist), would be better
off raised by *criollos;* he therefore convinced his former girlfriend to adopt
his baby. However, Ramona Sr. soon fell ill and handed Ramona Jr. off
to her sister (*la señora* Moreno). Ramona (the daughter), then, is a *mestiza* but does not know it until *la señora* Moreno, furious that Ramona
has become involved with an Indian employee, reveals her family history to her. Rebelling against the blatant racism of *la señora* Moreno,
who is ashamed to have a *mestiza* in the family and finds her love affair
with an Indian to be disgraceful, Ramona elopes with Alessandro. Alessandro is himself something of a hybrid. Raised on a mission, he speaks
perfect Spanish and plays the violin, but it soon becomes clear that he
is devoted to his people. Ramona proudly assumes an Indian identity
and the two set off to seek their fortune in the racist U.S. Southwest.

On numerous occasions, it is made clear that the treatment of the
Indians under U.S. rule is much worse than it had been under the
Spaniards or Mexicans. While the Spanish had educated the Indians
in their missions and the Mexicans had more or less respected their
autonomy and granted them land, the newly arriving U.S. settlers are
greedy and violent. The novel evokes a nostalgia for an idyllic mission-
era past and criticizes the United States for its policies of Indian removal
and extermination. Eventually Alessandro is murdered by racist white

settlers, leaving Ramona and her daughter alone. Luckily, around this time Felipe appears, looking for his lost stepsister. He rescues and marries her. Soon the new couple realizes that they can never be happy in Alta California with anti-Indian and anti-Mexican attitudes thwarting their attempts to make a life there. Finally, they move to Mexico City where they are welcomed and presumably live happily ever after.

Written by Jackson, an activist on behalf of the Indians of the Southwest, as a protest of Indian removal policy, *Ramona* was a huge success. However, lamentably, instead of invoking public sentiment to rise up against racism, the novel served more to promote a romantic myth of a California history that never existed, a history of picturesque and tranquil missions where Spaniards and Indians lived in peace. The historian Kevin Starr writes, with much irony:

> No matter that the mission system itself was founded on ambiguity: the enforced enclosure of the Indian. No matter that the Spanish soldiers hunted them in the hills like so much prey and drove them down into the mission compounds like so much cattle. There, in churchly captivity, the majority of them declined—from the syphilis the soldiers gave their women, from the alien work the padres made them do, from the trauma of having their way of life and their tribal places so cruelly taken away. In Helen Hunt Jackson's version of it all (and by the 1890s it was official myth), grateful Indians, happy as peasants in an Italian opera, knelt dutifully before the Franciscans to receive the baptism of a superior culture, while in the background the angelus tolled from a swallow-guarded campanile and a choir of friars intoned the *Te deum*. (58)

Moreover, this invented mythical mission-era past utterly erased Mexico from California's history along with the war by which California and the rest of the Southwest were acquired as U.S. territory. California's only past prior to the gold rush, then, was a distant colonial one. Otherwise, it was severed culturally from the country it bordered, as if Alta and Baja California shared no recent past.

Ramona has gone through many dozens of reprints and remains one of the most popular novels of the U.S. Southwest. Its popularity was perhaps greatest in the first half of the twentieth century when it inspired multiple Hollywood film representations featuring such stars as Mary

Pickford, Dolores del Río, and Loretta Young. It has also seen numerous stage productions, including most prominently California's annual Ramona Pageant, which has played there every year in the Ramona Bowl, a large outdoor theater in the town of Hemet, since the 1920s. "Ramona," a song written for the 1928 Dolores del Río film, became a classic (see Figure 5). For much of the twentieth century there was a booming tourism industry built around Ramona, featuring women who claimed to be the real Ramona and various places identified as her birthplace, her house, her grave, her wedding place, and so forth (DeLyser).

The nostalgia for an idyllic vision of the Spanish colonial mission frontier in *Ramona* contrasts sharply with representations of the late-nineteenth-century post-mission borderlands in Mexican literature. While there were as yet no novels being published in the northwestern borderlands, the *veracruzano* José María Esteva, who had visited Baja California briefly when sent to set up a customs office in La Paz in 1856, drafted the novel *La campana de la misión* in 1858, a book which he finally published in 1894 in Xalapa, Veracruz (Hernández Hernández 12–13). It recounts the shipwreck of Mexican travelers on their way to San Francisco, which leaves a young couple stranded in the desertlike terrain of the Baja California peninsula. They frantically ring the bell of an abandoned mission, but after they lose hope for rescue, the romantic hero, Eduardo, sets off alone in search of help. He perishes in a storm and his lover, Laura, left alone in the abandoned mission, is never heard from again. In Mexico, there is no nostalgia for the frontier missions. Baja California is ominous wasteland; the abandoned mission of San Borja recalls only the perils faced by settlers of a most uninviting land. The bleak terrain of Baja California is not of the borderlands, the terrain connecting the two neighboring countries and their cultures. It is not a contact zone where these cultures interact. San Francisco remains utterly out of reach; Baja California is instead frontier territory, far from the comforts of either Mexican or U.S. civilization.

Ramona, in contrast, was beloved by Californians—and by readers from all over the United States—for the picturesque vision the novel evoked of the nation's western frontier. Furthermore, in 1887, José Martí, another *Ramona* enthusiast, published his own Spanish-language translation of *Ramona*, first in New York, and shortly afterward in Mexico

Figure 5. *"Ramona." Sheet music of the theme song from* Ramona *(1928), directed by Edwin Carewe, with Dolores del Río; theme song by Mabel Wayne and L. Wolfe Gilbert.*

City. Martí claimed *Ramona* as "nuestra," that is, a novel of "nuestra América," a sentiment endorsed nearly a century later by the Cuban cultural critic Roberto Fernández Retamar.[13] *Ramona* is "nuestra" because it is a novel that not only promotes a *mestiza* heroine but endorses her coupling with an indigenous American protagonist (Alejandro).[14] There is no need to go into the history of Americanist criticism of *Ramona* here.[15] It will suffice to say that while the Americanists tend to focus on important race issues in the U.S. Southwest, the addition of Martí into the mix in Susan Gillman's article *"Ramona* in 'Our America'" ends up making interesting but misleading implications about nineteenth-century Mexico that my reading of the Lola Casanova legend contradicts. It demonstrates once again how U.S. border studies criticism has trouble penetrating the border and comprehending the types of issues brought about by the particular cultural confrontations that occurred in the other borderlands of northern Mexico.

Gillman notes, reading *Ramona* via Martí and Fernández Retamar, that the novel is particularly *nuestra* (Latin American) not only because of its *mestizo* characters and interracial couplings but because it shows that Latin America, in stark contrast with the United States, is a haven for racial tolerance and racial mixing. Martí's "nuestra América" project was inspired out of a need to promote an opposition to Eurocentrism and U.S. imperialism by fomenting national and racial pride in Latin Americans. Martí's vision is utopian, and while it may have been a vision shared by other Enlightenment-inspired or nativist Latin Americans, it was not likely embraced by many *criollo* Mexican elites in the northwestern borderlands of the late nineteenth century.

As we have seen, Sonorans did not wish to promote Latin America or Mexico as a *mestizo* paradise whose attitudes concerning race, particularly when it came to indigenous and mixed races, were opposite of those prevailing among whites in the United States. In the 1880s, Sonoran *criollos* were still fighting Yaquis, Seris, and Apaches and did not wish to represent themselves mixing happily with their enemies. Martí's vision depended upon the assimilation of conquered Indians like the Aztecs or Tlaxcaltecs (and presumably Yaquis and Seris) into Mexican *criollo* culture so that the latter could unite with *criollo* culture in the rest of Latin America. *Ramona's* fairy tale ending may have soothed some of Martí's readers in New York, Havana, or even Mexico City, but had anyone read it in the Mexican borderlands, it would not likely have been well received.[16] *Ramona*'s popularity in Mexico has been generally muted. Martí's translation did not make a big impact, and the novel has not been in print in Spanish translation for many years. A 1946 Mexican film starring Esther Fernández was both a critical and a box office failure. In fact, *Ramona*'s success with Spanish-language audiences has occurred principally in the United States. A stage adaptation starring the great Mexican actress Virginia Fábregas broke box office records in Los Angeles in 1927 and went on to tour the U.S. Southwest (Monroy 146). More recently, Lucy Orozco's adaptation of the novel to the format of a *telenovela* for Mexico's Televisa network in 2000 received lukewarm reception in Mexico but was a resounding hit in the United States, recently being re-aired by popular demand on Galavisión, a cable network serving Spanish-speaking communities in the United States. This most recent reinterpretation of *Ramona* has been described as "arguably the strongest critique of American expansionism ever seen on television—nothing less than a postmodern masterpiece, a brilliant subversion of the myth of the Old West" (Stein 2). Historically, *Ramona* has appealed to Anglos and Hispanics alike in the U.S. borderlands but has not made much impact on Mexicans in Mexico—even less so in *la frontera*.

Nineteenth-century Latin America could accept figures like La Malinche who bonded sexually into the *criollo* (in her case Spanish colonial) mainstream, or Nicolás (of *El Zarco*) who rejected their indigenous background to assimilate into *criollo* culture, but not characters like Lola Casanova who rejected mainstream *criollo* culture to join insurgent indigenous groups whose continued autonomy prevented national and Latin American unity. Ramona, too, gave up a comfortable life among her adopted *criollo*/Mexican American family to become indigenous, adopting an Indian identity. She would have been as unsettling in ninteenth-century Sonora as Lola Casanova was.

Los indios bábaros de la frontera

The history of violent strife between Mexican settlers and the various autonomous indigenous groups of the Northwest is one of the defining

experiences of the epoch for the region (see chapter 1). The very future
of the northwestern borderlands for *criollos* as well as *mestizos* depended
upon the subjugation and incorporation of these recalcitrant groups into
mainstream Mexican society. Until such a time, Martí's dream of a united
mixed race Latin America would remain unthinkable in the Mexican
borderlands, where attitudes toward these troublesome enemies tended
to resemble those of *gringos* interested in developing the U.S. Southwest, with one significant difference. The project of annihilation favored
by many in the U.S. Southwest might have seemed tempting to Mexican *fronterizos*, but many were conscious that it would be shortsighted.
Those recalcitrant indigenous groups needed to be assimilated into the
mainstream in order to serve as manual laborers in a region not yet
sufficiently populated to supply the labor force needed to carry out its
projects of modernization.[17]

In general, the only Indians welcome in Sonora were those willing
to work—for wages inferior to those paid to white workers (Tinker Salas
134)—for white colonizers, and to assimilate into Mexican *criollo* culture. Ramona, for example, might have been welcome in Sonora, arriving as she did with her second husband, the well-connected *criollo* Felipe;
however, her relationship with her first husband, in which she assumed
an indigenous identity, would hardly have been embraced by Sonorans, even if Alejandro played the violin and spoke Spanish. Indigenous
migrants from the United States were not welcome in Mexico: displaced
U.S.–based tribes that tried in these years to relocate to the Mexican
side of the border were soundly rejected by Mexican authorities.[18] The
rhetoric of civilization and barbarism was the overt and unequivocal
doctrine of the regional oligarchy, and whatever ambiguity Mexico as
a nation felt toward Spain, the *criollos* of the northwestern borderlands
felt obliged to ally themselves with their Spanish colonial heritage in
the name of civilization. Mexico's Apache campaigns would finally bear
fruit in the late 1880s, when at last cross-border Apache assaults would
be controlled, though occasional raids would occur well into the twentieth century (Figueroa Valenzuela, "Los indios" 158). Likewise, inter-
mittent confrontations with the Yaquis and Mayos (see chapter 5) would
go on until the first decade of the twentieth century, ending in a ruthless campaign to take possession of their lands and subjugate them once

and for all: "the most bloody and brutal era of the *porfiriato*'s depredation was established; the deportation of Indians became big business, and upon arriving at their destination they were sold as slaves" (Figueroa Valenzuela, "Los indios" 161). The military medic Manuel Balbás identifies the cause of the conflicts in 1901 from a decidedly *criollo* perspective: "the false idea they have formed of their nation, considering it to be constituted not by the greater land called Mexico, but uniquely and exclusively by the very limited Yaqui River region" (128).

The case of the Seris, or Kunkaaks, was somewhat different.[19] Unlike the Apaches who attacked Mexican settlers in raids launched from the safety of their territory on the U.S. side of the border, or the Yaquis and Mayos who protected their own fertile homeland from Mexican *criollo* invasion until late in the century, the Seris maintained their autonomy simply by distancing themselves physically from *criollos*. Traditional nomads of the Northwest, they isolated themselves farther and farther into the deserts of the northwestern part of the state, often using Tiburón Island, located in the Gulf of California, west of Hermosillo, as their base of operations. Despite their relatively small number, "by the 1880s . . . the Seris were the only Indians of Sonora who, even counting the Apaches, had remained independent of any form of dominance" (Figueroa Valenzuela, "Los indios" 146).

Ever since the first Spanish colonizers had arrived in the region, relations with the Seris had been hostile. Nonetheless, the Seris lived in such difficult land—infertile, hot, dry, isolated—that it had never been a priority for *criollo* authorities to vanquish them. However, around the middle of the nineteenth century, ranchers began establishing themselves closer and closer to Seri territories, gradually inciting tensions. The late February 1850 attack on the convoy carrying Lola Casanova— one of many similar attacks along the road between Guaymas and Hermosillo—set off a major punitive campaign against the Seris. However, it was only when armed conflict broke out between the Seris and local ranchers in 1855 that major damage was done. At the end of the so-called Encinas wars (1855 to 1867), an estimated half of the Seri population had been annihilated (Córdova Casas, "Las guerras" 299). Still they remained autonomous until in the 1880s, when some 150 Seris were captured and placed on a reservation—although they soon revolted and escaped when they discovered that some of their food rations had been poisoned by Mexican authorities (Bowen 241–42).

The autonomy of one of the smallest and most "primitive" tribes of the area was an embarrassment to local elites, who continued to crack down on the Seris in the last decades of the nineteenth century, instituting a campaign of extermination in which not only did some bounty hunters collect three pesos per male Seri head but also "Seris were hunted for sport" (Bowen 242). An 1890 military campaign resulted in a major Seri defeat. However, causing greater impact was the reported murder of several *gringo* adventurers who had gone to Tiburón Island in the early 1890s, which triggered another punitive campaign that ended with a Seri surrender in late 1894 (Bowen 254–58), although no formal peace agreement would be signed until 1907 (Córdova Casas, "Las guerras" 302).

This ongoing war with multiple indigenous groups in the Mexican Northwest, which went on into the early years of the twentieth century, made the area anything but the paradise of *mestizaje* envisioned by Martí. The Mexican Northwest, in fact, resembled the U.S. Southwest in many ways. Both were rapidly developing areas whose modernization depended utterly upon the confiscation of territories traditionally belonging to indigenous groups. Both were areas whose economic development required a process of population by new settlers that could only occur once all indigenous groups were brought under control. And, as in the United States, white Sonoran elites strove to ensure that whatever racial mixing occurred in the region did not permeate the *criollo* oligarchy.

True, many individuals of indigenous heritage chose to learn Spanish, take jobs with Spanish-speaking employers, and otherwise adopt the dominant *criollo* culture of the Mexican Northwest, and thereby "melted into the racially mixed population of the *gente de razón*" (Radding 17). However, the tendency for white *fronterizos* to exalt their status by emphasizing that they were among "those not mixed with other races" (Pérez Hernández 466) is evidence of a deep-seated racism that formed an important part of regional identity as constructed by elite members of the borderlands oligarchy in cities such as Guaymas, La Paz, and Hermosillo.

Early Legends of Lola Casanova

Within this context, it is not difficult to understand why Lola Casanova did not become, like Ramona in the U.S. Southwest, a major character of regional literature in the late nineteenth century. Not that literature existed as an institution in those days in the Mexican borderlands. While local newspapers began publishing poetry, often that of local poets, as early as midcentury (Aldaco Encinas), no regional literary production would exist until well into the twentieth century. Still, Casanova's early omission from historiography even as she remained alive through oral traditions points to the importance of popular culture in the evolution(s) of her legend into the twentieth century, when in the 1940s she would eventually appear to be on the verge of becoming a national icon. Ultimately, Lola never became a major protagonist of Mexican national culture, although she continues to be remembered today as a marginal heroine of regional high culture (literature, historiography), and as a beloved if still troubling figure of popular culture of the Mexican borderlands.

The earliest versions of the Lola Casanova legend, which had been lost for many years, recount the events differently from the way they appear in the best-known and more recent versions.[20] On 23 February 1850, Lola Casanova was traveling with her mother, Anita Velasco de Casanova, and her brother Ramón from her hometown of Guaymas to nearby Hermosillo when their carriage was attacked by a band of about twenty Seri Indians. That particular stretch of highway was well known for such assaults, and this time thirteen of the Mexican travelers were killed. *La señora* Velasco de Casanova was among the dead, and Ramón Casanova escaped.[21] Within a few weeks, a punitive military expedition was launched against the Seris in which attempts were made to rescue the captives. At the same time, the emergency law that put a bounty on the head of Apaches was extended to apply also to Seris (Bowen 238).

On 28 March, a Seri leader, Coyote Iguana, agreed to meet with the Mexican military officers and reportedly promised to return the captives within a few days. When he returned at the agreed-upon time without the captives, claiming that he needed more time to transport them, the military became impatient and launched a new attack (Bowen 238–39).

Finally, some time in April, the rescue expedition learned that Lola Casanova had actually been executed in mid-March in retaliation for the killing of a Seri woman. This was the story as it was reported in official military correspondence dated 24 April 1850.[22]

There are a couple of important differences between the very early, unpublished, official version of events and those popularly remembered. First, there is no mention in official reports of any romantic or sexual relationship between Coyote Iguana and Lola Casanova. The former is introduced as merely a spokesman for his tribe. Lola herself would have had little time to develop any relationship with the Seris since she was apparently killed after only a few weeks in captivity. This is not to say that the official version reflects the truth—or even that the truth would have any bearing on the construction of the legend, which likely serves purposes that have little to do with remembering the truth.

Bowen argues that the Seris who told their enemies that Lola Casanova had been killed may have been lying, perhaps in the hope that the search party would be called off.[23] The Seris might not have wanted it to become known at that time that Lola Casanova had been chosen as a romantic or sexual partner for Coyote Iguana. It is equally possible that Cayetano Navarro, the author of the official 1850 Mexican military documents on the conflicts with the Seris, was lying. Navarro, in fact, had taken numerous Seri women captive (Navarro 241), a practice that would certainly have been endorsed as more morally justifiable if the Seris were known to be doing worse with the white women of Sonora. It is also possible that Navarro may have been shielding the name of the Casanova family, his neighbors in Guaymas, from the shame of having a daughter contaminated by sexual contact, whether consensual or not, with a Seri.

In any case, the story was not to be published as such. It took time for the news to reach the only major newspaper of the northwestern borderlands, the government sponsored *El Sonorense*. In a brief article appearing under the heading "Seris," the 3 May 1850 edition merely recounted, in general terms, the "horrific murders" being committed along the road between Guaymas and Hermosillo and reassured readers that Navarro and his men were pursuing the enemy "with much steadfastness and energy" (4). No other protagonists of the story were named.

Similarly, José Francisco Velasco, in his *Noticias estadísticas del estado de Sonora* (1850), mentions the incident, identifying it as an assault by "inhuman, utterly filthy and cowardly bandits, murderers, thieves" (317). Neither Lola nor any of the other less famed victims were mentioned by name, despite that fact that Velasco's own brother counted among the dead.[24] A month after the first newspaper report, and well over three months after the original assault, a second story appeared in *El Sonorense*, this time mentioning specific details of the 23 February incident and citing Navarro's 24 April report to the governor. This story named several of the captives, noting that five of them had been set free. It then noted that a young girl named Elena Islas had not been released, and that Dolores Casanova—and this is the first published reference of her name—had been "sacrificed in captivity" (7 June 1850, 4). Interestingly, Elena Islas disappears quickly from the public imagination, while the name of Lola Casanova remains very much alive.

Regardless of how it was that her story remained active in the popular imagination of the northwestern frontier region, it clearly occurred for a reason. Whether that reason had to do with rumors that emerged later about Lola's marriage to Coyote Iguana and her refusal to return to Guaymas, or with other colorful adornments to the basic story that appealed to the popular imagination, or to persistent fears among white Sonorans, the revised versions of the Lola Casanova story that would be recorded in written form several decades later would significantly alter the official story as related in 1850.

Lola Enters History

The historian Fortunato Hernández, in his elegant publication *Las razas indígenas de Sonora y la guerra del Yaqui* (1902), makes Lola Casanova the protagonist of a coherent written narrative for the first time. Navarro's reports and the newspaper stories that summarized them centered their attention on Navarro and his campaigns, with Dolores Casanova as merely one supporting player among many. After 1850 there is no published reference to her for the rest of the century, with one exception: the Smithsonian Institute ethnographer W. J. McGee acknowledged the existence of a legend that would appear to be Lola's in 1898, only to deny its veracity: "The romantic story of a white slave and ancestress of a Seri clan, sometimes diffused through pernicious reportorial activity, is without shadow of proof or probability" (132).

But in Hernández, Lola takes center stage in a true-to-life romantic drama significantly different from that related by Navarro. The historian raises the subject casually as an example in his discussion of Seri traditions. Several new details emerge immediately: first, Coyote Iguana is not a real Seri but a Pima; and second, the abduction occurred in 1854 (62). These details would become fixed features of the story, as would others recorded in writing for the first time by Hernández, namely, that Coyote Iguana and Lola Casanova married and bore children who were raised as Seris, and that Lola chose to live the rest of her life among the Seris.

Hernández's source was a servant girl named María Valdés, who at some time around the early 1880s noticed a white woman among some Seri women who had come to the ranch where she was working to draw water from a well. When María asked the white woman what she was doing "with those infamous people," the latter responded, "I am . . . Lola Casanova" (63). Lola then recounted her entire story to María, who some two decades later repeated it, as she remembered it, to Hernández: Lola had been traveling with relatives from Guaymas to Hermosillo when their carriage was attacked. She fainted, awaking later to find herself "in the arms of a savage" (63). No mention is made of what happened to her family. Her captor turned out to be the chief of the Seris, Coyote Iguana, himself an ethnic Pima who had been adopted into the tribe as a boy. Coyote Iguana, who had lived among Mexicans as a boy, immediately proclaimed his love for Lola Casanova in excellent Spanish. She was repulsed at first by his attentions—Hernández's story mentions only hugs and kisses—although she gradually began to return his affection, and ten months later, Lola gave birth to a son (Hernández 63). By this time she was becoming accustomed to "the horrors of the savage life" (64), but it was her maternal instinct that led her to choose to stay with her captor. After all, "woman is born *hembra* [female animal] and nothing more" (64). And if her decision to take up the primitive life of a Seri was shocking, it was mitigated by the fact that her husband was actually a relatively respectable Pima. On the other hand, it might even be excused by the animalistic instinct that drives even a white woman:

> That is the only way to explain that a woman born and raised in unadulterated civilization could have adapted to an atmosphere as savage as the one constituted by Seri customs, and giving up homeland, family, home, religion, society, present, past and future, could have committed to living for the savage male animal who succeeded in seizing, dominating and satisfying her sexual instincts, and could have felt for him and for his children that sublime love that elevates the female animal to the category of mother. (65)

She lived many years among the Seri, even returning to Hermosillo (never Guaymas) several times, but was never able to bring herself to part from her new family. Eventually, Coyote Iguana was killed, but a few years later their son became the new chief, Coyote Iguana II. After his death, another son would become Coyote Iguana III.

What had been a tragic captivity narrative was transformed a half century later into a love story. The author of the new story may have been an imaginative servant who lied about meeting a woman who had been pronounced dead thirty years earlier; or her story may have been embellished by Hernández himself. It is more likely however that the story was a product of a popular oral history shared by many *fronterizos*. Interestingly, several details appear in other documents that support elements of this story, details that contradict information of the original 1850 reports.

For example, an unpublished manuscript authored by Roberto Thomson, who knew the Seri people well and represented their cause to the Mexican government in the second decade of the twentieth century, confirms a few of the new elements in Hernández (Bowen 242). Thomson recounts the campaign of 1890 that ended in the capture of a large number of Seri prisoners. Among them, he claims, were none other than Coyote Iguana and his pregnant wife, Lola Casanova (Bowen 245). Whether or not it is likely that Casanova was indeed pregnant at age fifty-eight, it is possible that the idea of there having been an interracial romantic liaison between the two, a liaison that bore them at least one child, was in circulation well before the publication of the

Hernández text—although it is not possible to say whether Thomson's source for the legend is more probably Seri or Mexican.

Another 1890 source, official documents signed by Captain Luciano Rodríguez reporting on peace negotiations with a group of eighty-six Seris, among them Víctor Ávila, purportedly the son of Lola Casanova and Coyote Iguana (Córdova Casas, "Las guerras" 303), again confirms Lola's blood ties to the Seris. It is not clear who it is that identifies Ávila as the son of the notorious mixed-race couple; however, his reported existence further points to the strength of an oral history in which Lola did survive and did marry her captor, which was in circulation well before the publication of Hernández's book.

One final note regarding Hernández: although his recounting of the Casanova legend sets the stage for its conversion into literature, Hernández did not wish to promote Lola as a role model. On the contrary, he makes a point of correcting Lola Casanova's irrational story by following it directly with the story of another Lola, Lola Morales, a Seri girl taken captive by whites,[25] and raised as if she were a *criolla*. He ends his chapter on Seri social organization with this happy anecdote of how "love, charity and instruction . . . [turn] the daughter of a Kunkaak semi-beast into the noble, sentimental and illustrious *señorita* Lola Morales" (71). Lola Casanova is a fascinating aberration; Lola Morales is the model of how to achieve racial integration in the borderlands: through a whitening acculturation that does not require the sullying aspect of *mestizaje*.

Flapper Lola

Hernández authorized an oral history of the borderlands, transporting it to Mexico City where it was endorsed by the well-known *literato* Juan de Dios Peza in a review published in *El Correo Español* in August 1902, in which he highlights "the story of the famous Lola Casanova, beautiful woman of the white Sonoran race, and whom her lover Coyote Iguana, Chief of the Seri Nation, imposed on the tribe as Queen."[26] Through Hernández and Peza, the story took on new life in Mexico's capital, resurfacing sixteen years later in *El Universal Ilustrado* (15 February 1918) in an article by Miguel López clearly based on the Hernández version of the legend and titled "Lola Casanova, la reina de los seris."[27]

López tells his "entirely veridical" story, locating the events in 1854. He includes virtually all the important details reported by Hernández, adding his own interpretation of Lola's momentous choice to stay with the Seris: "Lola Casanova, regressing, reverting to savage life for the love of her children, is proof of the complexity of female psychology, of a mother's affection and martyrdom, of the mystery that envelops that delicate being called woman." Lola is now more than a female animal; she is a case study in female psychology. If her behavior still seems bewildering to the average male reader, at least it can be attributed to patterns explained by scientific theory.

A second article on Casanova appeared in the same journal some two years later. This one, attributed to a *licenciado* Vidriera, was titled "Escenas de la vida nacional: Una mujer blanca reina de los seris: El rapto de Lola Casanova" (8 July 1920, 14–15). Its first paragraph asserts: "The Seris are the most savage and bloodthirsty Indians in America; nowadays they lead a pacific life under the constant vigilance of the Government" (14), foreshadowing his troubling story's happy dénouement.

Lola, merely a woman (actually female animal) in Hernández, "beautiful woman" for Juan de Dios Peza, "lovely woman" for López, was now a woman of exceptional beauty: "Tall and striking, white, golden haired and blue eyed, she was a rare beauty" (14). Vidriera's customary assertion that his story was "absolutely true" (14) is called into question by its illustration, a drawing by Carlos Mérida, who had recently arrived in Mexico from his birth country of Guatemala (see Figure 6). Mérida imagines Lola as a woman of the 1920s, sporting a hat adorned in exotic feathers and a flapper-style bob. Lola's decision to remain with the Seris is a product of both "the love she felt for her husband and her maternal sentiments" (15). This new romantic touch moves the story beyond the guise of historic testimony employed by Hernández, or the scientific analysis of a curious incident of the borderlands seen in López, presaging its later conversion into a novel. Coyote Iguana was no longer an enemy warrior but a romantic hero: "tall, well built, his naked legs, arms and chest revealing a powerful musculature. His copper skin shone with golden highlights . . . His abundant black hair, falling across his back, was carefully cut at the ends like the long hair of an artist" (14).

(Dibujo de Carlos Mérida)

Figure 6. "El rapto de Lola Casanova." Illustration by Carlos Mérida from El Universal Ilustrado, *1920. Courtesy of the Estate of Carlos Mérida/SOMAAP.*

Vidriera's tale is more fantastic and sensational than previous written accounts. Its characters and plot are more fully fleshed out yet more romanticized than in previous tellings: in Vidriera there was clearly a mutual attraction, and Coyote Iguana was shown to have made an effort to ensure that Lola was welcomed among his people. Lola, a woman in love, expressed her joy by decorating her hut: "built out of sponges and sea shells, roofed with *maguey* leaves and tortoise shells. Inside, the floor was covered in lion and mountain lion skins, from the walls hung scalps of Comanche chiefs conquered by her valiant consort " (15). Lola's motivations now go well beyond mere maternal instinct.

Early Women's Writing in Sonora

The local press of the northwestern borderlands, including official state-sponsored newspapers, had been publishing short literary texts by local writers, texts that sometimes addressed local themes, since the mid-nineteenth century.[28] Gilda Rocha cites *Días de amor* (1911) by César del Vando as Sonora's first novel; as mentioned previously, a novel set in Baja California, *La campana de la misión* by the *veracruzano* José María Esteva was published in Xalapa in 1894; and the Sonoran journalist Aurelio Pérez Peña published his play *Heroína* in 1897 (see chapter 4).

However, it was not until the mid-twentieth century that the north-western borderlands began to see sufficient literary production by local authors to warrant discussion of the concept of a regional literature. Interestingly, almost as soon as novels, short stories, and chronicles began to appear regularly by writers of the borderlands and on topics related to local culture, Lola Casanova quickly was established as a prominent protagonist of multiple literary works. It is as if her charac-ter had been lying in wait for a regional literary culture to develop in order to assert her presence and make the move from popular legend to literary heroine. Furthermore, it is of great interest to note that two of the earliest writers of the borderlands to bring Lola Casanova to life in their literature were women.

In 1943, Carmela Reyna de León, a local author whose name is absent from literary histories,[29] even those of her home state of Sonora, pub-lished the romantic novel *Dolores o la reina de los kunkaks*, the first full-length literary representation of the Lola Casanova legend. Reyna de León, thought to have been a schoolteacher in Pitiquito, a town in the Seri region of Sonora, may have been well informed about Seri culture. The novel differs significantly from previous published versions—for example, Reyna de León dates the kidnapping of Casanova to 1879 (1), nearly thirty years after the actual events, and a full twenty-five years after the date given by Hernández—leading one critic to surmise that the novelist's primary source of information may have been Seri legend rather than the historiography of Fortunato Hernández.[30]

In this version, Dolores Casanova is a "lovely mixed race girl," pop-ular carnival queen of Guaymas (1). Her wealthy parents give her as a birthday gift a trip to Los Angeles, but before she can set sail her stage-coach is attacked by a band of mainly Yaqui Indians and her father is killed. Coyote Iguana, the chief of the Kunkaks (Seris), who partici-pated in the assault along with the Yaquis, is attracted to Dolores and decides to keep her as his captive. However, she does not fall in love with him; instead she is attracted to Valiente, another handsome tribesman, who acts as her protector. Valiente tells her in excellent Spanish that he was raised among whites and schooled in Sonora. Very soon, a fight erupts between him and Coyote Iguana—who turns out to have been an ethnic Ópata—in which the latter is killed.

Lola spends several weeks among the Seris, longing to see her mother but afraid that if she returns, Valiente, whom she plans to marry, will be mistakenly blamed for her capture and unjustly put to death. Meanwhile, she tells him of the great indigenous men of Mexican culture: Benito Juárez, Ignacio Altamirano, Ignacio Ramírez. She adds, "I've heard say that the Kunkak race is not indigenous . . . that . . . they are equals of the Europeans in everything except their color" (23). Lola's romantic interest in Valiente is made understandable both by his similarity to Mexican *criollos* and by the critical view she develops of her birth culture living on the outside. Just as she shows Valiente that indigenous men have played an important role in Mexican political and intellectual life, Valiente teaches her that *criollo* culture should not be idealized, opining that whites "are slaves of government, the city, clothing, everything," whereas indigenous peoples are free (23).

As Valiente's wife, Dolores learns Seri customs and adopts their lifestyle. However, their home "was not a makeshift hut, but a well organized house . . . : spacious, clean, elegant; carpeted with the most precious of seal and gannet skins, and its benches made of whale vertebrae" (36). Again, Lola's penchant for interior decorating shows Sonoran readers that her life among the Seris was not a regression to savagery, as previous versions of the tale had so often implied. Around this time, they have a baby, whom they name Juventino.

Eventually (a good eight years after her disappearance), federal troops arrive while Valiente is off on an expedition and detain Dolores. She begs them to allow her to stay, but they take her and her son back to her mother's house. There she sees Juventino mistreated by racist white children. Finally, Valiente comes to rescue her from her captivity in Guaymas. Her mother calls the police, but finally they decide to let Dolores go because, after all, she is an adult living in a free country. The tale ends happily on the Isla del Tiburón with the joyous Seris welcoming

Lola back home. They cry jubilantly, "Long live King Valiente and Queen Dolores!" (49).

Several of the details of the story indicate that Hernández was not its main source. Lola, formerly white, is now *mestiza;* both her parents are alive at the beginning and her father dies in the attack. Since Reyna de León identifies her father as a "rich Spanish businessman," it must be assumed that her mother is her source of mixed blood. In the 1943 borderlands, it would seem that a mixed-race woman who married a wealthy white man (for example, Lola's mother—or Ramona, in her second marriage) was perfectly acceptable. In fact, even a mixed-race woman who married an indigenous man and assimilated readily to his culture (for example, Lola Casanova—or Ramona, in her first marriage) could be a romantic heroine.

However, the Seris, always the most primitive and savage of borderlands Indians in the nineteenth century, were now noble. They were not ravaging thieves; some of them were merely misled by some criminal Yaquis and their Ópata chief. The Seris themselves were peace loving. In fact, far from a backward, ignorant, barbarous people, they were comparable to civilized Europeans "in everything except their color."

The idealized beauty of the young couple implies that their son will be a *mestizo* worthy of "the cosmic race" (Vasconcelos). In fact, the influence of Mexico's new postrevolutionary cultural politics—a doctrine that violently rejected the racist positivism of the *Porfiriato* in favor of an acceptance or even celebration of Mexico's racial diversity, with an eye toward eugenic evolution and modernization (Lomnitz 52–53)—is evident throughout the novel. While indigenous customs are respected, the novel's hero is not the crude Coyote Iguana but the Hermosillo-educated Valiente, who is elated to learn of Mexican history's illustrious indigenous leaders from his *mestiza* wife. The *indigenismo* of the 1940s, very briefly summarized, exalted the glorious indigenous past: Aztec empire, Mayan science, Alcolhuan culture, and so forth, while promoting a better future for Mexico's indigenous population through education (and their implicit assimilation into the national mainstream). Reyna de León altered the scheme a bit by celebrating an indigenous past that was not ancient, but rather recent. While the Seris of the late nineteenth century were not as accomplished as the once-great cultures of Chichén Itzá, Teotihuacán, or Texcoco, the peace and freedom they enjoyed on the Isla del Tiburón were admirable on a smaller scale.

Reyna de León may have adapted her tale from a Seri legend that idealized a past way of life for a tribe reduced nearly to extinction. She may also have felt her redemption of the Seris was justified by a dominant philosophy that was happy to view their culture idyllically, as long as it was relegated to the past. Most important, the Seris in 1943 no longer posed any threat whatsoever to Sonorans. *Dolores* could not have been written in 1850 when Lola was kidnapped or even in 1885 when Martí translated *Ramona*. In 1943, with the caste wars over and the nation poised to recognize the past contributions and engagements of indigenous peoples in the national context, Sonorans of all races were at last ready to read and enjoy the story of Lola Casanova, at least enough Sonorans to justify the publication of *Dolores*, though not enough to admit it to a regional literary canon.

A Darker View

Not all Sonorans saw things as Reyna de León did; not all were ready for the glorification of Seri culture, much less the celebration of a white or even *mestiza* woman's romantic flight from a relatively modern city such as Guaymas to the primitive Isla del Tiburón, well beyond the frontiers of civilization. Sonora's first great female journalist and notable short story writer, Enriqueta de Parodi, recounted a different version of the Lola Casanova legend in her *Cuentos y leyendas* collection of 1944.[31] While Parodi sees it as "a complicated and dark passage from the history of aboriginal Mexico," because it features "some almost unbelievable details," she prefers to classify it as legend, citing Fortunato Hernández as her main source (25).

Her attitude toward the Seris contrasts drastically with that of Reyna de León. Even Hernández and Dávila believed that the most recalcitrant indigenous groups of the borderlands could be redeemed by education. Parodi, on the other hand, writes, "there have been various Sonoran governments who have made praiseworthy efforts to assimilate the Seris to civilization and all of them have been in vain" (26). Later she comments on what little remains of the Seri culture in the 1940s:

the Seri tribe continues in its pilgrimage to oblivion, because it will have to be extinguished one day; no force, no example, nothing has been sufficient to tame its legendary rebelliousness, indolence, laziness" (31).

Parodi's Lola was enthroned "by force," and her story is much less romance than horrific tragedy. The most remarkable characteristic of Parodi's version of the legend is its unbridled and venomous hatred of the Seris. Parodi concludes that "perhaps in the long and painful existence of this tribe, nothing has been better or more beautiful than . . . the story of Dolores Casanova" (31), whom the author designates the founder of the Coyote Iguana dynasty. Clearly nineteenth-century racial antagonisms, which ultimately devastated the Seri population to a low point of less than two hundred in the late 1920s (Figueroa Valenzuela, "La revolución" 360), had not been resolved to the satisfaction of all *fronterizos* by the 1940s. If only in that decade could Lola's tale be told among Sonoran *letrados*, it still could only be told a certain way. It is perhaps no surprise that Reyna de León and her novel remain absent from Sonoran literary history while Enriqueta de Parodi and her writings, more representative as they are of the views of Sonora's intellectual elite of her generation, have been celebrated for their foundational role in Sonoran letters.

Lola Goes National

Francisco Rojas González, on the other hand, was relatively unknown in the borderlands, but his publication of a full-length novel based on the Lola Casanova legend in 1947 would bring the story to its largest audience to date, and in a context decidedly national. Rojas González, an anthropologist turned novelist, based his story on the text of Hernández but also included an attention to detail that reflected his personal interest in and commitment to Mexico's indigenous peoples.

It is this version that would become a key source for many scholarly studies of the legend.[32] Lola was now firmly established as the only *criolla* daughter of a Spanish immigrant widower. Coyote Iguana was a truly noble savage, handsome and strong, gallant and wise. After her kidnapping (in 1854, as in Hernández), Lola married him and had his children out of love for him, and she came to respect his culture and to

live happily as his Seri wife, eventually outliving her renowned and respected husband.

Despite its influence, the novel is not known as the best of the author's
work. The critic Joseph Sommers writes:

> The improbability of the main argument, with its exotic contrast
> between the highly educated woman and a primitive setting, make it
> eminently appropriate for a legend, romantic story or melodramatic
> film. On the other hand, the ethnological detail that appears in
> describing the life of the Seris shows the hand of the *indigenista*.
> Both elements, juxtaposed, generate an incongruence that spoils
> the novel. (96–97)

The most exotic element of the plot, that most incompatible with the
author's ethnographic objectives, is the protagonism of Lola Casanova,
the white woman—and in Rojas González, Lola is "blanquísima" [ex-
tremely white] (11)—who abandons civilization for barbarism.

The literary *indigenismo* of the 1940s, as mentioned above, aimed to
incorporate all the variety and complexity of Mexico's many indigenous
cultures into the national imaginary. Typical literary works such as *El
indio* (1935) by Gregorio López y Fuentes, or the best-known *indigenista*
films (for example, Emilio "el Indio" Fernández's *María Candelaria* of
1944) tend to focus on the conflicts between mainstream national culture and its indigenous periphery, reiterating a binary vision of civilization (modern man) and barbarism (noble savage), and repeating the
familiar allegorical theme of the violation of the latter (represented by
the indigenous woman) by the former (white man).

In this context, now national, the romantic regional legend of the
borderlands is transformed into a national allegory. Reyna de León also
located her story in national culture, for example, through references
to Benito Juárez; later in the novel, when Lola leaves Guaymas for the
second time, the government official assigned to her case tells her
mother, "In the Republic we are all born free. She is an adult; if she
wants to be a savage, so be it" (Reyna de León 47). Lola, of her own
free will, separates herself from Mexican national culture to join the
alien culture of the Seris. If there is a national allegory in Reyna de
León, it is a trope on racial diversity and a resulting fragmentation of

national culture. In utter contradiction with *indigenista* doctrine, it is easier for Lola to assimilate into Seri culture than for Valiente to assimilate into mainstream Mexican culture, which treats his mixed-race son
with racist disdain.

In Rojas González, on the other hand, interracial love is linked firmly
with the concept of *mestizaje*, which is presented as a solution to the
Mexican Indian problem; it is a *mestizaje* "based on mutual respect of
cultural tradition and on the shared cooperative effort to construct a
modern society" (Sommers 98). Lola, in Rojas González, is no longer a
damsel in love who finds fewer prejudices among the Seris than in *criollo*
high society but a symbol of interracial unity at the national level.

There is indeed prejudice among the *criollos* in Rojas González. One
of Lola Casanova's early suitors, a major villain of the story whom Lola
fears she may be forced to marry against her will, is known as a "yaquero"
[Yaqui hunter]. He tries to win Lola over by giving her a young Seri
captive boy: "he could be another adornment for your garden" (23).
Lola of course is not racist and takes in the boy, whom she treats with
motherly affection. Later this will pay off when she becomes a Seri captive and the boy, having returned to his people, steps in as one of her
main allies.

Much later, years after Lola's capture, there occurs a scene in which
the Seris, among them the already acculturated protagonist, visit Guaymas, where they have a brief encounter with a little white boy and his
mother: "The lady interrupts her step, then suddenly resumes: she
frowns, while raising her brocaded handkerchief to her nose. 'Let's go,
my son, these people stink'" (251–52). A few moments later, Lola realizes that she recognizes that woman from her childhood: she had been
her best friend. The national prescription is simple: the childhood friend
represents ignorance and cruelty; Lola is kindness and generosity. And
it is obvious which of the two is of use to the nation.

In contrast, while there are also tensions among the Seris concerning the presence of a white woman in their tribe, between Lola and the
Seris a possibility exists, uncomfortable though it may be, to live together
and to come to know each other. Lola serves, then, not as a symbol of
an antinational antimodernizing acculturation as in Reyna de León but
as an instrument of transculturation. While on the one hand Lola does

strive "to transform her own idiosyncrasy, to inferiorize her culture, to twist her faith" (Rojas González 223), she also offers the Seris her knowledge of modern medicine. She moreover works to open commercial relations with the "yoris" (nonindigenous peoples, whether white or *mestizo)* in order to cultivate intercultural cooperation—and interestingly it is the Seri women who establish these dealings in a style "quite different from that sustained by the warriors with the *yoris*" (238). As an inverted incarnation of the postcolonial hybrid trickster of Homi Bhabha,[33] Lola accommodates herself in Seri culture and subtly introduces elements of Mexican *criollo* culture to the Seris, thereby modernizing them even as she herself appears to have reverted to a primitive lifestyle.

The novel ends in the twentieth century in a place called Pozo Coyote, founded by those Seris who were open to the changes fomented by Lola and receptive to racial mixing, as evidenced by the fact that *mestizos* also lived and worked harmoniously in the town with the Seris. The more conservative Seris remained on the Isla del Tiburón, living in primitive isolation from modern Mexican society. Lola, of course, is among the first group, the group of the future, but also the group of assimilation, an idealized (and not destructive) assimilation:

> The elders die without ceasing to be Seris; the adults grow old aiming to become *yoris;* the children grow up as *mestizos* . . . Nonetheless, the land, "grandfather of the *kunkaaks*" and godmother moon preserve respectability and reverence, because if the people speak, dress and eat *yori* style, they do not stop feeling, enjoying and suffering like Seris. (268)

The ending is rather pragmatic, as it is implied that all the Seris need is land and education to achieve a utopian state. One of the Seris of Pozo Coyote assesses their situation:

> Mexico gave us a slice of desert land; we, in exchange, have given back farmland; [we] drew water from where there was none; from the midst of sand dunes a town has sprouted up . . . The *yoremes* [Indians] have not gone to Mexico, it has come to us. (273)

In this hybrid town where they speak both Spanish and Seri, the people "live with the exaltation of endless work" (267). It took the acculturation of a white woman to make possible the mutual cultural understanding necessary to enable the incorporation of the Seris into the Mexican mainstream—where a particular role awaits them: "The commerce [in Pozo Coyote] is also *mestizo:* the *yoreme* produces and sells, the *yori* consumes" (267). Finally, as Anne Doremus puts it, "Rojas González . . . considers *mestizaje* the Indians' only hope" (395).

This recasting of the legend makes its white protagonist less radical than in Hernández, where she leaves her people never to return or to have any relation with them again. The project of *indigenismo* demands that Lola be a cultural bridge that the "indios bárbaros" may cross to enter into the modern nation.[34] The story is still discomforting due to the fact that Rojas González does not dare to overturn the final outcome of the legend—that is to say, that Lola remains the woman who abandons her life in Guaymas to "be a savage," but ultimately she is no longer radically opposed to national integration as she had been in Reyna de León's border romance. Finally, it must be remembered that an *indigenista* point of view is not equivalent to an indigenous point of view: one critic notes that despite Rojas González's anthropological pedigree, some Seris who have read the novel have responded to the representations of their customs and history with mocking laughter (Lowell, "Sources" 30).

Lola la Rumbera

Nevertheless, Rojas González's *Lola Casanova* promptly caught the attention of the greatest female director of Mexico's golden age of cinema, the pioneer Matilde Landeta, who produced her film adaptation, also titled *Lola Casanova*, in 1948. Landeta's script was based closely on the Rojas González novel –with only a few minor changes (for example, Landeta does not follow the historically accepted dates, locating her drama between 1860 and 1904).

This film employed the conventions of the nationalist-inspired *indigenista* school of cinema of Emilio Fernández, but from the perspective— utterly out of the ordinary in Mexican cultural production in that era— of a woman. While one of Landeta's goals was clearly to feature women as protagonists in national culture, she was also quite conscious of the

inversion of the national *mestizaje* myth that was embodied in her protagonists, one of the reasons why she chose this text for her first full-
length feature film. Landeta attempted to capture the cultural detail
expressed in Rojas González's novel, and her film in fact does succeed
in making her protagonists more than generic *indios* usually seen in such
films (Arredondo 197): they are clearly Seris, although her small bud-
get limited her ability to capture their culture as accurately as she would
have liked (García Riera 291). The elements of the production perhaps
most attractive to the viewing public were, in fact, the most absurd features of the film. For example, the newly founded Ballet Nacional de
México bestowed on the production artistic legitimacy, but its modern
style of choreography hardly evoked a "primitive" culture, despite the
dancers' ragged costumes. To make things worse, the *rumbera* Meche
Barba, best known for her starring roles in musical melodramas such as
Yo fui una callejera and *Una mujer con pasado*, was cast against type in the
role of Lola, and her love scenes with the hunky B-movie actor Armando
Silvestre (as Coyote Iguana) were, according to the film historian Emilio
García Riera, "suggestive of the classic 'Me Tarzan, you Jane'" (291; see
Figure 7).

The film, as a visual medium, despite its faults, likely communicated
Rojas González's message with greater lucidity than did his book: Landeta's Lola was emphatically a female agent of a modernizing 1940s-
style *indigenista* and nationalist agenda. Susan Dever argues that Lola's
own metamorphosis is radical in itself, implying that transculturation
must go both ways (90–91); however, in the end only Seri culture is
altered by the new cultural cooperation with the *criollos;* Mexican national
culture does not adopt any of the Seri customs learned by Lola. Furthermore, in the end it is the white *criolla* who is the culture-transforming
heroine of the Seris, a posture that is "fundamentally patronizing and
racist" (Rashkin 52). Landeta's Lola, a civilizing and modernizing force
of love, never threatens the *criollo* culture she abandons. She reveals its
prejudices and their sometimes brutal consequences, but she never ceases
to be its representative, its missionary. Still, she makes something quite
significant out of what would to a typical Mexican woman screen protagonist have been basically a life-ending experience. She is a helpless

captive transformed into less a romanticized queen—as in Reyna de León—than a protofeminist cultural icon.

Lola's Last Stand as National Heroine

Another nationally recognized—although not best-selling—novel of the late 1940s would bring further attention to Lola Casanova. Armando Chávez Camacho's 1948 *Cajeme: Novela de indios* romanticized the life story of José María Leyva, the Yaqui resistance leader of the 1880s. Its main character is not Lola Casanova, but Chávez Camacho is unable to resist telling her story, dedicating a complete chapter to this deviation from his central plotline. This *indigenista* novel aimed to vindicate the Yaqui hero, who, idealized by Chávez Camacho, has much in common with Coyote Iguana, also made into a noble savage in literature and film. Cajeme, raised among *criollos*, speaks excellent Spanish and is fully equipped to assimilate but is morally incapable of watching his people lose their land to greedy colonizers (see chapter 4).

Figure 7. Lola Casanova and Coyote Iguana. Film still from Lola Casanova *(1948), directed by Matilde Landeta, with Meche Barba and Armando Silvestre. Courtesy of Agrasánchez Film Archive.*

Cajeme is not about mestizaje; it is a historic and biographical novel that seeks to revise historiographic accounts of the Yaqui wars of the late nineteenth century by viewing the events from a Yaqui perspective. Since the government that so oppressed the Yaquis in Cajeme's day was that of Porfirio Díaz, the novel is able to position the Yaquis as pre-revolutionary rebels whose clashes with the Díaz government presaged those that would cause the country to erupt in revolution several decades later. Cajeme, like Teresa Urrea and the heroes of Tomóchic (see chapter 5), would, according to the intentions of Chávez Camacho, enter the national pantheon as a great hero of the Mexican people.

In a single chapter of the novel, the author digresses to recount another legend that he encountered while investigating the life of Cajeme, that of Lola Casanova. Interestingly—and consistent with Chávez Camacho's aim to retell history from an indigenous point of view—Lola Casanova does not get top billing: the chapter is titled "The Great Love of Coyote-Iguana" (191).

His Lola, like that of Reyna de León, is mestiza, although white skinned (196). Nonetheless, unlike the case of the Sonoran author who likely had knowledge of a Seri legend of the Casanova story, it seems that Chávez Camacho's principal source was Hernández, as is indicated by his dating the kidnapping in the year 1854, as Hernández (and Rojas González) had done.[35] Once again, after a few weeks in captivity, Lola struggles to decide what to do: "Which did she prefer? Civilization or savagery? . . . Finally, her heart imposed itself: she had to confess that she loved Coyote-Iguana" (207). This brief chapter, presented as a curious background tale, giving the reader a breather from the novel's main plot, no longer concentrates on Lola's role among the Seris but instead draws attention to her simple choice, the fact that choosing the "savage" life of the Seris over the comfort of criollo culture was a logical option for her. Lola assumed the radical role of a woman who rejects national culture, but it was of course not the postrevolutionary culture of the 1940s that she rejected, but the prerevolutionary life of the 1850s, and as such the tale was hardly threatening to twentieth-century readers.

This is indeed why it was possible for Lola to enter briefly into a culture no longer just regional but national in the 1940s. Literate Mexico had resisted acknowledging her persistence in the popular (oral)

imagination of the borderlands for nearly a century—until the borderlands indigenous peoples had been fully subdued and the area largely
settled and modernized, and until the nation had been more fully con-
solidated, having better symbolically incorporated its racial diversity. In
the cultural ambience of the 1940s, Lola—regardless of what her role
may have been: that of critiquing racist state policy of the nineteenth
century, that of promoting assimilation of resistant indigenous cultures,
or even that of celebrating interracial love and the romantic rejection
of civilization—was no longer, in effect, so radical. She was an unusual
girl, the protagonist of a legend of times long past, and was admissible
now in a national culture more symbolically diverse than a century earlier. But what little attention Lola earned in the late 1940s would quickly
subside and her image would quite suddenly vanish from the national
imaginary.

Mestizaje: *Traditional Concepts of Race and Gender Reaffirmed*

In 1950, Octavio Paz published what would soon become the classic
essay on Mexican national identity, *El laberinto de la soledad*. One of the
most prominent components of the essay was an analysis of how *mestizaje* figures in the national imaginary in gendered terms. While on the
one hand Paz was merely synthesizing and articulating what was already
understood as *lo mexicano*, the enormous success of this essay engraved
his vision of Mexican national identity more deeply than ever into
the national culture, inspiring a whole generation of further studies on
similar themes.[36] Paz represented Mexican *mestizaje* in the well-known
allegorical terms of the Spanish rape of indigenous Mexico, placing Mexican indigenous culture in the role of the feminine. Paz located the
concept of "chingar," a term implying an assertion of power through
sexual violation, at the very core of the Mexican character. In Paz's
Mexican imaginary, gender roles traced back to the symbology of the
conquest, and *mestizaje* could be imagined only in specific gendered and
racial terms.

Paz's analysis implies that ever since the conquest, *mestizaje* has been
understood as the rape of an always female indigenous Mexico by an

always white conquering male; there is no competing allegory of national racial identity. Lola Casanova's bizarre story, then, simply does not fit with the Mexican national character. It is thus no coincidence that Lola's sudden rise to prominence in national cultural production in the late 1940s was fleeting. She utterly disappears from national discourse after 1948, never to return again. No one like her appears in *El laberinto de la soledad,* nor is her legend revived in the literary boom that would follow in the 1950s and 1960s. If Mexico was not ready for Lola in the nineteenth century because she was too shocking, too radical, by the mid-twentieth century she continued, despite *indigenista* and feminist efforts to make her a national icon, to be too discomforting for Mexico's national culture to absorb.

Historiography in the Borderlands

Meanwhile, ever since Fortunato Hernández recounted the Casanova legend in his history of the indigenous peoples of Sonora in 1902, Lola Casanova began to assume an increasingly prominent place in local historiography. The Hernández version was repeated in works by the journalist Federico García y Alva in 1907 (Córdova Casas, "Lola Casanova" 14) and by the historian Eduardo Villa in 1937 (31–37) before being reworked in the literary adaptations of the 1940s. However, it was perhaps with the publication of Laureano Calvo Berber's *Nociones de historia de Sonora,* a grade-school history textbook, in 1958, that knowledge of at least one version of the story would become widely disseminated throughout the state.

Calvo Berber benefits from the discovery in 1952 by the historian Fernando Pesqueira of the original Cayetano Navarro letters on the various clashes with the Seris in the early 1850s (Córdova Casas, "Lola Casanova" 14). Calvo Berber's is the first major work of historiography to date the Casanova kidnapping 23 February 1850 (164), citing Navarro's letters directly, including the one that reports the death of Dolores Casanova soon after her kidnapping. Without noting any possibility that Navarro might have lied or received bad information from his Seri informant, Calvo Berber pronounces, "This is the historical truth concerning the tragic end of the young Dolores Casanova" (165). If historiography were more powerful than literature and popular oral legend, this would have put an end to more elaborate and extravagant versions of the story in which Lola falls in love with the enemy and forever renounces her race. But this has not been the case.

Seri Lola

Whether or not young Seris were taught "their" history with Calvo Berber's textbook, they surely had their own opinions about the validity of Mexican historiography. Regarding journalistic writings—which had for decades habitually referred to Seris as "barbarous"—the Seris, who themselves had no traditional concept of the press, came to refer to them as "the lying papers" (Lowell, "Sources" 30), and, as mentioned previously, Seri readers have found novelistic representations of their customs quite risible. It is unlikely that they saw Mexican historiography any differently.

In the late 1950s and early 1960s, several Seri versions of their own oral history concerning Lola Casanova were compiled by Edith Lowell in her comprehensive 1966 study of what she calls "folklore themes" in the Rojas González novel.[37] Her detailed comparison of numerous versions of the legend ("A Comparison" 156–58) identifies a number of similarities between Seri legends and the best-known versions in circulation in the mainstream of Mexican letters, including especially those of Hernández, Rojas González, Landeta, and Calvo Berber—as well as some significant differences.[38]

All sources agree that the Seris attacked a caravan on the road between Guaymas and Hermosillo in which Lola Casanova, a beautiful young woman, was traveling with relatives. Seri versions insist that Coyote Iguana was indeed a Seri and not a Pima as reported by Hernández, although they do agree that Coyote Iguana had received formal Mexican-style education and was able to speak Spanish. While most sources agree that Lola became Coyote Iguana's wife (in some, she was elevated to the status of queen)[39] and bore at least one son by him, most Seri versions contend that Lola was forcibly removed by soldiers from the Seri camp where she had taken up residence with Coyote Iguana, and that she was pregnant at the time. And while every version of the

legend reports that Lola left at least one direct descendent among the
Seris, no Seri version makes the claim that she spent the rest of her life
living as a Seri woman.[40]

Lowell concludes that the Seri versions point to an error in Sonoran historiography. She believes that the Seris would have no reason to
invent an inaccurate historic narrative. And if the Seris were going to
embellish the story, they would have had Lola staying with them and
rejecting the *criollo* culture of Guaymas as inferior—they would most
certainly not have invented her return to Guaymas after only a few years.
Lowell concludes, "No record of her return has been found, though
some Mexican residents believe her return was kept quiet by her family"
("A Comparison" 158).

On the other hand, the official Mexican version, based on Navarro's
letters, which insists that Lola was killed within weeks of her capture,
is refuted by the Seri legends that assert that her son Víctor remained
with them and became a tribal leader. According to Lowell, many Seris
(she counts 119 in 1966) consider themselves to be descendants of Lola
Casanova and Coyote Iguana, and the name Lola or even Lola Casanova was not uncommon among Seris in the 1960s.[41] She believes that
ultimately "Seri oral tradition appears to reflect historical events more
accurately and completely in this instance than does the better known
Mexican version which has been influenced by romantic literature" ("A
Comparison" 158)—a conclusion that flatly contests that of the borderlands folklorist Ronald Ives, who had written a few years earlier,
"Although a small part of the legendary material that cannot be verified by the historical record *may* be true, the larger part of it . . . can be
dismissed, with confidence, as pure fabrication" (164).

Regardless of the veracity of the Seri versions, it is of particular
interest to note that even as the small surviving population of Seris
remained apart from the Mexican mainstream, they kept alive the story
of Lola Casanova that had been separately entertaining and discomforting their white and *mestizo* Sonoran neighbors for over a century. Of
course, Seri accounts focused principally on the history of Coyote Iguana,
with the Lola Casanova story inserted as brief anecdote in the biography of their great leader. Accounts collected by Lowell and Moser begin
with Coyote Iguana's birth and end with his death ("A Comparison"

148–52). Seri accounts naturally do not incorporate the nineteenth-century *criollo* rhetoric of civilization versus barbarism; when Lola opts to stay among the Seris, no Seri finds her choice illogical, although some were not used to seeing white women up close and "were amazed to see her" ("A Comparison" 148).

There is no doubt that she was an extraordinary personage for the Seris, and it is for that reason that she became a fixture in their oral histories of the era. She signified, first of all, booty, material evidence of the Seris' victory in battle that day on the road from Guaymas to Hermosillo. She was also something of a foundational mother of Seri *mestizaje*—her mixed-race descendants could, after all, be found only among the Seris. On the other hand, the Seris, who claim that Lola lived among them only for a few years, make no mention of the transculturation brought on by having a white woman living among them—the thesis developed in Rojas González and Landeta; in fact, they claim that she did not learn the Seri language ("A Comparison" 151). Nor does she come to signify any profound superiority on the part of the Seris since the Mexicans win in the end: she is ultimately kidnapped a second time by the Mexican soldiers and taken away from her Seri family.

However, it is not only the Seris who continued to keep the legend alive through their oral traditions. Ricardo Mimiaga writes:

> In our country there is a great variety of indigenous legends that have
> endured to the present era. Likewise, the number of tales . . . of
> *mestizo* and *criollo* origin that still animate and give flavor to many a
> serene night of chitchat, whether in the mountains, in the middle of
> the desert or in the coastal valleys, is remarkable. In the Northwest
> region, oral traditions are kept alive in both ways: the indigenous . . .
> and the other, that of whites and *mestizos*, more vulnerable to suffer
> modifications with the passing of time and due to the permeability
> of our national culture. (387–88)

While we may not agree that only white or *mestizo* culture changes over time—Mimiaga implies that indigenous cultures in fact never change—the case of Lola Casanova makes clear the power of legend, multiform legends often developing separately in different social sectors, in the construction of Mexican borderlands culture.

Recent Incarnations of Lola Casanova

In the 1960s, Fernando Galaz revived the Lola Casanova legend once
again in his popular chronicles of Hermosillo, this time dating her kidnapping in 1872, a date that agrees with that given in no other source. In
other details, however, the tale is quite recognizable. Lola is an eighteen-
year-old white, chestnut-haired beauty from Guaymas, kidnapped by a
tall, strapping, muscular youth (Coyote Iguana), who spoke excellent
Spanish. Coyote Iguana was, despite being an ethnic Pima, the king of
the Seris, and he wished to make Lola his queen, and Lola soon was
seduced. The lovely white captive, however, was not readily accepted by
the Seris, and eventually—"twelve years later" (306)—she fled back to
live with her sister "in el Barrio de 'La Chicharra' (bordered by Mon-
terrey, Yáñez, Morelia and García Morales Streets)" in Hermosillo (306).
There she got involved with a military captain with whom she lived for
"three or four months" until he suddenly died (306). Two weeks later,
Coyote Iguana came for her, kidnapping her once again from her sister's house. This time Lola would spend the rest of her life with him.
She was last spotted in 1901, in full Seri-style regalia, selling pearls and
shells to passersby in the Plaza de Armas in Hermosillo (306).

This new capricious, even promiscuous Lola is a curious personality of local folklore, but hardly a great romantic heroine. This time she
apparently never has any children and is finally neither a symbol of *mestizaje*, of transculturation, nor of racial superiority for either race. She
is merely a woman who loves, leaves, and returns to her men with a certain ease, and who despite her beauty never rises to a position of power
or prestige in either Seri or *criollo* society. She is also relocated within
Sonoran culture. Her early years in Guaymas receive no attention, while
her return to Hermosillo becomes an important chapter in her life, her
latter history marked by references to local streets and landmarks.

A decade or so later, Lola is brought to life again in Horacio Sobarzo's
major work of regional historiography, *Episodios históricos sonorenses* (1981).
Unlike Galaz, who cites no particular sources for his tale, Sobarzo does
cite Rojas González's novel as his main source. Sobarzo revives the critical vision of Lola as espoused in earlier Sonoran versions such as that
of Enriqueta de Parodi of 1944; he laments the reckless acts of

the unfortunate Dolores who had to trade her queendom—because in
her home she was queen—for that of the nomadic tribe; the unfortunate Dolores who had to leave behind the sweetness, the tranquility,
the pampering and indulgence of her paternal home to adopt a primitive and savage life, without any more cover than a dry tree branch
lean-to that did not even resemble the huts of sedentary Indians. (178)

Coyote Iguana was no longer a strapping cinema hero, nor even a
homely but noble savage; for Sobarzo he was "a troglodyte" (179). The
Seris were "repulsive," accustomed as they were to eating "raw and
spoiled meat," drinking "swamp water," and sleeping on the bare ground
(179). Sobarzo grants Lola her rightful place in regional history, but she
is neither a victim nor a heroine—and certainly not a queen or even a
happy décor-obsessed Seri homemaker; she is a woman whose acts are
utterly illogical and aberrant. Sobarzo's point of view on Lola Casanova
is not that unusual among Sonorans.

At some point before his death in 1954, the great *cronista* of old
Guaymas, Alfonso Iberri, wrote his version of the Lola Casanova story,
although it reached a significant audience for the first time only posthumously, in 1982. Iberri shares with Sobarzo and Parodi a disgust for
the Seris and an attitude of resentment toward the romanticization of
the Lola Casanova legend. Iberri bases his text on no particular source,
noting that the stories that circulate on these events are full of "fantastic descriptions and nebulosities" ("El rapto" 275), and he hesitates
to conjecture any specific dates. He negates the popular love story, arguing: "The truth, surely, is something different: the beauty of the prisoner enflamed the sensuality of the king" (276).

His victimized Lola was soon "made mother" of Coyote Iguana's
heirs and forced to adapt to life "among grubby, dirty, lazy savages who
lived in disgusting promiscuity with their women, pierced their ears and
noses . . . , satisfying her hunger by eating raw fish and turtle meat" (276).
She stayed with the Seris either because she had become "ashamed of
her pitiful condition" or because she had become attached to "the offspring that Coyote Iguana gave her" (276). She ended up dying among
the Seris, "and there her cadaver rotted beneath the thorny twigs they
threw over her—since the Seris do not bury their dead" (277).

There is no return to civilization, no mention of visits to Hermosillo either to hide out in her sister's house or to seduce local bachelors, or even to sell Seri handicrafts. As in Galaz, Iberri's focus is local, although this time confined to the city of Guaymas. These chronicles signal that Lola has not only been accepted into regional historiography but also been embraced at the local level, written into microhistories that place her in a particular house, on a particular street, in a particular neighborhood, all recognizable to readers. On the other hand, it seems that Lola's return to her roots brings her back to life in only the most negative terms.

Even today traces of this style of anti-Seri rhetoric can be found in public discourse in Sonora. Recent state attempts to take possession of Seri lands have met with Seri resistance and have resulted in renewed tensions, leading Sonoran governor Eduardo Bours to comment, "The backwardness of the Seris worries me, but they have a great opportunity to modernize as they inhabit one of the richest zones in the state for development in the tourism and aquaculture industries."[42] One wonders what Bours would say if his daughter ran off with a Seri leader today.

In recent years, Lola has continued to inspire research among historians, even as the few verifiable facts of the case became remnants of a more and more distant and forgotten past. The legend, however, remains alive, as do numerous Seris claiming to be Lola's descendants.[43] In fact, Ricardo Mimiaga happened in the late 1980s upon a woman, Rosa Virginia Herrera Casanova, who sparked his interest in the legend when she told him that "she was related to the famous Lola Casanova" (387). While Mimiaga's recounting of the legend adds little new information, it does note Lola's particular subversive role as a symbol of *mestizaje:*

> The lineage of the clan of the Coyotes was founded on Lola's Spanish
> last name, just as had occurred with the blood of the proud Aztecs
> and that of their conquerors. But there is a difference. The general
> pattern of *mestizaje* was the crossing of white man with Indian
> woman. There were many with the last names Pérez, Rodríguez or
> López who were sons of *yoris* [whites] and *yoremes* [Indians] . . . but
> sons of *yoremes* and *yoris*, there are only a few, the Coyote Iguana
> clan, who come from the Indian seed planted in white flesh. (395)

Lola, then, continued to point to something real, and something unique and perhaps still troubling in the borderlands: the Seris' continued refusal to give up their traditions and identity and assimilate into the Mexican mainstream. Mimiaga was amazed at the "racial pride" that keep the Seris living to this day apart from urban civilization (381), and the tangible links (for example, Rosa Virginia Herrera Casanova) to a past history that has never made sense to white and *mestizo* Mexicans, particularly those of the northwestern borderlands who know firsthand just how drastic the difference is and was between the lifestyles of the Seris and their *yori* neighbors.

Another recent account is that of the Sonoran *cronista* Gilberto Escobosa Gámez, titled "El secuestro de Lola Casanova: ¿Historia o leyenda?" (1995). Besides the usual historiographic sources, Escobosa Gámez draws from an informant, Doña Manuelita Romero viuda de la Llata, his great-aunt, "an old woman who possessed a prodigious memory" (*Hermosillo* 34). While the widow died (at age 100) in 1933, Escobosa Gámez is able to recall her words—and even the emotions he felt as a small child upon hearing them—in the greatest detail.

Escobosa Gámez recounts the familiar romantic tale of a kidnapping after which Coyote Iguana, Pima leader of the Seris, a movie heartthrob type, makes Lola his queen. Although he portrays Lola as victim of "the ferocious passion of that fearsome savage" (33), she soon came to assimilate to Seri society, quickly learning their language and customs. In an idealized representation of transculturation, Lola stays with the Seris and learns to live as they do, while introducing her knowledge of modern medicine to the tribe.

At this time, Escobosa Gámez appeals to his long-deceased great-aunt to fill in the blanks of what has become the official story. Auntie Manuelita, after all, had herself visited the Casanova family in Guaymas as a little girl and actually met the teenaged Lola. Manuela remembered: "*Señor* Casanova and his wife died a year after the kidnapping. When they could not manage to locate their daughter, they lost interest in going on living. Lolita's uncle took charge . . . and spent a fortune trying to rescue his niece" (35). According to Auntie Manuelita, he was not able to find her until some fifteen years after the assault. However, by that time, when they tried to get her to come back home, "Lolita was not willing to return to the civilized world. She said she loved Coyote Iguana" (36).

Escobosa Gámez's love story, with all its melodramatic touches, unites several features of the many strands of the legend circulating during the past fifty years in the Mexican borderlands. It assumes its authority both from historiography and from eyewitness testimony, removed as it had become with time from the actual events. He needed to recall some sixty-odd years after the fact his nearly one-hundred-year-old aunt's reconstruction of events that she had learned about and a girl she had briefly seen some eighty years before that. His *crónica*, then, is both official and personal, as is the more academic style textual analysis of Mimiaga, who cites historiography and literature, along with his own face-to-face encounter with a distant relative of the protagonists of the story. Lola, then, even as her story falls back into an ever more distant past, is brought down to an ever more personal and local level for present-day Sonorans.

A final version, the most recent of all, fixes Lola as a key symbolic figure not in national or in Seri history but in the history of the northwestern borderlands. Alejandro Aguilar Zéleny's 2005 adaptation of the legend for the theater, in the playwright's words, "represents an interesting chance to get to know, through recourse to the arts, the process of identity formation in the Mexican northwest." He goes on, "Between reality and fiction, the sometimes hostile and occasionally friendly encounter takes shape between two vastly different societies that came together to form the culture of Sonora and of the Mexican northwest."[44]

In Synthesis . . .

What began in 1850 as a typical captivity narrative of Mexico's northwestern frontier has evolved and mutated in the past century and a half to signify a variety of meanings both at the national and the regional (borderlands) levels. Interestingly, unlike the other border narratives of this study, Lola Casanova has not managed to translate to the U.S. side of the border, remaining part of a very local lore of Guaymas, Hermosillo, and the traditional Seri territories in which the legend first circulated in the late nineteenth century.

From the very beginning, legend contradicted the few written pieces of evidence on Dolores Casanova's kidnapping and its aftermath. Either she died and was kept alive only symbolically by a popular imagination fascinated by the possibilities implied in her failure to return to her family, or she indeed remained alive and was written off as dead by those who preferred, for whatever reasons, a less romanticized tale. This captivity narrative circulated actively through different sectors of the northwestern borderlands in the late nineteenth century, serving primarily as a cautionary tale to local elites regarding the dangers posed by the continued strife with unconquered unassimilated indigenous groups such as the Seris. The symbolic union of Lola Casanova with Coyote Iguana was a reminder to *criollos* of the victory of the Seris in one particular battle, and of the general threat of encroaching barbarity on the barely established outposts of civilization in the northwestern borderlands at the time. Lola Casanova was a fascinating character, but hardly a representation of any mainstream identity constructs in the Mexican borderlands in the nineteenth century. For this reason, her legend was not incorporated in written form into Mexican borderlands culture during her lifetime.

Once Fortunato Hernández reinvented her as a protagonist of Sonoran history in 1902, her image as white queen of the Seris began to draw attention at the national level. In this context, Lola Casanova was a Malinche turned upside down, a symbol of inverted *mestizaje* in which a white woman mixes with an indigenous man. By the 1940s, Lola was no longer just a white woman among the Seris but an instrument of transculturation who learned Seri culture in order to seduce the primitive Seris to learn from her. While there was a brief but intense period of interest in this vision of Lola Casanova, the reemergence of La Malinche as the female national icon of *mestizaje* erased Lola Casanova from the national imagination by midcentury.

Back in the borderlands, however, the fleeting national interest in her legend provided just the endorsement needed to give Lola Casanova a prominent place in the cultural production of the borderlands state of Sonora. She had previously been first romanticized then vilified—by Carmela Reyna de León and Enriqueta de Parodi, respectively—in the early 1940s. This schizophrenic treatment would continue in the region's cultural production, most particularly historiography and the more literary form of *crónica*, throughout the rest of the century, as later published versions of her story became ever more local and personal. At the same time, the legend would continue to circulate, in multiple forms, throughout the northwestern borderlands, some of the most interesting versions being those of the Seris themselves, who featured Lola as a supporting player in the oral biography of their great leader Coyote Iguana. Among the Seris, Lola's mark was also left in a growing genealogy of descendents, who continue to use her name. While the Seris remain marginalized and are sometimes still vilified in mainstream Sonoran culture, they are still present, and the fact that Lola Casanova appears to still be among them in one way or another is a reminder of the unique history of racial tensions that continue to shape Mexican borderlands identity to this day.

CHAPTER FOUR

THE HEROINES OF GUAYMAS

O N 13 JULY 1854, Count Gaston de Raousset Boulbon led a small army of mostly French mercenary soldiers in an attack on the port city of Guaymas, Sonora. He had sailed from San Francisco with the intention of conquering Guaymas and establishing Sonora's independence, along with that of other states in northwestern Mexico, under his leadership, and with ambiguous ties to his homeland, France. He was soundly defeated by Mexican forces under the leadership of General José María Yáñez, backed by patriotic local volunteers.

The story of the legendary battle has been told and retold in many forms. It is classic border history in that the multiple contexts and points of view of the borderlands revealed in its numerous official, revisionist or even fanciful—and frequently conflicting—retellings highlight the complexity of cultural relations in and with northwestern Mexico since the latter half of the nineteenth century. This reading of the many histories of the French filibuster invasions of the 1850s is not actually about French military protagonist Raousset but about several Mexican supporting players in the drama, thus pointing to the ways in which the play of exclusions and inclusions of historiography, literature, and journalism keeps history malleable—and alive. The particular players in question here, sometimes hidden from history but never erased from the public memory, demonstrate that representation is always more than a simple relationship between hegemonic writing subjects and their subaltern objects. All this is made particularly obvious in the sometimes stormy debates on the content of historiography in the multicultural context of the borderlands.

History has traditionally celebrated the glorious exploits of important men, leaving out the contributions of others less powerful. However, even if erased from official history, otherness does not disappear from other forms of representation, particularly when multiple voices of conflicting points of view are engaged in constant dialogue. Historiography has struggled to take into account both mainstream discourse and also histories of otherness to provide more complete insight into life in past epochs. This chapter examines how such struggles have constantly reshaped history in the context of the Raousset invasions and the culminating battle of Guaymas of 1854.

A parallel simplifying tendency exists in border studies scholarship, whose focus generally limits itself to conflicts between Mexicans or Mexican Americans and Anglos or *gringos*. Other borderlands cultural groups are often left out, and sometimes these other groups' roles are more important than one might imagine. Borderlands history, itself traditionally marginalized from mainstream national historiography in both the United States and Mexico, must go transnational in a way that is not reductive, that is, that considers the weight and diversity of the multiple cultures that have historically constituted its population, including not only Mexicans and English-speaking *gringos* but also Native Americans from both sides of the border, Latin American immigrants from Chile and elsewhere, European immigrants from France and many other countries, Chinese immigrants, and so on. Raousset, as the historian Joseph Stout observes, was neither American nor Mexican but was nonetheless clearly a "product of the frontier environment" (187) and a major protagonist of nineteenth-century borderlands history.

The story of 13 July 1854 is the tale of Raousset's adventure and of Yáñez's military victory. It is a tale of a battle between two larger-than-life male protagonists, each in one way or another representing his nation. The cultural debates that have raged on—among biographers, historians, literati, journalists, and cultural critics in Mexico, France, and the United States—in the ensuing century and a half have examined the roles of both men and have also brought into debate the roles of other participants in the battle, including foreign nationals who may have sided with either the Mexicans or the French, the women and other civilians of Guaymas, and even a Yaqui rebel chief, who would later become known as both one of Sonora's most "barbarous" enemy leaders and the bravest of heroes.

It is a story too often limited to the confines of a Mexican national or a Sonoran regional historiography, or a history of mostly U.S. imperialism in Mexico; yet to fully understand what happened when Raousset came to Sonora, it is necessary to be aware of the cultural complexities of the borderlands context in which his voyages occurred. The story is also about the important role the French played in North America in the mid-nineteenth century, a role that is often forgotten and is too frequently omitted from studies of the borderlands, even though France's suspicious presence in northern Mexico was the product of and perhaps challenge to the nascent U.S. imperialism that had northwestern Mexicans nervous and U.S. Southwesterners wound up about annexation for much of the latter half of the century.

French Fantasies of Sonora

Raousset's 1854 invasion of Guaymas was not his first trip to Mexico, nor was it the first French incursion of dubious motives into the Mexican Northwest. He had arrived in Alta California in the early years of the gold rush, though too late to make much of it. An "imperious, unruly, reckless" youth (Wyllys 69), "talented but frivolous" (Ruibal Corella 140), he had already squandered his family fortune when, at age thirty-two, attracted by the call to adventure and easy riches of gold rush California, he set out for the New World, arriving in San Francisco in August 1850. After failing to strike it rich quickly, Raousset set his sights on northwestern Mexico, a region reputed to be the next California.

The legend of Sonora's untapped wealth had been in circulation for decades. It was known that there were silver and gold in some parts of the state, but that much of the territory in question had not been exploited due to relentless Apache raids from the north. The Mexicans, devastated by the war with the United States and decades of political instability, had been unable to control the borderlands, let alone populate them. The northwestern border states of Sonora and Baja California, isolated from the rest of Mexico by the Sierra Nevada Mountains, were largely neglected, left on their own to deal with rebellious Yaqui, Mayo, and Seri Indians as well as the particularly brutal Apaches who most often made raids into Mexico from the United States.[1]

Rumors of hidden riches in Sonora were particularly prevalent among the French. J. C. Beltrami had claimed as early as 1830 that the Sonora countryside was "sprinkled with mines" just waiting to be plundered (quoted in Suárez Argüello 19). While Cyprien Combier's 1828–31 voyage to Mexico (including a visit to Sonora) did not result in a publication of his maps pinpointing Sonora mines until decades later, Eugène Duflot de Mofras's accounts of Sonora's treasures in which he painted Sonora as a fertile paradise (not a desert) rich in gold and silver mines were published in 1844 (Suárez Argüello 21). Novelists such as Paul Duplessis and Gabriel Ferry set literary tales of adventure in exotic Sonora, further developing its allure among French readers.[2] Much of the boom in French writing on the attractions of Sonora, in fact, occurred while Raousset was already in California and in the years immediately following his death. Nonetheless, it is clear that the content of early publications such as Michel Chevalier's *Les mines d'argent et d'or du nouveau-monde* of 1846 was popular knowledge among the French in California, and that much of what was being written about in Paris was being spoken about in San Francisco in the early 1850s; in fact, similar writings were disseminated regularly in French-language newspapers in California, such as *Echo du Pacifique* and *Le Messager* (Glantz, *Un folletín* 11). The historian Rufus Wyllys writes:

> Concerning Sonora in particular, it was very simple to draw a parallel
> between her situation in 1850 and that of California in the forties.
> Both Sonora and California had been left helpless by the supreme
> government, both were wealthy in minerals, both had been torn by
> internal strife, and one had successfully been revolutionized by
> Anglo-Americans. Might not the California revolution be duplicated
> on the soil of Sonora? (49)

France's role here was special. French writings on the wonders of
Sonora constructed a vision of the territory in which

> the climate was healthy, the land fertile for agriculture, the fauna
> abundant and commercial opportunities optimal; but the most inter-
> esting feature was the unexplored deposits of gold, silver and other
> metals that existed below the ground, awaiting only that someone
> come and exploit them and be rewarded with unlimited riches. That
> someone, of course, should be French. They mentioned superficially
> the difficulties that presented themselves in trying to obtain these
> riches—the savage Indians, the deserts, the sparse population—since
> they considered that such difficulties could be surmounted with the
> collaboration of a selective European emigration, which ought
> preferably to be Latin. (Suárez Argüello 27–28)

Raousset's idea, it would seem, like the thinking behind the French Intervention in Mexico a decade later, was based upon a new construct of
pan-Latinism, the French imperialist precursor of the anti-imperialist
Latin Americanism that would be promoted in later generations.[3] This
is not to say that French imperialists invented the cultural affinity that
in fact did seem to exist to some degree between the French and those
of Spanish heritage in the Americas. Certainly the groups tended to
bond in gold rush–era California, often because they felt similarly discriminated against.[4] And in Mexico, where fears of another U.S. invasion were running high in the years immediately following the U.S.–
Mexico war of 1846–48, the idea of promoting immigration to Sonora
among foreigners did come up, with the French being an important target group. The thinking was that settling the border area with French
"military colonists" and not the more available U.S. immigrants would
provide a buffer between Mexico and the United States (Wyllis 12–19).

   And certainly Mexicans' fears were not mere paranoia, as incursions
were indeed being made into the Mexican borderlands by U.S.–based
adventurers, identified invariably as filibusters. While filibusters were
essentially pirates, criminal bands unsanctioned by governmental authority out for personal gain, increasingly strident rhetoric of manifest destiny that promoted the annexation of Mexico's northwestern states made
Mexicans wary of the possible covert ties between filibusters and the
U.S. government.

The Age of Filibusterism

Although filibuster invasions had been embarking from the United States for various parts of Latin America (most commonly Cuba, Central America, and Mexico's northwestern borderlands) since the early nineteenth century, the term "filibuster" did not come into popular usage to describe them until they became commonplace in the 1850s (Charles Brown 3). Following the success of the U.S. invasion of Mexico in 1846, the spirit of expansionism in the country flourished. This spirit, especially prevalent among the adventurous pioneers and opportunists of California, was not always patriotic, that is to say, related to constructs of nation. The rhetoric of manifest destiny was often less national than racial, and many believed that certain key areas of Mexico (and other parts of what is today Latin America) were ripe to be conquered by any band of white men, whether national army or filibuster militia.

As one historian writes: "The filibuster spirit seemed to be as combustible as gunpowder in many parts of the United States . . . but nowhere did it become so easily ignited as in California. There, no matter how dubious the auspices or how dangerous the project, adventurers enthusiastically joined invasion parties to the Mexican states of Sonora and Baja California" (Charles Brown 157). It was, after all, not only French sources that built up the legend of Sonora's vast riches, with journals such as the *New York Times* stirring up the pot by printing stories written by travelers to Guaymas making wild claims, such as the following:

> I have talked with many of the residents of Sonora . . . and they
> appear to regard the question of annexation with a degree of favor
> totally unexpected by me. While no men would be more prompt to
> repel the unauthorized efforts of filibusterism, none would be more
> eager to meet the United States on the question of a fair and manly
> adjustment by barter. They wish for it, they hope for it, and in that
> hope we cordially sympathize. (10 December 1858)

And while the U.S. government was unwilling to make further overtly imperialist military advances into Latin America at that time, many individuals were.

In 1851, Joseph Morehead led an unsuccessful expedition into Mexico with the intention of obtaining the "independence" of Sonora and Baja California (Wyllys 52–55), initiating a trend that would affect everyday life in the borderlands for decades: on the U.S. side, the excitement of countless schemes to further expand into Mexican territory; on the Mexican side, the constant fear of imperious behavior aiming to take advantage of Mexico's vulnerability, particularly in the unpopulated borderlands. Writes the Mexican historian Luis Zorrilla: "In the northwest . . . the war of nerves was constant as letters from individuals, news in the press and rumors in general disseminated the imminence of filibuster expeditions" (304).

It was not just Anglo imperialists who coveted more Mexican terrain. Later in 1851, the Californio Juan Bandini and others in San Diego instigated an uprising at the Santo Tomás military colony in Baja California in the hope of achieving the peninsula's annexation to the United States. Again the attempt failed, but it put Mexicans further on guard (Wyllys 56). The relationship between Californios and recent Mexican immigrants, many from Sonora, in Alta California in the early 1850s is quite complex. Many Californios were resentful at having been abandoned by Mexico, particularly as their rights under the Treaty of Guadalupe Hidalgo were not being protected (Zorrilla 259–74). Meanwhile, many white Californios adopted what resembled Yankee-style xenophobia: "ironically, in trying to protect their former social and territorial privileges, they allied themselves with the North Americans in their goal of destroying all that related to Mexicans" (Ruibal Corella 116).

To return to the theme of the filibuster movement, these incursions, though largely unsuccessful, made Mexicans more nervous about the relative lack of defense infrastructure along the new border. The borderlands were vulnerable because they remained sparsely populated. Wyllys observes that "[b]y 1852 [the Apaches] had nearly wiped out the strictly rural population in the northern portion of Chihuahua and Sonora" (4–5), and that Sonora lost "more than ten thousand" to the gold rush (8), which figures as close to a tenth of its total population at the time (Ruibal Corella 116). Just as the United States had made a grab for Mexico's one time borderlands of Alta California, New Mexico, and neighboring territories, it would not be hard for the stronger country to invade and seize possession of Sonora as the inevitable next phase of the project of manifest destiny. President Mariano Arista proclaimed to the Mexican Congress in January 1852: "Baja California, Sonora, the entire northern frontier . . . fears the irruption of savages, the attack of filibusters or revolutionary movements. There are no forces to contain this danger" (cited in Trueba 10). A year later, the U.S. president, Franklin Pierce, in his inaugural address, "announced a policy of territorial acquisition that would 'not be controlled by any timid forebodings of evil from expansion . . .' He was the first president in history to proclaim territorial aggrandizement an aim of the incoming administration" (Charles Brown 109).

Mexico needed to settle its borderlands, and if it was not possible to get Mexicans to settle the border region in sufficient numbers, perhaps the answer lay in the promotion of immigration. The fact that there were many immigrants who had come from all over the world to Alta California in the hope of striking gold, but had been disappointed, signaled a ready population of colonizers. The French, discriminated against in the United States—Joseph Stout reports: "Many Americans considered the French the same as Mexicans and lumped them together under the inaccurate name 'greasers'" (50)—adored as the model of cultural erudition in mid-nineteenth-century Mexico, and reluctant to return to their tumultuous homeland, seemed the ideal target population.

In late 1851, the French fugitive adventurer Charles de Pindray launched an expedition of eighty-eight Frenchmen from San Francisco to set up a "frontier colony" in Sonora.[5] The expedition arrived heavily armed and was later reinforced by sixty or so more men. Apache assaults and suspicions on the part of local government officials as to Pindray's intentions quickly complicated the mission, which ended with Pindray shot dead under mysterious circumstances.[6] Sonorans were becoming wary not only of U.S. imperialism but of the French whom they had begun to invite to their state. Early colonization expeditions failed to secure the border. Moreover, Mexicans began to wonder how wise it was to allow heavily armed foreigners to gain a foothold in national territory. Their fears were not unfounded: the remnants of early expeditions would later join the more problematic Raousset project (Wyllys 64–65).

It was in this context that Gaston de Raousset Boulbon, an acquain-
tance of Pindray's in San Francisco, entered the scene. Determined to
accomplish what Pindray could not, and with much greater fanfare,
Raousset connected himself not only with useful French associates in
the region such as the French minister to Mexico, André LeVasseur; the
French vice-consul at Guaymas, José Calvo; and the French consul at
San Francisco, Patrice Dillon; but also with key Mexican figures including President Mariano Arista. He additionally secured the sponsorship
of a large Franco-Mexican banking house, Jecker, Torre and Company.
Like Pindray, Raousset meant to obtain a land grant in an area reputed
to be rich with minerals. He would bring in a sizable contingent of
French colonizers who would develop the land for agriculture, establish the mines, and keep the Apaches at bay. It was reported that "[m]any
Mexican citizens were optimistic about the French colonizers, hoping
settlements would help stabilize the frontier" (*Daily Alta California* 28
August 1852, quoted in Stout 63). His enterprise, the Compañía Restau-
radora, would move into Sonora to carry out its mission.

Conflicts with Sonoran officials, nervous about the potential presence of another foreign militia in their territory, and the behind-the-
scenes intervention of a competing bank reluctant to allow Jecker, Torre
and Company to gain important influence in the region complicated
Raousset's plans. Raousset arrived in Guaymas on 1 June 1852 with some
two hundred men, but he was not received well by all. Sonora's acting
governor, Fernando Cubillas, claimed that it was Raousset's intention
to use his army to take over the region and make himself "Sultan of
Sonora."[7] The military display of Raousset's men, who traveled armed
and in uniform with Raousset often riding regally at the head of his pro-
cession, alarmed Sonorans and sowed discord with his Mexican business
partners—and in his own writings, the frequent evocations of Cortés and
Pizarro leave little doubt as to his grandiose ambitions (Sobarzo, *Crónica*
99). With news of Pindray's unexplained death still fresh in the public
imagination, distrust was mutual, and eventually the Mexican authorities made the French visitors unwelcome, threatening to deport them.

Furious, the count attacked the city of Hermosillo and quickly seized
control of it, proclaiming: "Citizens of Hermosillo . . . We have fought
against your tyrants. You have been told that we are pirates. We are

soldiers of liberty; liberty is what we bring to Sonora."[8] His public rhetoric is clear here: his goals went beyond settlement and development:
he intended to obtain Sonora's independence, under his leadership. But
his victory was short-lived, as the Mexican military retaliated and soon
drove the French out of the country. Around this time Raousset fell
seriously ill with dysentery, though some speculated that he might have
been poisoned.[9] In any case, by early November, the colonization project or filibuster invasion was all over.

Raousset's arrival back in San Francisco "was a veritable triumph"
(Sobarzo, *Crónica* 151). Anxious to cash in on the excitement he had
stirred up among adventurers and armchair annexationists alike, the
count quickly launched a new campaign, this time openly proclaiming
that his plan was to liberate Sonora from Mexico. He claimed that Sonorans wanted nothing more than their independence, and that they only
needed external help to bring it about. These arguments were not entirely fanciful; Sonora's congressional deputy, Mariano Paredes, had articulated a fear of a separatist movement afoot in 1850, a rumor that soon
spread to Alta California (Wyllys 10, 49). Meanwhile, in the U.S. Congress, there was talk of "a deep-laid scheme of French imperialism aimed
at the restriction of the United States to its existing limits" (Wyllys
133), and U.S. officials began to pay greater attention to the filibustering
activities in the west, particularly as they began to involve foreigners.

In late 1853, William Walker, a Southerner, launched a filibuster
invasion of Baja California, capturing for a time the city of La Paz before eventually being driven out of Mexico. Back in the United States,
Walker was arrested on federal charges of filibusterism. The U.S. government was in the process of negotiating the Gadsden Purchase (known
to Mexicans as the Treaty of La Mesilla), which would essentially buy
what is today the southernmost land of Arizona and New Mexico, including Tucson, from Mexico. In order to smooth the negotiations, President Franklin Pierce encouraged a crackdown on filibuster activities in
the borderlands. This did not discourage Walker, who later would briefly
take over Nicaragua. He would relentlessly continue his efforts in Central America until finally being shot by a firing squad in Honduras in
1860.[10] Raousset, meanwhile, was conspiring to reenter Mexico with an
officially sanctioned colonization company. However, Mexico's newly

reinstated dictator, Antonio López de Santa Anna, remained unconvinced that he did not have something more sinister in mind. Raousset's plan to bring in French paramilitary troops to develop northern frontier lands and set up a buffer against possible U.S. invaders attracted only guarded support among some Mexicans, and indignation among others. His ties with French diplomats were at times helpful but only led to further suspicions about his intentions. His rhetoric back in the United States, on the other hand, was not about colonization but liberation. He drummed up support among disappointed French fortune seekers, as well as immigrants from Germany, Ireland, and Chile, with his designs to obtain the independence of not only Sonora but also Baja California and Sinaloa, along with perhaps Chihuahua and Durango. His machinations to form an alliance with a recalcitrant former governor of Sinaloa, Francisco de la Vega, further shaded his reputation (Wyllys 156n55).

In response, the Mexican government, indeed wary of U.S. expansionist rhetoric, decided to recruit a foreign legion to better fortify the northwestern border from possible U.S. aggression (López Encinas 25). In a sense, they stole Raousset's own men out from under him. In response to what U.S. authorities worried was to be a major French military presence on the border, both Mexican and French consuls in San Francisco, Luis del Valle and Patrice Dillon, were charged under filibustering law with "raising an armed expedition against a friendly foreign power," though subsequently acquitted (Wyllys 172–81; Zorrilla 310–11).

Then, in June 1854, Raousset Boulbon arrived in Guaymas and quickly took charge of the French mercenary soldiers that del Valle had already brought in.[11] After a few days of unsuccessful negotiations between the Mexican general, José María Yáñez, and Raousset regarding the status of the French troops, war broke out in Guaymas. Raousset called his men to arms with the following speech:

> Frenchmen: you already know the wretches against whom you are
> going to fight. The local armed forces of Guaymas are paper dolls
> that you will see demolished at the first gunshot. You can rest assured
> of the victory that will place Guaymas promptly into your possession:
> its riches and beauty will be yours to enjoy to the limit. (quoted in
> Murillo Chisem 126)

Although outnumbered, Mexican troops were joined by outraged locals and quickly defeated the French filibusters on the same day, 13 July. The French soldiers were deported and Raousset was sentenced to death by firing squad.

General Yáñez's much-celebrated victory in Guaymas did not put an end to filibuster expeditions to the region. The former French admiral Jean Napoleón Zerman led another expedition of French and American volunteers in the hope of instigating a revolution in Sonora and Baja California in 1855. Zerman and his men were immediately imprisoned in Baja California (Zorilla 311–12).

Two years later, the California politician Henry Crabb and his Mexican brother-in-law, Agustín Ainza, led yet another expedition into Sonora, again with the announced intentions of helping to colonize Mexico's northern frontier. Mexicans soon suspected them of being yet another filibuster troop. When residents of the Mexican village of Caborca came to this conclusion, they attacked Crabb's party. The bloody battle ended with the annihilation of Crabb's entire force and the beheading of Crabb. Not unlike the border *bandido* Joaquín Murrieta in the United States, Crabb survived only as a severed head displayed in a jar of mezcal (Stout 143–68).

Eventually, filibusterism died out, but only after a decade of constant activity in the borderlands, although rumors of imminent filibuster invasion plagued the Mexican Northwest for decades. To most Mexicans, filibusters were a constant threat to national sovereignty; to many in the United States, they embodied shared dreams of national expansion. To some Mexican *fronterizos*, they may have even represented a chance for a neglected and undeveloped region to obtain its autonomy. To adventurers such as Count Gaston de Raousset Boulbon, filibusterism provided a means to realize dreams of personal glory. To French authorities back home, filibusterism may well have represented a sign of turbulence indicative of an opportunity for European imperial interests in the Americas. An analysis of just a sampling of the representations of the Raousset expedition in different geographical locations at different historical moments by different types of authors demonstrates just how complex the multicultural borderlands of Sonora were and continue to be one hundred and fifty years later.

Raousset in the 1850s

A few examples of how the Raousset expedition was presented in newspapers in the 1850s show that, from the outset, there has been little consensus on how to represent the events in question.

Mexico City, so distant from the borderlands, was in the early 1850s much more concerned with negotiations regarding the possible alterations to the Treaty of Guadalupe Hidalgo that eventually would lead to the Treaty of la Mesilla, and with discussions (with U.S. concerns) over the construction of a canal through the center of southern Mexico in the region of Tehuantepec, than it was with security in the borderlands. Despite the conflicts with Apaches, Seris, Yaquis, and Mayos that would continue throughout the century, news of "indios bárbaros" of the Northwest only occasionally reached the capital in the 1850s, and usually as borderlands issues and not as national concerns. Likewise, scuffles with filibusters such as José María Carvajal in Tamaulipas and Nuevo León were border problems, which appeared more often in regional news reports rather than among the national and international news stories given prominence on the front pages of Mexico City dailies.

El Universal, one of the most influential Mexico City newspapers of the era, did cover the Raousset Boulbon expedition of 1854, although its stories tended to be dated—an aspect of the case illustrative of Sonora's distance and isolation from central Mexico—and sometimes distorted. For example, in May 1853 it erroneously reported that two expeditions, one French and one American (presumably those of Raousset and Walker), had joined forces and as many as "two thousand valiant men" were setting out for Sonora, "one of the richest destinations in the world" (*El Universal* 19 May 1853, 1). The anonymous reporter speculates as to how a foreign occupation might improve conditions in the region: "Businesses will open in Guaymas . . . and before long a steamship line will open between San Francisco and Guaymas" (1). The report concludes with a promise for more "interesting news from those locations" (1). The story, apparently translated from an uncited U.S. journal, runs without any editorial comment.

It seems as if Mexico City was more concerned with the ordeals of Mexican nationals in Alta California than with the daily tribulations of citizens living in the Mexican borderlands. In the late spring of 1853, reports began to circulate regarding the persecution of Mexicans in Calaveras County, this bullying ultimately taking the form of expulsion under threats of death (12 June 1853, 1)—as previously mentioned in chapter 2—and the general detention of Mexicans in Utah Territory at the order of Brigham Young (12 June 1853, 2), but when the Raousset invasion was finally given full treatment by *El Universal* on 4 August 1854, a full three weeks after the fact, it was reported not as national news but as just another regional crisis in the borderlands. As late as 30 July, seventeen days after Raousset's defeat, news of the invasion had not yet reached the capital, although a story reported that troops had been dispatched from Mexico City to protect Sonora from arriving pirates (3). *El Universal* noted Raousset's arrival in Guaymas on 3 August (3). Finally, the next day, news of the battle of Guaymas and Raousset's defeat on 13 July came in (2). Thereafter, the journal launched a series of stories on the French filibuster invasion, adding details, reprinting reports from various military officials and articles from other newspapers, until it finally affirmed Raousset's execution in early September, again weeks after the fact.

Basically, Mexico City heard the official story: Yáñez's glorious defense of Guaymas against the nefarious intents of foreign pirates. Raousset was "audacious" (4 August 1854, 2), "arrogant," "treacherous" (5 August, 1), "insolent," "cursed," "cowardly" (31 August, 2); his soldiers were "ungrateful," "miserable" (5 August, 1); his designs "sinister" (5 August, 1), "perfidious," "ugly" (9 August, 1), while Yáñez was "brilliant," "prudent," "modest" (9 August, 1), "intrepid" (31 August, 2). At the same time, the capital city journal could not avoid pointing out, with admiration, that Raousset was of noble blood (4 August, 2), nor could it resist signaling his "valor" (9 August, 1). The national significance that *El Universal* drew from the events was that Raousset was misguided, and that his behavior should reflect on neither the many foreigners living in Mexico nor on the French government, an esteemed ally (5 August, 1; 9 August, 1). He was evil, but brave; at his death, *El Universal* translated a story from the Mexican French-language journal *Trait d'Union* that declared that the count "died bravely, manifesting very Christian sentiments" (10 September, 3).

Coverage was naturally more prominent in the borderlands, for example, in the official state journal, *El Nacional* of Ures. A flyer insert dated 16 July 1854 and penned by José María Yáñez lashed out virulently at Raousset's "abominable conspirations," calling the count a "pirate" and comparing his men to "cannibals." Yáñez points to the date "July 13 1854!" as a glorious milestone in both Sonoran and national history "that will serve eternally as irreproachable and authentic testimony to the values of the patriotism, fearlessness and determination in Mexicans when the moment comes to appeal to force, to defend the primary and most vital interests of human society and homeland."

Interestingly, it was in Mexico City and not in Ures that additional protagonists began to emerge, beyond the official battle between a pair of great men, supported in each case by a mostly anonymous band of loyal male underlings. On 31 August 1854, *El Universal* printed a letter from "a person" from Hermosillo who repeated the well-known story of the battle of Guaymas, adding the reactions of concerned neighbors in Hermosillo, anxious for revenge since it was their city that Raousset had so arrogantly invaded two years earlier. The letter concluded with the addition of a minor detail that had been left out of Yáñez's official reports:

> It is assured that count Raousset, a man so praised by his own people, above all as vigorous and brave, on this occasion has behaved in a cowardly fashion: he sought asylum in the house of the French vice consul before the action had concluded and before learning of its result, hoping to take refuge under the flag of his nation, and there suffered the humiliation of being disarmed in a gallant manner by a Mexican señorita. (2)

This last detail would remain in the background as the legend of Raousset took shape, but from that moment on the presence or absence of this still mysterious woman would open the doors to additional signification in the telling of the tale.

It should be noted that reports on the Raousset affair also reached the United States. In fact, many California journals had been following Raousset for years. The *Los Angeles Star*, in both its English and its Spanish editions, the latter called *La Estrella*, took the point of view that

Raousset was a pirate and that his "criminal enterprise" deserved strong censure, especially in the face of the "perfect harmony" of relations between the United States and Mexico at the time (*La Estrella* 16 April 1853)—in other words, as Mexico was being pressured to cede land to a U.S. company for the construction of the Tehuantepec canal. However, the same journal also gave space to Raousset himself, publishing the English translation of a letter from the count to Dillon, the French consul, in which he defended his position. He was not a filibuster: "A stranger to Sonora, I have no right to take the initiative in its domestic affairs, even for its good"; Sonoran citizens merely "call upon me" to aid them in their "national revolution."[12]

After his death, the criminal was made into a hero. At his execution, he "displayed himself as more than a man!" (*Los Angeles Star* 12 October 1854, 12). This story, attributed to an unidentified "account in Spanish," makes some claims that do not coincide in the slightest even with the more unconcerned reports from Mexico City. The presumably Sonoran writer went on, "Notwithstanding the events of the 13th, the people of Guaymas, with rare exceptions, deeply regret the death of count de Raousset Boulbon, whose memory will be perpetual to Sonora!" (12) and whose execution is "one of the saddest events in their history" (12). General Yáñez, meanwhile, did not get equal attention. This same article mentioned him (referring to him as general Yanes), recognizing his "bravery" and his "integrity and humanity," but concluded: "We cannot do injustice to the victor, even though our feelings shall turn us often to the tomb of his illustrious adversary, Gaston de Raousset Boulbon! Most worthy of a long and glorious career, had Heaven so willed!" (13).

His reputation in the United States as a great man was extensive. John (in Mexico, known as "Juan") Robinson, United States consul in Guaymas for fifteen years in the mid-nineteenth century and resident of the city for some three decades, was a friend to local leaders in Guaymas for many years.[13] Upon Raousset's invasion of the city in 1854, his son, Thomas (Tomás), twenty-one years old at the time, enthusiastically joined in the defense of the city and was subsequently honored with a special commission under Yáñez as captain in the Auxiliary Guard and with a medal from the Mexican government (Juan Robinson 16). Any bias Juan Robinson might have felt in favor of the Mexicans did not prevent him from admiring Raousset, whom he described repeatedly in his memoirs as "a very brave man" (17). Of course, by this time Raousset was no longer a threat to Mexico's sovereignty, nor to U.S. expansionist designs.

Once Raousset had been put to death, *La Estrella* of Los Angeles did not hesitate to urge U.S. president Franklin Pierce to negotiate with Mexico to obtain not just the "Mesilla" but all of Sonora: "The annexation of Sonora to the United States will be a mutual blessing for both nations" (12 October 1854, 14). The *Star* imagined that Mexico would cede "the whole of it, even to the River Mayo" and that they would do so with "a perfect consent of the people of Sonora" (26 October, 16), displaying a rhetoric strikingly similar to that which the paper had condemned only eighteen months earlier in Raousset, back before he had been refashioned into a borderlands hero.

This is not to say that Raousset's adventure had any effect on U.S. expansionist designs, save perhaps to call attention once again to northwestern Mexico's riches. And throughout the 1850s, annexation rhetoric continued to run strong in the U.S. Southwest. For example, in 1857 the *Sacramento Daily Union* made an argument similar to that of the *Star* (and Raousset) in favor of taking over Baja California: "If the United States do not wish to see Lower California soon in other than their own or Mexican hands, they had better at once negotiate for it. The majority of the inhabitants are in favor of annexation" (14 May 1857). Two years later, the *Weekly Arizonian* of Tubac made a similar argument for "the seizure of Sonora" (3 March 1859, 2). In one of a series of reports on the mineral wealth and other untapped resources of the state, the paper argued: "If it is the 'manifest destiny' of this favored region to become a portion of the great American Republic, we hope the day is not far distant when the annexation will be consummated. Once open to the energy of Anglo Saxon labor, a new era will dawn upon Sonora, more brilliant than anything in her past history" (24 March 1859, 2). Such reports were commonplace through much of the latter half of the century.

To return to the reports of the *Star*, the mysterious woman who according to *El Universal* orchestrated Raousset's surrender reappeared, now with a more specific identity: "the sister of Calvo, the French consul." The anonymous Spanish-speaking source whose relation of the

battle of Guaymas was reported in the *Star* on 12 October claimed that
Raousset delivered his sword to this woman because he was "unwilling
to be disarmed by a Mexican," adding, "She asked him for his pistol,
but this, he said, he would retain for himself."[14] This time, this woman,
who would remain largely absent from official histories, did not illus-
trate one more aspect of Raousset's final humiliation but now instead
confirmed his lofty arrogance in the face of defeat before the unworthy
Mexicans.

One final perspective will complete our discussion of Raousset's shifting and conflictive image in the 1850s. In France, his early role was none
too clear. He appeared to be in collusion at times with certain French
officials. However, France was unwilling to publicly endorse or finan-
cially back his endeavors during his lifetime. Speculation goes that had
he obtained a victory in Sonora, France would have been more than
happy to accept Raousset back into the fold as a hero and use his ground-
work to get a foothold into the earthly paradise that they believed
Sonora to be. The Mexican historian Suárez Argüello writes:

> Raousset's adventures woke the admiration of the French people. The
> Gallic government, for its part, had officially denied being in cahoots
> with the adventurer, but this, after all, did not signify a lack of interest
> in the count's activities. Probably at some point the French government
> did think about the convenience in encouraging Raousset, so that if
> he were to be successful, France would not miss out on what he might
> offer. (43)

Stout hypothesizes that France was not yet willing to openly back an
expedition such as Raousset's, but that it did perhaps run "a conscious
propaganda campaign" in his favor in French newspapers (78).

Whether or not France's official interest in Sonora was fully conceived
in 1854, a French presence in the area would certainly have been conve-
nient in the 1860s when France embarked on its own imperialist invasion of Mexico. As the Mexican cultural critic Margo Glantz observes:

> Raousset is a symbol. The ideas he put into circulation became
> quite popular and during the French Intervention they turned into
> common currency. Sonora became the most coveted prize of the

> French government, brandishing its dual faces: that of a rich province
> where French emigrants would live in abundance and sweet wealth,
> and that of the potent and decisive border, Latin and Catholic, that
> the Old World, embodied in France, would oppose against the dreaded
> and odious expansion of the young democrats of the American
> Union. (*Un folletín* 39)

Back in Paris, numerous chronicles and memoirs came out in the
years immediately following the Raousset escapade, including several
by surviving members of the expedition.[15] In these accounts, Raousset
is at once portrayed as more human than in any early accounts available
in Mexico or the United States, and also more grandiose. It is in the
French accounts that his profile as a legendary hero takes shape. Additionally, Raousset's own writings began to surface: not only his letters
to colleagues and relatives but also his literary efforts. In 1855, Librairie Nouvelle rushed to publish his novel, *Une conversion*. The editors,
in an unpaginated preface, refer to their author as a "noble and intrepid
adventurer" who realized "heroic exploits" in America. They assert that
they have decided to publish the manuscript "as much to satisfy public
curiosity as to render sympathetic homage to that audacious French-
man who died so far from France, to that man who nature, fortune and
education showered with all their gifts." Nowhere is Raousset a filibuster, an international criminal, an arrogant usurper. In fact, he is not
even marked as a loser: the editors recognize that he died in Guaymas,
but the epithet they assign him is "the conquerer of Hermosillo."

Already in 1855, Raousset seemed to be many men at once. Over the
years his tale would only become more complex as additional protagonists began to materialize.

The Cast of Characters

The most influential sources of the 1850s on the subject, those that would
shape both historiographic and literary representations of the adventures of Count Gaston de Raousset Boulbon, were the numerous French
books and the official reports of Yáñez. The French and Mexican texts
offered different perspectives, but in either case, the glory belonged to
one of these two men. These early stories of great men included a series

of supporting characters, great men themselves: diplomats, politicians, and businessmen.[16]

Close readings of French sources brought out additional names of French participants in the battle: Raousset's senior officers, other men who performed key roles at different moments of the two campaigns. Yáñez concludes his official published report, a brief addressed to the commander general of Sonora, with a list of names including officers of his troops, a few common soldiers who showed special bravery, leaders of the local militia, a few senior members of the Chilean and Irish volunteer brigades, and a few intrepid civilians, including a surgeon, a mid-level bureaucrat, and a Spanish schoolmaster, all men of honor and social position (unpaginated appendix, following page 18). As Yáñez would have it, the great men of Mexico rose up in union against the foreign invaders. While he is careful to recognize the collaboration of foreign mercenary soldiers, the image of national unity that he constructs masks issues of social hierarchy that would become increasingly apparent as history was rewritten again and again over the next hundred and fifty years.

An obvious issue missing from the discussion is the role of the United States. Officially the *gringos* were condemning Raousset's actions and had made significant efforts to impede them; meanwhile, his popularity in the press and the continuing rhetoric of annexation in the Southwest showed that this was not just a French story. The presence of U.S. citizens along with other foreigners, many of them international businessmen, in Guaymas and elsewhere in Sonora, shows the region to be more multicultural than one might imagine.[17] In addition, the evacuation of French residents of Guaymas—another detail left out of Yáñez's report—further simplifies his story into one of a monolithic Mexico at war.[18] But this was not a monolithically national context; it was the borderlands. This is not to say that other parts of Mexico were not culturally complex in the 1850s: they were. Still, Sonora's proximity to post–gold rush California, Guaymas's status as a major regional port, and the well-disseminated legend of Sonoran treasures all served to make Sonora, despite its relatively small population, a growing center of international immigration. Just as it had been easy for Sonoran adventurers to cross northward into Alta California to join in the gold fever a few years earlier, it was equally easy for disappointed fortune seekers to cross the other way, not necessarily as filibusters, but perhaps as entrepreneurs or common laborers.

Meanwhile, it was not long before another important aspect of the battle of Guaymas began to become more prominent: the participation of Mexicans who were not foreign-born but marginalized for other social reasons. These are the unsung heroes (and heroines) who, when added into the historiographic mix, permit the reshaping of the cultural meanings that history transmits. To begin with, let us take a look at a few of the female supporting players whose participation adds interesting nuances to the basic story of imperialist invasion and patriotic victory of great men.

María Antonia, Wonder of This Sun Blessed Land

One of the characters who does not obtain prominence in early official historiography in Mexico and remains unmentioned by and probably was unknown to Yáñez (she played her role in 1852, two years before the battle of Guaymas), but who is featured in several early French versions of the adventure of Raousset, is a woman from northern Sonora named María Antonia. The count met her just before his march on Hermosillo during a sojourn in Magdalena, while reveling happily among Sonorans at a local festival.

The count himself put it as follows in a letter:

> I was obliged sometimes to traverse the endless spaces that separate these isolated towns to rouse enthusiasm for national revolution in a town thirty or forty leagues from the camp, or to pursue Indians, or also to ride fifteen leagues on horseback through the desert to untangle the blonde braids of a young Mexican girl in love. Because in Sonora, my friend, and this is one of the wonders of this sun blessed land, there are blonde women among the many lovely dark skinned, shapely ladies with nervous feet, black eyed gazes and hair that seems to have been darkened in the waters of the Styx. The women of Sonora are beautiful, pleasant and spiritual. The soul of the race is concentrated in them. Everything gallant in the Spanish character from the immortal times of Cortés has been maintained in them: they alone have preserved the noble tradition one would seek in vain

among the men. A few days after the government of Sonora declared
me a rebel and a pirate, at the moment in which I became an outlaw,
and in which any individual might have killed me like a rabid dog,
receiving praises for it from the fatherland, I met at the festivals of
Magdalena, where the best and most select people of high society
congregate, a young and tall beauty named *doña* María Antonia.
She belongs to a family of importance; her father, who is one of
the principal authorities of the area, figures necessarily among
my enemies. I was being spoken of. I was attacked; she took up
my defense. Her aunt, a most intelligent elderly lady, said to her
pointedly, "Are you in love with the chief of the pirates?" Dear
Edmé, Antonia stood up impatiently, gracefully thrust herself into
her shawl, and with the greatest coolness replied, "Yes, I am in
love with that man whom you call a pirate! In this cursed moment
for Sonora, there is only one man who is truly thinking of saving
her from ruin: the count! If the men of this country were not so
spineless, they would take up arms as he does to shake off the yoke
of Mexico. Yes, I love the count, and I love him dearly!" Antonia,
dear Edmé, is tall, beautiful and blonde. Amid her dark companions,
she looks like a rose in a bouquet of black tulips. Yesterday, before
five or six thousand people, Antonia came to my camp and entered
my tent. I do not tell you this to satisfy the fatuity common in
animals of our species, but to give you the opportunity to judge the
worth of the women of Sonora and whether I am mistaken in believing
that I have support in this land. (quoted in Sobarzo, *Crónica* 116–17)

A nineteenth-century romance novel uniting the gallant Gaston de
Raousset Boulbon with the rebellious María Antonia would have allego-
rized the French and Mexican unity that Raousset and later Napoleón
III dreamed of.[19] Tacitly excluded are vulgar Americans who doubtless
could not equal Antonia's blue blood, as well as the dark-skinned rab-
ble of Indians and *mestizos* that the French believed was holding Mexico back.

Mexicans have thus treated this character warily. Apart from Raousset's letter, the main source on María Antonia is the French author
Maurice Soulié's 1926 romantic biography, *The Wolf Cub*. In *The Wolf
Cub*, Raousset first meets his paramour through some French friends of
his who happen to be her aunt and uncle (145). She is promptly dis-
owned by her family and becomes Gaston's spy (158). Importantly, it is

Antonia who, fed up with Mexico's neglect of the frontier, convinces him to attack Hermosillo "with the warmth of a patriot and a lover" (160). She joins him on multiple occasions as his adventure continues: in Mazatlán where he recuperates from dysentery (175–76), in Mexico City when he goes to meet with Santa Anna (186–88), and finally in Guaymas at the time of the fatal battle (222–23). While in Mexico City they make a point of staying in different lodgings; in Guaymas "her lover went to see her at nightfall and stayed with her till the song of the lark was heard" (223). She not only visits him in jail (235) but stays in town to witness his execution. Just before he is shot: "Suddenly a heartrending cry burst from one of the balconies; a woman was carried away in a faint" (243).[20] She later attends his burial, where she retrieves a gruesome souvenir, digging her fingers inside his cadaver to pull out the bullet that killed him (244). Finally: "After Gaston's death, María Antonia entered a convent and never came out" (255).

Most Mexican sources, on the other hand, either ignore María Antonia or include her only with serious reservations. Two Mexican historians who published new histories of the Raousset Boulbon filibuster assaults in 1954 to mark the centenary of the battle of Guaymas, Alfonso Trueba and Horacio Sobarzo, agree that the love affair about which Raousset spoke in his letter to his friend back home was nothing more than a "creation of the overwrought imagination of the count."[21] However, Sobarzo does not leave out a second reference to María Antonia from the early French sources. He quotes A. de Lachapelle:

> Later, in San Francisco, M. de Raousset was speaking to us of his campaign in Sonora. An intelligent and graceful narrator, he knew how to adorn the aridity of certain tales with a sentimental anecdote, full of charm. When we asked him if he was referring to Antonia, the daughter of the prefect of Altar, the blonde haired Mexican woman, the one who detained him for so long in Magdalena, he denied, with a huge smile, possessing such weakness. (*Crónica* 118–19)

Soborzo, then, vacillates between believing her to have been a real-life embodiment of "tender and generous, and at the same time violent, passion, one that leaps, in a fit of blindness, beyond prejudices and convenience" (118) and a mere invention. She was not, for Sobarzo, a symbol of the count's seductiveness for white Mexican high society—many members of which would later support the French Intervention and feel privileged to be ruled not by a weak president such as Arista or a corrupt dictator such as Santa Anna, but by an Austrian aristocrat.

Still, she seems to leave Mexican historians uncomfortable. Most prefer to disregard her entirely rather than admit that the count was capable of seducing Mexicans into union with him. The more recent history of Francisco López Encinas revives her—citing the count's 1852 letter (quoted at length above) as his source and adding some minor but interesting embellishments—such as referring to her as "María Antonieta," perhaps in a gesture to the arrogant French queen. María Antonieta "surrendered herself before the overpowering personality of the pirate, and was seen entering his tent at twilight and returning at daybreak" (37), bringing the element of sexual scandal into play from the start.

The marginal role of women in traditional historiography makes them especially interesting figures in borderlands texts. They so often fail to take on a clear role in official history, appearing only anecdotally. However, when they do appear, since they have not been assigned a fixed function in historical narrative, they remain amorphous. They are inserted into histories at will and are deployed to multiple strategic ends, depending upon the rhetorical goals of the author. María Antonia represents the golden seductiveness of Sonora; she is the element of the Sonoran population that does believe in and support the count's good intentions to liberate the state; her bond with the count suggests what a French military presence in Sonora could have been; and at the same time María Antonia/Antonieta represents the decadent Sonoran aristocracy ready to corrupt itself in any way to lure in the French. But the fetching María Antonia was not the only female supporting player in the Raousset drama.

La Señora Guadalupe Cubillas

As mentioned previously, early newspaper reports claimed, for conflicting reasons, that Raousset Boulbon surrendered his arms to a woman. Whether it was evidence of his humiliation, emasculation in the face of defeat, or an act of defiance and disrespect for his Mexican conquerors, it was a curious detail, noted only occasionally in French sources and omitted entirely from Yáñez's official documentation of the battle. Nonetheless, its memory lived on in the annals of local history, in which the woman in question was formally identified as Guadalupe Cubillas, apparently the sister of the French vice-consul's wife (López Encinas 107; Murillo Chisem 131). Important early Mexican histories (Iberri's *La jornada*, García Cubas, Sobarzo's *Crónica*, Trueba) omit Doña Guadalupe, relating only that when it became clear that the French had lost the battle, Raousset retreated to the vice-consul's house from which he had a white flag of surrender hung.

This is not to say that Cubillas remained absent from Mexican historiography until the late twentieth century. Francisco Dávila's 1894 book, *Sonora histórico y descriptivo*, whose title page advertises it as a "historical review of the most important events occurring from the arrival of the Spanish to the present and a description of [Sonora's] agricultural lands and pastures, its mines and livestock, its forests and rivers, mountains and valleys, its cities, towns, climate, etc.," was published in Nogales, Arizona, and distributed chiefly in the borderlands. Dávila summarizes Sonora's history in a book that is designed to give potential investors and settlers an inviting introduction to the territory.[22] The book's sales pitch plays up the strength and integrity of *sonorenses*, including Sonoran women. He introduces the story of Guadalupe Cubillas as follows: "Mexican woman, who for her sublime heroism and selflessness would be the envy of the Greeks for their great epic poems, was faithfully characterized in this armed event by a distinguished Sonoran lady" (26).

His version of the Raousset invasion quotes Yáñez's official history in its entirety but adds bits of local color, including a sonnet composed in Yáñez's honor by a local poet from Ures (39–40) and a detailed description of his surrender to *la señora doña* Guadalupe Cubillas, sister-in-law of the French consul (here promoted from his usual role as vice-consul), who refused to let the count seek refuge in her home until he disarmed himself and removed his hat. Dávila stresses that he surrendered to "a Mexican woman" (26) only because by entering her home, still armed, he had "violated laws of honor" (26).

The most-cited studies from the early to mid-twentieth century, including those of Wyllys and Sobarzo, omit Cubillas, despite the fact that Eduardo Villa, also a distinguished Sonoran historian, had featured her prominently in his influential *Compendio de la historia del estado de Sonora* of 1937. She also appeared in Calvo Berber's history textbook of 1941 and a 1907 commemorative pamphlet assembled by Pedro Ulloa, which was reissued upon the centenary of the Guaymas invasion in 1954.

It was not until many years later that a well-documented Mexican version of the events, Francisco López Encinas's *Sonora, frontera codiciada* (1985), revived her. In López Encinas's retelling of Raousset's surrender, the count enters the wrong door of the vice-consul's house, finding himself in Cubillas's quarters by mistake; *la señora* Cubillas, "with a dignity worthy of her, seeing that the count remained with his hat on and his arms in his hands, made him see that this was not how he ought to appear in a lady's presence, and asked him then to surrender his sword, which the count handed nobly over to her" (107). It should be noted that López Encinas inserts the story in parentheses, in the middle of an extended citation from the classic Yáñez report, introducing it not as a fact verified in any cited source of historiography but instead as a gossipy anecdote repeated "according to the legend" (107). The historian of the city of Guaymas, Jorge Murillo Chisem, repeats this version nearly word for word a few years later (131).

Another very recent iteration of the story, the Sonoran novelist Miguel Escobar Valdez's novella *Morir antes que ceder,* primarily follows Yáñez but inserts Cubillas, once again cast as the vice-consul's non-Mexican sister, into the drama, as she had appeared in the *Los Angeles Star,* so that Raousset might "avoid the humiliation of surrendering his sword to a Mexican" (24). However, this time the author has Cubillas do double duty, as both a non-Mexican and a woman: the exclamation he uses to introduce the anecdote, "Supreme ignominy!" (23), points to the count's humiliation at having to surrender to a woman, just as *El Universal* had reported in 1854.

One early source that drew liberally from popular oral history did include Cubillas, though in a slightly different role. The circumstances under which the source in question, Aurelio Pérez Peña's play *Heroína,* came into being will be reviewed later in this chapter. This defiant retelling of the battle of Guaymas casts Guadalupe Cubillas as an unmarried neighbor of Vice-Consul Calvo, who happens to live in a house

attached to his. It is significant that Pérez Peña has distanced Cubillas
even more from Calvo; she is neither his sister nor sister-in-law but a
mere neighbor—this despite the fact that Pérez Peña's likely source for
the incident was Dávila.[23]

Cubillas is the protagonist of the third and final act of Pérez Peña's
play. As the curtain rises, Guadalupe is alone in her home, lamenting the
events of the day, with a pistol at arm's reach on the table. She curses
Raousset: "You were at once infamous, ungrateful and disloyal! Where
is your nobility? Where is the gleam of the escutcheon? What was, vile
one, your intention towards my homeland?" (33).

Whether or not the audience knows the legend in which Cubillas is
the Mexican sister (in law) of the French (vice) consul, Pérez Peña leaves
no doubt that she is fully Mexican. In fact, the very essence of her identity seems to be her Mexican nationality, as she calls up such figures as
Cuauhtémoc and Morelos in her opening monologue. She concludes by
exalting the valor and patriotism of her countrymen:

> Come in unbridled torrents, enemies of my homeland, Mexico; every
> Mexican is a soldier ready to die fighting for his rights. Come like
> Raousset: from here I dare you; and if the heavens remain silent, here
> we have our bodies as shields! (35)

At this moment, she is startled by the abrupt entrance of none other
than the count into her home, pleading for her to take him in: "They're
after me, I hear their howls; they're getting closer, the bandits will catch
me; protect me!" (35). Guadalupe informs the count that he has entered
the wrong building, and that the vice-consul lives next door. Her wits
about her, before he has a chance to ask anything further, she also quickly
directs him:

> But listen, distinguished guest: without knocking you have entered
> this house and you are still wearing your hat and bearing your arms.
> Are your emergencies so great, sir? Let it be known that no one may
> pass through the threshold of this door that you see without first
> disarming and removing his hat. (36)

The count is taken aback, flustered at the accusation that he has placed
self-preservation over the question of good manners: "Madame, pardon
me! I didn't know . . . ," to which Cubillas retorts, "What did you not

know, sir? That to present oneself before a lady in your present state can only be called a lack of respect or a discourtesy. Hand over your sword!" (36).

When he hesitates, she grabs her own gun from the table and forces him to comply, to which he responds, "I am cursed! Villainous luck!" (36). Cubillas then goes off on a tirade at what Raousset has done to the Mexican people, despite his noble lineage. He reacts, "Madame! You insult me!" to which she replies, "You have forgotten that I hold you prisoner and that you have been disarmed" (36). The count is "surprised": "Prisoner, you say?" (37). She never falters in applying her power over him, quickly turning him over to the local hero, Colonel Campuzano (not *chilango* Yáñez), who soon arrives on the scene.[24] Author Pérez Peña's mission is to tell not the official version that General Yáñez penned, nor any competing foreign version, but the local, popular version, the unrecorded version that focuses on the multiple heroes of Guaymas. For Guadalupe Cubillas, despite her bravery, is perhaps not the main heroine of the drama (since, as we will see, there are two female protagonists who take on heroic roles), yet, importantly, Pérez Peña gives her a voice for the first time.

Cubillas is, then, not only the Mexican woman who handed Raousset his ultimate humiliation, or the non-Mexican woman who allowed Raousset his final snub toward the Mexican people. She is also a symbol of the patriotism of the citizens of Guaymas, of the strength of Mexican woman in a time of war, and of the sense of honor and pride of the Mexican people. However, her continued parenthetical treatment further points to Mexicans' ambivalence about opening official history to include not only great men but their wives and even sisters-in-law: notwithstanding Pérez Peña's project of launching a distinctly Sonoran counterdiscourse on Raousset's adventure, Cubillas remains absent from much Mexican historiography and, as we will see, continues to be a subject of controversy.

Doña Loreto Encinas de Avilés

Much of the Mexican historiography positions itself against a more global history of filibusterism that has made Gaston de Raousset Boulbon something of a mythic hero. Typical in Mexico are accounts such as the one by Abelardo Rodríguez titled "La jornada heroica" in which he duly describes "The Count, His Life and the Facts" in one section but dedicates another section to "The Hero of Guaymas" (190–91). Unlike the U.S. historian Rufus Wyllys, who focuses exclusively on Raousset's life story and only brings Yáñez in as he relates to Raousset's adventure, Rodríguez gives equal time to Yáñez, providing background information on his life story and career history leading up to the events of 1854. *Gringo* historians of filibusterism such as Joseph Stout limit themselves to the point of view of the adventurers whom their readers are meant to warily admire. The chapter of his classic history of filibusterism, *The Liberators*, in which Stout recounts the battle of Guaymas is titled "Sultan of Sonora" (not "The Hero of Guaymas"). Rodríguez contests this posture with a patriotically Mexican point of view, titling his section covering the same events "The Glorious Day" (197).

Aurelio Pérez Peña, although not a historian, had actually gone a step further several decades earlier, challenging both foreign accounts and also official Mexican history by introducing a series of marginal characters, thereby drawing attention away from Raousset and "the hero of Guaymas" to focus on Guaymas's heroine, or actually heroines. For while Pérez Peña features Guadalupe Cubillas acting in a heroic style in his third act, by the time she disarms the count the Mexicans have in fact already won the battle. Pérez Peña gained more notoriety for introducing another female protagonist into the story, also in a heroic role, this time as the Mexican who prevented a sneak attack by the French that might otherwise have had tragic consequences. Doña Guadalupe Cubillas is joined for the first time in Pérez Peña by Doña Loreto Encinas de Avilés (see Figure 8).

The most well-known source on Doña Loreto is Eduardo Villa's *Compendio de historia del estado de Sonora* of 1937. Villa presents her as an honorable local matron, already known for having been active in supporting the Mexican troops during the U.S. invasion of the 1840s (261–63). Nonetheless, what really distinguished her is that on 13 July 1854 she somehow found out that the French were planning a surprise attack, even though they were supposedly still in the midst of negotiations with Yáñez. Ever alert, "without worrying whether she was suitably dressed,

Figure 8. Portrait of Doña Loreto Encinas de Avilés.

or that she had to go with her little daughter Amalia in her arms, or that her actions may not have reflected a timidity proper to a woman, she hurried out, dashing to find the general, to whom she sounded the alarm" (264). Not only was her act helpful to the Mexican troops but, according to Villa, "one moment more and the surprise attack would have been consummated, perhaps presaging defeat" (264).

Yáñez, of course, never mentioned Avilés, nor any other woman, in his official report. And there has been considerable controversy over just what role she played on the day of the battle and how important any information she may have provided to the Mexicans was. Yáñez is never very specific about his sources, merely opting to portray himself as adroit in information management and in total control of the situation. He writes:

> Opportune warnings were reaching me at every instant regarding the operations of the enemy, and news reports were coming in one after another saying that Raousset was arming himself, that he was leaving his lodging and joining his compatriots, that he was haranguing them in a rousing rally to battle, and finally that they were in formation. ("Triunfo" 122; and in *Detall* 8)

Other sources have pointed to informants, perhaps German, within the Raousset forces (Wyllys 108n9, Murillo 125). Certainly in the first decades after the events in question, Doña Loreto fails to pass from oral to written history, even in the work of Dávila, *Sonora histórico y descriptivo*, who was appreciative of such anecdotes (although following the publication of *Heroína* he did incorporate her into his *Calendario guaymense* of 1902).

The source to which this legend is commonly traced is an unexpected one: Arturo Jáuregui y Bario, a lawyer from Mexico City who included the story in a commemorative discourse in 1886. But the one who really established it, prior to Villa, is the journalist Aurelio Pérez Peña.

Digression: Aurelio Pérez Peña and El Imparcial

Pérez Peña's own story is worth a digression. He was a journalist with literary aspirations; his newspaper, *El Imparcial*, was one of the most popular and longest-running independents of his day, beginning publication around 1889 in Guaymas and closing its doors only in 1910.[25] He was not really interested in disparaging the French, nor was he anti-*gringo*. In fact, he practiced a complex borderlands style ambiguity in his international politics that allowed him to become enraged at certain isolated acts, such as the Raousset invasion, without turning against the countries that he saw as important to Sonora's economic development—which is not to say that he was not racist but only that he reserved his most prejudicial attacks for other groups, including the Chinese and, oddly, Mexicans.

Looking to his journalism, his occasional reports on the United States censure, for example, "Yankee savagery," which tacitly sanctioned the lynching of a Mexican accused of robbing and killing his exploitative employer who had been cheating him out of earned pay. The legal prosecution of a Mexican criminal, even one whose crimes were committed under extenuating circumstances, would not have been problematic, but his lynching by a wild mob was "an act worthy only of savage tribes that lack any notion of morality and justice, and are only guided by ferocious instincts" (*El Imparcial* 2 September 1892, 3). The unsigned article[26] is critical of the behavior of some in the United States but notes that the U.S. government has recently paid indemnities to the families of other lynching victims in New Orleans. However, this Spanish-language newspaper in Mexico that included the English language tagline "The only newspaper published daily in Sonora. Largest circulation" was by no means anti-*gringo*—and it certainly did not wish to appear so, particularly to regular advertisers such as the International Drug Store of nearby Nogales, Arizona, or the Denver Public Sampling Works.

Nineteenth-century journalistic pioneers such as Pérez Peña greatly influenced not only how locals, whose news came to them through the filter of newspapers like *El Imparcial*, viewed the world but also how the world understood local cultures. *El Imparcial* and other local journals from outlying Mexican cities and towns became important sources of provincial news for major Mexico City dailies as well as for international journals. The fact that *El Imparcial* was published in the border state of Sonora made it of even greater interest beyond national borders. As Kirsten Silva Gruesz notes of nineteenth-century newspapermen,

"Editors on the border . . . became small-scale ambassadors of culture" (20) in the Americas of the nineteenth century. Pérez Peña was apparently quite conscious that his influence extended outside the city of Guaymas—or sometimes that of Hermosillo—where his newspaper was published, and that he was participating in a dialogue that crossed state and even national borders.

Another unsigned story published a few months later voiced concern that the Arizona legislature was discussing the state's need for a port on the Gulf of California and that expansionist movements were conspiring to take over some part of northern Sonora (1 August 1893, 2), but it came just weeks after *El Imparcial* stridently celebrated U.S. Independence Day on its front page: "Today all humanity joyously celebrates a grandiose event . . . We effusively salute our sister Republic on her glorious day, and we wish her all the best" (4 July 1893).

The full complexities of Pérez Peña's perspective with regard to the United States are revealed in two articles on the problems of Mexican emigrants. The first one, which he signs with his pseudonym Eliseo, lamented the fact that Mexico was often interpreted in the United States through the image of uneducated migrant laborers. He proposed that such "ignorant" Mexicans must not represent the country, and that the "true Mexicans" in the United States were those who had lived there prior to 1848. Pérez Peña, it seems, would have liked Mexico's image in the United States to be as palatable as possible to *gringo* prejudices. Therefore, the white Californios "are the ones who constitute the healthy part of our race in the United States; they are the ones who . . . because of their conduct, their intelligence and personality are actually necessary for us in that country where they have very scant idea of our history, our customs and our culture" (28 September 1892, 2–3).

An unsigned article a few years later responded interestingly to a movement in Texas to repatriate Mexican immigrants. *El Imparcial* found justification for the apparently racist attitudes of Texans, as the Mexican immigrants there were truly inferior beings: "In the United States, there is no woman, no matter how low in self esteem, who would be capable of entering into relations with Chinese and blacks, yet we know of an infinite number of Mexican women who utterly degrade themselves by maintaining illicit friendships with individuals of those two races"

(12 June 1895, 1). The article ultimately came out in favor of repatriation, proposing that "work and schooling might well regenerate those men and awaken in them love for the fatherland" (3). *Gringos* were not wrong in looking down on Mexicans, because the Mexicans they knew best were indeed worthy of their scorn.

Likewise, Pérez Peña bore no general ill will toward the French, and just as he celebrated U.S. Independence Day in the summer of 1893, he dedicated front-page space to Bastille Day a week and a half later, in which the featured article screamed, "Long live France!" (14 July 1893, 1). Again, the numerous French businesses that advertised in *El Imparcial* (for example, Vicent Toussaint's Restaurant Francés, D. Bastón's Mercería Francesa) undoubtedly helped shape its attitudes.

Interestingly, it must be noted that the fervor of *El Imparcial's* articles on the United States and France hardly compares with the grandiose treatment reserved in the same month of July 1893 for the heroes of Guaymas. Immediately following the aforementioned July Fourth celebration, the journal began publishing a series of "important documents," which were in fact José María Yáñez's official reports on the Raousset campaign (5 July 1893, 2; 6 July, 1–2; 7 July, 2). On 12 July the journal carried a front page story commemorating the 13 July holiday, listing the names of all surviving participants. Then on 14 July (the newspaper did not publish on the thirteenth because of the holiday), Pérez Peña contributed a poem in praise of "the July heroes" (14 July, 2).

However, Pérez Peña's most passionate writings were in a more negative vein. He, like many in late-nineteenth- and early-twentieth-century Sonora, loathed the growing population of Chinese immigrants. Guaymas in particular as an important regional port had always had some Asian presence, but while there had been isolated cases of Asian immigration to the area for decades, Chinese immigrants asserted a significant Asian presence in Sonora beginning in the 1870s. Their immigration to the Mexican borderlands grew in 1882 with the passing of the Chinese Exclusion Act in the United States and expanded further in 1893 with the signing of the Treaty of Friendship and Trade between China and Mexico (Hu-Dehart, "La comunidad china" 195). The Chinese population in Sonora would grow steadily through the second decade of the twentieth century. By 1919, it was the largest foreign resident group in the region, excepting that of U.S. immigrants. In the face of steadily increasing resentment and persecution, the Chinese Sonoran population would then drop off through the 1920s until 1931 when, following a series of nasty racist campaigns to rid the state of Chinese immigrants, they were expelled altogether from Sonora.

While the Chinese were successful in practically taking over certain local industries—for example, they thrived at running shoe and clothing factories—they were unable or perhaps unwilling to integrate themselves into the community, as many European or North American immigrants did. The "trenzudos" (braided ones) or "celestes" (celestials), as they were often referred to, seemed inherently different from the Mexicans in ways that made Sonorans remarkably uncomfortable. The historian Miguel Tinker Salas cites government communiqués that called Chinese "inferior immigrants" who are "prejudicial to natives" (224–25). As a consequence of these attitudes, Chinese in Sonora frequently suffered the kind of violent abuse that today would likely be characterized as racist hate crimes:

> By the late 1890s a newspaper in Magdalena reported that the authorities appeared helpless in preventing violence against Asians. An editorial in the *Correo de Sonora* indicated that for the previous three years, Chinese were being murdered in the district and authorities had brought no one to justice. Even though local officials regularly arrested Mexicans involved in altercations with Asians, violence against the Chinese continued to escalate. (Tinker Salas 228–29)

Thus, Pérez Peña's persecution of the Chinese in *El Imparcial*, a treatment reserved for no other group, is typical of Sonora of the time.[27] While most of the items are short, the titles speak for themselves in terms of their bias: "Demented Chinaman" (28 March 1893, 2), "A Queer People" (5 April 1893, 2), "Crazy Chinaman" (8 August 1893, 2), "Scandalous Chinese" (22 September 1893, 2). These stories reported that opium addiction, cannibalism, fetid odors, adultery, and rampant prostitution, among many other strange and barbarous traits, were typical of Chinese culture.[28] Notwithstanding the regular advertising from the shoe manufacturer San Chong and Company, the clothing and shoe factory Siu Fo Chong and Company, or the shoe store Quon Fo Long and

Company, 1893 and 1894 saw the publication of an especially large quantity of anti-Chinese virulence as President Porfirio Díaz negotiated and signed into law the above-mentioned trade agreement with China.

Pérez Peña worried about the effects of Chinese immigration not only on local culture but also on Mexico's image in the United States, where the Chinese had not been welcome for years. Another article, titled "The Treaty between Mexico and China: Unfavorable Opinion in the American Press," reported that since the treaty would permit Chinese immigration to Mexico, U.S. newspapers, fearing that the newly arriving Chinese might use Mexico as a platform to migrate northward, were raising the issue of a possible war with Mexico (8 August 1894, 2). *El Imparcial* expressed its own outrage—siding with the U.S. press—a few days later: "We have found it strange that the national press has remained silent about a subject that is going to bring us serious harm and even trouble with the United States" ("The Chinese" 11 September 1894, 2–3).

Pérez Peña's writings on the Chinese reflected a preoccupation with national identity, a national identity that could not help but be in dialogue with the United States. This digression was intended to provide some background to the cultural tensions of the borderlands in the late nineteenth century and to help show why the publication of *Heroína* was an important intervention into the representation of Sonora in the context both of national culture and the transnational culture of the borderlands.

Back to Doña Loreto

Above all, Pérez Peña worked hard to promote a positive image of Mexico, especially Sonora, in order to encourage profitable relations with countries like the United States and France. Therefore, when he decided in 1897 to publish his first and only book, and in fact Sonora's first locally published literary book, the dramatic play *Heroína*, he was not concerned with bashing the French or recording a verbal retaliation against expansionist rhetoric in the United States. What did interest him, and quite passionately it would seem, was to reconstruct the battle of Guaymas, focusing on the heroism not only of the Mexicans who defended the city but particularly of local participants who had been marginalized from official histories. While not critical of Yáñez, he clearly felt a need to contest the Mexican general's official telling of the story in order to make it less a struggle between two great men and more a community victory over a foreign interloper in the name of the nation.

For this reason, a few of his supporting players are unknowns, such as Jorge Martinón and Leandro Méndez, who represent local volunteers given short shrift by history; "a townswoman," who comes with her two young sons to volunteer them to fight; and "Old Man Moreno," who despite his advanced age eagerly seeks arms so that he can join in the fray. The dialogue is peppered with names of participants in the battle whom locals in 1897 might have recognized as relatives or neighbors but who are barely mentioned if not passed over entirely by Yáñez, who might have known his own troops' leaders but could not possibly have kept inventory of all of the local volunteers who spontaneously took up arms that afternoon. Interestingly, there is one name that does not appear in Pérez Peña's play: José María Leyva, an omission I will address shortly. Of particular note, however, is the inclusion of two women who, as local legend would have it, played major roles in the day's events: Guadalupe Cubillas and Loreto Encinas de Avilés.[29]

Like Villa, who may well have based his historical anecdote on Pérez Peña's play,[30] Pérez Peña makes Doña Loreto a heroine. At the time she appears, it seems that the town is already in an uproar. Dozens of volunteers, including a whole school of boys, have shown up in General Yáñez's quarters offering their services. She arrives running and screaming, "They're coming, sir! They're coming! The count is wearing a red shirt and they are coming with banners and rifles! They have left the barracks! I have seen them, sir! I have seen them!" (28). In the next scene, she delivers a monologue in which she recites a patriotic prayer. In fact, she is the featured character of the end of the second act. In its last three short scenes, she receives news of the battle from Old Man Moreno, treats the wounded lieutenant Iberri, and finally hears Moreno's reports of what he sees through the window as the Mexicans take first the occupied Díaz house, sending various Frenchmen including the count fleeing into the streets, and then Hotel Sonora, which had been a French stronghold throughout the battle. This last development signals the battle's end: Moreno shouts, "Victory!!!" and then Loreto joins in with him as both fall to their knees, "Thank you, God, thank you!!" and the orchestra breaks into the national anthem as the curtain goes down. Loreto is an Everywoman *guaymense:* Moreno is an eyewitness to the battle, but Loreto hears, along with the audience, his blow by blow description of the action. The audience is meant to identify with Loreto, to react as she does, and to share her every emotion.

Whether Avilés or Cubillas is Pérez Peña's heroine is in the end irrelevant. All *guaymenses* are heroes: military officers, common soldiers, leading citizens, schoolboys, young mothers, society matrons. The author's prologue to the book is telling. He remarks that he has come across documents relating to the 13 July battle and advises that he has chosen to write a play and not a newspaper story in order to reach a broader public. He makes reference to the show's opening night and how gratified he was to hear enthusiastic applause, particularly from two groups: children and women—two groups, it should be noted, that were left out of official history. His play consciously puts such players in the role of protagonists and not minor supporting actors. He uses those who were excluded from official history to rouse more local pride and bring the story closer to home, without detracting from its national importance. Doña Loreto and Doña Guadalupe were players not only in local history but in national history, as Yáñez's monologue of the play's final scene makes clear: "Sonorans . . . may heroism remain without limit in our breasts, and whenever there is danger, let the world know that there is a land, Sonora, whose sons and daughters are a model of honor and patriotism" (43).

Nonetheless, the United States, though never mentioned, plays an important role. *Heroína*, in fact, was born out of a burst of patriotic outrage. In early 1893, an unsigned article appeared in *El Imparcial*, undoubtedly penned by Pérez Peña, titled "Historical Pornographies." In it, the author complained bitterly of the misrepresentation of Mexico in the U.S. press. In this case, the journal in question was not a typical daily or weekly newspaper but a popular men's magazine called the *National Police Gazette*. It specialized in sensationalistic crime stories, updates on the careers of alluring stage actresses, and coverage of the

boxing circuit and other sporting events. The popular illustrated journal stayed in business for well over a century beginning in the 1840s,
entertaining men with stories of sex, scandal, crime, athletic competition, and manly aggression.

Pérez Peña reports reading a story on Raousset in the *National Police
Gazette*. The precise source is most likely the Spanish-language edition
of the journal, which ran for approximately eleven monthly issues in 1893
before abruptly folding and attained significant distribution throughout Mexico and Cuba, in parts of the United States with large Spanish-
speaking populations or links to Latin America, and in a few South
American and Central American countries.[31] The journal was advertised as being "lively, spicy and sensational" (*National Police Gazette* 18
February 1893, 1), and there is no doubt that the well-known story of
Count Gaston de Raousset Boulbon's filibuster invasion of Sonora fit
its criteria. Pérez Peña's reaction to the story was shrill indignation; the
Police Gazette version presented the count's deeds as "gallant and chivalrous" (*El Imparcial* 16 February 1893, 2), making him into a legendary
hero and implicitly condoning his acts. Pérez Peña counters:

> Eyes less accustomed than ours to tears would cry upon reading the
> relation of the errant disgraces occurring in Sonora to the most
> *saintly*, virtuous and likeable gentleman that legend has known . . .
> We would take the famous legend as a laughable joke from a clown
> with his face smeared in white for a town fair if it were an isolated
> case, but other North American newspapers have published such
> extraordinarily colossal nonsense on the same subject, such despicable
> slander, that we are sorry to be unable to write *that's enough* with the
> tip of a shoe dipped in dung rather than with an honorable pen.
> (16 February 1893, 2; emphasis in original)

It was not unusual for Mexican journalists of the era to take offense
at what they found to be outrageously incorrect or biased stories published in U.S. newspapers, but the level of fury in this case was unprecedented in *El Imparcial*. The *Police Gazette* story not only made a hero of
an enemy of Mexico but also reduced Sonora's greatest contribution to
national sovereignty to the tragic culmination of the illustrious career
of a French adventurer, and further, it presumably overlooked the heroism of Mexicans such as José María Yáñez. What for Sonorans was

a major moment of national history, a heroic victory for the Mexican nation, became a forum for exalting the image of a gallant outlaw, as if his military assault on Guaymas was just one more Wild West–style skirmish best suited not for history but for the entertainment of rambunctious boxing fans or worse. For *El Imparcial*, these were "absurdities, like those that are printed only in journals of scandalous *pornography* destined to circulate among libidinous old men, corrupt youngsters or shameless hussies" (16 February 1893, 2; emphasis in original).

It is no surprise that Pérez Peña a few years later published a new version of the battle of Guaymas that glorifies not only *chilango* Yáñez but also the local community, Pérez Peña's own neighbors and readers. His incorporation of what had been taken as largely extrahistorical local lore into his new literary representation of history made an immediate impact on borderlands historiography in Mexico.

Although the play's influence did not carry over into every major work of historiography on the topic—important works including those of Wyllys, Sobarzo, and Trueba, for example, exhibit no familiarity whatsoever with Pérez Peña's version of events—it did have an immediate and important influence. Pedro Ulloa's 1907 commemorative pamphlet on the battle of Guaymas (republished in 1954) tells of the local civilian mobilization in a form that practically plagiarizes Pérez Peña, listing, in fact, only those names of locals included among the play's cast—the Spanish schoolmaster (now Jorge Martión),[32] Leandro Méndez, Jesús Preciado, Sr. Basozábal, Miguel Ramón Peralta, Juan Casillas, Sr. Huerta, and even "a townswoman, whose name was not recorded by tradition nor by History" with her young sons (49). An interesting difference is the inclusion of two names not mentioned by Pérez Peña, those of two students from the local school, whose last names were La Cruz and Leyva (49). José María Leyva's role in the battle and its retelling will be discussed later. In addition, both Loreto de Avilés's (here "la Sra. Doña Loreto Avilés") warning (49) and Guadalupe Cubillas's disarming of the count (53) are related faithfully. In 1941, both women were featured prominently in a history textbook.[33] Some other sources, however, would openly take issue with Pérez Peña's populist revisionism.

Some years later, in an article by the Sonoran historian Ramiro de Garza,[34] the author cites a witness once removed from the events of

1854, "an elderly and honorable neighbor from Guaymas" who knew numerous witnesses and participants in the battle. *El señor* Torcuato Marcor complains vehemently about the "obstinacy among people with little inclination to investigate historic realities" (Garza, "El caso" 376) in their insistence on highlighting Doña Loreto's role in the battle of Guaymas. "Nothing could be further from the truth," maintains Marcor. He notes that this error was promulgated first by the aforementioned Arturo Jáuregui y Bario, a source deemed questionable because he was from Mexico City and not Sonora, and second by Aurelio Pérez Peña, whose "drama-sketch enhance[d] the figure of the referenced lady to the point of exaggeration" (377). He further notes that Yáñez's associates were unanimously in agreement that the dramatic last-minute warning by Encinas de Avilés never occurred. Yáñez, according to Marcor's sources, was well informed and already preparing for battle because his spy, the Jewish baker for the French troops, was keeping him carefully updated as to Raousset's movements.

Garza, who had clearly not read *Heroína* himself, confines his arguments to Villa's 1937 biographical sketch. His principal concern is that historiography that does not stick to the facts of "official history" will be harmful to students. He recognizes the importance of an impulse that began to gain momentum around the second quarter of the twentieth century to develop a regional historiography ("to bring to light all of the past of our local homeland *[patria chica],*" 377) and to better disseminate information about Sonora's past to the Sonoran population. However, he is alarmed by the tendency, even among prominent historians such as Villa, to "falsify historic truth" (378).

This feeling is echoed, albeit less stridently, by Laureano Calvo Berber, who mentions neither Villa nor Pérez Peña directly but insists that "there is no way that it could have been the isolated news that Doña Loreto Encinas de Avilés is said to have supplied that saved" the Mexicans (*Nociones de la historia de Sonora* 184). He goes on, "To accept such an assertion without reservations is tantamount to an assault on the recognized prestige and the unrefuted expertise of the superior military chief" (184).

I have argued that official history's tendency to exclude female protagonists allows revisionists to deploy such protagonists—whose reputed roles in local events are kept alive by local, unofficial, oral history—to diverse ends. Garza is no doubt correct that they distort official history, although he might not recognize that their exclusion is another distortion. Nor would it be difficult to argue that he, perhaps along with his own sketchy source Torcuato Marcor, is plagued by a sexist bias when he grumbles: "And every female character who passes through the yellowing pages of a Sonoran book, like *la señora* Avilés or the distinguished lady Doña Guadalupe Cubillas, is turned into yet another heroine" ("El caso" 378). The reference to the women as heroines would almost seem to allude directly to Pérez Peña except that there is no evidence anywhere in the article that Garza has read or even knows the title of the play. In any case, his complaint is not about literary or dramatic works but about historiography: "All this would be a 'peccata minuta' if it were only a question of a discourse at a literary reading or a toast at a commemorative festival, but unfortunately these exaggerations are being taught to schoolchildren, who accept them as dogma" (378).

It is ironic, then, that the contemporary historian who wishes to understand how figures such as Avilés and Cubillas came to be incorporated into a more or less official historiography sees that Garza is correct: literature and even commemorative public discourses have played important roles in reshaping official history, as have oral history, local legend, and gossip. They are, after all, often the only available sources capable of responding with authority to the "falsehoods" of official history.

Francisco López Encinas devotes an entire chapter to Avilés in his 1985 book *Sonora, frontera codiciada*, relying primarily upon Villa for his information; Villa had quoted from Arturo Jáuregui's 1886 discourse, which Villa claimed the historian Horacio Sobarzo held in his private archive.[35] López Encinas further amplifies the story by interviewing Oralia Avilés de Ferreira, great-grandniece of Doña Loreto. According to Avilés de Ferreira, Loreto lived in front of the house where Raousset was staying and very near the barracks of the French troops. She intentionally kept her eyes and ears open. Family legend states that Doña Loreto, having figured out that an attack was brewing, went running in search of Yáñez with her daughter Amalia in her arms. The French tried to detain her, but she escaped them, even as they shot at her, by hiding behind a tree. She then left Amalia behind at the house of the family of

Don Torcuato Huerta and continued running, the French hot on her tail, until she reached the Mexican barracks. Writes López Encinas, "She heroically saved the Mexican troops from a surprise attack; with her action she risked her life to contribute to the preservation of national territory" (103); he then concludes his treatment of this heroine with a discourse pronounced by a former governor of Sonora, Luis Encinas, recognizing Loreto's role during the festivities of the centenary of the battle of Guaymas in 1954, the same year in which Sobarzo and Trueba's histories excluded Loreto once again. More recently, local historians have unearthed lost documents such as Avilés's 1889 obituary to further make the case for the inclusion of a worthy figure who has been "ignored, even by many historians."[36]

Perhaps the most ironic treatment of Avilés occured shortly before the publication of López Encinas's history, in a 1984 Sunday supplement to a Hermosillo newspaper (ironically named *El Imparcial*).[37] It includes two articles commemorating the battle of Guaymas. One is a reprint of Eduardo Villa's oft-cited profile. The other is an article by Erasmo Gómez Araujo, an expanded version of an article he had written for a similar Sunday supplement story in 1982. While he adds information to what he had offered two years earlier, and despite the fact that the Villa article appears just one page earlier, he does not mention any female protagonists.

To sum up, Doña Loreto came to symbolize the patriotism of the women of Guaymas, as well as that of all the citizens of Guaymas that history forgot. She represents the role of the local in the national and the ability of the local to resist exclusion from the national. Moreover, she is an icon of the everyday heroism of *sonorenses* that made the failure of Gaston de Raousset Boulbon's contemptible misadventure inevitable. However, her rise to the status of heroine has sometimes been construed as an affront to the image of Yáñez and old-school historiography that sees only great men as protagonists.

One Final Hero of Guaymas

Of all the once-marginalized Mexican protagonists of the Raousset incident that have danced in and around the event's historiography for the past hundred and fifty years, there is one whose continued exclusion from major historical studies, including recent ones such as that of López Encinas, or even literary dramatizations such as Escobar Valdez's recent novella, remains especially puzzling. It is puzzling because authors focusing on the Raousset invasion inevitably omit him, while biographers of his own life or historians of events of which he was a leading protagonist rarely fail to mention his participation in the battle of Guaymas. I refer here to the great Yaqui leader José María Leyva, better known as Cajeme (see Figure 9).

In brief, Cajeme is known for leading the Yaquis in a period of resistance to Mexican control from 1875 until his capture in 1887, after which he was put to death. The Yaquis were one of those borderlands tribes that had never really been conquered by either the Spanish or the Mexican creoles. They got along with Mexicans without assimilating into mainstream national culture. While many Yaquis lived among white and *mestizo* Sonorans—for example, there was a substantial Yaqui population in the city of Guaymas in the 1850s (Wyllys 82)—and were in fact respected as hard workers and as good soldiers in the Mexican armed forces, they preserved their cultural identity to a much greater degree than other groups, and, more important, maintained control of their ancestral lands in southern Sonora (Martínez, *Troublesome Border* 74–76).

When Cajeme came into power among the Yaquis, he declared their independence from Mexico and expelled foreigners—including nonindigenous Mexicans—from Yaqui territory (Hu-Dehart, *Yaqui Resistance* 93; Figueroa Valenzuela, "Los indios" 151). He was known as an astute political leader and military strategist and led a robust resistance for years. When he was at last captured, a local politician and journalist, Ramón Corral, made a point of interviewing him before he was killed, revealing in the biography he culled from these death row discussions, first published in the state newspaper *La Constitución* in 1887, a certain admiration for his adversary that has played a significant role in the construction of Cajeme as a major hero in local history. Corral's position is paradoxical since he had "considered the Yaqui war a civilizing crusade," yet he produced a most "sensitive description of Cajeme" (Ruiz, "Genesis" 201).

The construction of Cajeme's image in historiography is the result of

Figure 9. Cajeme (José María Leyva). Courtesy of Arizona Historical Society, Tucson; Photographic Archives: Out of State—Mexico: Soldiers, Wars, and Revolution.

an unintended collaboration between the subject of interview (Cajeme) and the author (Corral). It is impossible to say to what extent either one manipulated facts, although a recent study by Palemón Zavala Castro interestingly attempts to contrast the likely Yaqui-style thinking of Cajeme with the creole perspective of Corral. Miguel Tinker Salas claims that "[b]y depicting Cajeme as a noble figure, Corral hoped to coopt the defiant character of the Yaquis" (217). What complicates any interpretation of Cajeme's life, including the version of it constructed in Corral's biography, is the fact that Cajeme is, perhaps more than any other personage of the Raousset story, a hybrid, a shape shifter, a product of the borderlands. Corral may have manipulated what Cajeme told him to suit his own purposes, but Cajeme's intelligence should not be underestimated: he just as likely put a spin on his life story with the intention of manipulating Corral's interpretation. Cajeme, after all, had the special advantage of having lived and participated socially and politically in both the Yaqui and the creole worlds, exemplifying in many ways Mignolo's concept of border gnosis.

Young José María Leyva had been educated in his adolescence in a creole household, albeit in the role of a servant. But his experience in the service of Cayetano Navarro—the local official who tried to rescue Lola Casanova a few years earlier (see chapter 3)—led him eventually into the Mexican armed forces where he engaged in several battles against the Yaquis,[38] earning the rank of captain. Later, he achieved such confidence with Mexican authorities that he was sent by them to be mayor (*Alcalde Mayor*) of the Yaquis "with the goal of keeping the tribe pacific through the influence of a chief of their own race, who with his skills could dominate them while remaining faithful to the government that gave him control of the [Yaqui] River" (Corral 154). The government had not counted on Leyva reverting to a Yaqui identity, taking up the Yaqui name Cajeme (meaning "he who does not drink"), and becoming perhaps the most fierce and astute rebel leader in their history of conflicts with Mexico.

In 1849, at the age of twelve, young Leyva had gone with his father to Alta California in the wave of emigration brought about by the gold rush. There, he "fell into the milieu of Joaquín Murrieta" (Zavala Castro 111). Soon afterward, he returned to Sonora where his father got him a position in the house of the Navarro family. According to Corral, Leyva was then enrolled in the local school run by the Spaniard Jorge Martinón.[39] He was there in 1854 when the French invaded, and, like any patriot, the young Leyva took up arms and joined in the defense of Guaymas. There is no way to verify any of the information that Cajeme gave to Ramón Corral about this period of his life. Yáñez, for example, did not name local boys, particularly indigenous ones, nor did any other creole witnesses see any value in recognizing the participation of individual Indians, despite the fact that a Yaqui brigade of the army likely played an important role in the Raousset's defeat (Wyllys 211). Therefore, two conflicting historiographies have developed: one based on Yáñez's official story in which Cajeme did not participate in the battle of Guaymas, and another based on Corral's official biography in which Cajeme decidedly did.

And these stories have tended not to intersect. Even as the incorporation of figures like Loreto Encinas de Avilés and Guadalupe Cubillas has caused controversy and reshaped official historiography, the figure of Cajeme has not even come up in debate. One rare source that acknowledges both Yáñez and Corral is Jorge Murillo Chisem's history of Guaymas, which concludes a long narration on the details of the battle—based on Yáñez but including references to both Avilés and Cubillas—with a list of known participants in the defense of Guaymas that includes ninety-six names (of the three hundred reported participants), the last one being José María Leyva (138–41).

However, the source that had been to date the great vindicator of the little guy, Pérez Peña's *Heroína*, showed itself in the end to be as racist as the author's newspaper's treatment of the Chinese. Even though Corral's biography of Cajeme had come out a decade before the publication of the play, the role of the young José María Leyva was not rescued. True, it was hardly the time for Sonorans like Pérez Peña to want to attribute even a piece of the credit for the most grandiose of achievements of local history to a Yaqui, let alone a great Yaqui rebel chief. In the 1890s, after all, war with the Yaquis raged on as Mexico demanded control of their fertile territory for private development projects; the Yaquis were officially scorned as *indios bárbaros* in the era of their most cruel persecution. The Porfiriato executed a crackdown on indigenous

insurgency that inflicted the punishment of deportation to other parts
of Mexico where Yaquis were virtually enslaved; at some moments, the
ruthlessness of the campaigns reached the proportions of what appeared
to be nothing less than genocide (Figueroa "Los indios" 161). To many
Sonorans, the Yaquis had been a nuisance for long enough and it was
now time to break their will and beat them into submission. In 1894,
Pérez Peña had celebrated their imminent "pacification" as "of the greatest importance to the progress of Sonora" ("Carta" iii). For him, the
Yaquis were "the enemy" (*El Imparcial* 19 September 1892, 2).

This is not to say that Corral's Cajeme was swiftly put aside. In the
same book where Pérez Peña had celebrated the defeat of the Yaquis in
his prologue, Dávila, describing an 1886 battle, waxes about how the
Yaquis under Cajeme "heroically resisted the advancement of the national
armed forces, making supernatural efforts to hold firm in their trenches"
(*Sonora* 312). Still, his overall approach is condescending, his greatest wish
regarding Sonora's indigenous people being that the government "dedicate the attention necessary to the indigenous race, seeking the means
to regenerate it" (325).

Pérez Peña's *Imparcial* exhibits a similar attitude, publishing a long
treatise in multiple installments, signed by "Espartaco," titled "La re-
generación de la raza indígena," promoting "education" as the key to the
problem (15 August 1893, 2). While Pérez Peña's main concern overall
seems to be promoting a better life for bourgeois *sonorenses* through
increased economic development, in an early article (signed by Eliseo)
titled "Costumbres indios" he reports on various traditions of Yaquis
and Mayos in order "to awaken the curiosity of aficionados to research
in the greatest possible detail what remains of the traditional customs
of *our race*" (10 September 1892, 2; emphasis mine). The journal also
reports frequently on the abuses suffered by the laborers of el Boleo, a
copper mining company located in Baja California whose workers were
"almost exclusively . . . Yaqui Indians" (Cota Meza 106; see, for example,
El Imparcial 8 March 1893, 1). *El Imparcial* argues that the poor treatment of Yaqui workers has the undesirable consequence of inciting rebellion (14 March 1893, 1). Pérez Peña is glad to accept Yaquis as part
of Sonoran society, as long as they are peaceful and do not interfere
with progress.

In 1902, Fortunato Hernández copied word for word Corral's description of Cajeme as an "Indian warrior who recalls to us the legendary heroes of the epoch of Xicoténcatl" and whose fame "has acquired colossal proportions" (Corral 149; Hernández 123). But if Corral had underscored that Cajeme had "told him of many of the incidents that occurred in Yaqui territory during his reign, placing great emphasis on his patriotism as a Mexican," as he protected tribal land from exploitation by *gringos* (191), in 1905, Francisco Troncoso, like Hernández deriving his information largely from Corral, makes him out to be less of an epic hero and certainly not a patriot, but instead a treacherous adversary of "both the government of Sonora and of the national federation" (64).

In the United States, two different biographies were in circulation in the 1880s. In the first, Cajeme was born in 1843 to Pantaleón Leiva Cajeme and Hilaria Bultemea (*Tombstone Daily Record and Epitaph* 18 October 1885, 3), while in the second Fernando Leyva and Juana Pérez gave birth to him in 1837 (*Tucson Daily Star* 15 May 1887, 4). In this latter case, after traveling to the United States, his father sent him to school in Guaymas; in the former, he was a teenage runaway who "refused to work," preferring to "scour the deep forests with his bow and arrows," a wild Indian. In the second story, undoubtedly based on Corral's biography, he participates in the defense of Guaymas in 1854, while in the earlier story, he does not. Cajeme is "savage" *(Epitaph)* or "clever" *(Star)*, but never both in the same biographical sketch.

With time, however, Cajeme's heroic image came to take a more fixed shape. Once the Yaquis were defeated and no longer a threat to the economic progress of the state, Cajeme was rescued and reconstructed again into another indigenous hero of the national pantheon. In 1948, Armando Chávez Camacho brought the character to life in an award winning *indigenista* novel *(Cajeme)*. The gesture was not isolated, and in fact Cajeme, as he is remembered today, has in many ways grown directly out of the hero making and nationalist positioning performed by Corral in 1887.

In the twenty-first century, Cajeme is a regional hero of indigenous power and resistance. Alejandro Figueroa Valenzuela writes: "Cajeme— along with the Yaquis in general—was reassumed into dominant non Indian society as if he represented the root of Sonoran strength" ("José

María Leyva" 31). This revisionism lauds Cajeme alongside the very creole military leaders who sought to destroy him. Figueroa sees a certain
hypocrisy in Sonoran culture, a culture that fancies itself whiter than
that of other parts of the country. Nonetheless,

> Sonorans . . . have reinforced their identity by creating and giving
> content to symbols such as those of Cajeme and the Yaquis; with
> these two symbols as a bulwark, Sonorans imagine themselves to be
> distinct from other Mexicans and they strive, as they did in colonial
> times, to maintain their difference. ("José María Leyva" 32)

Cajeme gives a name to a city, to monuments, to streets, schools, and
social organizations in Sonora.

Corral and Cajeme's collaborative reconstruction of Cajeme's life has
won out. However, Cajeme's version of history must not be confused
with that of the Yaquis in general. María de los Ángeles Orduño García
cites Yaqui sources that deny Cajeme's heroism, claiming that Cajeme's
negotiations with the Mexican government were done "on his own"
and not in representation of the Yaquis, many of whom distrusted him
and saw him as an outsider. His career ended in shame when "Cajeme
tired and fell ill. He fled to San José de Guaymas to hide. A Yaqui woman
discovered him there and sold him to the whites" (105–6).

In the end, it is quite clear that Yaqui history and Mexican history
(whether national or regional) do not easily intersect. Even when a hybrid
character like Cajeme plays prominently to both audiences, there is no
agreement as to what he should represent, or—as we have seen in the case
of the Raousset invasion—whether he is even worthy of representation.

Conclusions

Alfonso Iberri recalls how cosmopolitan Guaymas was in the latter half
of the nineteenth century, listing all the examples he can recall of foreigners living in the city. The list goes on for two pages and includes immigrants from the United States, France, Germany, Spain, China, Italy,
the Philippines, Norway, Algeria, Guatemala, Poland, Austria, Ecuador,
Chile, Sweden, Portugal, Canada, England, Peru, and the Middle East
(71–73). Sonora's multiracial citizens migrated north with the gold rush.

Sonora also welcomed immigrants who respected national sovereignty such as Juan Robinson but rejected *gringo* annexationists and French filibusters and had little trouble with the presence of foreign businesses in the state (as long as they were not Chinese). Border dwellers often lived multiple identities (Cajeme) and held complex, even conflictive opinions (Pérez Peña) with respect to the U.S.–Mexico relations that determined so much of the region's history in the latter half of the nineteenth century. The presence of French, Chinese, or even local indigenous groups in the region further complicates the national and racial dynamic well beyond the cliché of antagonism between Mexicans and *gringos*.

Old-fashioned histories of great men, such as Yáñez's relation of the battle of Guaymas, attempted to fix a static and even simplistic vision of local culture within a strictly national context. Oral history, journalism, literature, theater, and even commemorative toasts have helped open dialogue about what constitutes history, how it is shaped, and who its actors can be. Personages once marginalized from official history, but kept alive in other forms, reinsert themselves strategically to reshape local history and reposition it within not only a national but an international context, most frequently and most appropriately a transamerican one that positions Sonora not merely as a piece of Mexico but as a part of the supernational culture of the U.S.–Mexico borderlands of which its local history is inevitably an important product.

CHAPTER FIVE

OF SEDITION
AND SPIRITISM:
LA SANTA DE CABORA

A FINAL BORDERLANDS ICON emerged in the public spotlight in late 1889 from rural Sonora. Identified as a nurse, a witch, a revolutionary, a traitor, a miracle worker, a fraud, a protofeminist, a hysteric, a mystic seer, an entertainer, a lover, an innocent, and a saint, Teresa Urrea, better known as La Santa de Cabora, was a woman of unprecedented will and charisma. A *mestiza* bastard child raised in poverty until adolescence by her indigenous single mother, and other maternal relatives, she somehow not only managed to penetrate her wealthy father's privileged world but also achieved enormous fame and influence in her own right. Many, including Mexican president Porfirio Díaz, would admire or fear the authority she came to exert on her followers. Cast into the public eye, she became public property, and her image took on a life of its own. While at times she certainly succeeded in manipulating it, she was only one of many who did so.

La insólita historia de la Santa de Cabora

Teresa Urrea's life story has taken on so many contradictory forms in its many retellings since she first became famous throughout North America in the early 1890s that it is impossible to recount as a series of factual events. It is perhaps not surprising that the most complete and authoritative text on this remarkable woman is the novel *La insólita historia de la Santa de Cabora* by Brianda Domecq.[1] Many would agree with the author when she states that "the character from the novel today turns out to be much more real and alive to me" than the Teresa Urrea constructed from historic documents (Domecq, "Teresa Urrea" 12). The critic Deborah Shaw agrees in an article in which she sets out "to demonstrate how the Teresa of fiction reaches levels of profundity and complexity denied the historic personage" (285); and Gloria Prado finds that Domecq "fills, through fiction, the blank spaces and omissions in the historical sources she found" (171).

My interest here lies not in determining what Teresa was really like, what she really did, or what she really thought. Teresa Urrea is a cultural icon of the borderlands, and what is important to this study are her significations in the many different contexts in which her public persona became eminent both during her lifetime and in the century since she died. As the cultural critic José Manuel Valenzuela Arce puts it: "The myth becomes detached from the personage, like clothing stripped from a body, and is transported, reinvented, and for that reason the character is not as important as its popular impact" ("Introducción" 17). A summary sketch of how Teresa's life has generally been portrayed will help to introduce the intricacies of representation to which her image has been subjected.

She was born Niña García Nona María Rebeca Chávez (Holden 10) in Ocorini, Sinaloa, in October 1873 to the wealthy *hacendado* Tomás Urrea and a young Tehueco Indian woman, Cayetana Chávez.[2] Being an illegitimate daughter of an employee on Urrea's ranch, she was raised in her early years by her young mother and an aunt. Tomás Urrea was forced to leave Sinaloa for political reasons and moved in 1880, with most of his family and employees (though not his wife), to another of his properties, the San Antonio de Cabora ranch in Sonora (Domecq, "Teresa Urrea" 15–16).

By the late 1880s, Teresa's mother had left the ranch, impelling Teresa to seek the protection of her father in 1888. At this time he invited her to live in his house and she began to use his last name. In late 1889, Teresa suffered some type of cataleptic attack that rendered her unconscious for thirteen days and then sent her into a trance for several months. Afterward, she began to heal the sick and handicapped. Her apparently miraculous powers soon attracted great attention, and people from all over the area began to make pilgrimages to the Cabora ranch to meet or seek treatment from the young woman. Moreover, since she and her followers believed that her powers were a gift from God, many of them identified her as a living saint. From this time, she was known as Santa Teresa de Cabora (Domecq, "Teresa Urrea" 17–19).

Among the pilgrims who gathered daily at the ranch were many local Yaqui and Mayo Indians, as well as other peasants and even a few wealthier Mexicans. Some accepted her as a Catholic miracle worker; some believed what she represented lurked behind a Catholic facade in indigenous traditions; some understood her powers through the perspective of spiritism, a mystic belief system in vogue at the time in Europe and the Americas;[3] still others viewed her as an alternative or even oppositional icon to what they saw as despotic Catholicism. Urrea, in addition to her healing powers, had also become known for preaching social justice, openly criticizing both the Mexican government and the Catholic Church for their mistreatment of the poor and disenfranchised. The Cabora ranch soon became "a point of reunion not only for the infirm, but also for political malcontents who met there, exchanged opinions or laid plans" (Domecq, "Teresa Urrea" 19).

Urrea was not the only "living saint" who had been adopted by locals, who felt alienated by heavy-handed Catholic authorities, into the scheme of everyday religious practice in the northwestern borderlands. Indeed, the proliferation of such figures—immensely powerful among their worshipers—began to worry authorities, who rounded up a sizable number of "living saints" in the early 1890s, some of whom were killed (Aguirre 120). Teresa was not arrested, most likely because of her father's wealth and social position (Domecq, "Teresa Urrea" 20–21).

However, when rebellions began to occur in her name, things quickly changed. In May 1892, a band of Mayo Indians staged an armed insurrection in the town of Navojoa, Sonora, rallying to the war cry "Viva la Santa Teresa de Cabora." Meanwhile, a group of rebels from the town of Tomóchic in the state of Chihuahua had traveled to Cabora to meet Teresa. The government was following what they perceived to be seditious activities among this group, and federal troops soon became involved in armed skirmishes with the *tomoches* or *tomochitecos*, as they were called (Domecq, "Teresa Urrea" 21–31).

At this time, Teresa Urrea and her father were arrested, held briefly in Guaymas, and then exiled to Arizona. There, first in Nogales and later in other towns near the border, they settled, and Teresa continued receiving throngs of ill and admiring pilgrims, almost all Mexicans. Soon after her exile, the townspeople of Tomóchic engaged in a major insurrection; among the many reasons for their rebellion was that local church officials refused to allow them to worship the image of Santa Teresa de Cabora in the town's Catholic church. Soon federal troops laid siege to the town, and the long and bloody battle that resulted ended in Tomóchic's utter demolition and the annihilation of most of its residents. Dramatized in a novel by the federal soldier Heriberto Frías (*Tomóchic* 1893), this rebellion made heroes out of the rebels and went down in history as a major precursor to the Mexican revolution of 1910. Although La Santa de Cabora had already been exiled at the time of the uprising, the Tomóchic story would forever be associated with the name of Teresa Urrea.

Urrea, while in exile in the United States, also became increasingly involved with Lauro Aguirre, a Mexican journalist originally from Guaymas who had dedicated himself to instigating in any way possible the overthrow of the Díaz government. He worked primarily out of El Paso, Texas, where he published first *El Independiente* and then *El Progresista* from the mid-1890s to the early 1900s. The Urreas at one point moved to El Paso to work more closely with Aguirre (Domecq, "Teresa Urrea" 32–40).

In August 1896, while the Urreas were living in El Paso, a group of Yaqui rebels attacked Nogales, Sonora, as part of a plot to supposedly spur a larger scale rebellion. Among the articles found on the bodies of several of the rebels who were killed in the skirmish were documents implicating Teresa Urrea. Specifically, a letter mentioning La Santa de Cabora and a photograph of Urrea once again indicated that she was, if not an instigator of the insurrection, nonetheless an inspiration to the rebels. While Mexican authorities pressed to have her extradited for prosecution, U.S. authorities could find no direct evidence against her and refused to cooperate (Domecq, "Teresa Urrea" 40–44).

After this incident, the Urreas returned to live in Arizona, distancing themselves from Aguirre and his politics. In 1900, Urrea became involved with a young Mexican miner named Guadalupe Rodríguez, who persuaded her, against her father's wishes, to marry him. He soon seemed to go crazy and threatened to kill her. The day after their wedding he was arrested, and a few years later she divorced him, claiming that he had been a spy sent by the Díaz government to assassinate her (Domecq, "Teresa Urrea" 44–46).

Immediately following Rodríguez's arrest and subsequent internment in a mental institution, she went to California, where she received considerable attention from the San Francisco press. She was soon hired by a "medical company" to tour the United States performing her miraculous healing in public auditoriums. Since she did not speak English, she had a friend from Arizona send her bilingual son to translate for her. She and the young man soon fell in love and eventually had two daughters together (Domecq, "Teresa Urrea" 46).

Within a few years, Teresa became disillusioned with her work, extricated herself from her contract, and returned—without her young common-law husband but with her two daughters—to Arizona, where she used the money she had earned to build a small hospital in the town of Clifton. A few years later, on 11 January 1906, she died of tuberculosis at the age of thirty-three.[4]

Urrea, launched as a public figure when the borderlands and Mexico City press got wind of her local popularity in the last weeks of 1889, did not die in the public eye in 1906. She lived on in newspaper and magazine stories, novels, local and national histories, and eventually in biographical texts published in English and Spanish, on both sides of the border. The uses made of her image during her lifetime often reflect the important social issues of the borderlands at the turn of the century. This was, of course, a moment when revolutionary dissent was brewing in Mexico, while in the United States imperialist energies were being directed toward Latin America in a concrete fashion with the greatest intensity since the war with Mexico—although this time U.S. attentions were directed mainly toward the Caribbean. Issues of race, class, religion, national integrity, land rights, economic development, and gender roles played out in the many interpretations of the Santa de Cabora legend, as they would continue to do for decades to come.

The Birth of a Legend: 1889–92

Once Teresa Urrea's healing powers became known in late 1889 and people began to flock to the Cabora ranch to meet with her, her fame quickly spread, attracting the attention of both believers and nonbelievers from Sonora and beyond. Reports appeared in the Mexico City press as early as December of that year. One of the first was on 21 December in *El Monitor Republicano*.[5] The modern journalists of the capital were not easily convinced of Teresa's miraculous gifts, as is revealed in the headline that introduced her to its urban readership, "The Supposed Saint of Cabora." The report states that "superstitious people have declared her a saint, saying that she cures the blind, the crippled, lepers, etc. with dirt, which is false. They list an infinite number of miracles, all of which are fictitious." The story shows an apparent concern for her ignorant victims: "It is believed that someone is advising the charlatan with the goal of exploiting and cheating her believers, taking advantage of the ideas that delirium excites in their heads."[6]

In January 1890, despite its skepticism concerning her abilities, the same newspaper sent a reporter to Sonora to investigate firsthand. Mario Gill cites an article that appeared in the 3 January edition, which included what would become a legendary story of a balding pilgrim who showed up on Don Tomás Urrea's ranch looking for "la Santa de Cabora." Don Tomás was still skeptical of his daughter's abilities at this point and was not happy about the throngs who were arriving daily and camping out on his property. "Santa my foot! My daughter will be a saint the day that you start growing back your hair," he barked. A little while later, Don Tomás was stunned to see the same man coming out of Teresa's room sporting the beginnings of a new and very full head of hair. This story also spread Teresa's putative doctrine that "all acts of the government and clergy are evil" (quoted in Gill, *La doncella* 8). It furthermore reports another legendary story of a blind and deaf man who came to Teresa seeking help. When Teresa told him, "You have eyes that do not see. You have ears that cannot hear," he in fact understood her and began to hear even better when she mixed some cotton wads with dirt and placed them in his ears (quoted in Vanderwood 169).

El Monitor Republicano's apparent motive in repeating these stories was to show just how ignorant and ingenuous Teresa's believers were. An anonymous Mexico City reporter did, in fact, interview Teresa and claimed to have seen her "in one of her cataleptic or hypnotic moments" (quoted in Domecq, " Teresa Urrea"18), but he did not grant her space to tell her story in her own words and was not shy about repeating rumors of Teresa's reputedly lurid love life. He related two variations of a story about Teresa's passionate love affair with a miner named Millán from nearby Baroyeca, in which her first seizure occurred either after being raped by him or after catching him having sexual relations with another woman. Following something of a screaming tantrum, she fainted and then "declared herself a saint, inspired by God."[7]

El Monitor Republicano's investigative account concludes with a manifesto of scientific skepticism representative of the positivist doctrine promoted by the modernizing government of Porfirio Díaz:

> It is certain that she is not a saint, but the result of the highest ignorance. There is no catalepsy, no hypnosis, only a young girl imprisoned by nervous attacks and a multitude of imbeciles who pay her tribute because of their lack of intelligence. Saints do not belong to these times; their age has passed, and fortunately for the honor of civilization and progress, they will never return. (quoted in Vanderwood 174; translation his)

The skepticism of *El Monitor Republicano* contrasts with the sarcasm of *El Siglo XIX*, which argued that in the midst of a flu epidemic Santa Teresa should be persuaded "of the utility of a trip to Mexico City" since Mexico was "greatly lacking in saints" (4 February 1890, 3). In short, these early representations portrayed her as both a fascinating social phenomenon and a possible social problem for the superstitious and gullible *provincianos* of Sonora.

The attention paid by Mexico City journals heightened a few months later when they learned that parishioners in Guaymas were asking Sonora's Bishop Herculano to bless images of Santa Teresa de Cabora as if she were a Catholic saint. Paul Vanderwood paraphrases a report from

El Diario del Hogar of 23 October 1890: "By then an entrepreneur named Fermín Tapico had sold for fifty centavos each thousands of such images in Sonora, and more rolled off the printing press every day. In a surge of disgust the bishop ripped off his cassock and angrily swept it like a majestic broom through the pile of icons to be blessed" (176). Urrea had become more than a local sideshow; errant Catholics were treating her as a legitimate saint. She was challenging the authority of the Catholic Church with more than rhetoric; she was insinuating herself into the belief system of many Catholics of Sonora. Sophisticated Mexico City readers, of course, knew better.

Other Mexico City journals took her less seriously, calling her "a hysteric of the mystic genre," reporting that "she goes off with God, speaks to Saint Peter about you, and exchanges letters with the Holy Spirit," and adding that "she sells secrets for extirpating calluses, fulminates anathemas against Catholic priests, and eats dirt topped with tomato" (*El Siglo XIX* 9 January 1890, quoted in Domecq, "Teresa Urrea" 19). Still, it is clear that, from the very beginning of her public life at the Cabora ranch, she was to have a national reputation, as evidenced by the fact that around this time José Guadalupe Posada took an interest in her, illustrating a *corrido* dedicated to her in which federal agents carry her off, tied to a cross, while her supporters rally in rebellion (see Figure 10). On the other hand, since her divine mission did not coincide with the image of Mexico as the modern, progressive, and rational nation that the ruling elites of Mexico City wished to promote, they—unlike the popular classes whose interests were represented in the works of Posada and who embraced La Niña de Cabora as a new icon of popular culture—wrote her off, at least at first, as a hysteric and a fraud, a product of the ignorance of the Indians of the borderlands.

Through 1892, *El Monitor Republicano* continued to treat her with irony, informing readers that "the so called Santa de Cabora has managed to get rich with the miraculous healings that, according to common folk, she performs. So it is not so bad, the occupation of saint" (18 February 1892, 3, quoted in Romero 144). This report was stridently contested by General Refugio González, founding editor of *La Ilustración Espírita*, a few days later in a letter to the editor of *El Monitor Republicano*, reprinted in several different journals. He insisted that Teresa never charged for her work, and that her father had been forced to open up his ranch to provide lodging for the many pilgrims who came to visit. He added, "As for the portraits, . . . thousands have been sold—not by her, but by American speculators."[8] In fact, around this time, *El Monitor Republicano* began to give in a little, admitting: "The different versions recounted about the heroine are contradictory, but what stands out is the fact that many of her treatments are effected by suggestion and the laying of hands, exactly the way in which Dr. Charlot describes

Figure 10. "La Santa de Cabora." Illustration of the corrido *by José Guadalupe Posada. Courtesy of Editorial RM.*

the famous hypnotists." In the end, the journal began to wonder if the positivist science of the day would be so quick to dismiss her acts: "For us this is an admirable case of a medium, worthy of study through the formal observation of science" (26 April 1893, 3, quoted in Romero 145).

Meanwhile, in Sonora, it would seem that she was something of an embarrassment. There is no evidence of any coverage of Urrea in the state's official newspaper of the period, *La Constitución*, prior to 1892. Unfortunately, most of Sonora's early independent newspapers have been lost, and there is little evidence among what little remains of early Sonoran reports on the activities at Cabora. After *El Imparcial* of Guaymas broke the story in December 1889 (see *El Siglo XIX* 2 January 1890, 3), coverage did not appear to be a top priority for the local press. One early item did appear in Hermosillo's *El Sábado* on 28 December 1889, claiming that Teresa Urrea was selling a concoction of soil and cooking oil as a holy remedy, and that she was charging her pilgrims outrageous prices for basic food supplies.[9] It further observed that her followers "claimed to feel relief, despite continuing to be as crippled as before" (quoted in *El Diario del Hogar* 10 January 1890, 3). Another early Sonoran report in *El Eco del Valle* of Ures was titled "The So-Called Saint" and mentions a homeless man who had been "an epileptic or semi-invalid" and who came home from Cabora in much-improved condition. This time the article, published several months after that of *El Sábado*, admits that la Santa de Cabora may indeed have some kind of "magnetic power" (reprinted in *El Fronterizo* of Tucson 9 May 1890, 2). However, *El Sábado* went on rejecting such ideas. In its 3 May report, "Fraudulent Saint of Cabora," the editors refused to print a letter from a reader praising Santa Teresa, which they found "to border more on barbarous than absurd," because their newspaper was not "a vehicle for fanaticism and ignorance" (quoted in *El Fronterizo* 9 May, 2). Another local report ironically asserted, "This supposed saint who attracted so many fanatics to the Cabora ranch a few months ago has realized her ultimate miracle, fleeing from home on the wings of love, in the company of a local cowboy. Neither the church nor the Civil Registry have intervened into this miracle" (*El Sábado* 29 March 1890, quoted in *El Diario del Hogar* 9 April 1890, 2). While this gossip was not corroborated in any other source of the period, it contributed to Urrea's local image as a fraud well known for duping her followers. One other Sonoran report a few months later (from *El Sábado*) continued to chastise those who believed in "the farce of Cabora" (reprinted in *El Fronterizo* 12 July 1890, 2). With a few exceptions, the local strategy seems to have been either to ignore her entirely or to disparage her. She did little to give credibility to the region as an up-and-coming contributor to the nation's progress toward modernization.

Early Views from the North, 1890–92

Word of her celebrity had quickly begun to spread northward as well. By April 1890, reports were appearing as far north as Las Cruces, New Mexico, in the journal *El Tiempo*. News of the great *tianguis* (open-air market) of Cabora had spread throughout the borderlands region, drawing not only ailing and adoring pilgrims but also vendors of *milagros* (metal replicas of body parts in need of healing), crucifixes, printed images of La Santa de Cabora, scapularies, and all kinds of handicrafts. They also hawked food, coffee, *mezcal*, and similar items. *La feria de Cabora* was rather a grubby, seedy affair, according to this account.

The same story also reported that Teresa, in addition to her rhetoric of "charity, equality and love for one's fellow man," spoke adamantly against the Catholic Church and its rites, including confession and marriage (quoted in Domecq, "Teresa Urrea" 29). One of the earliest known U.S. portrayals of Urrea, then, saw her as more troubling than did Mexican journals, which were content to make light of her antics and chalk up her fame to the ignorance of her followers. *El Tiempo*'s insinuations regarding the Urreas' corruption and Teresa's radical subversion vis-à-vis the Catholic Church foreshadow later U.S. representations of Urrea as an outlaw and instigator of revolution. However, this was not the only image of La Santa de Cabora that reached the U.S. Southwest in the early 1890s.

The first mention of Teresa in a U.S. newspaper appears to have been in Tucson's *El Fronterizo* on 29 March 1890, in the form of a letter to the editor from R. G. Moreno of Opodepe, Sonora.[10] Moreno felt obliged to make known the facts regarding a phenomenon that had been inciting rumors throughout the region for several months. He reported that the young woman in question, "legitimate daughter of don Tomás Urrea," was on her way to becoming "the honor and glory of Mexico" (1) and cited several eyewitness reports of her healings. In each case she cured the sick instantaneously by rubbing simple dirt and water on them. Moreno quoted one witness as saying, "I believed before visiting the hacienda that Santa Teresa's fame was the product of some kind of money-making speculation on the part of her parents, but I was convinced that I had been mistaken" (1).

Moreno then related additional examples of Urrea's saintly miracles. One case involved three curiosity seekers, society women from Guaymas who visited Cabora just to see what all the fuss was about. Feigning belief, they gained an audience with La Santa, and when she realized that they were mocking her, she told them that one of the three was cursed. When they asked her to tell them which one, she replied, "I wouldn't know the answer . . . but I will tell you that the one who does not hear three rings of a bell upon leaving here is the cursed one" (1). Then, to the ladies' surprise, as they were leaving, two of them, one after the other, did hear three chimes. The women were immediately shocked into belief, and the condemned woman flew into a panic, rushing back to gain audience with Santa Teresa to plead with her to tell her how she might save herself.

> In response to her plea, Santa Teresa answered, "That is why I am
> here, little sister; you must rid yourself of half of your wealth, which
> is abundant because it was dishonestly earned, and dispense it to the
> poor, leaving you the other half with which to remake your life in
> an exemplary fashion." And so the poor condemned lady was saved,
> returning to Guaymas determined and converted, along with her two
> friends. (1)[11]

El Fronterizo, in fact, dedicated considerable space to the Santa de Cabora phenomenon over the course of the following months. The second item it published on the topic was another letter in the issue of 19 April 1890, signed only "A Catholic," in support of Moreno's position. Any Catholic knows, the letter posits, that miracles do occur and that that is how saints are made: "If this is a revelation by God, it is shameful that the Mexican people lower themselves to the level of Jews with their incredulity and stubbornness, since not even the miracles of Jesus himself sufficed to convince them" (2). This writer appealed to theological and medical authorities to investigate and was appalled that so many would write La Santa off without giving her a chance to prove herself.

On 2 May a third letter appeared, sent in by T. Quiñones, responding directly to Moreno's original letter, which Quiñones found nonsensical: "I, dear Editors, who live a short distance from the ranch in question, and who have seen and observed on different occasions the *so called* saint, can assure you that everything that is reported in the above mentioned letter to the editor is a web of lies and foolishness" (1; emphasis in original).

On 17 May, *El Fronterizo* allowed R. G. Moreno of Opodepe to respond to Quiñones. Moreno remained adamant that La Niña de Cabora was part of a glorious Catholic tradition going back centuries to the times of the ancient prophets. He argued that she could not be a witch, as many said she was, because "far from fleeing from the sacred that necromancers so detest and disdain, she strives to invoke the Supreme Being to perform her healings" (3).

Then on 30 May, *El Fronterizo* for the first time mentioned La Santa de Cabora in its own "news" story (as opposed to a letter to the editor). It did not investigate the facts of the case but merely compared them to a new sensation, the Wandering Jew of Chihuahua, which apparently was causing great alarm there since it was capable of consuming six cows at a time. The story then mentioned a mysterious white shadow that was appearing in Tucson, cast by a ninety-foot-long monster with a one-hundred-sixty-foot wingspan and a head eight feet in diameter, resembling a hairless bat or reptile.

A month later, on 28 June, the paper published a letter from Miguel Trevizo of Ariveche, Sonora, who again supported the idea that Urrea's gifts were "the designs of Providence" (2). He quoted from a letter written to Santa Teresa de Cabora by a man from Jalisco, who had once been paralyzed but now could walk. He claimed that although he had been immobilized and in immense pain since 1877, her treatment with "blessed dust" and "divine hands" cured him (2). Trevizo argued, "What would the Edisons and the Mesmers say if their electromagnetic instruments could cure the infirm from long distances away . . . as Teresa does—and in an instant?" (2).

Finally, *El Fronterizo* seemed ready to close the matter when in its 12 July edition it reprinted a story from *El Sábado* of Hermosillo titled "The Farce of Cabora." This article explicitly criticized *El Fronterizo* for printing letters from "ignorant fanatics" who believed in the healing and seeing powers of Teresa Urrea (2). *El Sábado* insisted: "Our editorial offices have been visited by a person who came from Cabora. Curiosity, he says, took him there, and it is surprising how the multitude of unfortunates who surround Teresa, despite having received palpable proof that she possesses neither saintliness nor miraculous faculties, continues to grow" (2). *El Fronterizo* did not reply directly to this editorial but neither did it continue publishing letters or any other articles about Teresa Urrea.

Brianda Domecq reported, in fact, that in her extensive research she could find no newspaper reports on Urrea for the rest of 1890, nor for all of 1891, in Sonora, in other parts of Mexico, or in the U.S. borderlands ("Teresa Urrea" 21). It would seem that Teresa Urrea had had her moment of fame. She had piqued society's interest; it had debated her case and then forgot about her.[12] In the United States, borderlands journals like *El Fronterizo* or *El Tiempo* relied mainly upon reports from their Mexican counterparts. For them, La Santa de Cabora was perhaps more entertainment than news, and it would seem that there was only so much that could be said about Teresa's miracle cures before readers might prefer to read about gigantic flying reptiles and cattle-devouring monsters. In those early years, her anti-Catholic rhetoric might have been seen as amusing or threatening, depending on the opinion of the reader—and considering that only Spanish-language papers took up the story at first, it can be assumed that most U.S. readers of the Santa de Cabora story were, in fact, Mexican American Catholics. But whether she was a new generation prophet, a mystical healer, or a fraud, she had no great effect on most who read about her in the United States, at least in those first few months.

Teresa and the Spiritists, 1890–92

Aside from traditional Mexican and Mexican American newspapers, there was one nonmainstream journal that did take a sustained interest in Teresa Urrea in the early 1890s. That journal was *La Ilustración Espírita*, a specialized journal published in Mexico City and dedicated to the subject of spiritism.

Spiritism was a popular fad in turn of the century Mexico. Although some did take it more seriously, as a kind of alternative to conventional religion and philosophy, many mocked it as just another silly fashion imported from Paris. And if most found it harmless, some of its critics claimed that belief in spiritism was a "precursor of insanity" (*El Siglo XIX* 12 February 1892, 2). José Valadés writes:

> Spiritism in Mexico was for some the revelation and for others the
> entertainment of the turn of the century. Chronicles of society . . .
> report that both in the capital of the Republic and in the provinces,
> there was no private social gathering that did not feature experiments
> with magnetism and hypnotism, and they reveal how people worried
> excessively over the little jerks with which their legs kicked chairs
> or tables while under the magnetic influence of other party goers.
> (*La Opinión* 173, 7 March 1937, 1)

Mexican spiritists adhered to a varying range of beliefs that shared the notion of linking spiritual mysticism to science. Many believed in life after death, in communication with spirits, in reincarnation, in spiritual powers (such as hypnotism and faith healing), and so forth. Spiritists, keeping with the fashionable positivistic principles of the era, investigated, analyzed, and tested theories about their paranormal experiences. Many recast less scientific aspects of Catholic or other religious belief systems in spiritist terms, thus attaching a certain scientific legitimacy to what many would consider to be superstitious aspects of religion (Vanderwood 179).

In Mexico, spiritist groups began emerging in the late nineteenth century in major urban centers such as Mexico City and Guadalajara, and also in smaller cities such as Mazatlán, Guaymas, and Hermosillo—and even in small towns such as Baroyeca, a little hamlet not far from the Cabora ranch (Vanderwood 178). Among the first intellectuals to take Teresa Urrea seriously were spiritists such as Lauro Aguirre.[13] Unlike progressive businessmen of Sonora or arrogant *letrados* of the capital, the spiritists saw in Teresa Urrea not only a possibly believable and legitimate

paranormal phenomenon but also one that would validate their own theories of mediumship and spiritual power.

The first spiritists to visit Cabora were those of the small circle that
had formed in neighboring Baroyeca, Sonora, who first made the trek
in November 1889 "at the time when Teresa was lapsing in and out of
convulsions and trances . . . Teresa was too childlike to hold any coherent conversation, and the Spiritists declared her insane" (Vanderwood
178). However, fellow spiritists remained unconvinced that she was not
worth a closer look. The group from Baroyeca was asked to return in
early 1890, and this time they spoke at length with a more lucid young
Urrea and left persuaded that she did have spiritual powers. They published a series of firsthand reports on La Santa de Cabora in *La Ilustración Espírita*, beginning in the 1 January 1892 issue (255–60), which
is the most complete biographical source on Urrea from her early years.
The journal, in addition, reprinted many newspaper stories from Sonora,
Mexico City, and elsewhere and published investigations of Urrea by
spiritists whenever possible. The journal first reported on Urrea in its
1 January 1890 issue (288, a reprint of a story from *El Monitor Republicano*) and continued its coverage regularly through September 1892, concluding with Lauro Aguirre's interview with Urrea from Arizona.

The spiritist coverage of Urrea often strove to counterbalance the
ridicule she suffered in other journals. Among the reports was one based
on an interview granted by Teresa to a doctor, E. P. Schellhous, who
had come to visit Cabora from the United States. Schellhous found her
to be in excellent health and additionally proclaimed her to be a spiritist medium. "She is simple, innocent, and without pretensions and has
a lucid understanding of her elevated mission and complete knowledge
that she is only the instrument of superior and benevolent spirits who
consider her invaluable in spreading good and kindness to suffering
humanity" (*La Ilustración Espírita* 1 June 1891, 50–51, translated in Vanderwood 192). Regardless of whether Teresa was won over by such spiritist fans, they were the intellectuals most likely to take her seriously in
the early years. For the generation of mainstream writers on Urrea in
the 1890s, almost all of whom were journalists, positivist thought dominated their perspective, and they found Urrea to be as strange as the
spiritists themselves (Vanderwood 192–93).

The Mexican spiritists of Baroyeca invited Teresa and Tomás Urrea to join their group and attend their meetings; in fact they declared Teresa Urrea their "honorary president." The most orthodox of the spiritists rejected many traditional Christian beliefs including the divinity of Jesus Christ, the concept of the Holy Trinity, and the Catholic tradition of the saints, beliefs that Teresa Urrea adamantly held. While she eschewed many aspects of organized religion, she did not question Catholicism's underlying principles. The spiritists endeavored to influence Teresa's thinking and claimed to make headway, although there is no evidence that she ever referred to herself as a spiritist or radically changed any of her rhetoric with regard to religious concepts (*La Ilustración Espírita* 1 February 1892, 281; 1 March, 314).

In addition to testing la Santa de Cabora's spiritist credentials, or endeavoring to lure her into the movement as its Mexican poster girl, *La Ilustración Espírita* contributed effectively to shaping Teresa's legend by focusing especially on her unusual powers. For instance, it repeated a story previously published in a letter to the editor of *El Siglo XIX* (4 February 1890, 3): it seems a skeptic from a nearby town challenged Teresa to a game of *vencida*, a competition akin to arm wrestling. La Santa did not deign to participate herself but instead had him battle her close friend Josefina Félix, who agreed reluctantly to the contest. To everyone's surprise, delicate young Josefina beat her burly challenger. The journal portrayed Teresa engaging in bizarre feats of strength, lifting heavy patients, and exerting such exceptional willpower as to prevent visitors from raising her arms as she lay in bed (*La Ilustración Espírita* 1 April 1891, 367–68; 1 January 1892, 259; 1 February 1892, 279).

The spiritist journal also linked La Santa de Cabora's unusual abilities to her knowledge of indigenous culture. While her miraculous powers came from her communion with spirits (according to their interpretation), Lauro Aguirre reported in the 1 September 1892 issue that as a young girl she had learned herbal cures, shamanistic healing rituals, and incantations from the housekeeper of the Cabora ranch, a *curandera* named Huila (141). *La Ilustración Espírita* would eventually claim Teresa as their own, declaring that through the influence of Baroyeca's spiritists Teresa eventually became convinced that Jesus Christ was not divine (1 March 1892, 314).

While Aguirre's story for *La Ilustración Espírita* was dated 28 July 1892 and therefore written in Arizona where both the Urreas and Aguirre were living in political exile, the historian José Valadés asserts that Aguirre had in fact known the family for well over a year at that time.[14] According to Valadés, he had been an early visitor to Cabora after word of Teresa's first healings became public (perhaps arriving with the spiritists from Baroyeca): "From this moment on, the engineer Aguirre became Teresita's spiritual guide. It is known that it was don Lauro who convinced don Tomás to permit Teresa to dedicate herself to tending to the hundreds of persons who sought out her aid" (*La Opinión* 173, 7 March 1937, 2). Whether or not this assertion is true, Aguirre's first published writing on Urrea is hardly political. He strives to disassociate her from any insurrections in Sonora and Chihuahua, and rather than raise a protest about her expulsion to Arizona, he merely comments blandly that "the exile of Señorita Urrea of Sonora has visibly augmented her fame."[15] Aguirre's role in the making of the myth of La Santa de Cabora will be addressed in greater detail.

Teresa and the Mayos of Navojoa, 1892

Teresa's exile was initiated with her arrest on 19 May 1892 and realized on 4 June of the same year, when she was deported to Nogales, Arizona, together with her father and other members of the Cabora ranch household. The immediate motive for their exile was an uprising of Mayo Indians on 14 May in Navojoa, Sonora. The rebels assassinated the town's mayor, among others, in a brief but bloody insurrection roused on with the rallying cry "¡Viva la Santa de Cabora!" Local authorities advised President Díaz that Teresa Urrea was inspiring a rebel movement characterized by a dangerous fanaticism, and the president knew already that armed insurgents linked to her name were also active in the state of Chihuahua, in the town of Tomóchic (Domecq, "Teresa Urrea" 24–25).

Díaz had Teresa and her father promptly detained and taken to Guaymas where they were placed under house arrest. He instructed military leaders to keep her away from the common soldiers "because they too are ignorant and can be led astray" (quoted in Domecq, "Teresa Urrea" 26). Once in Guaymas they were given two options: to be sent across the border into Guatemala, or to be exiled in the United States. The Urreas chose the latter.

Interestingly, in Domecq's extensive research on Urrea, she is surprised "not to find in the newspapers of the era any public accusation made toward Teresa and her father, nor any suggestion of her alleged implication in the uprising, nor even a mention of her arrest" ("Teresa Urrea" 26; see also Romero 158). Sonora's official journal, *La Constitución*, stated merely that in the course of the assault the usually "pacific" Mayos shouted out the name of La Santa de Cabora as an inspirational cry (20 May 1892, 1). A week later, another report added that after being driven from town, the Mayos retreated toward Cabora (27 May, 2). However, aside from those two stories, which at most insinuate Urrea's possible involvement with what was a minor revolt, her name was not mentioned in *La Constitución* for at least the next several years. Not only did the newspaper not report on her exile but it also gave minimal space to subsequent rebellions in the region, including those of Tomóchic and Temosachic, Chihuahua, never associating her name with any of them.

Independent newspapers did report Teresa's arrest, and in fact this period saw a good deal of colorful coverage of her weeks spent detained in Guaymas. *La Reserva* of Ures expressed relief "that that focal point of fanaticism has been suppressed" (25 May 1892, quoted in *El Monitor Republicano* 1 June 1892, 3). Pérez Peña's *El Imparcial* reported that a meteorite flew across the sky while Urrea was under house arrest in Guaymas, leading her fanatical worshipers to believe that "heaven was venting its rage" for her imprisonment (17 May 1892, quoted in *El Monitor Republicano* 4 June 1892, 3). *El Eco del Valle* of Ures portrayed Teresa as perfectly happy, singing, playing guitar, and making jokes with the military officials who kept her under detention.[16] The local journals neither took her arrest seriously nor paid attention to whether it was indeed justified. Furthermore, they portrayed her move to Arizona as voluntary. No local newspaper picked up on the fact that she was deported against her will. For example, *El Estudio* of Hermosillo reported on 6 June merely that Teresa "departed . . . , heading in the direction of Nogales" (quoted in *La Ilustración Espírita* 1 July 1892, 83). As a result, most major U.S. and Mexico City newspapers also did not pick up on Teresa's apparent political subversiveness at this time. She

remained principally a folk hero, a living saint to her believers, an entertaining quack to her doubters. Readers who knew of her from previous
news stories certainly would have been surprised to learn that she had
been arrested or exiled.

The reports that did spring up outside Sonora tended to play up
Teresa's putative supernatural powers but were ignorant of the Mexican
government's concern over the political implications of her activities.
El Monitor Republicano joked about her "emigration" to Nogales (26 June
1892, 1). *El Siglo XIX* mused over her application for U.S. citizenship:
"In the depths of her heart, how will she value the great loss of the country in which she was born? Who knows!" (19 July 1892). However, it
did not concern itself with the circumstances of her exile or her possible political subversion.

El Universal of Mexico City is the journal that perhaps took the
story most seriously. One of its first reports stated clearly that Urrea
was removed from Cabora "with the objective of suppressing the fanaticism that [she] has awakened" but added only that she "would be living
for some time in Guaymas" and not that she was actually under arrest
(2 June 1892, 3). Its stories proceeded to address what happened in
Guaymas upon her arrival: the meteorite, the chaos caused by the arrival
of her followers (5 June, 3; 10 June, 3; 15 June, 3). Then, abruptly, the
next report described her arrival in Nogales, without ever mentioning
how or why she came to move there (21 June, 3). The journal even
reprinted parts of an interview from a Nogales newspaper but left out
any mention of Teresa's conflicts with the Díaz government (5 July, 3).

Even when journals such as Ireneo Paz's *La Patria* referred directly
to Teresa's "arrest," which "follows from the recent uprising of the Mayo
Indians" (5 June 1892, 2), they failed to evaluate whether or not she was
guilty of anything. Once again, her ultimate punishment—forced exile—
was never noted. *La Patria* stated: "The deluded Teresa Urrea has left
for Nogales, Arizona," adding ironically that "over there they will not
accept any miracles or revelations beyond those of Mechanics, Physics
and Agriculture" (15 June, 3).

While news of Teresa's exile did reach the United States (*Los Angeles Times* 4 June 1892, 4), it was not the only information circulating
about her. The *New York Times* cited sources that claimed Teresa had

been arrested and convicted of witchcraft and sentenced, along with her father (a goatherd), to be shot. Her arrest had to do with her growing fame among indigenous militants in Sonora and Chihuahua. She was stirring up some kind of annoying paganism that was turning the Indians away from reason. While her sentence had been commuted to imprisonment, the *Times* noted that angry Mayos had reacted by going on the warpath (16 June 1892, 1; published previously in *The Brooklyn Eagle* 15 June 1892, 4). It is important to observe here that the cause and effect were confused: for the *Times* the Urreas were not arrested for having stirred up a Mayo rebellion; on the contrary, the Mayos were rebelling because the Urreas had been arrested. The root of the problem was the fanatical religious devotion of the ignorant indigenous groups of northwestern Mexico, not any kind of political subversion on the part of Teresa Urrea. The *Times's* correction of its error a couple of weeks later continued to miss this point; it recognized that she had been exiled to Arizona but reported that the government had only circulated rumors of her trumped-up death in order to "quell the excitement among restless Indians flooding to Nogales to see her for cures" (*New York Times* 29 June 1892, 10; published previously in *San Francisco Examiner* 28 June 1892, 1). Her exile thus served not to enhance her image as a political dissident but to play up her tendency to arouse superstitious Indians, who might follow through on their zealotry in irrational and unpredictable ways.

Teresa and Tomóchic, 1891–93

The case of Tomóchic, Chihuahua, is much better known than that of Navojoa. Navojoa's conflict consisted basically of one day of violence and was more or less resolved immediately. Tomóchic was another story. It involved an entire town's population that felt alienated by both local governmental and ecclesiastic authorities. Although fervent Catholics, upon being treated disrespectfully by Church leaders the townspeople turned to the "living saints" of the region who had been attracting so much attention in recent years (Sobarzo, *Episodios* 63). After all, the war of *la Reforma's* anti-Catholicism, encroaching Protestantism from the United States, and the new spiritist movement all contributed to the

Catholic Church's being especially weak in the northern borderlands—
the Yaquis, for example, had overtly broken off relations with the Church,
forming their own religion (Domecq, "Teresa Urrea" 30).

Holden notes that under these circumstances, the citizens of Tomóchic also "developed a schismatic theology of their own" (120), and one
of the figures to whom they were most drawn was Teresa de Cabora,
whose innocence, selflessness, and articulate nature with regard to issues
of social justice were particularly appealing to a group in search of both
a revised religious doctrine and a political rhetoric that favored the
poor and exploited. A dramatic moment of the break with the *tomoches*
in their already contentious relationship with Catholic authorities came
when Father Manuel Castelo had a public altercation with a local resident, Cruz Chávez, over whether Teresa Urrea was indeed a saint and
whether her image could be displayed in the town's church. Castelo reported this incident to *El Universal* of Mexico City (2 November 1892,
cited in Saborit, *Los doblados* 38–39). Around this time, Castelo visited
Cabora in person and witnessed Teresa Urrea performing her miracles,
which convinced several nuns who had accompanied him—but apparently not the priest—of her divine powers.[17]

The unrest in Tomóchic lasted much longer and was much more
threatening to the Díaz administration than had been the case with other
borderlands rebellions of the era. After a series of skirmishes between
the *tomoches—mestizos/criollos* quite skilled at warfare, having toughed
out generations of assaults by marauding Apaches (Vanderwood 116–
17)—and federal troops, in which the latter were repeatedly embarrassed,
in the late summer of 1892, the Mexican army set out to lay siege to
the isolated mountain town of Tomóchic. When the long battle concluded at the end of October, the greatly outnumbered *tomoches* were
finally defeated by their attackers when the latter essentially annihilated
the town, killing everyone still present, including women and children.
Their leaders, including the brothers Cruz and Manuel Chávez, would
quickly become heroes.

It was a truly shocking story—writes Mario Gill, "Of all the crimes
of porfirism, surely the most monstrous were those committed against
two mountain towns of Chihuahua, Tomóchic and Temosachic" (*La
doncella* 5)—much more so than any other event associated with Teresa

Urrea, and one that allied her again with superstitious "fanatics." Aside from the townspeople's fervent revised Catholicism, prominently featuring the worship of Santa Teresa de Cabora, more important roots of the conflicts in Tomóchic have gone largely ignored. The historian Jesús Vargas Valdez writes,

> Outside of Chihuahua, a defense of liberty or of dignity, much less a revolution against the government, was not spoken about. The ex-military man, Heriberto Frías spread the myth of a holy war centered around Teresita Urrea and located the heroic gesture of Tomóchic in the same atmosphere as that promoted by the propaganda of the Díaz government, i.e., one of religious fanaticism. ("Tomóchic" 177–78)

The enormity of the news of Tomóchic in 1892, and the fact that the rebellion would later go down in history as one of the most important antecedent events to the Mexican revolution (Vanderwood 284, 291), would make its legend key to the shaping of the nascent Teresa Urrea legend, even though she was already exiled from Mexico at the time it occurred, and it is unlikely that she ever met or had any other contact with the *tomoches*. What is interesting is that it is newspapers—none of which appears to have had the means to realize accurate reporting on a story playing out in an isolated small town way off in the mountains of the northern borderlands—and a novel, Heriberto Frías's *¡Tomóchic!*, that form the basis for all historiography in the case. Communications between government and military leaders of course do outline details of the military campaign against the *tomoches* but offer little insight into the motivations and personalities of the enemy, whom they saw as barbarous fanatics of the always problematic northern borderlands.

A pattern of the circulation of misinformation about the *tomoches* goes back at least to 1891 when, after a scuffle regarding the ownership of some religious paintings that had been on display in the town's church, the governor of Chihuahua informed his brother-in-law, President Porfirio Díaz, that the root of the problems in Tomóchic was "banditry." He soon added the term "fanaticism" to his descriptions of the recalcitrant citizens of Tomóchic, to whom he also referred as "Indians." While it is quite clear that all Tarahumaras who had lived within the

limits of the town had been driven out by the end of the nineteenth century (Holden 118), the term "indio" came to be used frequently in the
reporting on the rebellion.[18] In fact, the "indio" moniker was absorbed
into popular culture where a *corrido* referred to the Tomóchic conflict
as an "Indian uprising" (Saborit, *Los doblados* 122). As recently as the
1970s, Mexican historians continued to refer to the *tomoches* as "an abundant group of indigenous people from a remote place in Chihuahua"
(Corbalá Acuña 265), while U.S. historians have been particularly sloppy
on this point, one referring to the *tomoches* as a "religious tribe" (Larralde,
Mexican American Movements 63), and others repeatedly identifying the
rebels as "the Tarahumara Indians from the village of Tomóchic" (Rodríguez and Rodríguez 183).

Meanwhile, the putative "fanaticism" of the *tomoche* rebels has been
one of the greatest points of contention for their defenders. The fact
that the term was repeated not only by politicians but by newspapers,
and more importantly in the critically successful and widely read novel
by Frías, has established it firmly as part of the story: the government's
actions were unconscionable, but their victims were crazed with an irrational religious fervor. Aurelio Pérez Peña's *El Imparcial* of Guaymas
called them "stupid fanatics" (31 August 1892, 3). Regardless of whether
their ideas on religion were in synch with those of Catholicism or with
any modern belief system, the focus on their "fanaticism" and association
with the often-lampooned Santa de Cabora—referred to on occasion as
"a female religious fanatic" (*New York Times* 12 September 1892, 5)—
draws attention away from a number of rational reasons for their discontent, including serious issues regarding land rights, forced military
conscription, and local government abuses.[19] Nonetheless, there are few
contemporary sources that do not assume that fanaticism played a key
role in triggering the uprising. Horacio Sobarzo, for example, cites the
rebels' "spiritual regression, edging toward a primitive fanaticism—since
cases of such intense and blind obsession as that of which they were victims can only be observed among tribes that existed in the distant past"
(*Episodios* 60), and Mario Gill, who lauds the revolutionary valor of
the *tomoches*, nonetheless concludes that "the town appears to have been
attacked by a collective psychosis of mysticism" (*La doncella* 13).

The legend of Teresa's involvement with the Tomóchic rebellion is more complicated. While there was certainly a tendency in some reporting to belittle the movement by implying that "la neurótica de Cabora"[20] was the mastermind of their hapless rebellion, it is more difficult to learn to what extent she really may have been in contact with the *tomoches*, to what degree they took her as an ideological inspiration, or to what point her role was exaggerated later—particularly by Lauro Aguirre—for the purpose of inciting further rebellion.

Most sources agree that while some *tomoches* may have visited Cabora in the early years (Valadés, *La Opinión* 180, 14 March 1937, 1), the delegation of rebels that went specifically to meet her—under the observation of the Mexican armed forces, with whom they eventually battled—never even saw her, since she had gone into hiding when she heard they were coming, in order to avoid trouble. Vanderwood cites the sworn statement from July 1892 of a Tarahumara man who claimed to have found near Tomóchic a bag containing several letters from Teresa Urrea to several prominent residents of Tomóchic dated 1891 and 1892, although no trace of such letters can be found today.[21] Domecq notes that most sources agree that Urrea never met the *tomoche* leaders, although William Curry Holden "invents a story that he attaches to Francisco Almada, but there is nothing in Almada's book to sustain the supposed encounter between [Cruz] Chávez and Teresa."[22] She cannot resist, however, imagining a face-to-face meeting between Chávez and Urrea in her novel (*La insólita* 222–26). Incredibly, other researchers then cite Domecq for her description of this "meeting that would be decisive in the lives of both" (Osorio 84). Valadés insists that Teresa Urrea had been an advisor to the *tomoches* from early on (*La Opinión* 180, 14 March 1937, 1), although her role was later usurped by Lauro Aguirre, who, once he and the Urreas were exiled and living in Nogales, established an informal "conspiracy center" from which he issued instructions to the rebels and "put the *tomoches* and Indians [Yaqui and Mayo insurgents] in touch with sellers of arms and munitions" (*La Opinión* 187, 21 March 1937, 1), although it should be noted that Aguirre insists that Urrea and Cruz Chávez never met (133, 138). The Sonoran historian Manuel Corbalá Acuña nonetheless asserts that "she dedicated many long hours to attending and listening to" Cruz Chávez and the other *tomoches* (266), and Mario Gill calls her "the inspirer and organizer" of the rebellion (*La doncella* 6). Luis Urrea—who dares to make a buffoon of Tomóchic's hero, Chávez—portrays the two meeting and exchanging a most playful correspondence (*The Hummingbird's Daughter* 366–77, 388–90, 420–24); they later communicate telepathically as Tomóchic comes under siege by government troops (464–69). Regardless of her actual degree of involvement, opposition newspapers enjoyed mocking Díaz for nearly losing a battle inspired by "a saint/banker/financier" (*El Hijo del Ahuizote* 6 November 1892, 2).

Back in Sonora, the press paid little attention to the tumult in Chihuahua. The state's official newspaper, *La Constitución*, did not cover the Tomóchic rebellion, although it did print a story on a related flareup in neighboring Temosachic a few months later (28 April 1893, 2). It made no mention whatsoever of Teresa Urrea during this period. Independent journals such as *El Imparcial* were also surprisingly skimpy on their coverage. While a 31 August story did link Urrea to the Tomóchic story, it gave hardly any space at all to the events as they unfolded. However, once they were over, a series of reports, all borrowed from *La Frontera* of Chihuahua, excised Urrea and gradually even stopped calling the *tomoches* "fanatics." Post-massacre, the wild-eyed fanatics suddenly became "valiant" and the siege of Tomóchic by federal forces became "glorious episodes in that memorable struggle" (21 November 1892).

This shift in tone can also be seen in Mexico City. *El Diario del Hogar* clearly outlined the new interpretation of the events: "We know what the origin of that disastrous revolution was: it was not fanaticism as has been claimed, but defense of lives under threat, honor and interests trampled by serious violations" (20 December 1892, quoted in Gill, *La doncella* 27). *La Voz del Pueblo* articulated dramatically that "the insurgents all perished in the battle, holding their position with heroic valor; when they had used up all their cartridges and there were only five or six of them left, they defended themselves with knives" (13 November 1892, 3). The massacre of a small group of maltreated townspeople by a government force seven times their size (sixty *tomoches* versus four hundred federal troops, according to *La Voz del Pueblo*, 13 November 1892, 3) was quickly transformed into an everyman's legend of gallant resistance against the extravagant tyrannies of the Díaz regime. A similar vein of reporting also materialized in the United States, where the Tomóchic battle was called "a second Alamo."[23]

However, the newspaper that most influenced how Tomóchic and La Santa de Cabora were interpreted in the 1890s and would continue to be for decades was *El Demócrata*, the Mexico City daily that from 14 March to 14 April 1893 published the twenty-eight installments of the original version of the novel *¡Tomóchic!*, written by their own war correspondent, Heriberto Frías, who participated with the federal troops in the siege of the town. The focus of Frías's novel is the Tomóchic spectacle of which Teresa Urrea is merely a minor player, although her image looms large in the background. The novel follows the saga of the *tomoches*, whose portraits vacillate between extravagantly eulogistic and condescendingly comic. On the one hand: "They were admirable marksmen, heroic, intelligent, chivalrous, exceptional . . . They were demigods; invincible, intrepid, audacious; mountain tigers who would crush all forces sent after them" (26). On the other: "They did not know about the country, nor its governors, nor its religion, nor its priests. And what was strangest of all was that they were not a barbarous tribe. They were not Indians; they were creoles" (54). They were obsessive in their worship of the "living saint," Teresa de Cabora, and they declared one of their own, Cruz Chávez, "His Highness the Pope of Chihuahua and Sonora, in the name of the grand power of God" (61). Their rebellion was "as obstinately imbecilic as it was heroic" (27). The ambiguous representation of the *tomoches* is perhaps reflective of Frías's position as a liberal who was shocked by the brutality of the Díaz regime, and as a Mexico City *letrado*, a city boy who could not help but cringe at the backwardness of these misguided, even suicidal, rubes from the remotest of provinces.

Teresa de Cabora never actually appears in the novel, except in the form of an image, scavenged from the rubble of Tomóchic after the battle is over. Teresa Urrea is portrayed as "a humble daughter," "a poor hysterical girl," a "sweet, sick child." La Santa de Cabora is something of an unbalanced innocent whose image was somehow distorted and exploited by the "delirium" and "armored insanity" of the raging *tomoches* (225). Frías denudes her of any possibility of agency or even inspirational force. She is not a rebellious orator, nor even a common *curandera*, but merely an ill child. Like the Mexico City newspapers in which Frías had first read about Teresa Urrea, he did not take her seriously in any way.

In the absence of eyewitness news coverage of the event, except on the part of government troops, it has been difficult for historians to reconstruct a balanced story about Tomóchic without resorting either to fancy or to literature. Frías's novel offers, after all, the only firsthand report that is reasonably sympathetic to both federal soldiers and *tomoche* rebels. There are very few historians of Tomóchic who do not mention Frías, and there are many who cite him freely, as an eyewitness source, without warning readers that the only thing he wrote on what transpired in Tomóchic was a novel. More often, revisionists criticize Frías for factual errors they discover in his novel, as if it were in fact historiography.[24] All this goes to show not the foolishness of historians who do not know a work of fiction when they see one, nor the sloppiness of Frías, who could not be bothered to correctly recall every detail of what he witnessed during the course of the battle, but the fact that the genre to which the text has been assigned is irrelevant. It has been read for over a century as the most authoritative source on these events. In this sense, the *New York Times* "news story" of 12 September 1892 is more fictitious than *¡Tomóchic!* because it lacks eyewitness authority and liberally twists the facts: Teresa Urrea was not from "Tomasachic" nor were the rebels "Indians" as the *Times* claims. Frías's novelistic portraits, on the other hand, are much less easily dismissed. Nor is it surprising that the most popular contemporary source on Teresa Urrea is Brianda Domecq's rigorously researched historical novel.

Teresa in Arizona, 1892–96

Now we return to the events surrounding Urrea's deportation to Arizona in June 1892. Her exile began with great fanfare upon her arrival in Nogales. Believers and curiosity seekers flocked to the city to catch a glimpse of her, or, better yet, witness a miracle. Local merchants saw to it that she was well taken care of, even going so far as to take up a collection to rent and furnish her a house in Nogales. After all, if she left town, the throngs of pilgrims would follow her, and Nogales would lose the chance to sell its wares to them (Valadés, *La Opinión* 187, 21 March 1937, 1).

Public interest surged quickly, particularly in the southwestern borderlands. At first much of the newspaper coverage focused on her miraculous healing powers and remarkable popularity among Mexicans, particularly the "ignorant and superstitious lower classes" (*Arizona Daily Star* 4 June 1892, 1). She was not, the press emphasized, loved by all Mexicans. Certainly longer-term middle-class residents of the United States, who did not necessarily sympathize as Teresa did with the plight of Mexico's indigenous poor, were not thrilled with her presence. Such

> Mexican families stayed away, afraid of being identified with the
> motley groups of Indians. Their ambition was to conceal their
> mestizo traits, learn English, cover up their Latino background, and
> become accepted by the "whiteys," or at least by the "Hispanics" who
> claimed to be directly descended from Spaniards. It was a difficult
> struggle, almost impossible, and the arrival of the alleged saint with
> her following of ragged Indians complicated things. (Domecq, *The
> Astonishing Story* 279 [*La insólita historia* 295])

Regarding her treatments, the *San Francisco Examiner* reported that a man who had been blind and mute for four years had gained significant sight and speech after meeting with Teresita (28 June 1892, 1). The *Arizona Daily Star* cited a case of a man who regained the use of a paralyzed leg, thanks to Santa Teresa, and another whom she cured of near blindness (6 July 1892, 4). This Teresa, with her amazing healing powers, was the one that U.S. newspaper readers got to know (at least at first).

The circumstances under which she had arrived, her sudden exile from her home country, generated great sympathy, though many were skeptical of her powers. Most reports in the English-language press noted that it was only Mexicans who visited her seeking cures. However, the mocking reports calling her a neurotic or witch subsided at this time. One report in a small Nogales, Arizona, journal presented "scientific data" to show that her magnetic healing powers could be genuine, "so that the public might be more moderate in their criticism of the above mentioned young lady, and so that they can see that she might possess an extraordinary magnetic fluid" (*El Atalaya* 9 June 1892, 1–2).

The U.S. press's sympathy toward Urrea might also be interpreted as inflammatory toward Mexico: "she was characterized as martyr" (Illades 75), as having been "persecuted, stripped of her assets, and expelled from the republic by the Díaz government" (Ramos Luna 296). There was actually much confusion as to why she was expelled. One reporter who interviewed her through an interpreter wrote: "A war took place between two Indian tribes a while back and the Mexican officials claimed that she had incited the trouble" (*Arizona Daily Star* 28 June 1892, 4).

The *gringos* became particularly outraged when Mexican officials crossed into U.S. territory to harass her. Military authorities sent Mayor Manuel Mascareñas of Nogales, Sonora, into sister border town Nogales, Arizona, to pressure the Urreas to move further away from the border (Domecq, "Teresa Urrea" 33). It was around this time—that is, not when she was first arrested or exiled, but several weeks later, at the time of the Mascareñas visit—that Teresa Urrea began to be portrayed as politically subversive. It was certainly not the dominant element of her public image—she was still primarily a source of entertaining anecdotes or evidence of Mexican superstitiousness. Nonetheless, it began to sink in that Mexican authorities would not have gone so far as to banish her from the country if she were a mere sideshow attraction. And while the fact that her name was apparently being used as a rallying cry by rebels in various locations in the northwestern borderlands did not necessarily implicate her as an instigator of revolution, it did give cause to ponder her relationship to the insurgents. For this reason, her image in the U.S. press from this time on assumed a new facet.

For example, *El Fronterizo* of Tucson, which had allowed its readers to debate Urrea's saintly character in the spring and summer of 1890 until finally writing her off as "the farce of Cabora" (12 July 1890, 2), carried a story originally printed in *El Progreso* of Chihuahua expressing amazement about the latest news on Teresita Urrea: she was to start writing for a newspaper: "A saintly journalist! Let's see: to whom might such a thing occur? . . . for there to be saints who after performing a half a dozen miracles, take up a pen and zas! . . . make themselves available, notebook in hand, to go, in newspaperwoman's attire, glasses on, in pursuit of a big story, that could only happen in the final lustrum of this

shimmering century" (*El Fronterizo* 18 November 1893, 1). While historians and biographers agree that Urrea did not get directly involved with
journalism until Lauro Aguirre founded his politically incendiary *El Independiente* in El Paso a few years later, it seems that rumors of her connection with Aguirre and his projects were already in circulation in 1893.

Another 1893 story holds that Teresa returned to Mexico where she
was welcomed by "hundreds of Indians and ignorant Mexicans" (*New
York Times* 21 June 1893, 3), a rumor not believed by any historian or
biographer of Urrea, although Teresa herself confirmed it in two separate interviews, one in 1896 in which she is quoted as saying, "We were
permitted later [after her exile] to return to another district" only to be
expelled again shortly thereafter (*Los Angeles Times* 20 September, 19),
and another in 1900 (*San Francisco Examiner* 27 July, 7).

Then, in the spring of 1895, not far from the Mexican border town
of Ojinaga (near El Paso, Texas), a woman appeared carrying a stone
idol that she claimed had been a gift from heaven. Some took her to be
La Santa de Cabora, and as word of mouth spread, she began attracting hundreds of followers to the area. She did not perform healings, but
she did preach to her devotees messages that she claimed came directly
from her conversations with God, and she also made substantial cash
collections. Mexican authorities attempted to arrest her, but she escaped
to the U.S. side of the border. They did succeed in arresting some of
her followers, whom they jailed in Ojinaga. In response, rioters attempted
to raid the jail and free the prisoners, until troops arrived from Chihuahua to scare them away (Vanderwood 296–97).

The details as to why this woman was identified as La Santa de Cabora—her physical appearance? the exact content of her preachings? —
have never been recorded. The Chihuahua historian Francisco Almada
attributes these events to "an adventuress who was called 'Sister María'"
(*La rebelión* 135). Still, it is interesting to note how this story was covered in the press. An article from the 6 April 1895 issue of the *Oasis*,
titled "Santa Teresa Once More," reported that "a woman calling herself 'Teresa de Covra' *[sic]* and claiming to perform miracles" had appeared near El Paso and "has so excited the people there that they are
simply crazy" (reprinted in the *New York Times* 14 April 1895, 3). It then
concluded:

This is the same woman who was the cause of a bloody revolt at
Temochio [sic] about fourteen months ago, and which resulted in
the authorities making the woman leave the country. She crossed
to Nogales, Arizona, where it is claimed by the Mexicans that she
performed wonderful cures. She disappeared from Nogales and two
weeks ago made her appearance in the village of El Palyo, where 400
armed men are protecting her. (3)

Teresa never admitted to involvement in this incident, nor has any biographer or historian ever hypothesized that the woman involved was likely
her (Vanderwood 297).

La Santa de Cabora resurfaced in the press in September 1895, when
the same journal announced that the Urreas would soon be leaving town
and moving to Solomonville, Arizona: "We regret the departure of this
virtuous young lady from her present residence, where her numerous
friends always found a hearty welcome from the amiable señorita" (the
Oasis 18 September, 8). Soon after their move, Lauro Aguirre moved
to Solomonville as well and began publishing his radical newspaper *El
Independiente*. One of its earliest initiatives was to disseminate a procla-
mation denouncing the Díaz regime and outlining plans for a new government. While evidence suggests that the Urreas supported Aguirre's
ideas and were likely working with him prior to their move (Domecq,
"Teresa Urrea" 36–37), Teresa was careful to promote herself in her
new hometown as the saintly heroine of Mexico's poor and infirm, and
not a revolutionary agitator. Once settled, she quickly granted an interview to Solomonville's *Graham County Bulletin*, whose representatives
she received in her house, not while curing the sick or plotting revolution but "surrounded by a number of callers, representing the leading
Mexican families . . . entertaining them with her singing and music"
(8 November 1895, 3). In her interview, in which she spoke with the
English-speaking reporter through an interpreter, she told of how
she first came to realize that she "possessed great magnetic power," an
ability she defined as not supernatural but more like a "wonderful will
power and magnetism strong enough to cure any and all diseases." She
bragged, "I seldom fail. I have cured hundreds and hundreds and if
I fail to effect a permanent cure on some, I have never yet failed to
greatly benefit them" (3). Neither political issues nor the circumstances

surrounding her exile were raised, and, apart from the crowds of pilgrims she continued to attract, it appears that she kept a relatively low profile in Solomonville.

Nonetheless, U.S. government investigations of Aguirre led them to open a file on Teresa Urrea as well. Although she was never implicated strongly enough to be charged by U.S. authorities, this did not keep the press quiet about her alleged involvement (Domecq, "Teresa Urrea" 38). Indeed, the *New York Times* reported that Urrea, "the sensational crazy saint" (12 March 1896, 1) "takes no interest in either political or religious affairs" (11 March, 3); however, her name continued to come up in articles on possible revolutionary plots against Mexico originating from the borderlands (e.g., *New York Times* 3 April 1896, 13; see Vanderwood 298).

Soon afterward, Aguirre would relocate his operation to El Paso, Texas, and in June 1896 the Urreas would move there as well. Despite her association with Aguirre and her rumored participation in subversive activities in Mexico or the United States, the press treated Teresa as a celebrity clown. The *Los Angeles Times* noted her move to El Paso, reporting that "this alleged saint . . . receives the lame, the sick, the halt, the maimed and the blind, and people with more ails, aches and pains than there are colors on the mucous membrane of the stomach of a delirium tremens patient" (27 June 1896, 6). Taking her more seriously was the *Tombstone Prospector*, which cited an interview with Teresa's father, Tomás, in the *El Paso Herald* in which he praised "the press for the fairness shown himself and his daughter." The article concluded, "The doctors of divinity and medicine do not seem to be as favorable to the fair healer" but made no mention of her alleged political activities (11 July 1896, 4).

Tomóchic Revisited

Upon the Urreas' move to El Paso, and Teresa's incorporation as a central figure into Lauro Aguirre's revolutionary propaganda, her public image became even more contradictory than before. For example, in an early editorial in his *Independiente*, Aguirre deployed her as a symbol of the victimization of Mexico's most helpless citizens at the hand of an evil dictator. Teresa is "a woman who works always for the good of aggrieved humanity, without the slightest material interest, and who possesses such brilliant moral gifts," yet she "is persecuted and hunted by the Mexican government." Aguirre goes on, "What guarantees does the Mexican man have when a weak woman is persecuted and deported from her homeland simply because she dedicates herself to doing good for her fellow man?" (*El Independiente* 25 June 1896, quoted in Valadés, *La Opinión* 229, 2 May 1937, 1).

Shortly after her arrival, Aguirre began to publish installments of a text titled "¡Tomóchic! ¡Redención!," which he would later assemble into a book that he would sell to his readers, and of which Teresa Urrea was listed as coauthor. This bombastic retelling of the Tomóchic saga maintains Teresa Urrea's distance from the uprising—Aguirre contends that she never met nor corresponded with any of the rebels—yet, unlike Frías, makes her a major protagonist of the story. In addition, it is no longer a novel, much less "the novel full of falsehoods of Heriberto Frías"; it is a "historico-philosophical narration" addressing the "legendary and unequalled deeds of Tomóchic."[25] Better than a novel, even without eyewitnesses, is a history based on legend.

Safely publishing from the U.S. side of the border, unlike Frías, he is able to openly criticize the Díaz government, "which has been the most criminal and monstrous Government that there has ever been in Mexico" (116). He fleshes out Teresa Urrea so that she is more than a doll-like infant who happens to rouse some wild-eyed fanatical mountain men (as she was for Frías); instead, in Aguirre, she represents good in the face of the evil of Díaz. She is a young woman who "distinguished herself in Cabora for her abnegation and charity toward all unfortunate souls" (109). He also redeems the *tomochitecos* and other followers of Santa Teresita de Cabora. Frías had repeatedly called them fanatics—and parenthetically it must be added that Aguirre himself had a few years earlier portrayed the rural poor of the Mexican borderlands as "indigenous peons and Roman fanatics of the most ignorant kind" (*La Ilustración Espírita* 1 September 1892, 138); now Aguirre softens his stance: "This fanaticism is not only forgivable, it is natural and logical because for people who do not judge using any more criteria than their sensory impressions, without first finding out the hows and the whys of things, fanaticism is inevitable. They surrendered to the facts and, unable to explain them, they gave them the rational explanation of being miracles" (113–14). Tomóchic, then, is repositioned. No longer an isolated aberration in local borderlands history, Tomóchic is now a major symbol of the tyranny of the Díaz regime and an early cry of rebellion that will ultimately lead to revolution. Its protagonists are no longer merely simple mountain folk and a mentally disturbed girl:

> Tomóchic is, as we will see later and we are sure that history will confirm it, the awakening of the poor, the illiterate, the socially segregated, the homeless to the life of mankind . . . Heroic *tomoches!* Your sacrifices . . . have not been sterile; they have been the glorious prelude to the redemption of those who earn their living through work and performing duties. (107)

The story of the battle itself obviously must rely upon Frías, whose was the only widely circulated account of what occurred, and, importantly, the one that most poignantly questioned the government's ethics. Aguirre merely repositions the events laid out in Frías's novel in a context of national social unrest, a context into which Frías's *¡Tomóchic!* would eventually be recast by critics, but only after the revolution in the years following 1910 (Saborit, *Los doblados* 14).

This new "history," like Frías's "novel," is also personal. Frías was an eyewitness as was his protagonist, Miguel Mercado; here Aguirre makes himself a protagonist of his version of events. The first chapter begins, "I was a prisoner. The rages and persecutions of the most monstrous of tyrants that mankind has ever known weighed on me, because I had committed the crime of telling the truth" (93). Aguirre had never been to Tomóchic and was not part of the rebellion there, yet he is the character who introduces its story. The second character to appear (in a dream) likewise was only peripherally involved: Teresa Urrea nonetheless becomes a driving force of the story told by Aguirre as her biography is intertwined with the history of the insurrection of the *tomoches*. He traces out her cataleptic fits, her first healings, her rise to fame in Sonora, her good will, her sense of social justice, her popularity with oppressed peoples, the misunderstandings that led to her exile, her sympathy for the *tomochitecos*, whom she never met.

It is especially interesting that Aguirre lists Urrea as his coauthor, although the story is told with the first-person narrator representing him and Urrea referred to only in the third person. Critics have wondered whether Teresa directly participated in the revolutionary conspiring of Aguirre, or whether she was merely lending her name to a cause she (or her father) believed in; in other words, whether we ever really hear the voice of Teresa Urrea, even when her name appears as author. With her very limited education, it is unlikely that she was able to write something on her own, and indeed no text was published under her name after she left El Paso.

Finally, it should be mentioned that Aguirre's "¡Tomóchic! ¡Redención!" would never reach a significant readership. Despite his prophetic wisdom in locating the Tomóchic rebellion within a national context of popular insurgency, his distribution did not extend far beyond El Paso, and few copies survived beyond the revolution—unlike Frías's novel, whose fame and prestige would only grow with the fall of the Díaz regime in 1911. Aguirre's pamphlet's importance to Urrea's image is that this treatise politicized it, as did the other items printed about her in *El Independiente*, sometimes under her name. She was no longer just a miracle worker; she was a political activist.

There might be some irony in an article attributed to Teresa in *El Independiente* of 7 August 1896, when in response to a letter about her, she wrote, "I do not know for what reason, but it is a fact that everyone who has written something about me twists my ideas and leads them toward their own ideas, which results in things being attributed to me that I have not even thought of saying" (1). How much of the writing attributed to Urrea that was published in *El Independiente* was not likewise subject to fastidious intervention, in this case on the part of Aguirre?

Teresa and the Raid on the Nogales Customs House, 1896

In early August 1896, turbulence along the U.S.–Mexico border began to increase, first in Ojinaga, and then in Nogales. During this time, the Urreas, Aguirre, and other agitators were in close contact in El Paso. In addition, they had produced flyers featuring prayers to and images

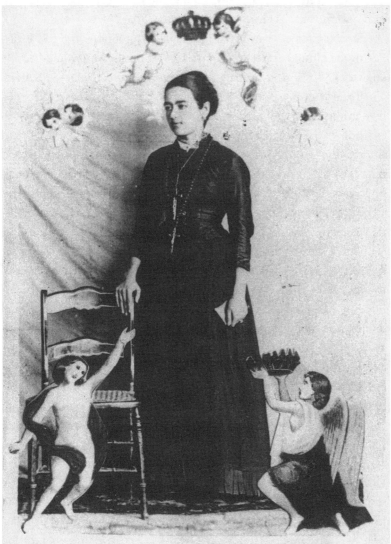

Tereeita Urrea. La Sta: Niña de Cabora

Figure 11. "Teresita Urrea, la Santa Niña de Cabora." Courtesy of Arizona Historical Society, Tucson; Photographic Archives: Portraits: Urrea, Santa.

of Santa Teresa de Cabora (see Figure 11), printed on the reverse side with revolutionary propaganda that called her "the Mexican Joan of Arc" (Domecq, "Teresa Urrea" 39–40) and urged the overthrow of the Mexican government (Illades 83–84).

The Nogales case attracted major media attention both in Mexico and in the United States. A group of Yaqui rebels, who would become known as "Teresistas," raided the customs house in Nogales, Sonora. Their stated goal was to steal sufficient money to buy arms and spark a revolution that would quickly spread southward toward the capital. In addition to the fact that once again "¡Viva la Santa de Cabora!" served as a rallying cry, Teresa Urrea and Lauro Aguirre both were implicated directly as instigators of the insurgency. Among items found on Yaqui casualties were images of Urrea, copies of *El Independiente*, and a letter signed by "Teresita Urrea and John the Baptist," urging them to battle (Domecq, "Teresa Urrea" 41).

The events of Nogales resulted in something of a media blitz for Teresa Urrea, who had appeared little in the press—aside from that of the towns in which she had resided—since her move to the United States. Back in Mexico City, journals such as *El Mundo* resuscitated and built upon terminology that had been used to denigrate her in the capital years before. She was "hysterical," suffering from a "psychopathy," and responsible for "the fanaticism of a human mass." It also sarcastically linked her back again with "the great men of Mexican spiritism" (Domecq, "Teresa Urrea" 201). Before long, she was being called an "ultracelebrity" as journals rushed to publish not only stories on her but "authentic" photos of her (*El Mundo* 25 October 1896; see Figure 12).

In Sonora, numerous journals made clear the connection between La Santa de Cabora, Lauro Aguirre, and the Yaqui rebels. Even the state's official newspaper, *La Constitución*, which had taken pains to avoid mention of Urrea a few years earlier, named her this time (18 September 1896, 2). Aurelio Pérez Peña summed up the local press's position with regard to the rebels in an article he wrote for *El Imparcial* titled "For the heroes, a tribute to those of Nogales (those attacked by the Yaquis)" (29 August 1896, 1). Certainly in Sonora, where war with the Yaquis had been essentially ongoing for decades, any rebellion instigated by that particular group was unlikely to rouse the sympathy of

even the most liberal press—not that Sonoran journals had ever treated
La Santa de Cabora as anything other than an embarrassment.

Mexico City newspapers such as *El Universal* tried to get to the bot-
tom of whether or not Teresa was guilty this time, first reporting "with
certitude" that she was (18 August 1896, 3), then reversing themselves a
few days later, claiming that some "cowboys of Arizona are the leaders

Figure 12. "Teresa Urrea, in a Mystic Attitude." Illustration from El Mundo,
25 October 1896.

of the movement" (29 August, 3). However, interest in Urrea among Mexican journals again quickly faded.

On the U.S. side, on the other hand, newspapers began adding information as they welcomed Teresa Urrea back into the public eye. In the borderlands, the *Oasis* of Nogales, Arizona, claimed that the raiders of its Mexican sister city were not only Yaquis but also "Mexicans, . . . Pima and Tomóchic Indians, and Mestizos" (15 August 1896, 1). A similar story in the *San Francisco Examiner* listed the participating groups as "all sorts—Pima Indians, Mexican peons, Yaquis and Mesitos *[sic]*."[26] The story began to assume outlandish proportions. The Yaqui invaders were "crazed" and "fanatical" (*New York Times* 14 August 1896, 1); the *San Francisco Chronicle* identified the skirmish as "the beginning of a revolution instigated by Teresa de Cabora," then contradicted itself by speculating that the raiders may actually have been Apaches realizing "a retaliatory move" for having been chased out of "Old Mexico" (13 August 1896, 1). The *New York Herald*, unable at first to place the "Santa Teresa" whose name was found on pictures and documents found on the bodies of the casualties of the "savages" who had "descended upon Nogales" (13 August, 12), later reported that she was "the patron saint of the Yaqui Indians" and furthermore situated her in the middle of the action: "She, it is said, led the advance in the attack" (17 August, 7).

Teresa Urrea was both "innocent" and forceful, having "obtained complete control" over the Yaquis (*New York Times* 13 August 1896, cited in Woodbridge 426–27). An anonymous *Los Angeles Times* correspondent, who claimed to have met "Terese" in Nogales a few years earlier, used his story on "the famous Mexican Joan of Arc" to repeat stereotypes of Mexicans as antimodern and actively ignorant:

> The Mexicans are intensely conservative and show no inclination
> to change their methods. The Mexican peon is contented with his
> condition and does not cudgel his brains about new inventions or the
> changes in the styles of dress. He wears his shoes with rawhide soles,
> the same as he did a hundred years ago, without a thought of higher
> heels or sharper toes, and his serape thrown about his shoulders is
> perfection, according to their ideas of comfort and style. They cele-
> brate their periodical fiestas the same as they did in olden times, and

would revolt against the idea of letting a fiesta day pass without the usual ceremonies and festive sports. (16 August 1896, 25)

Another correspondent, the novelist Maude Mason Austin (cited as "Maud Mason Austin"), authored another story on Urrea a few days later in the same journal. Austin lauds Urrea as the embodiment of "charity, love, self-abnegation and all those cardinal virtues which pulpit orators bepraise" (23 August, 18). Austin, who appears to have understood Spanish, insists that Urrea's powers are not supernatural ("any more than electrobiology is mysterious") and that she is "truly saintlike" (18). She also makes a point of clarifying misinformation circulating regarding Tomóchic, asserting that "the inhabitants of Tomochic are Mexicans, not Tarahumares" and that their insurrection was not a mere expression of fanaticism but also a response to "oppression and poverty" (18). In addition, Austin captures the heroism popularly attributed to the rebels in Mexico: women and children were "shamelessly butchered and Tomochic burnt. Before this was accomplished, however, fifty-eight valiant rebels killed 580 . . . soldiers—in one encounter" (18). Of course, for Austin, Teresa was not involved: "This gentle girl could never have revelled in bloodshed" (18).

This opinion was reaffirmed in a later *Los Angeles Times* article that claimed that Teresa's name was only brought into the Nogales affair when a Mexican customs officer was captured by the Yaquis and tried to obtain his release by claiming to be American:

"Will you swear it? What will you swear by?" said the Yaquis. "I swear," said the wily Mexican, "by Santa Teresa. Vive *[sic]* Santa Teresa!" he yelled, hoping to please them. Then the Yaquis took up the cry of "Vive *[sic]* Santa Teresa!" and forthwith she became an element in the little rebellion." (7 September 1896, 5)

If all this were not confusing enough, just a month later, *Overland Monthly* printed a story titled "Santa Teresa" that presents itself as her biography. In it, young Teresa is an orphan and is not assigned a last name (Woodbridge 422–23). When she was an adolescent, she had some kind of fit, after which she saw visions of angels. Her community was convinced that she was insane and they made her sleep in a pigpen (423).

Soon after that, she was kidnapped by Yaquis who planned to rape her. However, when they went to touch her, she gave them an electric shock, which convinced them that she had supernatural powers (424). From this time on, she became locally famous and took on the role of "instrument by whose means it was destined that the Yaquis were to shake the yoke of the Mexican government from their necks" (424–25). When Mexican troops attacked and killed the Yaquis with whom she lived, they took her prisoner as well and soon decided to execute her. However, when the firing squad was about to shoot, "[t]he ground suddenly opened beneath their feet and the twenty-one soldiers were sucked down into the abyss" (425).

The author, Bradford Woodbridge, was presented as a bona fide researcher, having submitted his story from Minas Prietas, Sonora. He swore that "[t]he main facts are true, although I cannot vouch for all the incidents. Teresa, like Jeanne d'Arc and the girl of Lourdes, is a psychological problem, and no doubt the accounts of her remarkable powers have been somewhat exaggerated" (426).

By the fall, Mexican authorities were attempting to extradite Lauro Aguirre and Teresa Urrea back to Mexico, where they wished to try them for sedition (Domecq, "Teresa Urrea" 43). However, a *New York Times* story quoted at length in the *Overland Monthly* claimed that the Díaz government in reality believed that "a mistake has been made" with regard to Mexico's treatment of her—that is, her deportation—and that "President Díaz . . . sent a deputation to invite her to return to Mexico" (427) as a free citizen.

Teresa's response to all this commotion, now much more politically tinged than ever before, was to issue a statement to the *El Paso Herald* to defend herself, and to publish a lengthy article in *El Independiente* outlining her political ideas. In the latter case, Domecq concludes that "by dint of its wording and content, this article could not have been written by Teresa and it is most likely that it came from the pen of Aguirre" ("Teresa Urrea" 42). Meanwhile, another theory holds that her father was behind some of her writings. For example, he took responsibility for the text on the reverse of her images as photographed by A. C. Rose around this time (Illades 83–84), and some news stories declared that the Yaqui prisoners interrogated after the Nogales assault "say her father

is more to blame than she, as the girl does about as he wants her to."
This report concluded, however, that "Aguirre is the worst, they say, as
he has complete control over Teresa's father" (*New York Times* 20 August
1896, 1). The term "complete control" harks back to the report from
the same paper of four days earlier, which maintained that Teresa had
"complete control" over the Yaquis (Woodbridge 427). Aguirre controls
Tomás controls Teresa controls the Yaquis, as the *Times* would have it—
although the newspaper cast doubt on its own whisper-down-the-lane
theory of control by adding that "Aguirre is a highly educated man . . .
but is said to be dissipated" (20 August, 1).

In any case, the article signed by Teresa Urrea in *El Independiente*,
"My Ideas on Revolution," that came out on 21 August closely resembled the verbose writings of Aguirre that commonly filled the journal.
For this Teresa Urrea, the revolutionary movements springing up around
Mexico "are a response to a profound public discontent regarding the
government's despotism." Her voice continued, "the most rational, just
and logical interpretation is that what happened in Nogales is a response
to the same causes as those of the many movements in Mexico, and not
to me, because it is stupid to believe that of twenty revolutionary movements there are nineteen that result from one cause, public discontent,
and that one of them be a totally different case" (quoted in Illades 82).
It is the voice of a revolutionary who, although she denied involvement
with the Nogales insurgency, would not hesitate to support such actions.
It is the Teresa Urrea that, according to Valadés, "continued working
to organize new expeditions" (*La Opinión* 236, 9 May 1937, 1). Some
historians indeed report as a fact that Teresa was a lead organizer in the
assault on Nogales (Gill, *La doncella* 30).

Her letter to the editor of the *El Paso Herald*, just a few weeks later,
painted a totally different picture. She was no longer a revolutionary
concerned with Mexican tyranny but an innocent victim, resentful of
the unjust treatment to which she was subjected:

> The press generally in these days has occupied itself with my humble
> person in terms unfavorable in the highest degree, since in a fashion
> most unjust . . . they refer to me as participating in political matters;
> they connect me to the events that have happened in Nogales,
> Sonora . . . where people have risen in arms against the government

of Sr. General Don Porfirio Díaz. I am not one who encourages such
uprisings, nor one who in any way mixes up with them, and I protest
. . . against the imputations of my enemies. (11 September 1896,
quoted in Putnam 256)

A few weeks earlier a revolutionary, she was now suddenly outraged
that anyone might imagine her "participating in political matters." She
continued:

> I have noticed with much pain that the persons who have taken
> up arms in Mexican territory have invoked my name in aid of the
> schemes they are carrying through. But I repeat I am not one who
> authorizes . . . these proceedings. Decidedly, I am a victim since in a
> most unjust way have I been expatriated from my country since May
> 19, 1892 . . . Oh, that heaven may pardon this ingratitude of which
> I have been made the victim by the president of the Republic of
> Mexico. (quoted in Putnam 257)

She concluded by appealing to her readers: "Am I to blame because my
offending compatriots demand of the government justice for me? I think
not, and appeal to the judgment of every sensible person" (quoted in
Putnam 257). Such writings lead other critics to follow Frías in concluding that Teresa was just an innocent girl who never involved herself in politics and was only manipulated by others who wished to take
advantage of her popularity. Frank Bishop Putnam writes: "Teresa stead-
fastly refused to have any part of the political affairs of Mexico" (256).

Still, whether or not she really was involved in politics, the Mexican
government believed that she was, and she (and her associates) knew it. In
January 1897, things came to a head when there was an attempt reportedly made on Teresa's life (Perú 20). The *Los Angeles Times* reported that
Urrea felt herself to be "in hourly dread of being kidnapped" (12 June
1897, 2; see also 14 January 1897, 1; 30 June 1897, 9). La Santa de Cabora's political life—real or invented—was becoming too high profile, and
things were getting risky. By summer, then, the Urreas decided it was
time to move back to Arizona. They chose the quiet town of Clifton, not
far from Solomonville (Domecq, "Teresa Urrea" 44). Around this time,
the *San Francisco Call* published a story claiming that Teresa Urrea, "the
Sonora Witch for whom men gave up their lives," had been invited by a

promoter in San Francisco "to be a freak," that is, to become "a star the-atrical attraction" (27 August 1896, quoted in Edwards 56). However, nothing came to pass. Perhaps Teresa felt that it was time to lie low.

Teresa in Clifton, Arizona: 1897–1900

Brianda Domecq may have been accurate in portraying Teresa's great relief at leaving El Paso and moving to quiet Clifton ("For the first time ever Teresa experienced real tranquility. In Clifton nothing ever hap-pened": *The Astonishing Story* 325; *La insólita historia* 345). Still, it is hard to believe that Teresa's life back in Arizona was truly quiet. The crowds continued to follow her and she went on treating the infirm. As Valadés puts it, "The throngs of ailing pilgrims were interminable" (*La Opinión* 243, 16 May 1937, 1). However, in the last years of the 1890s, Teresa kept a lower profile and roused much less controversy than she had before. "Those were happy days," reminisced one of Teresa's half-sisters, "She played the marimba and the guitar, and sang beautifully. I remem-ber so well how she charmed everyone" (quoted in Putnam 258). This image of Teresa as a musician and entertainer foreshadows the way in which her public persona was to develop in the coming years. In the United States, it seems that she would attain greatest popularity nei-ther as a spiritist or religious mystic, nor as a political insurgent, but as a star performer. But she did not become a professional entertainer while she was in Clifton. Her father, in fact, was more the breadwinner then, running a dairy and a woodyard, both of which were quite successful (Putnam 258).

Still, she had not yet escaped her reputation as an anti-Díaz militant and friend of the Yaquis. In 1899, as armed conflict with Yaqui rebels mounted in Sonora, rumors surfaced in the States that Teresa was actu-ally in the Yaqui River valley, heading up the insurgency. The *El Paso Daily Herald* of 29 July 1899 reported, "The young Mexican woman María Teresa Urrea . . . can presently be found in Sonora among the Yaquis, and although they are the most ferocious tribe in the Republic, and the most irreconcilable with people of reason, they venerate Teresa and obey her as if she were a queen" (quoted in Valadés, *La Opinión* 243, 16 May 1937, 1). It claimed that Mexicans saw her as "the mother of Moctezuma, the dreamed of Mexican Messiah, who would come to emancipate peons from the servitude in which they are found and to restore the splendor of the throne that Cortés plundered and destroyed" (quoted in Valadés, *La Opinión* 243, 16 May 1937, 2).

Another story reports a hoax in which someone writing in Teresa Urrea's name "offered $10,000 and the rulership of 5000 [Yaqui] Indians to any American who would wed her" (*Los Angeles Times* 22 May 1899, 4). This story also claims that Urrea had moved "to some obscure hamlet in Sonora" (4), although it does not place her among insurgent Yaquis, a few days later adding that her return to Mexico was possible because she had been "released from the disfavor of the state" (24 May, 13).

Most historians agree that Urrea never returned to Mexico. In fact, less than a year later, in June 1900, she found herself at the center of another scandal in Clifton. Against her father's wishes, she got involved with a young miner named Guadalupe Rodríguez and eventually accepted his proposal to marry. The next day, he tried to get her to go back to Mexico with him, and when he attempted to force her at gunpoint, he was arrested (Domecq, "Santa Teresa" 46). Rodríguez wrote numerous irate letters to protest his arrest, but the consensus was that "he is mentally unbalanced and no doubt when he is released from jail he will be tried for lunacy" (*Arizona Bulletin* 27 July 1900, 1). All this was seen as bad luck for Urrea. The same journal concluded its reporting on the topic: "Santa Teresa has the sympathy of the Americans here, as well as the Mexicans, in her troubles" (1). Some months later, Teresa herself described these events in an interview, emphasizing Guadalupe's "strange" and irrational behavior following their wedding ceremony, which culminated in his ordering her to follow him as he set out walking along the railroad tracks toward Mexico: "He began to run. I ran, too. He had his gun and he started to shoot. The people ran out and made me come back. Then they caught him" (*San Francisco Examiner* 27 July 1900, 7).

By this time, Teresa Urrea had been largely forgotten in Mexico. Once stories about her in U.S. journals ceased to have major political implications, Mexican newspapers stopped reporting on her almost altogether. Her marriage in 1900 did generate a minimum amount of coverage in Mexico City, where *El Universal* printed a mocking story under the headline "Saintly Things," noting that Santa Teresa's brand-new husband had just been arrested for attempting to murder her (1 August 1900, 2). The same journal would repeat this story a couple of months later after Urrea had arrived in San Francisco, this time deriding her further by reporting that she "has resolved to marry" with her new husband-to-be identified as a Mr. Duger, a putative arms supplier to insurgent Yaquis (28 September 1900, 1). Despite the issues raised (among them polygamy and treason), *El Universal* neglected to follow up on the leads and the story was quickly forgotten.

A few years later, in her divorce proceedings, Teresa would speak out on her marriage, claiming that Rodríguez had been an agent of Porfirio Díaz sent to bring her back to Mexico, dead or alive. She also claimed that the marriage was never consummated (Holden 176–77). Whether or not any of this was true, Domecq contends, "The incident with Rodríguez marked the end of her being implicated in politics" ("Teresa Urrea" 46). In fact, it was in the summer of 1900, just after her short-lived marriage broke up, that her public persona would take on yet another facet when Teresa made a trip to California.

The trip was arranged by friends in Clifton. A local medical doctor, L. A. W. Burtch, befriended her, impressed as he was at the progress she appeared to make with some of his most incurable patients. He introduced her to the family of a wealthy banker, C. P. Rosencrans, whose son was suffering from a debilitating disease. When Teresa was credited with improving the boy's condition, the Rosencrans family took her under their wing. Given her father's lingering anger over her disobedience in marrying Rodríguez, she was uncomfortable back home with him, but a few days after her return, Mrs. Rosencrans invited Teresa to accompany her to San José, California, where a friend, Mrs. A. C. Fessler, had a daughter also in dire need of treatment (Putnam 259–60).

Teresa Goes to California: 1900

On 27 July 1900, the *San Francisco Examiner,* the same journal that had previously facetiously reported on the exile of "'Saint' Teresa" (28 June 1892, 1) and the "Sonora Witch" (14 August 1896, 1–2), did a major feature story on Teresa Urrea, now referred to respectfully as "Santa

Teresa, celebrated Mexican healer" (7). This often-quoted story includes an interview with Urrea and an extended first-person autobiographical narrative attributed to Teresa herself. However, given the fact that "Santa Teresa speaks only Spanish," it must be taken into account that the English-language text was first translated by Mrs. A. C. Fessler and then shaped by the reporter Helen Dare.

Although the text is considered an important source since it is one of only a few in which Teresa herself speaks at length,[27] it opens with a series of factual errors. It states that Teresa was first imprisoned in Mexico for "causing an uprising of the Yaqui Indians," "has been the cause of uprising and bloodshed wherever she has appeared in Mexican towns or villages," and "was . . . the real cause of a bloody attack on the custom-house in Nogales, Sonora, Mexico some four years ago, by a religiously crazed band of Pima Indians, Mexican peons, Yaquis and Mesitos [sic]" (San Francisco Examiner 27 July 1900, 7). It also asserts, regarding the Díaz government's decision to deport her in 1892, "the decree caused the Tomóchic Indians to go on the warpath." It adds that "to bring about peace," she was allowed to return to Sonora in 1893, enabling her to set up her healing operation anew in Cabora. Soon after, it claims, she was arrested again in Presidio del Norte when a fight broke out between her followers and Mexican authorities.

Teresa's own narrative speaks to her healing powers, which she herself confesses not to understand, but she concludes, "I believe God has placed me here as one of his instruments to do good" (7). She mentions her methods: "Sometime I rub; sometimes I give also medicines or lotions that I make from herbs I gather. I pray, too, but not with the lips but I lift up my spirit to God for help to do his will on Earth" (7). The article features three photos—one a full-length portrait of Santa Teresa and two smaller ones of her miraculous hands—and focuses principally on her healing powers.

However, Urrea does briefly address her troubles with Mexican authorities, declaring: "I had nothing to do with the Yaqui revolution . . . I have cured the Indians and they love me for it, but I do not tell them to make revolutions" (7). And while it was the Fessler child whom "she saved from death" (7), it was an emotional Mrs. C. P. Rosencrans who got the chance to put in her two cents about Teresa's treatment of her son Alvin who "was dying of cerebro-spinal meningitis" and had gone blind. Dare quotes Mrs. Rosencrans: "'Santa Teresa . . . has been caring for him for six months and he can move and talk, he is fat again, and I believe,' and the little mother's heart choked up into her throat, 'that she will cure him and make him see again'" (7).

Helen Dare paints a most sympathetic portrait of Urrea as a gentle woman, in fact an ordinary woman whose life was made extraordinary by circumstances not in her control. However, she hesitates to take a position on Urrea's authenticity: "Whether Santa Teresa is a spiritual healer or not is not given for me to know—nature has not endowed me with faith" (7). Nonetheless, her emphasis on Teresa as a healer and not a political agitator is important at this stage of Urrea's public career.

About six weeks later, Teresa was back in the public eye in San Francisco. On 9 September, all the major local papers printed stories as part of a publicity blitz—arranged by a "wide awake press agent"—for a series of public appearances at the city's Metropolitan Temple where Urrea was scheduled to "treat the sick free of charge" (*San Francisco Call* 9 September 1900, 40). Urrea in effect gave a press conference at which she demonstrated her healing powers to local reporters. Besides laying her hands on all willing reporters ("There was no malady to be experimented upon, but the magnetic influence was sufficiently proved," wrote the *Examiner* reporter: 9 September, 23), she treated a whisky drummer named P. J. Hennelly for spinal paralysis, after which he was able to stand without the aid of a cane for the first time in years. He stated, "I do not think she has given me any relief that will be permanent. I will say, however, that the temporary effects of her treatment were wonderful" (*San Francisco Call* 9 September, 40).

The stories treated her rather lightly. They reviewed her legendary past and reputation, dramatically described the techniques Urrea demonstrated on Hennelly and others, briefly addressed the rather inconclusive results, then announced the dates of her public engagements. Her denials of political involvement were taken at face value, and little effort was made to drum up old news stories of Mayo insurgencies, the Tomóchic massacre, or Yaqui rebellions. The *San Francisco Bulletin* avowed, "She abhors the idea of war. She implored the Yaquis to submit, but the Mexican government was cruel and faithless" (9 September, 20).

The *San Francisco Chronicle* was alone in its blunt skepticism, object-ing that Hennelly's reported temporary improvement "was not apparent to the observer" (9 September, 5). The *Chronicle*'s doubts about Urrea's abilities point to its anonymous reporter's distrust in journalism in gen-eral, since it is in newspapers that her image took shape:

> Little truth, mixed with much fantasy has been written about this
> woman and her mystic charm has been exploited from one end of the
> land to the other. Fable and fiction have been so interwoven with the
> grains of reality that she is now heralded as being possessed with
> divine powers and is credited with the performance of miracles. Like
> all people of her class, she attracts the superstitious and ignorant. (5)

Yet, the *Chronicle* alone provided significant followup on the press con-ference. It sent a reporter to her first session at the Metropolitan Tem-ple, where it was observed that "a half dozen men and women climbed laboriously to the platform and one by one underwent the ordeal of manipulation at the hands of Santa Teresa. Some of these professed that they had been benefited, if not cured of their ailments" (13 Sep-tember 1900, 9).

It also covered the story of the arrest of J. H. Suits, "the enterpris-ing manager of Santa Teresa," for false imprisonment of his client. The "Spiritualist" Madame Young had been trying to meet with Urrea to go into business with her. Unable to reach her directly, she contacted her through a mutual friend, Beatrice Castro: "they came to the conclusion that Santa Teresa was held as a prisoner from the fact that she had on several occasions refused an invitation to dine out" (23 September 1900, 10). Whether indeed Urrea was being exploited, whether this was merely a plot to discredit her manager,[28] or whether in fact Teresa simply did not wish to dine with Madame Young, the story points to the shift in Urrea's image from political dissident to popular performer. Teresa Urrea was entering the entertainment business.

In fact, these appearances in San Francisco launched a five-year tour that was to pay Urrea ten thousand dollars. A "medical company" run by "clever promoters" (Putnam 261)—or as others see it "scheming pro-moters" (Rodríguez and Rodríguez 196)—sent her on a "Curing Cru-sade" to such cities as St. Louis, Los Angeles, and New York. She was no longer healing hordes of impoverished Mexican pilgrims at dusty Cabora Ranch or in arid border towns. She was now part of a business enterprise that took her to glamorous modern cities and brought her to audiences of largely Anglophone curiosity seekers. Her new career made her a media star wherever she went, but, no longer a threat to *la paz porfiriana*, she largely disappeared from the Mexican press.

Santa Teresa on Tour

Aside from what can be ascertained from the news feature stories promoting her tour, little is known about the details of Teresa's life in the first few years of the new century.[29] She traveled the country with her promoters and a young interpreter named John Van Order, whose mother was a friend of the family from Arizona, and with whom she eventually would have two daughters.

Around this time, the first novel about Teresa Urrea was published in New York. Largely forgotten, William Thomas Whitlock's *Santa Teresa: A Tale of the Yaquii Rebellion* (1900) remains unread by nearly all Urrea biographers and historians. Whitlock casts Teresa as a mysterious and beautiful Mexican faith healer in a Wild West romance in which her sweet character is contrasted with that of her evil sister, a bandit named Jovita. The stockbroker John Deware is brokenhearted when he falls in love with Teresa only to discover that she is unwilling to give up her sainthood to become his wife. Although she dies in the Colorado desert in the early 1890s, in the book's epilogue, her name appears again in a newspaper story about a "Yaquii" uprising, causing the narrator to wonder whether she really died and further adding to her mystique. Like Woodridge's fanciful treatment of her in 1896, her romanticized portrayal in this adventure yarn only serves to embellish her already extravagant image.

Returning to La Santa's tour, in March 1901, while in New York—and reportedly on her way "to London and Paris [and] [a]fterward to India" (*New York Journal* 3 March 1901, 23)—she granted an interview to the *New York Journal*, again providing flamboyant publicity photos demonstrating her healing techniques (see Figure 13). In this interview, in which Urrea was presented as "the heroine of a melodrama in real life," she reiterated in some detail her personal history and experiences as a healer (3 March 1901, 23). She also spoke at length about the plight of the Yaquis in Sonora, whom she called "the bravest and most persecuted people on earth." The interview concluded with Urrea declaring that her two great wishes in life were "to heal all humanity" and "continued peace for the Yaquis" (23). Her activities in New York are not well documented, although it is believed that she engaged in activities beyond treating the ill and crippled: rumor has it, in fact, that she entered and won a beauty contest there as well (Putnam 262).

In 1902, her father died, but she continued on tour. Later that year she returned to the west coast, briefly taking up residence in Los Angeles, where she was taken as a "Yaqui girl." The *Los Angeles Times* reported: "As admitted by an old Mexican woman, who is one of her circle, she uses medicinal compounds of her own concoction in dealing with the afflicted, and probably many of her alleged cures are effected through her Indian knowledge of healing herbs" (15 December 1902, 5). In Los

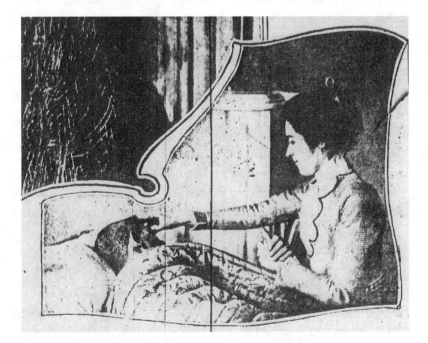

Figure 13. "Santa Teresa, the Fanatical Mexican Miracle Worker in New York." Illustration from the New York Journal, *3 March 1901.*

Angeles, the press was less friendly than in San Francisco. The *Los Angeles Times* emphasized that "the majority of Mexicans" believed in Santa Teresa's "supernatural powers" and further implied that the "pitiful throng" of "the halt, the blind, the inwardly distressed, paralytics almost helpless and others ravaged by consumption" along with all kinds of "cripples" who were arriving in Los Angeles to see her were only Mexican, as if no one else would be so foolish (15 December 1902, 5). Another report claims that even Urrea was sick of these forlorn hangerson, and that she asked for police assistance in getting rid of them: "Santa Teresa told the officers that she does not care to heal any more . . . All she wants is to be left alone" (*Los Angeles Times* 30 October 1902, A2).

Meanwhile, her lifestyle was changing remarkably with her new income, and in mid-1903 she went to Santa Barbara for a lengthy vacation. It was also during her sojourn in southern California that she filed for divorce against Guadalupe Rodríguez (*Los Angeles Times* 18 December 1902, A2; 27 May 1903, A2; 27 November 1903, A4; 24 January 1904, 10). When her house in Los Angeles burned down (*Los Angeles Times* 27 August 1903, A6), she decided to get out of her contract with her promoters, and she returned in mid-1904 to Clifton, Arizona (Vanderwood 305).

The Fall of La Santa de Cabora

She arrived back in Clifton with her two daughters, but without their father. She used her savings to build a small hospital and settled down into a quiet life as a mother and healer, although some believed that since she was no longer a virgin, she had lost her healing powers. Valadés writes:

> Upon realizing that she had lost her faculties, Teresa went into hiding, and although she continued living in Cliffton [sic], several major U.S. reporters wrote of her disappearance. Some said that she had been kidnapped by the Mexican government; others that she had gone into the interior of the Sonoran sierra to prepare a new Yaqui Indian insurrection. (*La Opinión* 243, 16 May 1937, 1)

Others contend that she continued curing until the very end of her life. For example, in a storm that flooded parts of Clifton in 1905, it is said that "Teresita was in the cold rain and water for hours rescuing people and their possessions" (Putnam 263). In the midst of a drought, the rain had been welcome, and some went so far as to attribute the rain itself to Urrea: "The flood predicted for Clifton by 'Santa Teresa' arrived several days late, but near enough to reestablish the prestige of the seeress in the eyes of the Mexican population" (*Los Angeles Times* 27 March 1905, I11).

Whether from this selfless act or from other causes, Teresa herself fell ill with tuberculosis and died in early 1906. Despite her low profile in the last couple of years of her life, she had endeared herself to the population of Clifton, and her funeral was said to be one of the largest that had ever been held there. But later that year, a local newspaper commented that by the end of her life "[h]er magical power had disappeared. The 'sainted girl of Sonora' had been forgotten" (*Tucson Citizen* 22 December 1906).

Teresa Urrea would remain relatively forgotten for awhile—except in literature, where Frías's *Tomóchic* alone kept her alive in the Mexican national imagination. During her lifetime, she had been the darling of the spiritists, the folly of superstitious Yaquis, the inspiration of the fanaticism of the *tomoches*, a threat to the Porfiriato, a miraculous healer, a sensational spectacle, a neurotic witch, and a seasoned entertainer. She shifted shapes as she crossed borders from Mexico to the United States and from the company of the poor and infirm to the society of people of wealth and power.

In Mexico City, she represented first provincial ignorance and superstition, then became the emblem of the alternative belief system of the spiritists, then became a hysterical girl who inspired dangerous fanaticism in borderlands Indians and peasants. In the Mexican northwestern borderlands, although she was a major local celebrity whose reputation as a saint and/or fraud spread rapidly in the early 1890s by word of mouth, the local press considered her largely an embarrassment unworthy of attention. In the U.S. southwestern borderlands, she became a signifier through which multiple attitudes toward Mexico could be expressed. Mexico was unjust for expelling her; Mexicans were superstitious for believing in her; Mexicans were fanatics for being inspired to rebel by her. Although it did not really take her seriously, the U.S. borderlands press was largely sympathetic to her. Later, when Lauro Aguirre began actively promoting her as a symbol of resistance to Porfirian excess and brutality, her figure grew in proportion. Then, when she withdrew from Aguirre's propaganda and became a performer, her witch and healer persona ballooned even more as she turned into a celebrity, more likely to compete in a beauty pageant than instigate armed insurrection. But Teresa Urrea was not forgotten forever. She may have been buried in an unmarked grave (Vanderwood 306), but La Santa de Cabora was not to disappear from the multiple contexts in which she moved during her lifetime.

Teresa Urrea after 1906

After Teresa's death, it would be decades before her image was revived. Interestingly, while it has primarily been historians who have joined in a continuous process of reshaping and correcting her image, the most complete and most often read texts about her have been literary. No historiographic study of La Santa de Cabora would be complete without citing Heriberto Frías's *Tomóchic*. In fact, Frías's novel is a major source for many historians. Valadés, who acknowledges the novel's "great documentary value" (*La Opinión* 166, 28 February 1937, 1), quotes verbatim over twenty paragraphs of *Tomóchic* in his seventh chapter (*La Opinión* 208, 11 April 1937, 1–2). Frías likewise takes a prominent place in the bibliographies of Gill, Sobarzo, Vanderwood, Domecq, Illades, Rodríguez and Rodríguez, and Romero, among many others. The historian Jesús Vargas Valdez notes that Francisco Madero himself acknowledged the importance of Frías's novel for its "historical value" ("Introducción" 15).

And in recent years, despite a resurgence of interest in La Santa de Cabora among historians at the centenary of the Tomóchic rebellion, the most often read text on Urrea has been Brianda Domecq's novel *La insólita historia de la Santa de Cabora*.[30] Unlike Frías, Domecq did not have eyewitness authority to lend her credibility, but she has the authority today for being the historian[31] who has most profoundly researched Urrea. Her historiographic essay "Teresa Urrea: La Santa de Cabora" boasts a rich bibliography of newspaper articles, historiography texts, biographies of Urrea, and, of course, Frías's novel, as well as additional materials from Mexican military and diplomatic archives, and is the definitive source on Urrea prior to 1900. But as she herself puts it, "the character of the novel has turned out much more real and alive than that of the documents" ("Teresa Urrea" 12). She adds, "If history capriciously overlooked such a fascinating character, the novel would revive her forever" ("Teresa Urrea" 12).

Among the first texts to revive the name of La Santa de Cabora was the serialized book by José Valadés, *La Santa de Cabora y la insurrección de Tomóchic en 1892*, published on twelve successive Sundays in the winter and spring of 1937 in *La Opinión*, a Spanish-language newspaper in Los Angeles.[32] It would finally come out in book form in Mexico only posthumously in 1985, retitled *Porfirio Díaz contra el gran poder de Dios: Las rebeliones de Tomóchic y Temosachic*. Valadés, a historian, was also known as a militant revolutionary in his early years. It is unclear why he chose as a venue for his work a newspaper geared primarily toward emigrants in the United States. However, it should be noted that the journal did reach a significant audience in the northwestern Mexican borderlands (Holden xiii). Valadés, whose writings included numerous texts on the Mexican revolution, wished to publicize some of its precursor movements. He aimed to challenge the notion of the Porfirian era as peaceful and to incorporate some early rebel heroes into Mexican historiography—among them, Cruz Chávez, Lauro Aguirre, and Teresa Urrea.[33]

This impulse to make a prerevolutionary heroine of La Santa de Cabora, to revive her image as the "Mexican Joan of Arc," was repeated by other Mexican historians such as Mario Gill in the 1950s. Gill insists that Teresa's "attitude was that not of a miracle worker, but of a revolutionary" ("Teresa Urrea" 643). He applauds her for tormenting Porfirio Díaz and salutes her as a precursor to the celebrated revolutionary agitator Ricardo Flores Magón ("Teresa Urrea" 644).

However, this image of Teresa Urrea would not stick. Valadés's ephemeral newspaper story was soon forgotten and Gill's essay, published in an academic journal, never reached a wide audience—that is, until a few decades later when the Mexican government published a widely distributed booklet by Gill through its Conasupo supermarket chain.[34] By the last decades of the twentieth century, researchers had taken up anew the effort to vindicate Urrea as a recalcitrant heroine of the Porfiriato.

Contemporary researchers including Brianda Domecq and Lilián Illades have been adamant about resuscitating Urrea to show that she was not the sweet and innocent creature portrayed in Frías but rather a strong-willed woman, "a first order participant . . . in the prerevolutionary movements that preceded and undoubtedly inspired the Flores Magón brothers" (Domecq, "Teresa Urrea" 12). Both conclude their articles by locating Urrea "in the list of precursors of the Mexican Revolution" (Illades 88). This is not to say that these latter portraits of Urrea are one-dimensional; Domecq's in particular is quite complex. However, both do share with Valadés and Gill a goal of rewriting the history of the Porfiriato in order to add the important interventions of a key personage of the opposition.

Another cluster of texts in which the name of Teresa Urrea was revived is concerned less with the Porfiriato, the revolution, and national history than with the local history of the northwestern Mexican borderlands. An important early contributor to this trend was Plácido Chávez Calderón, whose *La defensa de Tomochi* was first published in 1964. The author, son of Manuel Chávez and nephew of Cruz Chávez, both leaders in the Tomóchic rebellion, relies upon the memory of his mother, Clara Calderón, for an alternative eyewitness account to that of Frías. Moreover, its local *tomoche* perspective has been a source of local pride in the (rebuilt) town, where it is considered "the true history" (Vargas Valdez, "Introducción" 17).

Chávez Calderón writes his book to set the record straight. He concerns himself with errors he found in the histories of the rebellion written by Francisco Almada in 1938—a highly influential text said to have "structured local memory about the events" (Vanderwood 319)—and by José Carlos Chávez in 1943. The former, he surmises, was forced to rely on official government documents, and the latter on the eyewitness testimony of General Francisco Castro; both, then, despite their intentions to incorporate the *tomoche* insurgents into national history as heroes (in the same vein as Valadés), gave too much of a one-sided view of the events. Meanwhile, he announces that he will simply "discard" Frías as unreliable and inaccurate. This text, much like those of Almada and Chávez, focused as all three are on the regional history of Chihuahua, offers little on the figure of Teresa Urrea. Chávez Calderón in fact asserts that his father and uncle Cruz never even met La Santa de Cabora. She was an inspiration to them, clearly, but not a real character in the drama he recounts.[35]

Thus it is little surprise that later Mexican borderlands accounts that focus greater attention on Urrea do not succeed in treating her with any less sexist bias than Frías did. For the Sonoran historian Horacio Sobarzo, for example, hers was a "story determined by the hysteria of an abnormal woman" (*Episodios* 64). Just as we have seen to be the case with Joaquín Murrieta, Lola Casanova, and the heroines of Guaymas, Urrea has not been embraced into local history. And it is not unusual for local historians to simply omit her from their work, just as the official newspaper *La Constitución* frequently left out reports on Tomóchic and the various incidents of conflict with the Díaz regime in which Teresa Urrea was implicated. For example, Gilberto Escobosa Gámez, in his *Crónicas sonorenses*, relates the 1896 Yaqui rebel raid on the Nogales, Sonora, customs house as an important occasion of "solidarity between both Nogaleses" (262), yet he never once mentions that exiled Teresa Urrea was thought to have instigated the uprising. Important histories by Calvo Berber and Villa, despite their interest in other celebrities of local legend such as Lola Casanova and Loreto Encinas de Avilés, ignore her entirely. The six-volume *Historia general de Sonora* only mentions her name once, as the battle cry of the Mayos in their short-lived 1892 rebellion (Figueroa Valenzuela, "Los indios" 160).

The Sonoran historian Manuel Santiago Corbalá Acuña does report her story—with numerous nuances that go against the commonly accepted historical record—in 1977. Most of his divergences are minor ones, repeated elsewhere, such as the identification of the *tomoches* as "indigenous" (265), or popular stories largely discredited by historians in recent years, such as the alleged meeting between Urrea and the *tomoche* rebel leaders, which Corbalá claims lasted "many long hours" (266). However, his most interesting assertion is that Urrea was the legitimate daughter of Tomás Urrea. In fact, unlike other biographical sketches of Teresita, all of which focus primary attention on *mestiza* Teresa's close relationship with her white *criollo* father, Corbalá recounts detailed stories about young Teresa's close relationship with her white mother, Doña Loreto Esceberri de Urrea. Other accounts are in agreement that

Doña Loreto was estranged from her womanizing husband, who, from just before he took his bastard daughter Teresa into his household at Cabora, took up with a much younger common-law wife. Doña Loreto in fact never lived at Cabora, remaining with her legitimate children on another of Don Tomás's properties back in Sinaloa. Otherwise, Corbalá keeps most of the legend intact: the Tomóchic rebellion, the crowds of worshipers converging on Cabora, the Mayo uprising at Navojoa, Teresa's and Tomás's subsequent deportation to Arizona, and Teresa's death there in 1906. His emphasis is on her ties to important rebellions by such celebrated national heroes as the "valiant tomochitecos" (268). Having not altered any other details, his subtle whitening of Teresa comes across therefore as all the more believable.

Santa Teresa de Cabora is not the folk hero one might expect her to be for Sonoran historiographers; perhaps they are still discomfited by her reputation as a spiritist, *curandera*, or even fraud, for which Mexico City newspapers had ridiculed her. Or perhaps, like Aurelio Pérez Peña, some have continued to insist upon promoting Sonora in the most palatable way possible to a racist world. *Mestiza* Santa Teresa, emblem of religious fanaticism and superstition that recalls a barbarous indigenous past, is best left out of official history, or cleverly incorporated in such a way as to obscure her most discomforting traits.

It is indeed that indigenous link that has been least pursued by historians and biographers of Teresa Urrea. Although she came to be well known, particularly in the United States, for her deep connections to the Yaquis (indeed she was sometimes assumed to be a Yaqui), contemporary scholars deny Urrea's importance in Yaqui culture. One major historian of Yaqui culture asserts "there is no evidence anywhere that the Yaquis were caught up in the messianic movement . . . or influenced by her in any other way" (Hu-Dehart, *Yaqui Resistance* 255n87); another agrees: "Yaquis . . . were not interested" in Santa Teresa and other living saints (Spicer 149).

The Mayos, on the other hand, did become attached to Urrea: "The whole Mayo country was stirred during 1890, as Mayos from all over left the haciendas where they were voluntarily or forcibly employed and went to hear [Urrea and other] prophets preach" (Spicer 149; see also Crumrine, *The Mayo Indians* 134–35). Santa Teresa has apparently continued to signify powerfully for the Mayos, who celebrate her with a saint's day on 3 May each year (Crumrine, *The Mayo Indians* 125). Although it remains unclear exactly what Santa Teresa signifies for the Mayos, one ethnography recounts a relatively recent Mayo myth of Santa Teresa that pits her not against oppressive Mexicans but against invading French forces:

> During the time of Santa Teresa, Napoleon was leading his cavalry and riding his horse through the Mayo area. His horse and his men were very tired. Napoleon said, "We must go on, we are going on!" And he continued to drive his horse. When he came through here Santa Teresa said, "Now look it's time you should rest." Napoleon replied, "I'm not going to rest." And on he went. Because he disregarded what Santa Teresa said, because he didn't respect Santa Teresa, suddenly his horse's sweat turned to blood. The horse was sweating blood out of his body. This was the miracle that was performed because Napoleon did not respect Santa Teresa.[36]

It would seem that Santa Teresa's opposition to Napoleon would implicitly ally her with nineteenth-century Mexican liberals and nationalists, an alliance of little interest to Urrea and the Mayos of the 1890s. Twentieth-century Mayos have perhaps redeployed Urrea to reposition their own culture within Mexican history. Unfortunately, this fragment of Mayo oral narrative is hardly enough to draw any powerful conclusions about Urrea's continued presence in Mayo collective memory.

Teresa Urrea's story has, on the other hand, been retold on numerous occasions by historians of the U.S. Southwest, providing ample evidence of her significations in the north. The first local U.S. borderlands historian to pay notable attention to her was James M. Patton, who included significant data on Urrea in his 1944 master's thesis on the history of Clifton, Arizona. Focusing primarily on her years in Clifton, he relies upon personal interviews with José Urrea—presumably a relative of Teresa's—to reconstruct Teresa as an affectionately remembered eccentric personality of local history. Emphasizing neither her political subversiveness nor her great fame, the author concludes:

> Talk concerning her usually lends to the question of whether or not she was a faker. The truth of the matter probably is that she shared

the quality, be it spiritual, psychological, or physical, which all faith
healers have to make her patients feel that they were well. She was
successful as all of her kind are because there are always people who
are ill only in their minds but think they are ill physically. Be that
as it may she was a good woman and richly deserved to be called
"The Saint of Cabora." (143)

Patton published his thesis only in 1977, and even then it reached few
readers outside Clifton.

However, Patton was not the only Arizona historian to write about
Urrea. Several magazines ran stories on her in the latter half of the
twentieth century. For example, a pair of articles in the 1950s from the
newspaper supplement *Arizona Days and Ways* portrayed Urrea as "Arizona's only female saint" (Ridgway 22) and the "Witch of Nogales"
(Willson 22). Sources include "oldtimers" such as Mrs. Eppley, who "told
of taking her sister, Susie to . . . see Teresa. 'She never helped my sister
but she was a beautiful woman and had a magnetic personality'" (Ridgway 22). The authors' intention was to drum up colorful tidbits from
the past to contribute to local lore. For instance, Teresa's exile is dramatized as follows: "A troop of soldiers was sent to arrest Teresa but
were ambushed by Yaquis near Cabora. The skirmish that ensued resulted in 25 deaths and was the spark that ignited the Tomachic *[sic]*
war" (Ridgway 22). The story of the customs house raid at Nogales was
also reshaped:

> It was found that a woman about 25 years of age living at or near
> Carbo *[sic]*, a small village below Magdalena, was behind it all. She
> was Teresa Urrea, a mestiza, who, while still in her teens, was said to
> have had a disappointing love affair, which caused such despondency
> that she sought death by refusing to eat . . . She planned attacks on
> the rich ranches, and against the Mexican authorities, which her
> Indian and mestizo followers carried out, thus securing cattle, horses
> and plunder that were taken to mountain hideouts. (Willson 23)

The fabricated or distorted events of her life are vibrant, yet from such
a distant past that she is hardly threatening, even when cast as a rebel.
The slanderous ending of one of the versions seems quaint in the 1950s:
"Eventually she faded into oblivion and became a dirty, unkempt old

woman, who in her last years was known as 'The Witch of Nogales'"
(Willson 23).

Frank Bishop Putnam put more serious research into a 1963 article
on Urrea for *Southern California Quarterly*. Putnam cites numerous U.S.
English-language newspaper articles on Urrea, placing emphasis on stories of her miracle cures and on a few additional bizarre (and unsub-
stantiated) details: "For instance, the chemistry of her body was such that
her perspiration had an odor similar to perfume" (251).

Putnam's methodology is typically nationalist and monolingual.
Although California and Arizona are on the border, just as Chihuahua
and Sonora are, and although Teresa Urrea spent about half her life on
each side of the border, Mexican historians tend to limit themselves to
Mexican sources and to focus on her years in Mexico, while U.S. researchers tend to consult only English-language texts about the period
following her exile to Arizona. While there are notable exceptions, particularly in the last decade or two, the borderlands legend of Teresa
Urrea spent years in a posthumous double life, and it was not until the
1970s that Mexican Teresa's life began to be sutured onto that of Mexican American Teresa.

Later sources often do recognize Urrea as a borderlands icon. One
cites "Teresa Urrea's lasting contribution to the history of the United
States–Mexico border country" (Edwards 57) but still fails to present a
transamerican research methodology, relying on only U.S. newspaper
reports. Despite its central presence in Mexican historiography on Urrea,
the Tomóchic insurrection is given minimal attention, and Frías's landmark novel is never mentioned by most U.S.–based Urrea historians.

The 1970s was a decade in which La Santa de Cabora received revi-
talized attention in the United States, this time from early Chicano
studies scholars eager to establish an ethnic history to contest mainstream
U.S. historiography, which tended to marginalize Mexican American
culture. The first such vision of Teresa was an article by Richard and
Gloria Rodríguez first published in 1972. The bilingual authors made
a major breakthrough by citing both English- and Spanish-language
sources, bringing together Frías, Gill, Putnam, Willson, Ridgway, Chávez
Calderón, Patton, and even Woodridge. Here Urrea is cast into the "history of Aztlán" (179), taking on more substance as she moved beyond

the one-dimensional role of a national heroine, a cultural embarrassment, or a local eccentric.

A few years later, Carlos Larralde devoted a chapter to the "Chicana saint" in his 1976 book *Mexican American Movements and Leaders* (59). Interestingly, the cross-cultural Teresa Urrea first established in the Rodríguez article began to acquire a new postnational form as an icon of Chicana/o resistance. Larralde's Urrea "mixed religion and politics with astonishing results . . . She gave the era much of its color and verve . . . and thrilled the public with her miracles. Teresa's activities penetrated into American history and is *[sic]* now part of our Chicano heritage" (*Mexican American Movements* 59). Despite a couple of odd quirks that Teresa assumed in Larralde (for example, "she startled her admirers by sleeping in a coffin": *Mexican American Movements* 59), this new Teresa was constructed principally so as to be attractive to 1970s-style social and political rebels. Larralde emphasized her use of indigenous herbs in her treatments: her famous cataleptic fit had a new source: an "overdose" of hallucinogenic "mushrooms" (*Mexican American Movements* 61). Two years later, Larralde would embellish this aspect further by having his Teresa take "a sacred intoxicant to make her soul explore the universe. It was made of sacred mushrooms, roots of peyote, serpents' blood and portions of her powders" ("Saint Teresa" 23). This psychedelic Chicana Teresa is also less the simple country girl swept up by extraordinary circumstances than a veritable star. On her "Curing Crusade Campaign," she traveled about in "flamboyant gowns" (*Mexican American Movements* 66) and "gave in to the temptations of the theaters, exotic cafes, and the bright and variable social events of each season" (67–68). Furthermore, she became more than "queen of something or other": "For publicity purposes, her promoters encouraged her to enter beauty contests. Elected queen of many social events, Teresa loved the pageantry with all its glittering robes and the dazzling crowns" (68). Larralde then makes his embellished Teresa an important player in Los Angeles's Pacific Electric Strike of April 1903 and later, back in Clifton, captures her "distressed to see her people suffering from oppression at the hands of the Arizona Rangers. The Mexicans were denied political or labor rights so that the mining companies would have a strong political force and a source of cheap labor. The Rangers made sure that the Mexicans stayed in their place" (68–69).

Another book from the same era calls her "a Chicana counterpart to La Virgen de Guadalupe" and "a symbol of resistance to oppression for contemporary Chicanos" (Mirandé and Enríquez 86). The bicultural reconstruction of Urrea by Chicano/a scholars, then, does more than bind two culturally distinct interpretations of the Urrea legend; it transforms her from a Mexican or southwestern borderlands icon into a veritable Chicana hybrid.

Another interesting text from the 1970s is Teresa's only book-length biography, *Teresita* by William Curry Holden. Curiously, this is not usually taken to be the definitive text on Urrea. Domecq, for example, accuses Holden of naively taking Lauro Aguirre's writings on Urrea at face value, questions his ability to understand Spanish-language sources, and concludes that his supposed biography is "quite novelized."[37] The Mexican critic Rubén Osorio bitingly criticizes Holden's descriptions of the rebels of Tomóchic, claiming his comparisons of Cruz Chávez to William Jennings Bryan, John Brown, Buddist monks, and Joshua are "incomprehensible" and the product of a "fanciful imagination," and that his comparisons of the *tomoches* to Amish folk are "absurd" (78). It also does not help that *Teresita* was published by a minor publishing house and has received a relatively limited distribution. Holden was an anthropologist of the borderlands whose work took him to Texas and to Sonora at different moments of his career; the Urrea biography was a pet project of his for many years. Although it includes an extensive bibliography and has been described as "careful anthropological work" (Vanderwood 360n2), Mexican scholars have accused him of not giving Teresita enough credit. The title infantilizes his heroine, and, like Putnam before him, he denies Teresa political agency (Domecq, "Teresa Urrea" 53n96).

If Holden is antifeminist in belittling Teresa's character and fortitude, feminists have also claimed La Santa de Cabora in recent years for their cause, and this latter group has empowered its heroine. Vanderwood cites a 1995 film that exalts her as "a woman who on her own became a dominating force in a man's world" (323). Likewise, critics have noted the feminist impulse—albeit a complex and multilayered one—present in Brianda Domecq's 1990 novel. The literary critic Deborah Shaw notes: "History is also a space that traditionally has obviated or distorted women, the reason why Domecq affirms that Teresa demanded to be represented in a novelistic form" (299). She further notes that Domecq's Teresa is more than an unusually gifted girl: "Teresa enjoys her powers not only because she can do good with them, but also because they give her a social position and a freedom otherwise denied her as a woman" (306).

Domecq's perspective is not, however, that of a one-dimensional feminism. She also appreciates and stresses the remarkable ascendancy in social class that Urrea managed to achieve. While many of Teresa's interviews and all her biographical sketches mention that she was born illegitimate, *mestiza*, and poor, they tend to take for granted that she was easily able to escape poverty because her father was wealthy. None asks what happened to all the other illegitimate children Tomás Urrea had with his servants and employees. Domecq concerns herself with the ingenuity Teresa needed to exercise just to get into her father's house, and from there to escape the subservient roles to which most women, even wealthy ones, were limited in the late nineteenth century. The issue here is more than one of portraying Urrea as a powerful woman; she is also the daughter of a servant, who rises up to a position of power, which she uses to further the cause of those of the class into which she had been born. Moreover, to attain such a level of social influence and be such a threat to the mighty dictator Porfirio Díaz was extraordinary. And Domecq's novel more than any other source remains conscious of that fact and presents a vision of how it was all possible.

This is not to say that Domecq's Santa Teresa is necessarily more true to life than Holden's or Aguirre's or even Frías's. The many clues left behind in the multiple sources available from which Domecq drew— "facts, gossip, rumors, curses, truths, lies" (Domecq, "Teresa Urrea" 12)—gave her ample material from which to construct an Urrea of interest to her. If she did not dwell on Teresa's romantic entanglements,[38] or if she chose not to develop in detail the evolution of Teresa's close friendships with certain women (her mentor Huila, her best friend Josefina Félix, her servant Mariana),[39] or if she failed to explore the bonds Teresa developed with key powerful members of the communities in which she lived, or if she left out Teresa's identity as a mother to her two daughters, it was because other aspects of Teresa Urrea's character—her ability to enter public life and become an important public figure, despite being a woman and a bastard—interested her more; it was not because anyone is sure that Teresa was not really sexually active, or did not really have a tendency toward close bonds of friendship with women, and so on.

Domecq's Teresa Urrea is not just an extraordinary woman. Her role as an herbal healer is also important in Domecq. Deborah Shaw writes: "Domecq has declared that her environmentalist activities were what motivated her to finally describe the character who had obsessed her for fifteen years" (288). Certainly Teresa Urrea would not interest many readers if she did not appeal to contemporary topics of interest. And if spiritism was not a major topic of discussion in the 1990s, it does not behoove Domecq to focus excessive attention on Teresa's connections to Mexican spiritists—and she does not do so. Environmentalism and herbal healing were more likely, on the other hand, attractive themes for a 1990s literary audience.

Recent critics have focused greater attention on Urrea not as a flesh and blood woman but as a symbol. And for most people, including those whom she met, it was her public image, her social signifying function, and not her intimate essence, that they encountered, and that influenced them. Vanderwood reviews many of the posthumous materializations of Santa Teresa de Cabora and the particular social circumstances or ideological beliefs that attracted different authors or groups to her (317–29); although he does not say as much, the fact that this section forms the conclusion to his book implies that he understands her as more an icon than a person. The final scene of his book recounts the initiation of a Saint Teresa festival to drum up tourism in sleepy Clifton, Arizona, in the 1990s. There she is compared to Sor Juana Inés de la Cruz and Mother Teresa, assuming yet one more new role and attracting new potential enthusiasts (324–29).

Especially convincing is the Mexican scholar Saúl Romero's thesis that "the cult of Teresa Urrea was only the banner" that brought people together and around which they rallied (142). She did not inspire a wild fanaticism that caused her followers to act irrationally; she merely gave them a symbol that they could share and that they could employ to inspire them to undertake acts that they needed to undertake for reasons unrelated to her. The *tomoches* had serious disputes with civil and ecclesiastic authorities in Chihuahua. The Yaquis and Mayos were being viciously exploited in Sonora. Their rebellions were the product of tangible grievances, and Urrea became a symbol of the moral values for which they fought.

However, when he writes that "Teresa Urrea *was* a symbol" (162, emphasis mine), he tells only half the story. She still *is* one, but she bears multiple meanings. In recent years, Elena Díaz Björkquist has performed Teresa Urrea, channeling the spirit of La Santa de Cabora in Arizona and elsewhere, representing her as "a border person, . . . a heroine to Mexican revolutionary peasants and a darling of the Arizona Anglos" (Díaz Björkquist); Wynne Brown has included Urrea in her project to reshape the history of Arizona by incorporating "the experiences of the women who helped build it" (vii), making her something of a founding mother of state culture; and most recently Luis Alberto Urrea, a "distant cousin" of Teresa ("For True Healing"), published (in English) the biographical novel *The Hummingbird's Daughter*, in which he plays up Teresa's early training as a *curandera* and emphasizes her "mystical" indigenous knowledge.

At Cabora, in the Yaqui River valley, throughout Sonora, off in Tomóchic, in fact all around Mexico, then later in the U.S. Southwest, and from California to New York: Teresa Urrea signified in multiple ways throughout her life and continues to signify in ever evolving ways even today. She continues to be, like Joaquín Murrieta, Lola Casanova, and the heroines of Guaymas before her, a border-crossing, shape-shifting, multifaceted icon of the borderlands.

CULTURAL ICONS
OF THE
OTHER BORDERLANDS

THIS STUDY'S MAIN FOCUS has been the culture of the northwestern borderlands of Mexico in the late nineteenth century.
However, the cultural icons that have provided the basis for
the study have been rather unwieldy border crossers whose temporal
correlations have been slippery, as each has circulated and continues to
circulate in multiple contexts. This epilogue serves to look broadly at
some of the more important cultural contexts that have appropriated
the icons and to review the kinds of cultural meanings each has tended
to produce through these icons.

None of these contexts are truly discrete cultural units; each overlaps
with others; each fragments from within; each is unstable over time.
However, each can be understood to represent, however imperfectly,
shared ideas that can be identified with a particular time, place, and
community. To draw definitive conclusions about any such cultural context without interrogating it in detail and teasing out its imprecisions
would be an intellectually unsound exercise. However, such categories
do serve the purposes here: those of noting general observations regarding patterns of representation and of signaling ideologies underlying
such representations within a given roughly defined but recognizable
cultural context.

Of the many contexts in which the cultural icons in question have surfaced, those of greatest interest to this project are precisely those with which the Mexican borderlands as an imagined community most directly dialogues and defines itself. Those contexts are those of (1) Mexico, in the sense of centrist, nationalist conceptualizations of the nation; (2) the United States, as the encroaching Anglo-Protestant imperialist power; (3) Aztlán, the Mexican American U.S. Southwest; and (4) indigenous Mexico, particularly the northwestern region.

Mexican Icons in the United States

U.S. representations of Mexico, especially those by non-Mexicans, tend to see Mexico as a monolithic other. Mexico is what the United States is not, and cultural differences within Mexico, particularly regional ones that are so important to questions of *fronterizo* identity, go virtually unnoticed. A few of the patterns emerging from representations of Joaquín Murrieta (the novels of Yellow Bird and the *California Police Gazette*), Helen Hunt Jackson's *Ramona*, the *National Police Gazette*'s controversial representation of the 1853 invasion of Guaymas, William Curry Holden's *Teresita*, and the various U.S. newspaper reports on all the icons studied here, to name some key examples, follow.

Mexicans were assumed in the latter half of the nineteenth century to be criminal, corrupt, and immoral. The only recourse when confronted by figures such as Joaquín Murrieta was to kill them. The perceived inherent lack of law and order in Mexico is why so many believed that Mexicans would be happy to be liberated by *gringo* (or French) filibusters, and why rebellions such as those allegedly incited by Teresa Urrea seemed so logical. It is part of the reason why Mexico has been thought by many to be unable to progress and modernize, and why Mexicans in the United States have been deemed unworthy of status equal to that of Anglo-Americans.

On the other hand, Mexico has often been imagined as a paradise of racial solidarity. Mexicans are categorized as either mixed race or indigenous—certainly not white. Their cultural acceptance of miscegenation is why Ramona felt so at home there, but it is also why Mexico is so resistant to modernization. *Gringos* imagine nonwhite Mexicans to be superstitious—as can be seen in the fanatical followers of Teresa Urrea. Their backwardness implies a need of protection by "superior" races such as the Anglo-American race. It was after all not the mixed-race Mexicans but the Spanish colonizers who so successfully pacified the Indians through their missions.

Mexicans are assumed to be weak, and it is only by luck that they were able to hold off the incursions of the gallant French adventurer Gaston de Raousset Boulbon, at least in the opinion of the *National Police Gazette*. Despite all the fuss made over La Santa de Cabora's miraculous healing powers, she was really only a little girl named Teresita, hardly capable of masterminding rebellion or promulgating a cohesive rhetoric of insurgency. After all, if Mexicans were strong, they would not have lost half their territory in the U.S.–Mexico war.

Finally, racial differentiation in Mexico is so unimportant to U.S. observers that it makes little difference whether the rebels of Tomóchic are erroneously represented as Tarahumara Indians—or even as "Tomoche" Indians, a race that does not exist. That is also why it makes little difference whether Joaquín Murrieta was swarthy or blond: as Frank Latta points out, his head can still be confused with that of any Indian.

When these borderlands icons travel to the United States, they cease to represent the borderlands and come to signify facets of Mexico as a unified (nonwhite) whole. No matter how heroic such figures may be to some Mexicans, they repeatedly fail to attain such status when translated into Anglo-American cultural contexts.

Borderlands Icons in Aztlán

The context of Mexican American culture in the United States is quite different from the Anglo context described above. In several cases, for example, those of Lola Casanova, Cajeme, and the heroines of Guaymas, such icons display no presence whatsoever in the Mexican American imaginary. Loreta Encinas de Avilés and Coyote Iguana have no special meaning to Chicanos of the southwestern borderlands. Such figures demonstrate to what extent the geopolitical border does exert a certain force on culture. Not every Mexican borderlands icon, fascinating as he or she may be to Mexican *fronterizos*, appeals to border dwellers on the U.S. side.

Icons such as Joaquín Murrieta and Teresa Urrea who have attracted the attention of Chicano cultural expression have not done so as *fronterizos* or even as Mexicans. Both Murrieta and Urrea were after all migrants, Mexican Americans, who lived significant portions of their lives in the United States and who, according to Anglo-American accounts, died in the United States. Such figures have been appropriated into the pantheon of Mexican American culture as is evidenced by such reference texts as Mirandé and Enríquez.

Chicano deployments of these borderlands legends say little if anything about the Mexican borderlands. Instead they represent either Mexican (American) resistance to racist Anglo-American oppression in the United States—in the case of Murrieta—or Mexican (American) defiance of Mexican national oppression as expressed from the United States— in the case of Urrea. Both serve as models of strength to Mexican migrants to the United States and their descendants. The only differences among Mexicans are the product of migration and geopolitics; there are only two kinds of Mexicans: Mexican nationals living in Mexico and Mexicans who have migrated to or were born in the United States. Murrieta's and Urrea's particular circumstances of race, social class, region of origin, religion, or political beliefs are of little import. Their status in the United States is determined only by their having emigrated from Mexico.

White and Mestizo Icons and Indigenous Cultural Autonomy

Indigenous cultural autonomy is too infrequently brought into meaningful dialogue with national or regional ideologies in investigations of Mexican culture. Indigenous cultures within Mexico are often too autonomous to make such dialogues feasible on any level other than that of microanalysis. In the Mexican Northwest, there is no way to represent the Seri, Apache, Yaqui, and Mayo cultures with a single voice. The Mayos and Yaquis may share many traits and some history, but they have little to do with the Seris, and less with the Apaches. Nor is it easy to judge what translations of indigenous cultural production are made available to scholars who are not experts in those cultures.

The most vividly recounted indigenous representations of the cultural icons studied herein are the Seri oral histories of the life of Coyote Iguana, including the anecdote of his relationship with Dolores Casanova, reported in English translation by the U.S. literary scholar Edith Lowell. Lowell works with anthropologists and missionaries to obtain and presumably to translate this material, but she does not make key elements of the process by which the materials were obtained sufficiently transparent. It is not fully clear what relationship her Seri informants had with those who collected the stories, nor for what purpose the Seris believed they were telling them. Nor are the mechanisms by which the Seri-language tapescripts were translated into English revealed.

Yaqui and Mayo sources are even more problematic. Yaquis and Mayos were protagonists in many key historic events of the late-nineteenth-century borderlands. They migrated to the United States during and after the gold rush. They formed brigades in the Mexican military, fending off filibuster invasions and Apache incursions. They participated as workers in most every enterprise of modernization in the region. Their involvement with the stories at hand is most apparent in the cases of the invasion of Guaymas and the uprisings inspired by Teresa Urrea. The legendary Yaqui rebel leader Cajeme is believed by many to be one of the heroes of Guaymas, just as the Yaqui and Mayo rebels of Navojoa and Nogales were protagonists in important precursor rebellions to the Mexican revolution. Yet there exist no academic-style Yaqui sources recounting the details of their roles in these events. It is never clear to what extent Ramón Corral embellished his biography of Cajeme; meanwhile stories of "Teresista" rebels are never recounted from a Yaqui or Mayo point of view.

What few materials exist that present—albeit indirectly, through un-elucidated filters—fragments of indigenous perspectives on Mexican borderlands culture do offer some tentative insights into the racial schisms and hierarchies that persevere in the northwestern borderlands. These indigenous accounts, for example, assert indigenous protagonism in borderlands history. Cajeme insists on putting a name—his own—to at least one of the many anonymous Yaqui participants in the Mexican military, here in the nationally important defense of Guaymas. Seri descendants of Lola Casanova retell her story as one small piece of the larger biography of Coyote Iguana, whose feats as a warrior dwarfed those of his wife, a mere captive woman. Mayo storytellers make allies of the Mayos and Mexicans in the face of French invasion through Santa Teresa de Cabora.

These accounts draw attention to the representations indigenous cultures tend to take within Mexican borderlands discourse. Seris, Apaches, and Yaquis are all *indios bárbaros*, and even when they ally themselves with Mexicans such as José María Yáñez, they are not worthy of individualization. At best Yaquis are differentiated culturally from Seris—by Fortunato Hernández or Francisco Dávila. At worst, their role in Mexican military history is omitted or reduced to a minor one, subordinate to that of lighter-skinned celebrities such as Teresa Urrea and Lauro Aguirre.

Regional Icons in National Culture

Mexican national discourse exhibits two main tendencies with regard to the cultures of its peripheries: either it subsumes and appropriates them as national or it marginalizes them, at times failing entirely to recognize them. If they are important enough to generate cultural meaning recognizable in the center, they become part of the national imaginary. Others that are less aligned with existing national projects are derided as provincial, antiquated, barbarous, or uncouth.

When Ireneo Paz published the translation he obtained of the *California Police Gazette*'s plagiarism of Yellow Bird's Murrieta novel, although he did make the important identification of Murrieta as Sonoran, regional identity and culture were not the issue. Paz was reclaiming Murrieta for Mexico after his name had circulated for years in the Spanish-speaking world only as a Chilean hero. While Paz preserved the scenes relating to Murrieta's journey to Mexico City and his humiliation on the ranch of President Santa Anna, it was highly unlikely that his intention was to distinguish Murrieta's Sonoran or *fronterizo* identity from that of his Mexico City rivals. Santa Anna was, after all, the Mexican president responsible for the ceding of the U.S. Southwest to the United States. For many Mexican readers, his Mexico City ranch represented less a centrist Mexico City vis-à-vis Murrieta's peripheral home state of Sonora than an old-guard corruption in contrast with Murrieta's forward-thinking ambition and integrity. Murrieta could as easily have been read as a modernizing force that was driven to look northward due to the outmoded thinking that was holding Mexico back. The fact that Paz's translation was never published in Sonora but only in Mexico City and Los Angeles supports the contention that his objective was not to appeal to a border identity or a *fronterizo* cultural autonomy.

Likewise, the newfound popularity of Lola Casanova in the 1940s did not follow from any particular interest of Mexico's nationalist cultural oligarchy in better understanding the borderlands, but rather from the Lola Casanova story's conformity to paradigms promoted in the nationalists' *indigenista* doctrine. Once she was firmly supplanted in the national imaginary by the return of the more traditional national icon, La Malinche, she did not remain popular as a regional icon for a national audience: she simply went away, disappeared from national level discourse.

Regarding the alternative regionalist history produced by Aurelio Pérez Peña and some Sonoran historians regarding the important roles of certain local personages in the defense of Guaymas from the invasion of the filibuster army of Raousset Boulbon, it simply never became known to a national audience. It has been debated at the regional level for over a century, but it has never received any national attention whatsoever.

Finally, the case of Teresa Urrea is the most complex example of national attitudes toward *la frontera*. Mexico City newspapers at first ridiculed Teresa Urrea and her fanatical followers for their superstitiousness. Spiritists embraced her for her unquantifiable powers, abilities incomprehensible to modern science. Teresa was a slap in the face of the all-consuming positivism that had gained so much prestige by the last decade of the nineteenth century. Later she became a symbol in newspapers like *El Hijo del Ahuizote* of the paranoiac cowardice of Porfirio Díaz, who felt so threatened by the antics of a crazed teenage girl that he banished her from the country. Heriberto Frías denied Teresa's importance on the national stage, portraying her as a little girl, an example of provincial ignorance and irrationality. Later interpretations by Valadés and Gill recast Teresa as a protorevolutionary heroine, an example followed by later historians, including Brianda Domecq, who added a feminist appreciation of Urrea's astonishing story, making La Santa de Cabora into a greater national revolutionary icon than ever. When she is a national heroine, her relation to the borderlands is unimportant. She might just as easily have emerged from a town in Oaxaca or Michoacáon or from some *barrio* of Mexico City. In the national spotlight, she is not connected to a specifically Sonoran history. The insurgency she provoked had less to do with Sonora's history of conflicts with the Yaquis and Mayos or the autonomy desired by Chihuahua's borderlands peasants than it did with the general dissatisfaction brewing in the Mexican underclasses on the eve of revolution.

Sources writing from a nationalist point of view have either embraced Teresa Urrea as a national heroine or scoffed at her. In the latter case, however, she carries no weight from a national perspective. She is a laughable example of the lack of sophistication in the Mexican borderlands. Her involvement in national affairs such as the rebellions of Tomóchic or Nogales is tangential. She was a poor ignorant peasant girl swept up in extraordinary circumstances that she barely understood, let alone controlled. At the national level, regional borderlands culture only exists under old frontier paradigms of borderlands barbarism versus central civilization. The northwestern frontier was still an antimodern wasteland in the national imaginary of the 1890s, as it was in the decades following the revolution (Valadés, Gill), and as it remains to a large degree even in the meticulous historiography and measured creativity of Brianda Domecq in the late twentieth century.

The Northwestern Borderlands and Its Icons

The icons of the borderlands produce multiple meanings from the cultures that meet and mingle within the contact zone of the Mexican Northwest. If Mexican nationalists, *gringos*, Chicanos, and even the indigenous peoples of the region are outsiders, whites and *mestizos* of the region are its insiders. They undoubtedly identify as Mexicans, but they see themselves as culturally distinct from their countrymen and women from further south, just as they set themselves apart from Mexican Americans living to their north in the United States, as well as from

Anglo-Americans in general and from indigenous Mexicans from their own region. In the contact zone of the Mexican Northwest, these distinctly *fronterizo* Mexicans are those for whom these icons are of greatest significance. These icons are the raw material from which they construct their cultural distinctness in opposition to the cultural imaginaries of the other cultural groups with whom they come into contact. In particular, they use these borderlands icons to dialogue with these other cultural groups. If some *fronterizos* have not easily embraced some of these icons, it is because their peculiar stories have not conformed readily to the images that they have strived to project of their own regional culture. In fact, the struggles of representation that have played out through these icons among different sectors of *fronterizos* have often been of greater import than the clashes between the images produced in the borderlands versus those of other cultures with which the *fronterizos* come into contact.

The cultural oligarchy of the northwestern borderlands did not take the lead in heralding the roles played by the icons examined herein in local history and culture. In the case of Joaquín Murrieta, most major traditional histories of Sonora prior to the late 1980s did not mention him at all. The Sonoran historian Eduardo Villa, for example, despite having assisted Frank Latta in 1936 in his interviews with relatives and other oldsters with memories of or tales about Murrieta in Sonora, omitted the legendary bandit from his 1937 landmark text, *Compendio de historia del estado de Sonora*. Murrieta was a criminal, an enemy of the English-speaking population of the U.S. Southwest. Moreover, he was an emigrant who had abandoned his homeland of the northwestern borderlands at a time in history when the region needed to build population.

Newspapers in the early 1850s expressed outrage at the anti-Mexican campaigns in Calaveras County and other regions of the Mother Lode, but they did not claim Joaquín as a hero for the banditry and vengeful murders he committed. On the other hand, migrant Mexicans—wherever they may have been located—and the *fronterizo* laborers with whom they associated in cantinas and other public spaces—did embrace Murrieta's story. The adversity he met in the United States summoned up great empathy on the part of migrants and other working-class Mexicans who had felt the sting of Yankee racism in the borderlands.

Murrieta did not become an important borderlands legend because of the many literary works that have popularized his story in both the United States and in Mexico (and in many far-off lands as well). Nor did borderlands historiography ever play a role in keeping his name alive in the Mexican borderlands. Only oral legend and popular ballads have enabled his story to live on in the popular imagination of the Mexican Northwest.

The story of Lola Casanova is a bit different, probably because it took place in the borderlands themselves and not in Alta California, as was the case with Murrieta. Early histories such as those of Velasco and Dávila do not mention Lola by name, and it is only through the influential 1902 study of Fortunato Hernández on the history of indigenous conflict in Sonora that her story entered historiography.

Hernández's account, based on oral history from a single source, was repeated by several historians during the first half of the twentieth century, including Villa's 1937 history of the state of Sonora. Other early histories including Laureano Calvo Berber's 1941 textbook did not mention Lola. While Carmela Reyna de León's novel—sold as a popular romance—did put in writing a more elaborate and in some ways probably more accurate, if romanticized, rendering of the story, Lola was not embraced by the borderlands' *letrado* classes during the 1940s. Enriqueta de Parodi and Alfonso Iberri did include her in their chronicles and stories of local culture, but they treated her with heavy-handed disdain.

It was only after *indigenista* novelists such as Francisco Rojas González brought Lola's legend to a national audience in the late 1940s that borderlands historians began to pay her serious attention. And after the Sonoran historian Fernando Pesqueira discovered the lost letters of Cayetano Navarro documenting the events surrounding the Casanova kidnapping, she began to take a more prominent place in regional history. Calvo Berber, for example, who had ignored her story in 1941, added her to his 1958 history text. However, borderlands historians would continue to deny her any kind of status, preferring to see her as a victim, or worse: a woman who would leave white society to live with primitive Seris was either incredibly foolish or simply treacherous to her own people.

From the beginning the problem was that Lola's story did not construct the image of the region that borderlands *letrados* wished to exhibit,

whether to national peers or to their racist neighbors in the United
States. The story of what they saw as racial regression, of resistance to
modernization, went against their ideals. They preferred to report vic-
tories over Indians and not emphasize defeats. If Lola Casanova had to
be discussed, it was better to imagine her dead than married to the savage Coyote Iguana.

Still, the story of Lola Casanova circulated orally as a captivity narrative, a cautionary tale that signaled the fear in which *fronterizos* lived
throughout the nineteenth century regarding the various autonomous
indigenous peoples with whom they shared territory. Lola Casanova's
legend has survived not as an interracial romance pointing to a new
national paradigm for *mestizaje*, nor as a celebration of indigenous power
(although for Seris, this may indeed be a major part of the legend's
appeal), but as a symbol of unresolved racial conflicts in the borderlands.

The trajectory of the various unsung heroes of Guaymas is also
unique. Many sources have taken the traditional path and denied them
entry into history. Alfonso Iberri kept them out of his 1948 account of
the battle of Guaymas. Francisco Almada made no mention of them
whatsoever in 1952. Laureano Calvo Berber did mention briefly the roles
of Loreto Encinas de Avilés and Guadalupe Cubillas in the defense of
Guaymas in 1941, then argued against their historical significance in
1958. Horacio Sobarzo, despite possessing documents suggesting the
importance of Encinas de Avilés as early as 1948, left her (and Cubillas)
out of his 1954 version of the events.

Aurelio Pérez Peña, of course, is the one who stridently inserted these
two women into history in 1897, and some historians including Pedro
Ulloa (1907) and Eduardo Villa (1937) drew from this historiography
as revised by literature and popular legend. However, this revisionism
was hardly accepted by the mainstream of borderlands historiography.

The roles of additional minor icons associated with the French invasion of Guaymas have even less prominence in borderlands letters. Raousset's young lover, Antonia, is rarely mentioned at all, and when she is—
for example by Horacio Sobarzo in 1954—the veracity of her story is
treated with suspicion. José María Leyva, the Yaqui rebel chief also
known as Cajeme, occupies an even more questionable spot in official history. The primary source regarding his participation is Ramón Corral's

biography of Cajeme, which was based on interviews with Leyva himself. Whether Cajeme was an audacious liar or an eyewitness aiming to set the historical record straight, his own youthful participation in the battle of Guaymas is largely ignored by historians, although often accepted as fact by his biographers.

Much of the controversy here is about race and gender. Some historians have been uncomfortable elevating the names of the women of Guaymas, while the individual male heroes who risked their lives in battle are habitually singled out for their heroism. Likewise, Cajeme, nemesis to projects of modernization in the borderlands in the late nineteenth century, has hardly been a candidate for hero status for many *fronterizos letrados*.

On the other hand, others have celebrated the roles particularly of Avilés and Cubillas because they were women. The surrender of Raousset to Cubillas, for example, implies his humiliation. And the fact that everyone, including unarmed local women and schoolchildren such as Leyva, fought off the French is a source of regional pride. Pérez Peña in particular revised histories already in circulation to negate the nationalist stance of Mexican historiography—condescending as it was to those of the borderlands—and to refute the anti-Mexican attitude of U.S. accounts of the events. The case of these figures does not present the class conflict seen in those of Murrieta and Casanova, yet once again these popular icons have not been absorbed readily into the *alta cultura* of the borderlands.

Finally, the case of Teresa Urrea once again illustrates the resistance borderlands culture has shown toward accepting its popular icons. During her lifetime, she was mostly ignored and sometimes mocked by the local press. Twentieth-century historiography largely ignores her. While she does play a role in some accounts by *chihuahuense* historians of the battle of Tomóchic, Sonorans ignore her wholesale. Only in 1981 did a major Sonoran history, that of Horacio Sobarzo, mention her, albeit as a hysterical troublemaker.

With the exception of Heriberto Frías's *Tomóchic*, in which her role is minimal, Urrea did not benefit from a literary presence, whether in Mexico or abroad—as was the case with Murrieta beginning in 1854, the heroines of Guaymas beginning in 1897, and Lola Casanova beginning in the 1940s—that is, until Brianda Domecq gave her her literary due in 1990. And although twentieth-century Mexican historiographers such as José Valadés and Mario Gill did revive her (following the lead of Lauro Aguirre), their heroic portraits of Urrea as a protorevolutionary orator had no important echo in the borderlands prior to Domecq.

Urrea and her followers drew attention to the putative ignorance and fanaticism of *fronterizos*, and the rebellions associated with her name highlighted the unrest in the region. Neither were qualities that elite *fronterizos* wished to publicize. Many locals, particularly those frustrated with the despotism of the Catholic Church, were thrilled at the prospect of having a living saint in their midst but could not convince their more skeptical peers that she was not a fraud or hysteric. And while Urrea may have continued to live on in popular memory after her exile, it seems to have taken longer in her case for popular interest to translate into writing.

Nonetheless, all of these icons have achieved a prominent presence in more recent historiography. Their ultimate ascent into *alta cultura* reflects the power of both popular oral legends repeated from generation to generation, and of literary and cinematic representations that bring history to life. Inevitable dialogues with other cultures also play an important role in determining which figures become historically significant and which do not. Murrieta's notoriety in Alta California and in Chile, Casanova's rise to fame in Mexico City, Raousset Boulbon's heroic status in New York, and Urrea's newfound celebrity status in both Mexico and the United States in the 1990s have required responses from the borderlands culture in which each originated. The fascinating trajectories of these cultural icons of the contact zone of the Mexican Northwest demonstrate that these "other borderlands" are deserving of greater attention by scholars of history, literature, and cultural studies in the Americas.

NOTES

Introduction

1. I am of course oversimplifying a bit here. For example, Valenzuela Arce's summary of approaches to the study of the border in his article "Centralidad de las fronteras" clearly points to a wide range of complex paradigms of inquiry including those of rhizomes, cultural intersection, transculturation, cultural recreation, cultural translation, interstices, etc. However, my point stands that the border metaphor does not encourage inquiry beyond the basic binary terms defined by whatever is on this or that side of the border.

1. The Other Borderlands

1. The list of border studies texts emerging from the field of Chicano studies is too long to reproduce here; a few key cultural studies texts, apart from Saldívar's, include Anzaldúa; Calderón and Saldívar; Gutiérrez-Jones; Limón; and Ramón Saldívar, *Chicano Narrative*.

2. See Rowe, *The New American Studies*; Powell, *Ruthless Democracy*; Rowe, *Post-nationalist American Studies*; Gruesz; also see Sadowski-Smith and Fox.

3. On the importance of this lecture and the work of Turner in general, see Weber 33–54; see also the anthology edited by Milner, along with essays by Noble, Thomas, and Weber and Rausch.

4. Turner also opposed the north-south axis that had shaped historiographic

inquiry in the late nineteenth century and that pinpointed the U.S. Civil War of the 1860s as the culminating event in the shaping of national culture, substituting in its place an east-west axis and his frontier hypothesis (Thomas 227).

5. Noble 263; see also Thomas 281.

6. There are, of course, exceptions, a major one being the historian J. Fred Rippy's 1926 study *The United States and Mexico*, which makes a serious attempt to understand Mexico's perspective in its political relations with the United States.

7. I am paraphrasing the arguments of Lauren Berlant as quoted in Curiel et al. 2.

8. While this book predates Rowe's *The New American Studies* by a couple of years, it came out at the same time as *Post-nationalist American Studies*.

9. Other Americanists who have productively applied a transamerican perspective to their work include Gruesz, Sánchez and Pita, along with the contributors to Belnap and Fernández, and Levander and Levine.

10. This and all subsequent translations from Spanish or French are my own unless otherwise indicated.

11. I develop this argument in greater detail in "¿Qué hacen los nuevos americanistas?"

12. Note that the Baja California chapters treat both Baja California Norte and Baja California Sur; this territory, which remained sparsely populated throughout the period in question, was not granted statehood (and divided in two) until the mid-twentieth century.

13. Mora-Torres 84; the author refers specifically to the state of Nuevo León, in northeastern Mexico; however, the processes he outlines concur roughly with those playing out in Sonora and the Northwest in the late nineteenth century.

14. See Poblete; Sommer, *Bilingual Aesthetics*; Castillo.

15. E.g., Tinker Salas cites fourteen Mexican archives and nine U.S. archives; he consulted over twenty U.S. newspapers and seventy from Mexico. His books and articles likewise cite primary and secondary sources that represent perspectives from both sides of the border.

16. Fox's own study of late-twentieth-century border culture follows from Mary Louise Pratt's notion of the cultural contact zone as a fundamental site of transculturation (Fox 13).

17. Mora-Torres's descriptor for Nuevo León (3) again applies readily to Sonora and the Northwest; see also Mártinez 111.

18. On the issue of Apache raids into Mexico, see Zorrilla 275–92 and Figueroa Valenzuela, "Los indios" 140–44.

19. On Mexican imperialism during the Porfiriato, see González Arriaga and Espinosa Blas.

20. Iberri 71–73; Tinker Salas agrees that in the late nineteenth century "in addition to Americans, economic growth along the border attracted significant numbers of Europeans, Middle Easterners, Asians, and Mexican emigrants" (223).

2. The Many Heads and Tales of Joaquín Murrieta

1. It is generally agreed that any "real" Joaquín that existed would have had the last name of Murrieta, a fairly common last name in Sonora, Mexico. John Rollin Ridge's 1854 novel fixed the name in public memory as Murieta, but Mexican Manuel Rojas claims, "Murieta is a printed barbarism, derived from the difficulty English speakers have in pronouncing the double 'r'" (*El "Far West"* 86). In this chapter, Murrieta will be the spelling generally employed, except when referring to specific works that themselves use an alternate spelling, in which cases the alternate spelling will be mimicked.

2. Leal notes that Paz was probably nothing more than the book's publisher ("Introducción" 25), yet Leal's Arte Público edition maintains Paz's name on the cover as author. The early Spanish-language editions in fact never listed Paz's name as author, and the 1904 ads for the first Mexican edition of the book which ran in Paz's own newspaper, *La Patria*, never listed an author for the text—meanwhile, books written by Paz were invariably advertised there under his name.

3. Luis Leal claims, "The first time that the name 'Joaquín' appears in the newspapers to refer to Mexican bandits, but without identifying any of them with a surname, is between 1850 and 1851" ("Introducción" 2), yet he cites no specific newspaper report, and no other source concurs with Leal on this.

4. Rojas notes that members of Joaquín's gang included at least one Yankee, "Jim Mountain" (*El "Far West"* 58n1) and another man who was half Seri Indian, half Chinese, el "Chino Molinero" (58n2, 149).

5. Sources do not make clear how Murrieta's name was spelled in this very early report: Leal uses "Murrieta" ("Introducción" 5–6) while Thornton uses "Murieta" (15), as do Castillo and Camarillo (39).

6. Leal, "Introducción" 6; Latta 35–38. "Joaquín" was first singled out in the *San Joaquín Republican* of 29 January 1853 (reprinted in Latta 37–38).

7. Quoted in Thornton 18; no date is given for the report.

8. See Susan Johnson 38 and 352n59; Thornton 20; Latta 602. Rojas concludes that the real names of these two latter were Juan Joaquín Batelas and

Joaquín Ochoa Merino (*El "Far West"* 30, 58, 105) or Ochoa Moreno (*Truthful Focuses* 25).

9. Latta (44) cites a reprint of the story in the *San Joaquín Republican*, 16 February 1853.

10. *San Joaquín Republican* 2 March 1853, reprinted in Latta 49. Latta claims that this man was a half brother of the real Joaquín Murrieta whose full name was Joaquín Carrillo Murrieta (12–13). Rojas contends that Murrieta's full name was actually Joaquín Murrieta Orosco (*El "Far West"* 44).

11. The large print on the ad identified the head as belonging only to the generic Joaquín. However, fine print listed his last name as Muriatta (Latta 599).

12. Quoted in Thornton 25–26; the author does not date the citation.

13. This same story was reprinted on 25 March 1853 in *El Sonorense* of Ures, then capital of Sonora (4).

14. *El Siglo XIX* 17 February 1853, reprinted in *El Sonorense* 8 April 1853, 4.

15. Second part of the same article from *El Siglo XIX*, reprinted in *El Sonorense* 15 April 1853, 4.

16. A few examples from *El Sonorense:* 15 June 1849, 3; 21 December 1849, 2–3; 3 May 1850, 4; 7 June 1850, 4; 18 February 1853, 4; 15 April 1853, among many others.

17. 15 April 1853, 4; this is the second part of an editorial copied from *El Siglo XIX* and dated 17 February.

18. On "sensational literature" as a genre in the late-nineteenth-century United States and its significations regarding Mexico and Latin America, see Streeby, *American Sensations*.

19. Most important, the previously mentioned early biographical sketch of Joaquín (reprinted in the *San Joaquín Republican* 16 February 1853).

20. Story from 18 April 1853, as noted earlier (Castillo and Camarillo 47–48).

21. Luis Leal routinely refers to the text as a biography (e.g., see "Introducción" 2); see also Jackson, "Introduction" xxxviii.

22. The *Pacific Police Gazette* of San Francisco launched the first installment in its inaugural May 1854 issue, then went immediately out of business when its publisher was murdered; in July of the same year, the *California Police Gazette* apparently published a complete story in serialized form, probably the same one that had been intended for the *Pacific Police Gazette*. Unfortunately only one installment survives (Farquhar vi).

23. According to Francis Farquhar, the serialized version was published weekly in ten installments between 3 September and 5 November 1859. The entire text was also published in pamphlet form in the same year, and then in

book form in 1861 (iii). For a somewhat truncated yet convincing analysis of the *Police Gazette*'s plagiarism, see Leal, "Introducción" 20.

24. Thornton notes that Nahl's first published engraving of Murrieta had appeared in the *Sacramento Union* in 1853 (95).

25. It did influence the California historians Hubert Howe Bancroft and Theodore Hittell in the 1880s (Thornton 104), but its readership would not rival that of the *California Police Gazette* version until the 1950s.

26. This Spanish version only saw a partial publication since *La Gaceta* went out of business before reaching the final episode. Publication ran weekly between 4 June and 20 July 1881 (see Leal, "Introducción" 24 and *La Gaceta* 16).

27. Robert Glen Cleland's *From Wilderness to Empire*, quoted in Thornton 130.

28. The *tlaxcaltecas* were the enemies of the *aztecas* who collaborated with the Spanish and facilitated Cortés's conquest of the great empire of Moctezuma.

29. See Thornton 121–24; Murrieta films include *The Gay Defender* (1927); *The Avenger* (1931); the Chilean silent film *Joaquín Murieta, el bandido chileno en California* (1931); a 1938 short, *Joaquin Murrieta;* a 1956 Mexican film, *El último rebelde; Firebrand* (1962); *Murieta* (1965—a Spanish production, in English); the TV movie *The Desperate Mission* (1969); Luis Valdez's short based on the Corky González poem "I Am Joaquin" (1969); and the Spanish dramatization of the Pablo Neruda cantata *Fulgor y muerte de Joaquín Murrieta* (1975). Murrieta has most recently turned up as a supporting character in *The Mask of Zorro* (1998) and its Mexican counterpart, *La máscara de Zorro* (2000).

30. Ironically, Frances Belle, in her 1925 translation, plays down the Mexican nationalist context Paz wished to revive in the legend, instead locating the story in those "picturesque years, when the styles of old Spain dominated the Golden State, and sombreros, sashes, bell trousers, mantillas, fans and shawls were the dress of the day" (ix), recalling Helen Hunt Jackson's romanticization of life in Alta California when it was part of "old Mexico" (see chapter 3).

31. Thornton 133; see also Alfredo Figueroa.

32. Luis Leal traces the best known Murrieta *corrido* to a different *corrido* from Zacatecas that dates back to 1853 ("El Corrido").

33. Thornton 134; Streeby ("Joaquín Murrieta") also argues, "It is easy to recognize the basic outline of the *California Police Gazette*'s version of the Murrieta story in the pattern of the typical heroic corrido" (169), but does not explicitly posit a theory of influence; instead, her comparison reveals that the two diverge significantly in perspective: "corridos attack the legitimacy of the new forms of power and law that the Police Gazette ends up defending" (170).

34. He means "güero," a commonly used Mexican term referring to some-one who is light skinned and relatively light-haired. Latta asserts that Murrieta was "decidedly blond" and "blue-eyed" (11) and that in his family his nickname was "El Huero" (12). Bilingual critics have taken Latta to task for his sloppy Spanish, which some claim calls into question his interpretation of data from Mexican sources (Humberto Garza 8).

35. For example, Neruda brought Murrieta to the Soviet Union, where Pável Grushkó wrote a libretto for a rock opera based on *Fulgor y muerte de Joaquín Murrieta*, which made its debut in Moscow in 1976 (Leal, "Introducción" 62). Alfredo Figueroa claims that Murrieta became an important figure of peasant resistance there (7).

36. Previously, Neruda had claimed that Murrieta's identity papers had been lost in an earthquake in Valparaíso (see Rojas *El "Far West"* 85).

37. Although Rojas is himself from the borderlands—as a child he lived near Mexicali (*El "Far West"* viii) and carried out much of his research as a pro-fessor at the Universidad Autónoma de Baja California (*El "Far West"* back cover)—he leaves no doubt that his perspective is primarily nationalist.

38. For example, one interesting document locates a man named Joaquín Murrieta and a companion, Carmen Feliz, in Altar where they were named god-parents of a little girl in 1849 (Rojas, *Truthful Focuses* unpaginated).

39. This last endeavor produced no conclusive evidence (*El "Far West"* 188–94).

40. Almada's *Diccionario* (494) lists his birthdate as 1809. This probable typo-graphical error then found its way into Porrúa's often-consulted 1964 dictionary of Mexican history, biography, and geography, perpetuating and multiplying the error's resonance in later sources. It is just hard to connect the popular image of dashing Joaquín Murrieta to the body of a forty-four-year-old.

41. *El "Far West"* 125; Rojas generally lauds Latta's work but makes a point of citing a ninety-two-year-old Murrieta relative in Sonora who claims, "That gringo is a liar" (*El "Far West"* 90).

42. Rojas (*El "Far West"* 55); note that some sources (among those old-timers who claim to be related to Murrieta) insist that Murrieta was not anti-Chinese and that some members of his band actually worked as coyotes, smuggling Chi-nese across the border from Mexico into the United States (Palazón Mayoral 38).

43. This theory is further confirmed by reports in the *Sentinel* of Santa Cruz and the *Alta California* of San Francisco in 1856 and 1879, respectively (for these and other later sources, see Leal, "Introducción" 30–31). An additional source, the diary of Daniel Martin, refers to an incident in which he met Joaquin Murrieta,

who was passing through the Carmel Valley in the autumn of 1877. When he asked him if he knew that he had supposedly been killed, Murieta answered, "I hear so, but I got away and went to Mexico," and he explained that he had come back to California (twenty-four years later) to retrieve "some treasures" he had left behind.

44. Thornton (141) also cites, not mentioning the author, a 1975 poem titled "Nuestro Ideales" *[sic]* listing Murrieta as a hero of the United Farm Workers. Leal recalls a pair of early 1970s poems by Sergio Elizondo that likewise follow from González's portrayal of Murrieta as an icon of Chicano resistance ("Introducción" 55–56).

45. Castillo and Camarillo 1; see also Thornton 141–42.

46. Vélez-Ibáñez and Humberto Garza are two examples of many; see Thornton 144.

47. In Huerta's Spanish-language articles, published in Spain, he goes by Albert, but in his English language articles published in California, he uses Alberto.

48. Corbalá 258; Murrieta has elsewhere been associated with women named Rosa, Carmen, Carmela, Clarita, and Ana, but never María. The great film actress María Félix, one of the most famous figures ever to come from Sonora, would undoubtedly have relished playing a bandit's lover in one of her films.

49. Susan Johnson observes: "Of the scores of Murrieta family members and acquaintances Frank Latta interviewed between 1920 and 1980, only one person (and then her offspring) remembered what had become of Rosa and Joaquín" (53).

3. Lola Casanova

1. For contemporary readings of the Malinche legend, see the collection edited by Glantz, *La Malinche: Sus padres y sus hijos.*

2. See Leal and Cortina xv; González Acosta argues forcefully that the anonymous author was actually the exiled Cuban poet José María Heredia. Anna Brickhouse has intriguingly proposed a collaborative effort among Heredia, Varela, and Vicente Rocafuerte (51–57).

3. The first Mexican edition appeared in 1853.

4. For a complete analysis of La Malinche in nineteenth-century literature, see Cypess 41–97.

5. This novel was written in the late 1880s about historic events of the 1860s, but it was not published until 1901. Doris Sommer identifies *El Zarco* as

Altamirano's masterpiece of literary nationalism (224). Note that Altamirano was himself son of an indigenous father and a mixed-race mother and identified as indigenous (Campuzano 12).

6. Such narratives were common throughout the Americas in the nineteenth century, although it seems that they were more popular in the United States (see Faery) and Argentina (see Rotker) than in most other places; see also Operé, especially 242–43.

7. Notes Faery of New England captivity tales, "Stripping the captive woman or ripping off her clothing is as much a stock trope in captivity tales . . . as is the habitual nakedness of Native women in representations of the 19th century and earlier" (177).

8. Interestingly, the anthropologist José René Córdova Rascón notes that despite frequent assaults by U.S.–based Apaches on settlements in northern Sonora, the urban populations of Sonora's larger southern cities were largely indifferent toward the Apache problem and unwilling to volunteer their services in military campaigns against them (162–65, 177).

9. This policy, unfortunately, inspired bounty hunters to randomly kill indigenous men from the area, including peaceful Tarahumaras and Yaquis (Tinker Salas 63).

10. Government decree to Sonorans published in *El Sonorense* 7 February 1850, quoted in Tinker Salas 63.

11. Writing on an analogous context in New England, Rebecca Faery comments: "Paradoxically, Indian captivity represented for Puritan women of New England an expansion of experience rather than what we might ordinarily think would be a contraction or restriction of experience" (31). Staying with the Indians, then, may not have been all that undesirable for nineteenth-century women, confined as they were by the patriarchal order. In Latin America, according to Fernando Operé: "Of the thousands of captives who enlarged indigenous communities, the vast majority either remained in forced captivity or integrated themselves voluntarily, turning down opportunities to return to their places of origin" (21). For women, it was particularly difficult to return: "The contact with the Indians had marked them for life, and that stain was not easy to erase"; their own captivity narratives "were stories of shame" (Operé 27).

12. "Of all the known Indian tribes in Sonora . . . there could scarcely be one more vulgar and uncouth than the Seris. They are perverse to the extreme; vicious without parallel in their drunkenness; filthy to the infinite degree, and bitter enemies of whites" (José Francisco Velasco, writing in 1850, quoted in Dávila, *Sonora* 317–18).

13. Gillman 91–95; for a more complete reading of Ramona from a Mexican *fronterizo* perspective, see Irwin, "*Ramona* and Postnationalist American Studies."

14. This is the name used in Martí's translation, fitting for an indigenous man educated by Spanish missionaries in old California; Jackson, as seen above, oddly employs the Italian name, Alessandro. Similarly, Martí Hispanicizes the last name of the elder Ramona (the protagonist's first stepmother) from the odd Ortegna to the more Spanish sounding Orteña.

15. See, for example, Venegas, Jacobs, Luis-Brown, Gutiérrez-Jones (50–79), Noriega, and Goldman (39–64).

16. The Mexican cronista and man of letters Manuel Gutiérrez Nájera avidly praised Martí's translation of *Ramona* because "it calms the nerves and tranquilizes the conscience." Although he found Jackson to have less talent than the great writers of the day, he concluded, "she makes one suffer less" (236) than those writers do. He overlooked the utterly radical racial configuration of the novel's interracial couple, Ramona and Alejandro, focusing instead on "the goodness of the whole, rich in vital juices, prodigious with life, full of love of nature and humanity" (239). His book review, originally published in *El Partido Liberal* 23 December 1888, 1, was a rare example of the scant attention Martí's translation received in Mexico City despite Martí's keen interest in promoting it there (see Fountain). There is no evidence that it received any attention whatsoever in the northern borderlands.

17. As late as 1901, Manuel Balbás insisted that Yaqui labor was absolutely necessary. "It would not be possible to rapidly substitute other elements because immigration to Sonora is not attractive at all to Mexicans from other parts of the country, and the problem of foreign colonization is so complex and difficult that its realization requires time" (131). See also Figueroa Valenzuela, "Los indios" 140.

18. Tinker Salas gives the example of the Maricopas, a group whose traditional lands spanned both sides of what became the national border in 1848 but were assigned to live in Arizona (109).

19. While "Kunkaak" is the term by which they refer to themselves in their language, virtually all studies of the group call them, following Mexican tradition, the Seris.

20. It was only when Cayetano Navarro's original letters were discovered by the historian Fernando Pesqueira in 1952 that the Casanova legend was incorporated into local history (Lowell, "Sources" 6). Meanwhile, early newspaper reports on the Casanova case have been ignored by historians. Even the most complete reconstructions of the events from recent decades (e.g., Lowell;

Bowen; Córdova Casas, "Lola Casanova") leave out the coverage in *El Sonorense* of Ures.

21. These details were extracted from initial reports from Cayetano Navarro to Governor José de Aguilar from late February 1850. See Lowell, "Sources" 6–8, Bowen 237. Navarro, coincidentally, was the same man who reputedly took the young José María Leyva into his household during the latter's boyhood (see chapter 4).

22. See Navarro; also Bowen 239; Lowell, "Sources" 9; Córdova Casas, "Lola Casanova" 15–17.

23. Bowen 239; Navarro named his source as the Seri interpreter Cheno, who died of fever a few weeks prior to the filing of his 24 April report (242).

24. Calvo Berber, *Nociones de historia de Sonora* 164; it is unclear whether Lola's mother, whose maiden name was Velasco, was of any relation to the author.

25. Actually, her mother "ceded her" to a presumably white family of ranchers when she was only eight months old (70).

26. The review, apparently published before the book was printed, appears as an unpaginated introduction to Hernández's text.

27. This same article was published a few years later in Hermosillo in *Alborada*, journal of the Sonora state high school and teaching academy (15 April 1922, 7).

28. See Aldaco, Ibarra Rivera.

29. Her only other known work is the manuscript "La voz de la sangre: Paisajes y leyendas del Distrito de Altar," which she wrote in Sonoyta, Sonora, in 1965.

30. Lowell, "Sources" 57; Lowell further notes that Reyna de León employs in her text Seri words that appear to be her own transcriptions since they do not follow the spelling used in published Seri vocabularies (153, 156).

31. On Parodi's professional trajectory, see Moncada O. 77.

32. For example, the most authoritative study of the multiple recountings of the Casanova legend to date (Edith Lowell's 1966 M.A. thesis) bills itself principally as a critical study of the Rojas González novel. In Sonora, Horacio Sobarzo's late-twentieth-century history of Sonora bases its Lola Casanova "episode" on Rojas González (and Hernández) (176).

33. Bhabha's hybrid infiltrates the dominant colonizing culture in order to subversively inject into it elements of the colonized culture (102–22). Lola becomes a different kind of hybrid trickster, infiltrating subaltern culture in order to inject into it elements of the colonizers.

34. Writes Doremus, "while [Rojas González] envisions a type of mestizaje

that values the indigenous and European heritages equally, his narrative in some senses contradicts this. Notably, it is a Creole and not an Indian who succeeds in improving the Indians' plight. The novel thus implies that the Indians lack the intelligence or willpower to do this on their own . . . Most tellingly, the author ultimately favors the destruction of Seri culture through mestizaje" (395).

35. Lowell notes that the novels of Rojas González and Chávez Camacho were likely written simultaneously, and that it is therefore nearly impossible that either exercised any influence at all over the other. While Rojas González did publish his a year earlier than Chávez Camacho (1947 vs. 1948), the latter won a literary prize for his novel in 1947, when it was still in manuscript form ("Sources" 51).

36. For a genealogical summary of discourse on *lo mexicano* from the Porfiriato to the latter half of the twentieth century, see Roger Bartra's *La jaula de la melancolía*.

37. It is important to note that Lowell, a literary scholar, undertakes no interrogation of the process of transmission from Seri informants to the anthropologists who recorded their stories, nor does she make clear how these narratives were translated into Spanish or English. Writing two decades prior to Clifford's landmark article, "On Ethnographic Allegory," she assumes communication to be utterly transparent.

38. Lowell uses four separate sources of Seri legend, including a study by the anthropologist William B. Griffen in 1959, an article on popular borderlands legend published in *Western Folklore* in 1962 by Ronald Ives, as well as a pair of versions collected and reported in the 1960s by Edward Moser and by Lowell herself ("A Comparison" 156–57; the latter accounts are transcribed in Lowell, "A Comparison" 148–52). It is significant to note that Moser and his wife Becky were missionaries associated with the Summer Institute of Linguistics, who spent over thirty years living among the Seri. However, it remains unclear whether the particular relationships forged between the Mosers (or Griffen or Ives) and the Seris likely brought about greater trust and honesty in communication or greater suspicion and rhetorical agility on the part of Seri informants.

39. This latter detail was repeated by Ronald Ives (161–62), but not by any other interpreter of Seri lore.

40. Again, Ives—who supplemented his investigations among the Seris with data supplied by the Sonoran historian Eduardo Villa, whose own historiography relies upon Fortunato Hernández for its account of the Casanova legend (Lowell, "A Comparison" 147)—diverges from other Seri versions in asserting

that Lola in fact remained with the Seris, never returning to Guaymas (162, 164). For this reason, Lowell classifies Ives's version as neither Seri nor Mexican, but "hybrid" ("A Comparison" 153).

41. "A Comparison" 155; Ives insists: "Genealogical studies of the Seri . . . disclose that no present-day Seri traces his descent to either Coyote-Iguana or Lola Casanova" (164); Lowell herself remarks that those claiming to be descendants of Casanova do not have any obvious Caucasian characteristics ("Sources" 40).

42. *La Jornada* online, 10 May 2005: http: //www.jornada.unam.mx/2005/may05/050510/037n1est.php.

43. Córdova Casas counts "over fifty" in the early 1990s ("Lola Casanova" 17).

44. *Cambio* online 4 March 2005: http://www.cambiosonora.com/Impresa/vernota.asp?notID=88427&pagID=55&secID=4&fecha=04/03/2005.

4. The Heroines of Guaymas

1. It was the responsibility of the United States, according to the Treaty of Guadalupe Hidalgo, to maintain peace with indigenous groups along the border. The U.S. government did not pay much attention to this duty (Rippy 60–69; Zorrilla 275–92).

2. On French writings on Sonora's riches, see Suárez Argüello 15–29; Sobarzo, *Crónica* 33–35; López Yescas.

3. Napoleon III's advisor, Chevalier, has been cited as having first articulated the concept of Latin America as a tool to promote the French imperialist project in Mexico. See Hanna and Hanna 61–67.

4. Wyllys 42; Sobarzo, *Crónica* 28; Ruibal Corella 116.

5. For an interesting if fantastic link between Pindray and Joaquín Murrieta ("Joachim Muretta"), see Soulié (88–90), who credits Pindray with capturing and killing Murrieta—although historic records show that Pindray died long before Murrieta became famous.

6. His death was rumored to be suicide, although speculation has also pointed to possible mutiny among his men or even assassination by nervous Mexican authorities (Wyllys 59–63). A more colorful source suggests that he was killed by a cowboy, jealous that Pindray had stolen his Dutch girlfriend, Elsa Kitchen (Sobarzo, *Crónica* 56).

7. Wyllys 87; his source is an article in *El Sonorense* from 1 October 1852. It was Cubillas and not Raousset himself, as is sometimes asserted, who came up with this moniker.

8. In Wyllys 258; the original document is dated 18 October 1852; see also Sobarzo, *Crónica* 114.

9. Various U.S. newspapers conjectured that the French had been bribed into submission (Stout 77 cites both the *Daily Alta California* of 18 December 1852 and the *New York Daily Times* of 1 January 1853). Wyllys finds the poisoning theory to be "quite ridiculous" and cites a *Daily Alta California* story of 23 December 1852 that attributes Raousset's illness to dirty drinking water (121n6).

10. It is interesting that despite Pierce's policies, U.S. military authorities signed an agreement with Walker while he was still in Mexico and employing the title "President of the Republic of Sonora" (Zorrilla 309).

11. Most of the non-French soldiers in this company—the small Chilean, Irish, and German contingents recruited by Raousset—elected either to fight on the side of the Mexicans or to remain neutral. Some in fact may have served as spies for Yáñez (Murillo Chisem 122, 124, 125; see also Wyllys 205, 208n9).

12. This letter is dated 19 May 1854, but it is not clear on what day the *Star* printed it. All these stories have been archived as clippings at the Bancroft Library of the University of California at Berkeley, where they are cataloged as "Raousset-Boulbon in Sonora: clippings from the *Los Angeles Star* and its Spanish section, *La Estrella*." Most are dated, but a few, including this one, are not.

13. The Guaymas historian Jorge Murillo Chisem considers his family "transcendent to regional history" (154). By the 1860s, he had perhaps become too Mexicanized, as U.S. authorities began "to question [his] citizenship" (Tinker Salas 25).

14. The *Star* 12 October 1854, 11. This detail also appeared in the *San Francisco Daily Herald* of 19 October 1854, according to Wyllys, who traces the story to one of Raousset's soldiers (Wyllys 212–13n24).

15. Suárez Argüello cites six books, all published within a decade of the battle of Guaymas (44–45n111). Substantial excerpts from several of them are included in Glantz, *Un folletín*.

16. The Guaymas historian Jorge Murillo Chisem laments the fact that "except for a few individuals, the names of the participants in the defense of Guaymas are not registered anywhere. On the other hand, those of the adventurers, who were joined by the majority of the French living in the port, can be found in detail in the archives of the Secretary of National Defense" (138).

17. Yáñez lists, additionally, among local volunteers a Spaniard, Antonio Rodríguez, and an Austrian, Emilio Davelichi (*Detall*, unpaginated appendices). According to Ramírez Cabañas, "various North Americans" also fought on the French side (180).

18. See Wyllys 214–19, especially notes 31, 40–42. Many of Guaymas's French residents, "even those who had lived for a long time in Guaymas and were married to Mexican women and had Mexican children," fought with Raousset's men (Ramírez Cabañas 180).

19. On interracial romance as national allegory, see Sommer, *Foundational Fictions*.

20. This incident, originally reported in Lachapelle, was repeated by Ramírez Cabañas (94–95) but is usually omitted from Mexican historiography.

21. Sobarzo, *Crónica* 118; Trueba's words are practically identical: "This is a passage created by the imagination of Raousset, surely" (35).

22. Such books were not uncommon at the time, and while Dávila's book was visually unassuming, similar books, such as J. R. Southworth's 1899 *Baja California ilustrada*, a bilingual text with attractive illustrations, were often more showy. As Southworth writes in his introduction, "The primary object of this book . . . is to attract the attention of intelligent capitalists" (3).

23. Pérez Peña, in fact, wrote the prologue to Dávila's 1894 book from the jail cell where he was imprisoned in 1894 while engaged in a legal battle over a newspaper story he had published in his popular independent journal *El Imparcial* attacking a local politician (Dávila, *Sonora* 2–4; on Pérez Peña's legal battles, see Moncada 44–48).

24. Yáñez lists Lieutenant Colonel Antonio Campuzano as one of his direct subordinates; Zavala Castro's map of Guaymas indicates that his was likely one of the most prominent families in the city (117). Pérez Peña's cast also includes, apart from Yáñez, several other military figures, among them Lieutenant Wenceslao Iberri, and local volunteers Jorge Martinon, the Spanish schoolmaster, and "el Viejo Moreno" as well as Leandro Méndez. Moreno is not lauded in Yáñez's report but is credited elsewhere as Juan G. Moreno; Méndez is occasionally listed elsewhere as Leocado and not Leandro (see Pérez Peña 4, Yáñez 127–29; Murillo Chisem 138–41).

25. Only about two years' worth of *El Imparcial* remain in the Hemeroteca Nacional de México; I have been able to locate only a few clippings from single issues in other archives. While the paper was primarily issued from Guaymas, around the time of Pérez Peña's incarceration, beginning around late 1893 or early 1894, it moved for a time to nearby Hermosillo (Moncada 26, 223, 226). On 15 November 1892, when the paper's founder, Ernesto Pelaez, officially ceded control of *El Imparcial* to Pérez Peña, he mentioned that he had originally established the journal "three years ago" (1). On the journal's success, see Almada, *Diccionario* 572.

26. This article may actually have been written by the newspaper's director at that time, Ernesto Palaez; it should be noted that Pérez Peña officially took over as director and editor on 8 March 1893. His contributions were frequently attributed to Eliseo, his pseudonym, although he likely was responsible for much of the unsigned content of the journal even prior to his assuming directorship.

27. Other Sonoran newspapers participating in the anti-Chinese propaganda campaigns include *El Tráfico* (Hu-Dehart cites multiple examples from 1899–1901: "La comunidad china" 200, 206), *Heraldo de Cananea, El Eco de Sonora, El Noticioso, El Criterio Público,* and *El Estado de Sonora* (all cited in Tinker Salas from the period 1897–1907: 226–29). See also articles in *La Evolución* 10 and 17 February 1905.

28. See, respectively, "Opium" (8 September 1893, 2), "Cannibals" (28 March 1893, 2), "Emergency" (1 April 1893, 2), "Tale of a Chinaman" (8 September 1893, 1), and "China: Notes from Today" (8 December 1894, 1).

29. The play's action takes place in the course of a single day, 13 July 1854; therefore, another secondary player, María Antonia de T., is not mentioned since her participation occurred in 1852 during Raousset's first expedition to Sonora. Only Soulié represents this as more than a fleeting romantic interlude of 1852.

30. While the play is cited occasionally by local historians, there is no record of an existing copy in any Mexican archive. One of the few existing copies is held in the Bancroft Library of the University of California at Berkeley.

31. An ad in the May 20, 1893 English edition of the *National Police Gazette* lists a distribution of nearly 4,000 for the Spanish edition, not counting distribution in New York, where it was printed (1). The last advertisement for the journal, sometimes listed as "the Spanish edition of the Police Gazette" and other times as *La Gaceta de Policía,* appeared in the November 15, 1893 issue (1). Unfortunately, I have been unable to locate any issue of this journal in any archive.

32. Note that the spelling Martinon, as given by Yáñez, is frequently used (Sobarzo, *Crónica* 206), although many other sources use the more likely Martinón (Iberri's *La jornada,* Ramírez Cabañas, Zavala Castro 120, Escobosa Gámez's *Crónicas* 172, Trueba), Martiñón (Rodríguez B. 200), or even Martión (López Encinas 106). Jorge Murillo Chisem is undecided, vacillating between Martinon (126) and Martinón (140). Ulloa uses "Martión" (49) in his main text and "Martinón" in his appendices (61).

33. Calvo Berber, *Nociones de historia del estado de Sonora* 47. Note that later the same author came to question the validity of their inclusion. A 1958 text by Calvo Berber expunges Cubillas and mentions Avilés only in order to argue that

her reported participation has been grossly exaggerated (184), as discussed in greater detail later.

34. This undated typewritten manuscript, "El caso de Doña Loreto," was likely written around the 1940s or 1950s.

35. A 1948 version of this text, the one that cites Sobarzo, is reprinted in Villa's "Sonorenses ilustres." Villa's insertion of Avilés into Sonoran history first occurred in 1937, seventeen years prior to the publication of Sobarzo's historical chronicle of the Raousset invasions; it is interesting therefore to note that Sobarzo makes no mention of Avilés in his book.

36. J. Gutiérrez 17. Additionally, in 1919, Jesús Avilés, Loreto's grandson, recited a patriotic poem lauding the leadership of Yáñez when his remains were shipped to Guaymas to be buried. Also of interest is a photograph from the same era of the dedication of a commemorative obelisk in Guaymas presided over by Don Jesús Avilés, Loreto's grandson (in López Encinas, following title page, unpaginated). These events indicate that in Guaymas the Avilés name clearly remained closely connected to the battle of 13 July 1854 well into the twentieth century, even without official historiographic endorsement

37. Clipping from the supplement *Sonora Ayer y Hoy* from July 1984 (specific date unknown).

38. One of the battles had a particularly bloody end as hundreds of Yaquis were reportedly taken prisoner and left in a sort of concentration camp in which nearly four hundred of them were massacred (Zavala Castro 135).

39. Zavala Castro believes this to be an invention and argues that no Indian servant would have been permitted to attend school (120).

5. Of Sedition and Spiritism

1. The 1990 publication of the novel in Mexico was followed by that of Kay García's English translation, *The Astonishing Story of the Saint of Cabora*, in the United States in 1998. While *The Hummingbird's Daughter* by Luis Alberto Urrea, a relative of Teresa's, purports its own textual authority based upon Urrea's access to family sources, its 499 pages cover only Urrea's years in Mexico, finishing upon her exile in 1892.

2. Domecq, in the historiographical study she carried out while preparing to write her novel, points out that while the critical consensus is that she was born in 1873, Teresa herself may not have been sure of her birth year, on at least one occasion indicating that she was born in 1872 ("Teresa Urrea" 48n2). Domecq also conjectures that her given name may have indeed been Teresa (48n3). In

general, Domecq's reluctance to draw definitive conclusions on the details of Teresa's life and her consultation of multiple sources make her recounting of it more convincing than the more authoritatively presented biography of Holden or other studies with less developed (often monolingual) bibliographies. For this reason, I will use Domecq's life summary of Urrea as the basis for discussion.

3. On Urrea's appeal to spiritists, see Vanderwood 178–81; see also the coverage on Urrea in the Mexico City journal *La Ilustración Espírita*, whose attention to the Santa de Cabora phenomenon began as early as April 1890 and continued regularly through the end of 1892 (examined in detail later).

4. Domecq, who argues that Urrea was likely born in October 1873, also insists that she died at age thirty-three ("Teresa Urrea" 46). The parallelism with the life of Christ is part of her legend, but it does not add up—the January 1906 death would put Urrea's age at thirty-two. Other sources, including her biography (Holden), make the same error.

5. *La Ilustración Espírita*'s report of 1 January 1890 (288) cites a previous story from *El Monitor Republicano*'s 19 December 1889 issue.

6. Quoted in Domecq, "Teresa Urrea" 17; a very similar story appears in *El Siglo XIX* on 2 January 1890, 3, which cites its source as *El Imparcial* of Guaymas, which in turn cites a wire report from Álamos, Sonora, dated 18 December.

7. Quoted in Vanderwood 172, translation his. See also *El Diario del Hogar* 10 January 1890, 3.

8. *El Monitor Republicano* 21 February 1892, 3, quoted in Romero 144; see also *La Ilustración Espírita* 1 March 1892, 327.

9. The story was later quoted in *El Monitor Republicano* 10 January 1890 (Vanderwood 175) and in fact printed in its entirety in *El Diario del Hogar* on the same date.

10. This letter was reprinted in *El Diario del Hogar* in Mexico City (9 April 1890, 2).

11. This story reached *La Ilustración Espírita* 1 September 1890, 159, via a report from Belgium; later Lauro Aguirre recounted the same story, this time reporting that the ladies were from Tucson (*La Ilustración Espírita* 1 September 1892, 140).

12. Holden does date an interview of Teresa with a reporter from the *Arizona Daily Star* in late 1891; however, his source is not the newspaper but a 1962 interview with someone who had heard of it through family folklore (3, 221, 229). *La Ilustración Espírita* continued steady coverage of Urrea throughout the years 1890–92 (as discussed later).

13. *La Ilustración Espírita* did not publish a story in Aguirre's name until

September 1892, when Teresa was already exiled to Arizona; however, the journal does mention receiving informal reports from Aguirre on Urrea as early as
1 April 1891, 366.

14. Domecq links Aguirre to the Urreas beginning "well before 1895," but
"from when exactly and on what the relationship was based are not known"
("Teresa Urrea" 36), but in her novel, Aguirre is a family friend and a frequent
presence at Cabora from the start. Other sources contend, without citing any
concrete proof, that Aguirre and Urrea began to conspire for revolution against
the Díaz regime from as early as 1891 (Edwards 53). Luis Urrea represents
Aguirre as a close friend of Tomás Urrea since childhood (*The Hummingbird's
Daughter* 4, 21).

15. *La Ilustración Espírita* 1 July 1892, 144 (note that this page number is
misprinted as 116 in the journal).

16. 3 June 1892, quoted in *El Monitor Republicano* 12 June 1892, 3; see a similar report from *El Occidental* of Culiacán also quoted in *El Monitor Republicano*
a few weeks later (29 June 1892, 3).

17. Vanderwood 49–50; he cites as his source *La Ilustración Espírita* 1 February 1892, 280, although the report of the Baroyeca spiritists that he cites names
this priest as Father Irigoyen; see also Holden, who identifies him as Father
Gustelúm: 103–5.

18. Gill, *La doncella* 21. See, for example, the Mexico City journal *Gil Blas*,
4 November 1892, cited in Saborit, *Los doblados* 123. In the United States, see
the *New York Times* 12 September 1892, 5. The story is a bit distorted in its details,
claiming that the "Indians" in question were from "Tomasachic in the State of
Sonora" and that the rebellion was instigated by Teresa herself when she "arose
at Tomasachic" and "charged that the clergy, from priest to Pope, were corrupt."
A few weeks later, the *Times* located the Indian rebellion in "Tamache" (3 October). The *Los Angeles Times* identified the insurgents as "Yaqai Indians" (25
October 1892, 2). A later report (16 November 1895) from *El Fronterizo* of Tucson (actually a reprint of a story from *La Opinión Pública* of Solomonville, Arizona)
also accused Teresa of stirring up "the Temasachic Indians" in 1892 (2)—the
date making it clear that the reference is to Tomóchic and not Temosachic, a
town whose 1893 rebellion was something of an aftershock to Tomóchic. Even
Mexico City's *El Monitor Republicano* at one point years later made accusations
regarding the 1896 raid on the Nogales customs house against "Yaqui and
Tomóchic Indians" (15 August 1896, 3). This error has been handed down to
contemporary literary critics, some of whom have referred to the *tomoches* as
indigenous rebels in their readings of Frías (see Lund).

19. On the many factors contributing to the conflict, see Romero 146–53. See also Chávez Calderón 31–36; Vanderwood 20–48; Vargas Valdez, "Tomóchic" 182–83.

20. This moniker appeared on repeated occasions in Pérez Peña's *El Imparcial*, often in stories borrowed from *La Frontera* of Chihuahua; e.g., 28 March 1893, 2; 14 April, 2. Mexico City newspapers such as *El Universal*, also borrowing from *La Frontera*, repeated that term (e.g., 2 November 1892, 3) and others such as "the disequilibrated woman of Cabora" or "Teresa the hysteric" (30 October 1892, 3).

21. Vanderwood 221; see also Osorio 98; Wagoner claims that similar letters were found, "miraculously undamaged, in the burned church at Tomóchic" (6).

22. "Teresa Urrea" 50n25; see also Holden 121–22. Holden in fact is not very meticulous about documenting his sources. The only source listed for the chapter in which he describes this meeting is Almada (*La rebelión* 230); nonetheless, he draws significantly on interviews with friends and family of Teresa, and their descendents, few of which he cites directly. It is likely that his source here is actually an uncited interview. Almada's position is that in the months preceding Teresa's exile, no local authority accused her of being involved, "which evidently proves that she had no prior knowledge of the events, and much less did she participate or hold responsibility for them." After all, "she had never met nor visited the tomoches and the only time they were in Cabora, they did not find her there" (*La rebelión* 79).

23. *El Paso Daily Times* 27 October 1892, 7, reprinted in *Arizona Weekly Citizen* 5 November 1892; cited in Vanderwood 283.

24. For example, see Chávez Calderón 28; Chávez 17; Osorio 78.

25. From an ad for the book, reproduced in Aguirre 191.

26. 14 August 1896, 1; this version also reached Mexico City's *El Monitor Republicano* (15 August, 3). Similar misinformation (that the invaders were not only Yaqui but also "Tomochi" Indians) found its way into military reports on the raid (Rodríguez and Rodríguez 189). The *Los Angeles Times* referred to "Yaqui and Tomochio Indians" (13 August, 5).

27. Previous sources include Teresa's writings in El Paso, most of which point to major collaboration (if not textual control) by Lauro Aguirre. While Aguirre's influence on Urrea has often been noted, Dare's story is generally taken at face value.

28. Larralde notes, "Beatrice [Castro] and Madam Young attracted huge crowds with the juicy tidbits of gossip about Teresa" (*Mexican American Movements* 67).

29. According to Holden, Teresa herself refused to talk about her life of this period to members of her household upon her return to Arizona (186).

30. It is no surprise that Domecq's "autobiographical narrator" (Shaw 304) admits to having first become intrigued by La Santa de Cabora by reading Frías (Domecq, *The Astonishing Story* 4; *La insólita historia* 10).

31. Domecq insists that she is not a historian: "My intentions were literary and not historic" ("Teresa Urrea" 12).

32. The same text was published concurrently in *La Prensa* of San Antonio, Texas. While I consulted and therefore cite *La Opinión*, it is *La Prensa* that was the main operation, and *La Opinión* the satellite (I am indebted to Juan Bruce Novoa for pointing out this detail to me).

33. Valadés's contemporaries were not in unanimous agreement with his revisions to official history, noting that, like Frías before him, his new history of Tomóchic, particularly as it referred to Teresa Urrea, was full of "fantasies" (Almada, *La rebelión* 128–29).

34. This small book, *La doncella de Cabora*, lists no publication date. However, all library sources that I have been able to locate date it 1987. Nonetheless, Vanderwood claims it first came out much earlier and lists a date of "1973?" in his bibliography.

35. All three texts take a similar stance: Teresa Urrea was a popular cult figure whom the *tomoches* had taken for a living saint and a spiritual inspiration. However, these local sources agree that she never met Cruz Chávez or other *tomoche* leaders nor bore any direct influence on them. See Almada, *La rebelión* 79, 82, 129; Chávez 78.

36. This is the seventeenth Mayo myth related in Crumrine, *Mayo Social Organization*, unpaginated. Crumrine's 1982 structuralist study does not account for how the myths he recounts were collected or translated, and while he does address the fact that these myths have changed over time and are the product of a complex history, he does not attempt to interpret their signification with regard to Mayo attitudes toward mainstream Mexican society or French invaders.

37. "Teresa Urrea" 13, 48n3, 48n1; Holden himself admits to having to use interpreters and to requiring "extensive translations" of Spanish-language documents (ix). On the occasions when he needed to communicate with Mexicans without interpreters present, he notes dryly that "communication was difficult" (199).

38. Rarely emphasized or explored in detail by any biographers or historians, Teresa's love life remains largely a mystery. Particularly puzzling are a series of poems that Teresa reportedly sent in 1895 to Carlos Lucero Aja, a leading

spiritist from Hermosillo, with whom Teresa had developed a friendship. Considering that there is no report of any romantic entanglement in Teresa's life—apart from the possible tragic affair with a miner around 1889—until her abrupt marriage in 1900, her biographers provide no context for a poem such as the following (quoted in Aguirre Vázquez 17):

> Take this flower and think that it is my life
> because I love you with ardent love
> Keep it then and think that in my mind
> nothing fits if not you
>
> That I knew not how to love, that is a lie
> Your image alone occupies my memory
> Without your love, I wish for not even glory
> I wish for death, I wish for death if I lose you

Whether or not these poems, unpublished until after Lucero Aja's death, are authentic, their meaning remains obscured by an interest in Urrea that has stressed the political and the spiritual, while neglecting the personal.

39. Holden's portrayal of these friendships suggests at times an extraordinary intimacy. For example: "So close was the bond between Mariana and Teresita that the two of them could communicate without words" (232). An 1892 newspaper report on Teresa's period of house arrest in Guaymas concludes: "she sang and danced endlessly with another 'girl'" (*El Monitor Republicano* 12 June 1892, 3). These close relationships with women are only touched upon by Holden and poorly developed by Domecq, in the end a result of an interest in Teresa always based on her public life. The private woman behind the public performer remains an utter mystery today.

BIBLIOGRAPHY

Aguirre, Lauro, and Teresa Urrea. "¡Tomóchic! ¡Redención!" [1896]. *Tomóchic: La revolución adelantada*, vol. 2. Comp. Jesús Vargas Valdez. Ciudad Juárez: Universidad Autónoma de Ciudad Juárez, 1994. 91–193.

Aguirre Bernal, Celso. *Joaquín Murrieta: Raíz y razón del movimiento chicano: Un enfoque histórico*. Mexico City: Lito Publicidad Internacional, 1985.

Aguirre Vázquez. "Teresa Urrea, Santa de Cabora." *Historia de Sonora* 80. 5 (1993): 16–17.

Aldaco Encinas, Guadalupe Beatriz. "La prensa decimonónica sonorense: El caso de *La Voz de Sonora* y *La Estrella de Occidente* (1856–1870)." *Memoria: XIV simposio de historia y antropología de Sonora*. Hermosillo: Instituto de Investigaciones Históricas, Universidad de Sonora, 1990. 361–73.

Allende, Isabel. *Hija de la fortuna*. Barcelona: Plaza y Janés, 1999.

Almada, Francisco. *Diccionario de historia, geografía y biografía sonorenses*. Chihuahua, 1952.

———. *La rebelión de Tomochi*. Chihuahua: Talleres Linotipográficos del Gobierno del Estado, 1938.

Altamirano; Ignacio M. *El Zarco* [1901]. México: Porrúa, 1995.

Anderson, Danny J. "La frontera norte y el discurso de la identidad en la narrative mexicana del siglo XX." *Nuevas ideas; viejas creencias: La cultura mexicana hacia el siglo XXI*. Coord. Margarita Alegría de la Colina, et al. Mexico City: Universidad Autónoma Metropolitana, Azcapotzalco, 1995. 127–50.

Anonymous. *Joaquin Murieta, the Brigand Chief of California: A Complete History of His Life from the Age of Sixteen to the Time of His Capture and Death in 1853* [1859]. San Francisco: Grabhorn Press, 1932.

Antochiw, Michel. "Textos sobre problemas indígenas" [1984]. *Sonora: Textos de su historia*. Comp. Mario Cuevas Arámburu. Hermosillo/Mexico City: Gobierno del Estado de Sonora/Instituto de Investigaciones Dr. José María Luis Mora, 1989. 405–7.

Anzaldúa, Gloria. *Borderlands/La Frontera: The New Mestiza* [1987]. San Francisco: Aunt Lute Books, 1999.

Arredondo, Isabel. "'Tenía bríos y, aún vieja, los sigo teniendo': Entrevista a Matilde Landeta." *Mexican Studies/Estudios Mexicanos* 18.1 (2002): 189–204.

Badger, Joseph. *Joaquin, the Saddle King*. New York: Beadle and Adams, 1881.

———. *Joaquin, the Terrible*. New York: Beadle and Adams, 1881.

———. *The Pirate of the Placers; or, Joaquin's Death Hunt*. New York: Beadle and Adams, 1882.

Balbás, Manuel. "Civilización y barbarie según un médico militar participante en la guerra del Yaqui" [1901]. *Sonora: Textos de su historia*, vol. 3. Comp. Mario Cuevas Aramburu. Hermosillo/Mexico City: Gobierno del Estado de Sonora/Instituto de Investigaciones Dr. José María Luis Mora, 1989. 125–32.

Bancroft, Hubert Howe. *California Pastoral*. San Francisco, 1888.

Barthes, Roland. *Mythologies* [1957]. Trans. Annette Lavers [1972]. New York: Hill and Wang, 1994.

Bartlett, John Russell. *Personal Narrative of Explorations and Incidents in Texas, New Mexico, California, Sonora and Chihuahua 1850–1853*, vol. 1 [1854]. Chicago: Río Grande Press, 1965.

Bartra, Roger. Introduction. *Warrior for Gringostroika*. By Guillermo Gómez-Peña. Saint Paul: Graywolf Press, 1993.

———. *La jaula de la melancolía: Identidad y metamorfosis del mexicano*. Mexico City: Grijalbo, 1987.

Belle, Frances P., trans. *The Life and Adventures of the Celebrated Bandit Joaquín Murrieta, His Exploits in the State of California* [1925]. By Ireneo Paz. Chicago: Charles T. Powner, 1937.

Belnap, Jeffrey, and Raúl Fernández, eds. *José Martí's "Our America": From National to Hemispheric Cultural Studies*. Durham, N.C.: Duke University Press, 1998.

Bhabha, Homi. *The Location of Culture*. London: Routledge, 1994.

Bolton, Herbert Eugene. *The Spanish Borderlands: A Chronicle of Old Florida and the Southwest*. New Haven, Conn.: Yale University Press, 1921.

Bowen, Thomas. *Unknown Island: Seri Indians, Europeans, and San Esteban Island in the Gulf of California.* Albuquerque: University of New Mexico Press, 2000.

Brickhouse, Anna. *Transamerican Literary Relations and the Nineteenth-Century Public Sphere.* Cambridge: Cambridge University Press, 2004.

Brown, Charles H. *Agents of Manifest Destiny: The Lives and Times of the Filibusters.* Chapel Hill: University of North Carolina Press, 1980.

Brown, Wynne. *More Than Petticoats: Remarkable Arizona Women.* Guilford, Conn: Twodot, 2003.

Burns, Walter Noble. *The Robin Hood of El Dorado: The Saga of Joaquín Murrieta, Famous Outlaw of California's Age of Gold.* New York: Coward-McCann, 1932.

Calderón, Héctor, and José David Saldívar. "Editor's Introduction: Criticism in the Borderlands." *Criticism in the Borderlands: Studies in Chicano Literature, Culture and Ideology. "* Ed. Héctor Calderón and José David Saldívar. Durham, N.C.: Duke University Press, 1991. 1–7.

Calvo Berber, Laureano. *Nociones de historia del estado de Sonora.* Hermosillo: Imp. Cruz Galvez, 1941.

———. *Nociones de la historia de Sonora.* Mexico City: Porrúa, 1958.

Campuzano, Juan R. *Ignacio Altamirano: Constructor de la nacionalidad y creador de la literatura mexicana.* Mexico City: Federación Editorial Mexicana, 1986.

Carr, Barry. *The Peculiarities of the Mexican North, 1880–1928: An Essay in Interpretation.* Glasgow: University of Glasgow, Institute of Latin American Studies, 1971.

Carrillo, Adolfo. *Cuentos Californianos* [c. 1922]. Guadalajara: Secretaría de Cultura de Jalisco, 1993.

Castillo, Debra A. *Redreaming America: Toward a Bilingual American Culture.* Albany: State University of New York Press, 2005.

Castillo, Debra A., and María Socorro Tabuenca Córdoba. *Border Women: Writing from la Frontera.* Minneapolis: University of Minnesota Press, 2002.

Castillo, Pedro, and Albert Camarillo. *Furia y muerte: Los bandidos chicanos.* Los Angeles: Aztlán Publications, Chicano Studies Center, University of California: 1973.

Chávez, José Carlos. *Peleando en Tomichi* [1943]. Chihuahua: Imprenta Moderna, 1955.

Chávez Calderón, Plácido. "La defensa de Tomochi" [1964]. *Tomóchic: La revolución adelantada,* vol. 1. Comp. Jesús Vargas Valdez. Ciudad Juárez: Universidad Autónoma de Ciudad Juárez, 1994. 25–74.

Chávez Camacho, Armando. *Cajeme: Novela de indios* [1948]. Mexico City: Porrúa, 1967.

Clifford, James. "On Ethnographic Allegory." *Writing Culture: The Poetics and Politics of Ethnography.* Ed. James Clifford and George E. Marcus. Berkeley: University of California Press, 1986. 98–121.

Corbalá Acuña, Manuel Santiago. *Álamos de Sonora.* Mexico City: Libros de México, 1977.

Córdova Casas, Sergio. "Las guerras de Encinas." *Sonora: Historia de la vida cotidiana.* Coord. Virgilio López Soto. Hermosillo: Consejo Editorial de la Sociedad Sonorense de Historia, 1998. 295–305.

———. "Lola Casanova: Al margen del mito y la leyenda." *Boletín de la Sociedad Sonorense de Historia* 68–69 (1993): 12–15, 15–19.

Córdova Rascón, José René. "Sonoreños contra apaches: La campaña de 1851." *Sonora: Historia de la vida cotidiana.* Coord. Virgilio López Soto. Hermosillo: Sociedad Sonorense de Historia, 1998. 155–78.

Corral, Ramón. "Biografía de José María Leyva Cajeme" [1887]. *Obras históricas.* Hermosillo: Biblioteca Sonorense de Geografía e Historia, 1959. 147–92.

Cota Meza, Ramón Blas. "La Compañía del Boleo: Una empresa minera francesa en el Golfo de California." *Francia en Sonora.* Coord. Ignacio Almada Bay. Hermosillo: Instituto Sonorense de Cultura, 1993. 103–14.

Couldry, Nick. Inside Culture: *Re-imagining the Method of Cultural Studies.* London: Sage, 2000.

Crumrine, N. Ross. *The Mayo Indians of Sonora: A People Who Refuse to Die.* Tucson: University of Arizona Press, 1977.

———. *Mayo Social Organization, Ceremonial and Ideological Systems, Sonora, Northwestern Mexico.* Greeley: Museum of Anthropology, University of Northern Colorado, 1982.

Cueva Pelayo, José Jesús. "El legendario Joaquín Murrieta." *Visión histórica de la frontera norte de México.* Vol. 4: *De la nueva frontera al porfiriato* [1987]. Ed. David Piñera Ramírez, Mexicali: Universidad Autónoma de Baja California/El Mexicano/Editorial Kino, 1994. 73.

Cuevas Aramburu, comp. *Sonora: Textos de su historia,* vols. 2–3. Hermosillo/Mexico City: Gobierno del Estado de Sonora/Instituto de Investigaciones Dr. José María Luis Mora, 1989.

Curiel, Barbara Brinson, et al. Introduction. *Postnationalist American Studies.* Ed. John Carlos Rowe. Berkeley: University of California Press, 2000. 1–21.

Cypess, Sandra Messinger. *La Malinche in Mexican Literature: From History to Myth.* Austin: University of Texas Press, 1991.

Dasenbrock, Reed Way. Introduction. *No Short Journeys: The Interplay of Cultures in the History and Literature of the Borderlands*. By Cecil Robinson. Tucson: University of Arizona Press, 1992. xv-xxiii.

Dávila, Francisco T. *Calendario guaymense para 1902*. Guaymas: Imprenta y Casa Editorial de A. Ramírez, 1902.

———. *Sonora histórico y descriptivo*. Nogales, Ariz.: Tipografía de R. Bernal, 1894.

DeLyser, Dydia. *Ramona Memories: Tourism and the Shaping of Southern California*. Minneapolis: University of Minnesota Press, 2005.

Dever, Susan. *Celluloid Nationalism and Other Melodramas: From Post-revolutionary Mexico to fin de siglo Mexamérica*. Albany: State University of New York Press, 2003.

Díaz Björkquist, Elena. "Teresa Urrea, la Santa de Cabora." http://www.elena diazbjorkquist.net/Elena/chautauqua.html#about. Consulted 5 May 2005.

Domecq, Brianda. *The Astonishing Story of the Saint of Cabora* [1990]. Trans. Kay García. Tempe, Ariz.: Bilingual Press/Editorial Bilingüe, 1998.

———. *La insólita historia de la Santa de Cabora*. Mexico City: Planeta, 1990.

———. "Teresa Urrea: La Santa de Cabora." *Tomóchic: La revolución adelantada*, vol. 2. Comp. Jesús Vargas Valdez. Ciudad Juárez: Universidad Autónoma de Ciudad Juárez/Gobierno del Estado de Chihuahua, 1994. 9–65.

Doremus, Anne. "Indigenism, Mestizaje, and National Identity in Mexico during the 1940s and 1950s." *Mexican Studies/Estudios Mexicanos* 17. 2 (2001): 375–402.

Edwards, Harold L. "They Raided Nogales: Santa Teresa and the Mexican Insurrection of 1896." *True West* 3 (1989): 52–57.

Escobar Valdez, Miguel. *Morir antes que ceder*. Hermosillo: Instituto Sonorense de Cultura, 2001.

Escobosa Gámez, Gilberto. *Crónicas sonorenses*. Hermosillo: Editora la Voz de Sonora, 1999.

———. *Hermosillo en mi memoria: Crónica*. Hermosillo: Instituto Sonorense de Cultura, 1995.

Esteva, José María. *La campana de la misión* [1894]. Xalapa: Universidad Veracruzana, 1998.

Faery, Rebecca Bevins. *Cartographies of Desire: Captivity, Race, and Sex in the Shaping of an American Nation*. Norman: University of Oklahoma Press, 1999.

Farquhar, Francis. "Notes on Joaquin Murieta." *Joaquin Murieta, the Brigand Chief of California: A Complete History of His Life from the Age of Sixteen to the Time of His Capture and Death in 1853* [1859]. San Francisco: Grabhorn Press, 1932. i–viii.

Fernández, Emilio "el Indio," dir. *María Candelaria*. With Dolores del Río, Pedro Armendáriz. Mexico City: Films Mundiales, 1943.

Fernández, Raúl. *The United Status–Mexico Border: A Politico-Economic Profile.* Notre Dame: University of Notre Dame Press, 1977.

Figueroa, Alfredo. Introduction. *Joaquín Murrieta, "El Patrio"* [1986]. By Manuel Rojas. Trans. Ilsa G. Garza. Mexicali: La Cuna de Aztlán, 1996. 1–9.

Figueroa Valenzuela, Alejandro. "Los indios de Sonora ante la modernización porfirista." *Historia general de Sonora.* Vol. 4: *Sonora moderno: 1880–1929* [1985]. Coord. Cynthia Radding de Murrieta. Hermosillo: Gobierno del Estado de Sonora/Instituto Sonorense de Cultura, 1997. 139–63.

———. "José María Leyva 'Cajeme': Un símbolo para la identidad sonorense." *Entre la magia y la historia.* Comp. José Manuel Valenzuela Arce. Tijuana/ Mexico City: Programa Cultural de las Fronteras, El Colegio de la Frontera Norte/Consejo Nacional para la Cultura y las Artes, 1992. 23–32.

———. "La revolución mexicana y los indios de Sonora." *Historia general de Sonora.* Vol. 4: *Sonora moderno, 1880–1929* [1985]. Coord. Cynthia Radding de Murrieta. Hermosillo: Gobierno del Estado de Sonora/Instituto Sonorense de Cultura, 1997. 353–78.

Fishkin, Shelley Fisher. "Crossroads of Cultures: The Transnational Turn in American Studies—Presidential Address to the American Studies Association, November 12, 2004." *American Quarterly* 57.1 (2005): 17–57.

Fountain, Anne. "Ralph Waldo Emerson and Helen Hunt Jackson in *La Edad de Oro.*" *SECOLAS Annals* 22. 3 (1991): 44–50.

Fox, Claire F. *The Fence and the River: Culture and Politics at the U.S.–Mexico Border.* Minneapolis: University of Minnesota Press, 1999.

Frías, Heriberto. *Tomóchic* [1893]. Mexico City: CONACULTA, 1998.

Galaz, Fernando. "Lola Casanova" (transcription). Instituto Nacional de Antropología e Historia, Hermosillo, Sonora. "Artículos históricos sonorenses." Vol. 2, Ficha 8225 [no date]: 305–6.

Gamio, Manuel. *Forjando patria* [1916]. Mexico City: Porrúa, 1982.

García Canclini, Néstor. *Culturas híbridas: Estrategias para entrar y salir de la modernidad* [1989]. Mexico City: Grijalbo, 1990.

García, Lorenzo. *Apuntes sobre la campaña contra los salvajes en el Estado de Sonora.* Hermosillo: Imprenta de Roberto Bernal, 1883.

García Riera, Emilio. *Historia documental del cine mexicano,* vol. 3: 1945–48. Mexico City: Ediciones Era, 1971.

Garza, Humberto. *Joaquín Murrieta: A Quest for Justice!* San Jose, Calif.: Chusma House, 2001.

Garza, Ramiro de. "Baroyeca . . . y la 'Santa de Cabora'" (transcription).

Instituto Nacional de Antropología e Historia, Hermosillo, Sonora. "Artículos históricos sonorenses." Vol. 2, Ficha 8225 [no date]: 278–80.

———. "El caso de doña Loreto" (transcription). Instituto Nacional de Antropología e Historia, Hermosillo, Sonora. "Artículos históricos sonorenses." Vol. 2, Ficha 8225 [no date]: 375–79.

Gill, Mario. *La doncella de Cabora*. Mexico City: Secretaría de Educación Pública/Conasupo, 1987.

———. "Teresa Urrea, la Santa de Cabora." *Historia Mexicana* 6.24 (1957): 626–44.

Gillman, Susan. "*Ramona* in 'Our America.'" *José Martí's "Our America": From National to Hemispheric Cultural Studies*. Ed. Jeffery Belnap and Raúl Fernández. Durham, N.C.: Duke University Press, 1998. 91–111.

Gipson, Rosemary. "The Beginning of Theatre in Sonora." *Arizona and the West* 9.4 (1967): 349–64.

Glantz, Margo. *Un folletín realizado: La aventura del conde Gastón de Raousset-Boulbon* [1973]. Mexico City: Fondo de Cultura Económica, 1988.

———, ed. *La Malinche: Sus padres y sus hijos*. Mexico City: Universidad Nacional Autónoma de México, 1994.

Goldman, Anne E. *Continental Divides: Revisioning American Literature*. New York: Palgrave Macmillan, 2000.

Gómez Araujo, Erasmo. "Cuando el conde Raousset-Boulbon invadió Guaymas." *El Imparcial* (Hermosillo), *Suplemento Dominical* 18 July 1982: 6–8.

———. "Semblanza de Raousset-Boulbon: Crónica y apuntes sobre la gesta histórica del 13 de julio de 1854." *Sonora Ayer y Hoy*, supplement to *El Imparcial* (Hermosillo), July 1984: 3–7.

González Acosta, Alejandro. *El enigma de Jicoténcal*. Mexico City/Tlaxcala: Universidad Nacional Autónoma de México/Instituto Tlaxcalteca de Cultura/Gobierno del Estado de Tlaxcala, 1997.

González Arriaga, Verónica, and Margarita Espinosa Blas. "Centroamérica y el Caribe en los imaginarios mexicanos del porfiriato." Unpublished conference paper, Southwest Council of Latin American Studies, Morelia, Michoacán, 2003.

González, Rodolfo "Corky." "I Am Joaquín" [1967]. *The Latino Reader*. Ed. Harold Augenbraum and Margarita Fernández Olmos. Boston: Houghton Mifflin, 1997. 266–79.

Gracida Romo, Juan José. "Génesis y consolidación del porfiriato en Sonora (1883–1895)." *Historia general de Sonora* . Vol. 4: *Sonora moderno, 1880–1929* [1985]. Coord. Cynthia Radding de Murrieta. Hermosillo: Gobierno del Estado de Sonora/Instituto Sonorense de Cultura, 1997. 17–74.

Gray, Carl. *A Plaything of the Gods: A Tale of Old California.* Boston: Sherman, French and Company, 1912.

Griswold del Castillo, Richard. "New Perspectives on the Mexican and American Borderlands." *Latin American Research Review* 19.1 (1984): 199–209.

Gruesz, Kirsten Silva. *Ambassadors of Culture: The Transamerican Origins of Latino Writing.* Princeton, N.J.: Princeton University Press, 2002.

Gutiérrez, David. "Significant to Whom? Mexican Americans and the History of the American West." *A New Significance: Re-envisioning the History of the American West.* Ed. Clyde A. Milner II. Oxford: Oxford University Press, 1996. 67–89.

Gutiérrez, Juan Ramón. "La defensa de Guaymas." *Historia de Sonora* 74 (1992): 16–18.

Gutiérrez-Jones, Carl. *Rethinking the Borderlands: Between Chicano Culture and Legal Discourse.* Berkeley: University of California Press, 1995.

Gutiérrez Nájera, Manuel. *La prosa de Gutiérrez Nájera en la prensa nacional.* Ed. Irma Contreras García. Mexico City: Universidad Nacional Autónoma de México, 1998.

Hanna, Alfred Jackson, and Kathryn Abbey Hanna. *Napoleón III y México.* Mexico City: Fondo de Cultura Económica, 1973.

Hazera, Lydia D. "Joaquín Murieta: The Making of a Popular Hero." *Studies in Latin American Popular Culture* 8 (1989): 201–13.

Hernández, Fortunato. *Las razas indígenas de Sonora y la guerra del Yaqui.* Mexico City: J. de Elizalde, 1902.

Hernández Hernández, Lucila E. Prólogo. *La campana de la misión.* By Jose María Esteva. Xalapa: Universidad Veracruzana, 1998. 7–28.

Herrera-Sobek, María. "Joaquín Murieta: Mito, leyenda e historia." *Entre la magia y la historia.* Comp. José Manuel Valenzuela Arce. Tijuana/Mexico City: Programa Cultural de las Fronteras, El Colegio de la Frontera Norte/Consejo Nacional para la Cultura y las Artes, 1992. 137–49.

Heyman, Josiah McC. "The Mexico-United States Border in Anthropology: A Critique and Reformulation." *Journal of Political Ecology* 1 (1994): 43–65.

Holden, William Curry. *Teresita.* Owing Mills, Md.: Stemmer House, 1978.

Howe, Charles E. B. "Joaquín Murieta de Castillo" [1858]. *California Gold Rush Plays.* Ed. Glenn Loney. New York: Performing Arts Journal Publications, 1983. 21–63.

Hu-Dehart, Evelyn. "La comunidad china en el desarrollo de Sonora." *Historia general de Sonora.* Vol. 4: *Sonora moderno, 1880–1929* [1985]. Coord. Cynthia

Radding de Murrieta. Hermosillo: Gobierno del Estado de Sonora/Instituto Sonorense de Cultura, 1997. 193–211

———. *Yaqui Resistance and Survival: The Struggle for Land and Autonomy 1821–1910*. Madison: University of Wisconsin Press, 1984.

Huerta, Albert. "Joaquín Murieta, el fantasma de la ópera." *Religión y cultura* 33.160 (1987): 513–30.

———. "Murieta y los 'californios': Odisea de una cultura." *Religión y cultura* 29.136–37 (1983): 615–50.

Huerta, Alberto. "Joaquín Murieta, California's Literary Archetype." *The Californians* 5.6 (1987): 47–50.

Hyenne, Robert. *Un bandit californien (Joaquín Murieta)*. Paris : L'écrivain et Toubon, 1862.

Ibarro Rivera, Gilberto. *Escritos y escritores de temas sudcalifornianos*. La Paz: Gobierno del Estado de Baja California Sur/Secretaría de Educación Pública, 1998.

Iberri, Alfonso. *La jornada gloriosa: 13 de julio de 1854*. Guaymas, 1948.

———. "El rapto de Lola Casanova" [1982]. *Sonora: Un siglo de literatura: Poesía, narrativa y teatro (1936–1992)*. Ed. Gilda Rocha. Mexico City: Consejo Nacional para la Cultura y las Artes, 1993. 275–77.

———. *El viejo Guaymas*. Hermosillo: Gobierno del Estado de Sonora, 1952.

Illades, Lilián. "Teresa Urrea y Lauro Aguirre." *Tomóchic: La revolución adelantada*, vol. 2. Comp. Jesús Vargas Valdez. Ciudad Juárez: Universidad Autónoma de Ciudad Juárez/Gobierno del Estado de Chihuahua, 1994. 67–90.

Irwin, Robert McKee. "¿Qué hacen los nuevos americanistas? Collaborative Strategies for a Postnationalist American Studies." *Comparative American Studies* 2.3 (2004): 303–23.

———. "*Ramona* and Postnationalist American Studies: On 'Our America' and the Mexican Borderlands." *American Quarterly* 55.4 (2003): 539–67.

Isla, Carlos. *Joaquín Murrieta*. Mexico City: Fontamara, 2002.

Ives, Ronald L. "The Legend of the 'White Queen' of the Seri." *Western Folklore* 21.3 (July 1962): 161–64.

Jackson, Helen Hunt. *Ramona* [1884]. New York: Signet Classics, 1988.

Jackson, Joseph Henry. "The Creation of Joaquin Murieta." *Pacific Spectator* 2.2 (1948): 176–81.

———. Introduction. *The Life and Adventures of Joaquín Murieta* [1854]. By Yellow Bird (John Rollin Ridge). Norman: University of Oklahoma Press, 1955.

Jacobs, Margaret. "Mixed-Bloods, Mestizas, and Pintos: Race, Gender, and Claims to Whiteness in Helen Hunt Jackson's *Ramona* and María Amparo

Ruiz de Burton's *Who Would Have Thought It?*" *Western American Literature* 36 (2001): 212–31.

Johnson, Benjamin. "Engendering Nation and Race in the Borderlands." *Latin American Research Review* 37.1 (2002): 259–71.

Johnson, Susan Lee. *Roaring Camp: The Social World of the California Gold Rush.* New York: W. W. Norton, 2000.

Kadir, Djelal. "Introduction: America and Its Studies." *PMLA* 118. 1 (2003): 9–24.

Kanellos, Nicolás. "Two Centuries of Hispanic Theatre in the Southwest." *Revista Chicano-Riqueña* 11.1 (1983): 19–39.

Kroeber, Karl. "American Indian Persistence and Resurgence." *Boundary 2* 19.3 (1992): 1–25.

Landeta, Matilde, dir. *Lola Casanova.* With Mercedes Barba, Armando Silvestre. Mexico City: Técnicos y Actores Cinematográficos Mexicanos Asociados, 1949.

Lape, Noreen Groover. *West of the Border: The Multicultural Literature of the Western American Frontiers.* Athens: Ohio University Press, 2000.

Larralde, Carlos. *Mexican American Movements and Leaders.* Los Alamitos, Calif.: Hwong Publishing, 1976.

———. "Saint Teresa: A Chicana Myth," *Grito del Sol: Chicano Quarterly* 3.2 (1978): 5–114.

Latta, Frank F. *Joaquín Murrieta and His Horse Gangs.* Santa Cruz: Bear State Books, 1980.

Leal, Luis. "El Corrido de Joaquín Murrieta: Origen y difusión." *Mexican Studies/Estudios Mexicanos* 11.1 (1995): 1–23.

———. "*La Gaceta* (1879–1881) de Santa Bárbara: Su contenido literario." *Ventana Abierta* 1.3 (1997): 11–17.

———. Introducción. *Vida y aventuras del más célebre bandido sonorense, Joaquín Murrieta: sus grandes proezas en California* [1904]. By Ireneo Paz. Houston: Arte Público Press, 1999. 1–95.

———. "Mexico's Centrifugal Culture." *Discourse* 18.1/2 (1995–96): 111–21.

Leal, Luis, and Rodolfo J. Cortina. Introducción. *Jicoténcal* [1826]. By Félix Varela. Houston: Arte Público Press, 1995. vii–xlvii.

Levander, Caroline, and Robert Levine, eds. *Hemispheric American Studies: Essays beyond the Nation.* New Brunswick, N.J.: Rutgers University Press, forthcoming.

Limón, José. *American Encounters: Greater Mexico, the United States, and the Erotics of Culture.* Boston: Beacon Press, 1998.

Lomnitz, Claudio. *Deep Mexico, Silent Mexico: An Anthropology of Nationalism.* Minneapolis: University of Minnesota Press, 2001.

López Encinas, Francisco. *Sonora, frontera codiciada.* Hermosillo: Sygma Gráfica, 1985.

López Rojo, Miguel. Introducción [1992]. *Cuentos californianos* [1922]. By Adolfo Carrillo. Guadalajara: Secretaría de Cultura de Jalisco, 1993. 9–22.

López Soto, Virgilio, coord. *Sonora: Historia de la vida cotidiana.* Hermosillo: Consejo Editorial de la Sociedad Sonorense de Historia, 1998.

López Urrutia, Carlos. "Apéndice: El Murrieta chileno (la historia de un fraude literario)." *Vida de Joaquín Murrieta.* By John Rollin Ridge "Pájaro Amarillo." Mexico City: Libros del Umbral, 2001. 133–42.

———. "Notas del traductor a la edición mexicana." *Vida de Joaquín Murrieta.* By John Rollin Ridge "Pájaro Amarillo." Mexico City: Libros del Umbral, 2001. 7–11.

López Yescas, Ernesto. "Ecos franceses en la historiografía de Sonora." *Francia en Sonora.* Coord. Ignacio Almada Bay. Hermosillo: Instituto Sonorense de Cultura, 1993. 119–27.

López y Fuentes, Gregorio. *El indio* [1935]. Mexico City: Porrúa, 1983.

Lowe, John. "'I Am Joaquin!' Space and Freedom in Yellow Bird's *The Life and Adventures of Joaquin Murieta, the Celebrated California Bandit.*" *Early Native American Writing: New Critical Essays.* Ed. Helen Jaskoski. Cambridge: Cambridge University Press, 1996. 104–21.

Lowell, Edith S. "A Comparison of Mexican and Seri Indian Versions of the Legend of Lola Casanova. *Kiva* 35.4 (1970): 144–58.

———. "Sources and Treatment of the Folklore Theme in the Novel *Lola Casanova* by Francisco Rojas González." M.A. thesis, University of Arizona, Romance Languages, 1966.

Luis-Brown, David. "'White Slaves' and the 'Arrogant *Mestiza*': Reconfiguring Whiteness in *The Squatter and the Don* and *Ramona.*" *American Literature* 69.4 (1997): 813–39.

Lund, Joshua. "They Were Not a Barbarous Tribe." *Journal of Latin American Cultural Studies* 12.2 (2003): 171–89

Martin, Daniel. "A Story of Joaquin Murieta the Bandit." Excerpt from unpublished diary. Monterey County Historical Society. http://www.mchsmuseum.com/murieta1.html. Consulted 30 March 2005.

Martínez, Oscar J. *Troublesome Border* [1988]. Tucson: University of Arizona Press, 1995.

————, ed. *U.S.–Mexico Borderlands: Historical and Contemporary Perspectives.* Wilmington, Del.: Scholarly Resources, 1996.

McGee, W. J. *The Seri Indians.* Washington, D.C.: Government Printing Office, 1898.

Mignolo, Walter. *Local Histories/Global Designs: Coloniality, Subaltern Knowledges, and Border Thinking.* Princeton, N.J.: Princeton University Press, 2000.

Millán, María del Carmen. Introducción. *El Zarco* [1901]. By Ignacio M. Altamirano. Mexico City: Porrúa, 1995. vii–xxvii.

Millares, Selena. "Los rostros de la eternidad: La aventura literaria de Joaquín Murieta." *Cuadernos Hispanoamericanos* 539–40 (1995): 203–12.

Miller, Joaquin. "Joaquin Murietta" [1869]. *Songs of the Sierras and Sunlands.* Chicago: Morrill, Higgins and Company, 1892: 293–309.

Miller, Nicola. "Contesting the Cleric: The Intellectual as Icon in Modern Spanish America." *Contemporary Latin American Cultural Studies.* Ed. Stephen Hart and Richard Young. London: Arnold, 2003. 62–75.

Milner II, Clyde A., ed. *A New Significance: Re-envisioning the History of the American West.* Oxford: Oxford University Press, 1996.

Mimiaga, Ricardo. "Lola Casanova y los seris (en la leyenda, en la historia, en la novela y en cine)." *Memoria del XIII Simposio de historia y antropología de Sonora*, vol. 2. Hermosillo: Universidad de Sonora, 1989. 379–99.

Mirandé, Alfredo, and Evangelina Enríquez. *La Chicana: Mexican-American Women.* Chicago: University of Chicago Press, 1979.

Moncada O., Carlos. *Dos siglos de periodismo en Sonora.* Hermosillo, Ediciones EM, 2000.

Mondragón, María. "'The [Safe] White Side of the Line': History and Disguise in John Rollin Ridge's *The Life and Adventures of Joaquín Murieta: The Celebrated California Bandit.*" *American Transcendental Quarterly* 8.3 (1994): 173–87.

Monroy, Douglas. "Ramona, I Love You." *California History* 81.2 (2002): 134–55.

Mora-Torres, Juan. *The Making of the Mexican Border: The State, Capitalism, and Society in Nuevo León, 1848–1910.* Austin: University of Texas Press, 2001.

Moreiras, Alberto. *The Exhaustion of Difference: The Politics of Latin American Cultural Studies.* Durham, N.C.: Duke University Press, 2001.

Morla Vicuña, Carlos [C.M.]. *El bandido chileno Joaquín Murrieta en California.* Santiago de Chile: Imprenta de la República, de Jacinto Núñez, 1867.

Murillo Chisem, Jorge. *Apuntes para la historia de Guaymas.* Hermosillo: Gobierno del Estado de Sonora/Instituto Sonorense de Cultura, 1990.

Navarro, Cayetano. "Resumen de las operaciones de campaña contra el seri"

[1850]. *Sonora: Textos de su historia*, vol. 2. Comp. Mario Cuevas Aramburu. Hermosillo/Mexico City: Gobierno del Estado de Sonora/Instituto de Investigaciones Dr. José María Luis Mora, 1989. 240–44

Neruda, Pablo. "Fulgor y muerte de Joaquín Murieta" [1966]. *Obras completas* 3. Buenos Aires: Losada, 1973. 129–42.

Noble, David W. "The Anglo-Protestant Monopolization of 'America.'" *José Martí's 'Our America': From National to Hemispheric Cultural Studies.* Ed. Jeffrey Belnap and Raúl Fernández. Durham, N.C.: Duke University Press, 1998. 253–74.

Nombela, Julio. *La fiebre de riquezas: 7 años en California*, 2 vols. Madrid: Imp. de Santos Larvé, 1871.

Noriega, Chon A. "Birth of the Southwest: Social Protest, Tourism, and D. W. Griffith's *Ramona*." *The Birth of Whiteness: Race and the Emergence of U.S. Cinema.* Ed. Daniel Bernardi. New Brunswick, N.J.: Rutgers University Press, 1996. 203–26.

Officer, James E. "La nacionalidad de Joaquín Murrieta" [1980]. *Temas sonorenses a través de los simposios de historia.* Hermosillo: Gobierno del Estado de Sonora, 1984.

Operé, Fernando. *Historias de la frontera: El cautiverio en la América hispánica.* Mexico City: Fondo de Cultura Económica, 2001.

Orduño García, María de los Ángeles. *En el país de los yaquis.* Hermosillo: La Voz de Sonora, 1999.

Orozco, Lucy, prod. and screenplay. *Ramona.* Dir. Alberto Cortés, Nicolás Echevarría, Oscar Morales, Jesús Nájera Saro, Felipe Nájera. With Kate del Castillo, Eduardo Palomo, Helena Rojo. Mexico City: Televisa, 2000.

Ortega Noriega, Sergio. *Un ensayo de historia regional: El noroeste de México 1530–1880.* Mexico City: Universidad Nacional Autónoma de México, 1993.

Osorio, Rubén. "Cruz Chávez: Los tomoches en armas." *Tomóchic: La revolución adelantada*, vol. 1. Comp. Jesús Vargas Valdez. Ciudad Juárez: Universidad Autónoma de Ciudad Juárez, 1994. 75–138.

Palazón Mayoral, María Rosa. "Las verdaderas leyendas de Joaquín Murrieta." *Revista Casa de las Américas* 191 (1993): 37–49.

Park, Joseph F. "The Apaches in Mexican-American Relations, 1848–1861" [1961]. *U.S.–Mexico Borderlands: Historical and Contemporary Perspectives.* Ed. Oscar J. Martínez. Wilmington, Del.: Scholarly Resources, 1996. 50–57.

Parodi, Enriqueta de. "La dinastía de Coyote-Iguana." *Cuentos y leyendas* [1944]. Hermosillo: Gobierno del Estado de Sonora, 1985. 25–31.

Patton, James M. *History of Clifton* [1944]. Clifton, Ariz.: Greenlee County Chamber of Commerce, 1977.

Paz, Ireneo. *Vida y aventuras del más célebre bandido sonorense, Joaquín Murrieta: Sus grandes proezas en California* [1904]. Los Angeles: Imprenta El Libro Diario, 1919.

————. *Vida y aventuras del más célebre bandido sonorense, Joaquín Murrieta: Sus grandes proezas en California* [1904]. Houston: Arte Público Press, 1999.

Paz, Octavio. *El laberinto de la soledad* [1950]. Mexico City: Fondo de Cultura Económica, 1989.

————. "Silueta de Ireneo Paz." *Vuelta* 21. 243 (1997): 4–8.

Pereira Poza, Sergio. "Joaquín Murieta, la expresión dramática de la rebeldía latinoamericana." *Indagaciones sobre el fin de siglo*. Ed. Osvaldo Pellettieri. Buenos Aires: Galerna/Facultad de Filosofía y Letras, Universidad de Buenos Aires/Fundación Roberto Arlt, 2000. 77–86.

Pérez Hernández, José María. "Industria, comercio, instrucción pública, beneficencia, razas, idiomas y religión" [1872]. *Sonora: Textos de su historia*, vol. 2. Comp. Mario Cuevas Aramburu. Hermosillo/Mexico City: Gobierno del Estado de Sonora/Instituto de Investigaciones Dr. José María Luis Mora, 1989. 464–72.

Pérez Peña, Aurelio. "Carta a guisa de prólogo." *Sonora histórico y descriptivo*. By Francisco T. Dávila. Nogales, Ariz.: Tipografía de R. Bernal, 1894. i–iv.

————. *Heroína: Drama histórico nacional*. Guaymas: Tipografía de A. Ramírez, 1897.

Perú, Leonel. "Teresa Urrea: Un caso de mesianismo." *Historia de Sonora* 86 (1993): 18–20.

Peza, Juan de Dios. "Una obra histórica de suma importancia" [1 August 1902]. *Las razas indígenas de Sonora y la guerra del Yaqui*. By Fortunato Hernández. Mexico City: J. de Elizalde, 1902. No pagination.

Piñera Ramírez, David, ed. *Visión histórica de la frontera norte de México*. Tomo 4: *De la nueva frontera al porfiriato* [1987]. Mexicali: Universidad Autónoma de Baja California/El Mexicano/Editorial Kino, 1994.

Poblete, Juan, ed. *Critical Latin American and Latino Studies*. Minneapolis: University of Minnesota Press, 2003.

Powell, Timothy B. "Historical Multiculturalism: Cultural Complexity in the First Native American Novel." *Beyond the Binary: Reconstructing Cultural Identity in a Multicultural Context*. Ed. Timothy B. Powell. New Brunswick, N.J.: Rutgers University Press, 1999. 185–204.

———. *Ruthless Democracy: A Multicultural Interpretation of the American Renaissance*. Princeton, N.J.: Princeton University Press, 2000.

Prado, Gloria. "Entre la historia, la magia y la santería, Teresa, la santa de Cabora." *Territorio de leonas: Cartografía de narradoras mexicanas en los noventa*. Coord. Ana Rosa Domanella. Mexico City: Universidad Autónoma Metropolitana—Iztapalapa, División de Ciencias Sociales y Humanidades/Casa Juan Pablos Centro Cultural, 2001. 163–172.

Pratt, Mary Louise. "Arts of the Contact Zone." *Profession* 91 (1991): 33–41.

———. "Criticism in the Contact Zone: Decentering Community and Nation." *Critical Theory, Cultural Politics, and Latin American Narrative*. Ed. Steven M. Bell, Albert H. LeMay, and Leonard Orr. Notre Dame, Ind.: University of Notre Dame Press, 1993. 83–102.

Putnam, Frank Bishop. "Teresa Urrea, 'the Santa of Cabora.'" *Southern California Quarterly* 45.3 (1963): 245–64.

Radding, Cynthia. *Wandering Peoples: Colonialism, Ethnic Spaces, and Ecological Frontiers in Northwestern Mexico, 1700–1850*. Durham, N.C.: Duke University Press, 1997.

Radding de Murrieta, Cynthia, coord. *Historia general de Sonora*. Vol. 4: *Sonora moderno, 1880–1929* [1985]. Hermosillo: Gobierno del Estado de Sonora/Instituto Sonorense de Cultura, 1997.

Rama, Ángel. *La ciudad letrada*. Hanover, N.H.: Ediciones del Norte, 1984.

Ramírez Cabañas, Joaquín. *Gastón de Raousset: Conquistador de Sonora*. Mexico City: Xóchitl, 1941.

Ramírez Saucedo, Mateo. "Otra de Joaquín Murrieta." *Recuerdos de papel: Crónicas del viejo Mexicali*. Comp. Aglae Margalli. Mexicali: Ayuntamiento de Mexicali/Instituto de Cultura de Baja California, 2001. 109–10.

Raousset-Boulbon, G. de. *Une conversión*. Paris: Librairie Nouvelle, 1855.

Rashkin, Elissa. *Women Filmmakers in Mexico: The Country of Which We Dream*. Austin: University of Texas Press, 2001.

Reyna de León, Carmela. *Dolores o la reina de los kunkaks*. Pitiquito: Imprenta Económica, 1943.

———. "La voz de la sangre: Paisajes y leyendas del Distrito de Altar." University of Arizona, Special Collections, Manuscript Collection, 1965.

Richard, Nelly. "Mediaciones y tránsitos académico-disciplinarios de los signos culturales entre Latinoamérica y el latinoamericanismo." *Dispositio/n* 22.49 (1997): 1–12.

Ridge, John Rollin (Yellow Bird). *The Life and Adventures of Joaquín Murieta* [1854]. Norman: University of Oklahoma Press, 1955.

Ridgway, William R. "Saint or Nurse? Arizona Historian Relates Poignant Story of Beauteous Teresa Urrea," *Arizona Days and Ways*, supplement to *Arizona Republic*, 27 September 1953: 22–23.

Rippy, James Fred. *The United States and Mexico*. New York: Alfred A. Knopf, 1926.

Robinson, Juan A. "Statement." Bancroft Library, University of California at Berkeley. Mexican Manuscript 375 [no date]: 278–80.

Rocha, Gilda, ed. *Sonora: Un siglo de literatura: Poesía, narrativa y teatro (1936–1992)*. Mexico City: Consejo Nacional para la Cultura y las Artes, 1993.

Rodríguez B., Abelardo. "La jornada heroica: Del 13 de Julio de 1854 en el puerto de Guaymas, Sonora contra fuerzas extranjeras" (transcription). Instituto Nacional de Antropología e Historia, Hermosillo, Sonora. "Artículos históricos sonorenses." Vol. 2, Ficha 8225 [no date]: 189–200.

Rodríguez, Richard. "The Head of Joaquín Murrieta" [1985]. *Days of Obligation: An Argument with My Mexican Father* [1992]. New York: Penguin, 1993. 133–48.

Rodríguez, Richard, and Gloria L. "Teresa Urrea: Her Life, as It Affected the Mexican-U.S. Frontier" [1972]. *Voices: Readings from "El Grito," 1967–1973*. Ed. Octavio I. Romano. Berkeley, Calif.: Quinto Sol Publications, 1973. 179–99.

Rojas, Manuel. *Joaquín Murrieta, el Patrio: El "Far West" del México cercenado*. Mexicali: Gobierno del Estado de Baja California, 1986.

———. *Joaquín Murrieta, el Patrio: Truthful Focuses for the Chicano Movement* [1986]. Trans. Ilsa G. Garza. Mexicali: La Cuna de Aztlán, 1996.

Rojas González, Francisco. *Lola Casanova* [1947]. Mexico City: Fondo de Cultura Económica, 1984.

Romero, Saúl Jerónimo. "Teresa Urrea y sus seguidores fanáticos revolucionarios." *Espacios de mestizaje cultural: III anuario conmemorativo del V centenario de la llegada de España a América*. Mexico City: Universidad Autónoma Metropolitana—Azcapotzalco, 1991. 137–67.

Rotker, Susana. *Cautivas: Olvidos y memoria en la Argentina*. Buenos Aires: Ariel, 1999.

Rowe, John Carlos. *Literary Culture and U.S. Imperialism: From the Revolution to World War II*. Oxford: Oxford University Press, 2000.

———. *The New American Studies*. Minneapolis: University of Minnesota Press, 2002.

Ruibal Corella, Juan Antonio. *Historia general de Sonora*. Vol. 3: *Periodo México independiente: 1831–1883* [1885]. Hermosillo: Gobierno del Estado de Sonora/ Instituto Sonorense de Cultura, 1997.

Ruiz, Ramón Eduardo. "Génesis de Ramón Corral (1882–1893)" [1984]. *Sonora: Textos de su historia*, vol. 3. Comp. Mario Cuevas Aramburu. Hermosillo/ Mexico City: Gobierno del Estado de Sonora/Instituto de Investigaciones Dr. José María Luis Mora, 1989: 195–202.

———. "Los perímetros del cambio, 1885–1910" [1983]. *Sonora: Textos de su historia*, vol. 3. Comp. Mario Cuevas Aramburu. Hermosillo/Mexico City: Gobierno del Estado de Sonora/Instituto de Investigaciones Dr. José María Luis Mora, 1989. 7–16.

Saborit, Antonio. *Los doblados de Tomóchic: Un episodio de historia y literature*. Mexico City: Cal y Arena, 1994.

———. Presentación. *Tomóchic* [1893]. By Heriberto Frías. Mexico City: Consejo Nacional de la Cultura y las Artes, 1998. 9–13.

Sadowski-Smith, Claudia, and Claire F. Fox. "Theorizing the Hemisphere: Inter-Americas Work at the Intersection of American, Canadian, and Latin American Studies." *Comparative American Studies* 2.1 (2004): 5–38.

Saldívar, José David. *Border Matters: Remapping American Cultural Studies*. Berkeley: University of California Press, 1997.

Saldívar, Ramón. *Chicano Narrative: The Dialectics of Difference*. Madison: University of Wisconsin Press, 1990.

———. "Narrative Ideology, and the Reconstruction of American Literary History." *Criticism in the Borderlands: Studies in Chicano Literature, Culture and Ideology*. Ed. Héctor Calderón and José David Saldívar. Durham, N.C.: Duke University Press, 1991. 11–20.

Sánchez, Rosaura. *Telling Identities: The Californio "Testimonios."* Minneapolis: University of Minnesota Press, 1995.

Sánchez, Rosaura, and Beatrice Pita, eds. and commentaries. *Conflicts of Interest: The Letters of María Amparo Ruiz de Burton*. By María Amparo Ruiz de Burton. Houston: Arte Público Press, 2001.

Sepúlveda, César. *La frontera norte de México: Historia, conflictos 1762–1983*. Mexico City: Porrúa, 1983.

Serna Maytorena, M. A. *En Sonora así se cuenta: Sonora en el corrido y el corrido en Sonora*. Hermosillo: Gobierno del Estado de Sonora/Secretaría de Fomento Educativo y Cultura, 1988.

Shaw, Deborah. "Las posibilidades de la escritura femenina: *La insólita historia de la Santa de Cabora* de Brianda Domecq." *Literatura Mexicana* 10.1–2 (1999): 283–312.

Sheridan, Thomas F. *Empire of Sand: The Seri Indians and the Struggle for Spanish Sonora, 1645–1803*. Tucson: University of Arizona Press, 1999.

Sobarzo, Horacio. *Crónica de la aventura de Raousset-Boulbon en Sonora*. Mexico City: Librería de Manuel Porrúa, 1954.

———. *Episodios históricos sonorenses y otras páginas*. Mexico City: Porrúa, 1981.

Sommer, Doris. *Bilingual Aesthetics: A New Sentimental Education*. Durham, N.C.: Duke University Press, 2004.

———. *Foundational Fictions: The National Romances of Latin America* [1991]. Berkeley: University of California Press, 1993.

Sommers, Joseph. *Francisco Rojas González: Exponente literario del nacionalismo mexicano*. Trans. Carlo Antonio Castro. Xalapa: Universidad Veracruzana, 1966.

Soulié, Maurice. *The Wolf Cub: The Great Adventure of Count Gaston de Raousset-Boulbon in California and Sonora 1850–1854* [1926]. Trans. Farrell Symons. Indianapolis: Bobbs-Merrill, 1927.

Southworth, J. R. *Baja California ilustrada* [1899]. La Paz: Gobierno del Estado de Baja California Sur, 1989.

Spicer, Edward H. *The Yaquis: A Cultural History*. Tucson: University of Arizona Press, 1980.

Starr, Kevin. *Inventing the Dream: California through the Progressive Era*. New York: Oxford University Press, 1985.

Stein, Marion. "My Ramona." Unpublished manuscript, 2000.

Stout, Joseph Allen, Jr. *The Liberators: Filibustering Expeditions into Mexico 1848–1862 and the Last Thrust of Manifest Destiny*. Los Angeles: Westernlore Press, 1973.

Streeby, Shelley. *American Sensations: Class, Empire, and the Production of Popular Culture*. Berkeley: University of California Press, 2002.

———. "Joaquín Murrieta and the American 1848." *Post-nationalist American Studies*. Ed. John Carlos Rowe. Berkeley: University of California Press, 2000. 166–99.

Suárez Argüello, Ana Rosa. *Un duque norteamericano para Sonora*. Mexico City: Consejo Nacional para la Cultura y las Artes, 1990.

Tabuenca Córdoba, María Socorro. "Aproximaciones críticas sobre las literaturas de las fronteras." *Frontera Norte* 9.18 (1997): 85–110.

Taylor, Lawrence D. "The Mining Boom in Baja California from 1850 to 1890 and the Emergence of Tijuana as a Border Community." *On the Border: Society and Culture between the United States and Mexico*. Ed. Andrew Grant Wood. Lanham, Md.: SR Books, 2001. 1–30.

Thomas, Brook. "Frederick Jackson Turner, José Martí, and Finding a Home on the Range." *José Martí's 'Our America': From National to Hemispheric Cultural*

Studies. Ed. Jeffrey Belnap and Raúl Fernández. Durham, N.C.: Duke University Press, 1998. 275–92.

Thornton, Bruce. *Searching for Joaquín: Myth, Murieta and History in California*. San Francisco: Encounter Books, 2003.

Tinker Salas, Miguel. *In the Shadow of the Eagles: Sonora and the Transformation of the Border during the Porfiriato*. Berkeley: University of California Press, 1997.

Troncoso, Francisco P. *Las guerras con las tribus yaqui y mayo del estado de Sonora*. Mexico City: Departamento del Estado Mayor, 1905.

Trueba, Alfonso. *Aventura sin ventura (Gastón de Raousset)* [1954]. Mexico City: Jus, 1957.

Turner, Frederick Jackson. "The Problem of the West" [1896]. *The Frontier in American History*. New York: Dover Publications, 1996. 205–21.

———. "The Significance of the Frontier in American History" [1893]. *The Frontier in American History*. New York: Dover Publications, 1996. 1–38.

Ulloa, Pedro N. *Folleto conmemorativo de la memorable jornada del 13 de julio de 1854* [1907]. Hermosillo: Laura Romandía, Viuda de Ulloa, 1954.

Urrea, Luis Alberto. "For True Healing to Begin, Simply Turn Off Your Western Mind." *Los Angeles Times* 23 May 2005. LATimes.com. http://www.latimes.com/news/printedition/opinion/la-oe-urrea23may23,1,2172211.story. Consulted 24 May 2005.

———. *The Hummingbird's Daughter*. New York: Little, Brown, 2005.

Valadés, José C. "La Santa de Cabora y la insurrección de Tomóchic en 1892." *La Opinión*, nos. 166, 173, 180, 187, 194, 201, 208, 215, 222, 229, 236, 243, Segunda Sección. 28 February–16 May 1937.

Valenzuela Arce, José Manuel. "Centralidad de las fronteras: Procesos socioculturales en la frontera México-EE.UU." *Fronteras de la modernidad en América Latina*. Ed. Hermann Herlinghaus and Mabel Moraña. Pittsburgh: Instituto Internacional de Literatura Iberoamericana, 2003. 159–82.

———. Introducción. *Entre la màgia y la historia*. Comp. José Manuel Valenzuela Arce. Tijuana/Mexico City: Programa Cultural de las Fronteras/El Colegio de la Frontera Norte/Consejo Nacional para la Cultura y las Artes, 1992. 13–19.

Vanderwood, Paul. *The Power of God against the Guns of Government: Religious Upheaval in Mexico at the Turn of the Nineteenth Century*. Stanford, Calif.: Stanford University Press, 1998.

Varela, Félix. *Jicoténcal* [1826]. Houston: Arte Público Press, 1995.

Varese, Stefano. "Indigenous Epistemologies in the Age of Globalization."

Critical Latin American and Latino Studies. Ed. Juan Poblete. Minneapolis: University of Minnesota Press, 2003. 138–53.

Vargas Valdez, Jesús. Introducción. *Tomóchic: La revolución adelantada*, vol. 1. Comp. Jesús Vargas Valdez. Ciudad Juárez: Universidad Autónoma de Ciudad Juárez, 1994. 9–24.

———. "Tomóchic: La revolución adelantada." *Tomóchic: La revolución adelantada*, vol. 1. Comp. Jesús Vargas Valdez. Ciudad Juárez: Universidad Autónoma de Ciudad Juárez, 1994. 139–235.

Vargas Valdez, Jesús, comp. *Tomóchic: La revolución adelantada*, 2 vols. Ciudad Juárez: Universidad Autónoma de Ciudad Juárez, 1994.

Vasconcelos, José. *Breve historia de México*. Mexico City: Botas, 1937.

———. *Indología: Una interpretación de la cultura iberoamericana* [1926]. Barcelona: Agencia Mundial de Librería, 1930.

———. *La raza cósmica* [1925]. Mexico City: Espasa Calpe, 1986.

Velasco, José F. *Noticias estadísticas del estado de Sonora, acompañadas de ligeras reflecsiones*. Mexico City: Imprenta de Ignacio Cumplido, 1850.

———. "Yaquis y mayos hacia 1850" [1850]. *Sonora: Textos de su historia*, vol. 2. Comp. Mario Cuevas Aramburu. Hermosillo/Mexico City: Gobierno del Estado de Sonora/Instituto de Investigaciones Dr. José María Luis Mora, 1989. 215–27.

Vélez Ibáñez, Carlos. *Border Visions: Mexican Cultures of the Southwest United States*. Tucson: University of Arizona Press, 1996.

Venegas, Yolanda. "The Erotics of Racialization: Gender and Sexuality in the Making of California." *Frontiers: A Journal of Women's Studies* 25.3 (2004): 63–89.

Villa, Eduardo W. *Compendio de historia del estado de Sonora*. Mexico City: Patria Nueva, 1937.

———. "Sonorenses ilustres: Loreta Encinas de Avilés (heroína sonorense), 1810–1889." *Sonora Ayer y Hoy*, supplement to *El Imparcial* (Hermosillo), July 1984: 2.

Voss, Stuart F. *On the Periphery of Nineteenth-Century Mexico: Sonora and Sinaloa, 1810–1877*. Tucson: University of Arizona Press, 1982.

Wagoner, Jay J. "Teresa: Healer or Saint?" *Arizona Days and Ways*, supplement to *Arizona Republic*, 2 December 1984: 5–7.

Walker, Franklin. "Ridge's Life of Joaquín Murieta: The First and Revised Editions Compared." *California Historical Society Quarterly* 16.3 (1937): 256–62.

Weber, David J. *Myth and History of the Hispanic Southwest*. Albuquerque: University of New Mexico Press, 1988.

Weber, David J., and Jane M. Rausch. Introduction. *Where Cultures Meet: Frontiers in Latin American History*. Ed. David J. Weber and Jane M. Rausch. Wilmington, Del.: Scholarly Resources, 1994. xiii–xli.

Whitlock, William Thomas. *Santa Teresa: A Tale of the Yaquii Rebellion*. New York: Town Topics Publishing, 1900.

Williams, Henry Llewellyn. *Joaquin: The Claude Duval of California, or The Marauder of the Mines (a Romance Founded on Truth)*. New York: Robert M. de Witt, 1865.

Willson, Roscoe G. "Deluded Yaquis Invade Town under Order of 'The Witch,'" *Arizona Days and Ways*, supplement to *Arizona Republic*, 18 March 1957: 22–23.

Wood, Raymund F. "Ireneo Paz and 'Vida y aventuras de . . . Joaquín Murrieta.'" *American Notes and Queries* 12.5 (1974): 77–79.

———. "New Light on Joaquin Murrieta." *Pacific Historian* 14.1 (1970): 54–65.

Woodbridge, Bradford. "Santa Teresa." *Overland Monthly* 28.166 (1896): 422–27.

Wyllys, Rufus Kay. *The French in Sonora (1850–1854): The Story of French Adventurers from California into Mexico*. Berkeley: University of California Press, 1932.

Yáñez, José María. *Detall y algunos documentos relativos al triunfo alcanzado en el Puerto de Guaymas el 13 de Julio de 1854 contra el conde Gaston de Raousset Boulbon y extrangeros que acaudillaba*. Ures: Tipografía del Gobierno a Cargo de J. P. Siqueiros, 1854.

———. "Triunfo mexicano sobre Raousset de Boulbon en Guaymas" [1854]. *Sonora: Textos de su historia*, vol. 2. Comp. Mario Cuevas Aramburu. Hermosillo/Mexico City: Gobierno del Estado de Sonora/Instituto de Investigaciones Dr. José María Luis Mora, 1989. 119–30.

Yellow Bird (John Rollin Ridge). *The Life and Adventures of Joaquín Murieta: The Celebrated California Bandit* [1854]. Norman: University of Oklahoma Press, 1955.

Yetman, Davis. *Where the Desert Meets the Sea: A Trader in the Land of the Seris*. Tucson, Ariz.: Pepper Publishing, 1988.

Zavala Castro, Palemón. *El indio Cajeme y su nación del Río Yaqui*. Hermosillo: Gobierno del Estado de Sonora/Secretaría de Fomento Educativo y Cultura, 1985.

Zavala, Silvio. "The Frontiers of Hispanic America." *Where Cultures Meet: Frontiers in Latin American History*. Ed. David J. Weber and Jane M. Rausch. Wilmington, Del.: Scholarly Resources, 1994. 42–50.

Zorrilla, Luis G. *Historia de las relaciones entre México y los Estados Unidos de América 1800–1958*, vol. 1. Mexico City: Porrúa, 1965.

Newspapers

Alborada, Hermosillo
Arizona Bulletin, Solomonville
Arizona Daily Star, Tucson
Arizona Silver Belt, Globe
El Atalaya, Nogales, Arizona
Brooklyn Eagle, Brooklyn
California Police Gazette, San Francisco
El Cambio, Hermosillo
La Constitución, Ures and Hermosillo
El Diario del Hogar, Mexico City
El Estado de Sonora, Nogales, Sonora
La Estrella, Los Angeles
La Estrella de Occidente, Ures
El Fronterizo, Tucson
Graham County Bulletin, Solomonville
El Hijo del Ahuizote, Mexico City
La Ilustración Espírita, Mexico City
El Imparcial, Guaymas and Hermosillo
El Independiente, El Paso
La Jornada, Mexico City
Los Angeles Star
Los Angeles Times
El Monitor, Hermosillo
El Monitor Republicano, Mexico City
El Nacional, Ures
National Police Gazette, New York
New York Herald
New York Times
Oasis, Nogales, Arizona
La Opinión, Los Angeles
La Patria, Mexico City
Sacramento Daily Union
Sacramento Steamer Union
San Francisco Bulletin
San Francisco Call
San Francisco Chronicle
San Francisco Examiner

El Siglo XIX, Mexico City
El Sonorense, Ures
Tombstone Daily Record and Epitaph
Tombstone Prospector
Tucson Citizen
Tucson Daily Star
El Universal, Mexico City
El Universal Ilustrado, Mexico City
La Voz del Estado, Magdalena, Sonora
La Voz del Pueblo, Mexico City
Weekly Arizonian, Tubac

INDEX

Robert McKee Irwin is associate professor of Spanish at the University of California, Davis. He is the author of *Mexican Masculinities*, also published by the University of Minnesota Press. He is also coeditor of *The Famous 41* and *Hispanisms and Homosexualities*.

Cultural Studies of the Americas (continued)

45 pictures
57

106
119
130

173
188

203
231
233

246